MODERN
LAND COMBAT

Above: Artillery deployment by Sikorsky UH-60 Blackhawk helicopter.

Above: A US Army Tow team prepares to engage a tank target.

MODERN
LAND COMBAT

David Miller • Christopher F. Foss

Portland House

New York

A Salamander Book Credits

This 1987 edition published by Portland House,
a division of dilithium Press Ltd.
distributed by Crown Publishers, Inc.,
225 Park Avenue South,
New York, New York 10003

© Salamander Books Ltd., 1987

Printed and bound in Belgium

ISBN 0-517-63854-1

Editor: Bernard Fitzsimons

Art Editor: Mark Holt

Designer: Nigel Duffield

Colour artwork: Mark Franklin, Terry Hadler, Ray Hutchings, Janos
Marffy, Maltings Partnership, David Palmer, Stephen Seymour

Diagrams: TIGA

Colour reproduction by Melbourne Graphics

Acknowledgements: The publishers wish to thank wholeheartedly the
many organizations and individuals in the defence industry, and the
armed forces of various nations, who have supplied photographs and
information used in the compilation of this book.

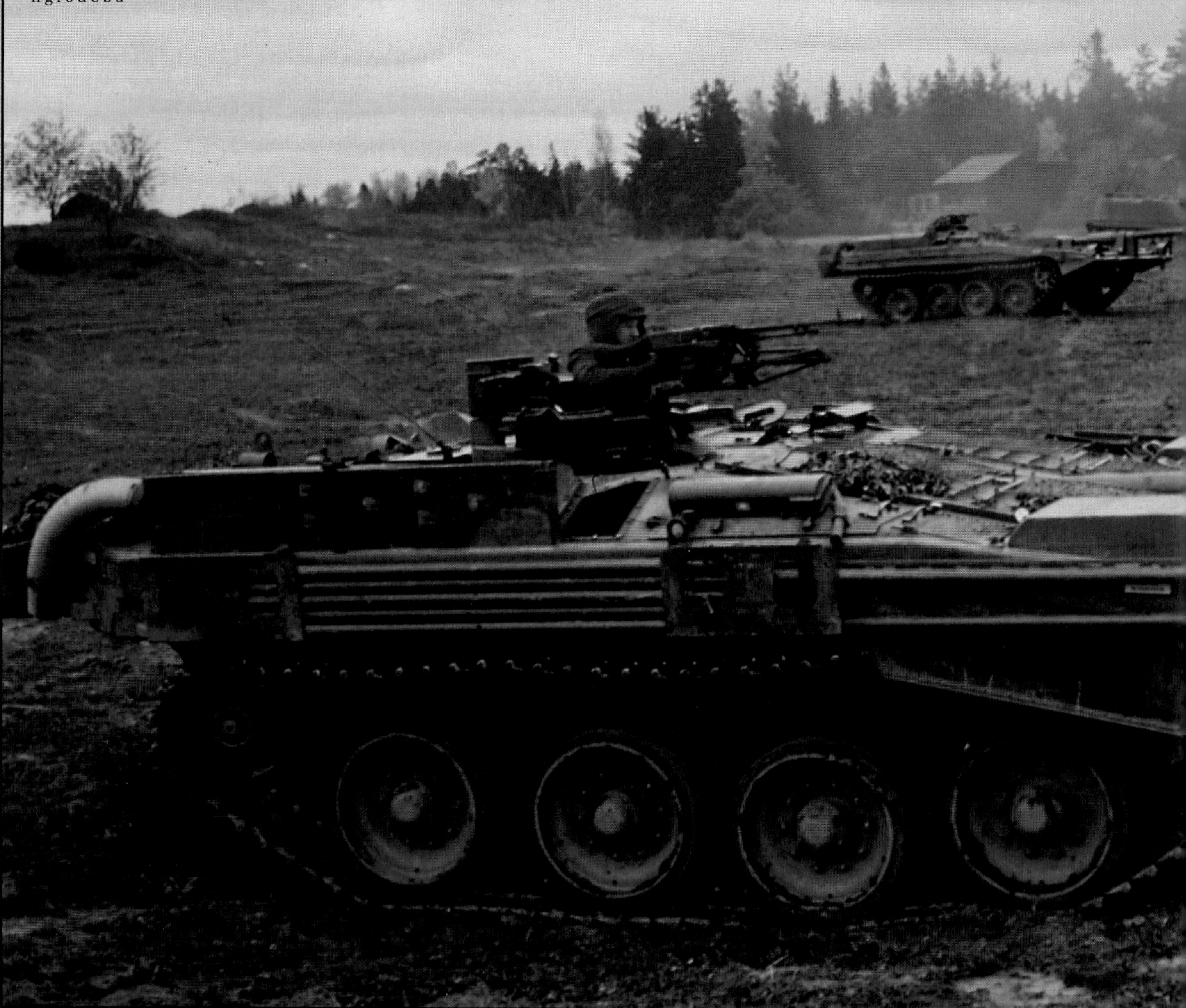

The Authors

Christopher F. Foss has made a detailed study of modern armoured fighting vehicles and their associated systems for the last 20 years and is recognised as a leading authority in this field. He has driven almost 40 different armoured vehicles and pursued his researches in countries as far apart as Brazil and China, as well as lecturing in a number of countries. He has written hundreds of articles on armoured fighting vehicles and artillery as well as many books, including *Armoured Fighting Vehicles of the World* (Ian Allen) and *Jane's World Armoured Fighting Vehicles*, and is currently Editor of *Jane's Armour and Artillery*. He was also consultant and chief author of Salamander's *Illustrated Encyclopedia of the World's Tanks and Fighting Vehicles* and his other work for Salamander includes contributions to *The Encyclopedia of Land Warfare*, *The Illustrated Directory of Modern Weapons* and *The US War Machine*.

David Miller is a serving officer in the British Army, a career which has taken him to Singapore, Malaysia, Germany and the Falkland Islands and which has included service in the Royal Corps of Signals, several staff jobs at Army headquarters and the command of a regiment in the UK. He has contributed numerous articles to technical defence journals on subjects ranging from guerilla warfare to missile strategy and is the author of *An Illustrated Guide to Modern Submarines* (1982) and *An Illustrated Guide to Modern Subhunters* (1984), co-author of *Modern Naval Combat* (1986) and *Modern Submarine Warfare* (1987) and a contributor to *The Vietnam War* (1979), *The Balance of Military Power* (1981) and *The Intelligence War* (1983), all published by Salamander Books.

Below: Mobility is vital on the modern battlefield. Here S-Tanks are supported by Pbv 302 APCs and dismounted infantry during a Swedish Army exercise.

Contents

Foreword	8	M1 and M60	82
		T-64, T-72 and T-80	84
Technology David Miller	**10**	Chieftain and Challenger	86
Introduction	12	AMX-30 and AMX-40	88
Tank Design	16	Leopard 1 and Leopard 2	90
Light Armoured Fighting Vehicles	30	OF-40 and TAM	92
Anti-tank Warfare	34	Merkava	94
Artillery	40	Type 63, SK 105 and Ikv-91	96
Surveillance and Target Acquisition	46	Scorpion and Stingray	98
Air Defence	48	AMX-10 and Fox	100
Infantry Warfare	56	Luchs and BRDM-2	102
Battlefield Helicopters	62	M113	104
Command, Control and Communications	64	LAV-25 and M2/M3 Bradley	106
Electronic Warfare	66	BMP-1 and BMP-2	108
Tactical Nuclear Warfare	70	FV432 and Warrior	110
Chemical Warfare	72	BTR-70, MT-LB and BMD	112
Low-intensity Warfare	74	Marder and Fuchs	114
Unconventional Warfare	74	AH-64 Apache	116
		Mi-24 Hind	118
Weapons Christopher F. Foss	**78**	Mangusta	120
Introduction	80	Lynx	122

2S5 and DANA	124	SA-80, M16 and AK-74	166
SP-70 and GCT	126	Valmet M76, FA MAS and Galil	168
M109	128	M249, RPK, MG3 and M60	170
Pershing and Lance	130	MO-120-RT-61, L16 and M-240	172
Pluton and Hades	132		
MLRS	134	**Tactics** David Miller	**174**
SS-1 Scud, SS-21 Spider and SS-23 Scarab	136	Introduction	176
BM-21 and RM-70	138	The Suez Canal, 1973	178
TR, FH-70 and Soltam	140	Combined Arms Operations	182
D-30 and S-23	142	Soviet Tactics	186
M198 and Light Gun	144	River-crossing Operations	186
Crotale, Shahine and AMX-13 DCA	146	Infantry Battalion Attack: Wireless Ridge	190
Wildcat, Roland and Gepard	148	Air Mobility	194
Bofors 40mmL/70 and ZSU-23-4 Shilka	150	Airborne Forces	196
SA-4, SA-6, SA-8, SA-9 and SA-13	152	Parachute Operations: Rescue at Kolwezi	198
Rapier	154	Artillery	200
M163 Vulcan and Patriot	156	Low-intensity Warfare	202
Artemis and Breda Twin 40L70	158	Special Forces Operations	204
Stinger, Blowpipe, Javelin and SA-7 Grail	160		
Armbrust, RPG-7 and Dragon	162	**Index**	**206**
Carl Gustaf, AT-4, Tow and Milan	164	**Picture Credits**	**208**

Foreword

The advanced weapon systems with which today's armies are equipped form the main subject of this book, which begins with an exploration of the role of technology in all the most important aspects of today's land warfare. The principal weapon on the modern battlefield remains the tank, with its unique combination of firepower, mobility and protection, and the first chapter explores the fundamental elements of tank design: new types of powerplant, advanced guns firing specialised ammunition and new forms of armour protection are described and illustrated and their performance and capabilities analysed.

Light armoured fighting vehicles, the subject of the second chapter, offer essential support and current examples are capable of bringing substantial firepower to bear. The same is true of modern anti-tank weapons, an enormous variety of which have been produced in an attempt to exploit any weakness in tank design. Thus specialised missiles have been designed to attack tanks' more vulnerable top armour and smart sensors have been combined with mines and rocket launchers to produce unattended, self-activating weapons.

The other source of heavy firepower is artillery, where the main thrust in recent years has been toward the production of self-propelled mountings. At the same time, improvements in the range performance and accuracy of artillery shells, new varieties of payload and enhanced surveillance and target acquisition capabilities have helped to enhance the value of artillery weapons, while the primitive multiple rocket launchers of World War II have been succeeded by both modern versions and by such sophisticated weapons as the Multiple Launch Rocket System.

Virtually all land operations nowadays are conducted under a constant threat of air attack, and the resources devoted to dealing with that threat are necessarily substantial. Once again there is a wide range of weapons available, ranging from long-range missiles and guns of various calibres to shoulder-launched missiles, new types of which are overcoming earlier limitations on engagement angle. Such weapons as Stinger and Blowpipe have been used in action from the Falklands to Afghanistan, and have proved their worth in both theatres, claiming several victims and severely degrading the effectiveness of hostile aircraft.

The provision of portable anti-tank and anti-aircaft systems is one major change in the role of the infantry: another is the almost universal provision of mechanised transport in the form of both armoured vehicles and helicopters, the latter having assumed the additional role of front-line anti-armour platform and added yet another threat to the battlefield environment.

Other aspects of modern land warfare considered in the first section include the fundamental role of command, control and

Left: Bofors RBS-56 BILL trials firing sequence. As the missile leaves the launch tube under the propulsion of its solid rocket motor the cruciform wings and control surfaces flip out.

Above: Surrounded by piles of equipment, men of the US Army's 82nd Airborne Division stand watch on a hill in Grenada during the October 1983 invasion of the island by US forces.

communications systems, electronic warfare, which has the monitoring, analysis and disruption of the latter as one of its primary functions and the specialised tehnology involved in tactical nuclear, chemical, low-intensity and unconventional warfare.

The book's central section is devoted to examples of specific weapon systems. Main battle and light tanks, reconnaissance vehicles, armoured personnel carriers, combat helicopters, self-propelled and towed artillery, battlefield missiles and rockets, air-defence and anti-tank weapons, small arms and mortars are illustrated and described to provide a panorama of more than 100 of the principal systems in current front-line service.

Even within specific categories, the range of weapons is remarkable, and it is notable that virtually all of them are produced by one of the super-powers or by European nations. This is a reflection of the extent to which weapon development relies on a strong industrial and technological base and substantial research and development budgets, though many Third World nations, and particularly China, are making strenuous efforts to establish or develop their own capabilities in the area of production, efforts which they hope will lead to indigenous research and development capability and lessen their dependence on Soviet, American or West European suppliers and their vulnerability to political pressures exerted through the control of arms supplies.

Once the weapons have been designed, developed, produced and sold, it is up to the customer armies to develop tactics to make the best use of what is invariably a substantial investment. Accordingly, the final section of the book deals with tactical considerations in several areas, beginning with an examination of the basic tactical doctrines followed by the armies of th Soviet Union, the United States and Britain.

Given that almost all armies base current tactical thinking on a study of military history, the section includes analysis of some particularly significant actions from the last two decades, including the battles waged over the Suez Canal during the 1973 Arab-Israeli War and the successful attack on Wireless Ridge by the 2nd Battalion of the British Parachute Regiment during the South Atlantic War of 1982.

There is also a discussion of the tactics involved in combined arms, airborne, artillery, low-intensity and special forces operations, and these are illustrated by examples taken from a variety of sources to illustrate Soviet practice in such areas as artillery displacement and river-crossing operations, as well as real-life examples such as the French Foreign Legion's rescue operation in Zaïre in 1978 and the rescue by the British SAS of hostages held in Iran's London embassy in 1980.

Above: A Norwegian Leopard 1 main battle tank participating in a NATO exercise. An infra-red/white light searchlight is mounted on the mantlet, and there is a firing simulator on the gun barrel.

Right: As the Bofors BILL reaches its target, a proximity fuze detects the tank and detonates the shaped-charge warhead, which is angled down at 30° to attack the more vulnerable top surfaces.

Technology

Below: Deployment of a Stinger
man-portable anti-aircraft missile,
an example of the new capabilities
advanced technology is making
available.

Introduction

Land combat is the ultimate form of warfare because all warfare is about people, the direction of their way of life and the control of the land on which they live. Naval and air combat are usually of immense importance in the outcome of a conflict, but they are never the final arbiter; the British in the 1982 South Atlantic War needed the air force for transportation and bombing support and the navy to provide transportation, close air support and fire support, but soldiers had to defeat their Argentinian counterparts on the islands and occupy the capital, Port Stanley, in order to achieve victory.

LEVELS OF CONFLICT

There are, in general terms, four levels of land combat, civil unrest, revolutionary war, limited war and general war, each with its own requirements in terms of tactical doctrine, weapons, surveillance systems, command and control structures and so on. Some may be usable in more than one type of warfare, out as the Americans found in Vietnam and the Soviets in Afghanistan, the systems and technology designed for general war are not necessarily effective in counter-revolutionary war. Of course the converse also applies, and some of the equipment developed by the Americans as a result of the apparent lessons of Vietnam is proving to be of limited value in the central European environment.

Civil unrest may stem from political, ideological, economic, racial or social causes and is normally an internal matter for the country concerned, though it is by no means unknown for an external power to foment such unrest for its own purposes.

Revolutionary war is a military undertaking by a political party or other organisation which has concluded that it cannot achieve power by any other means than a protracted campaign. Most revolutionary wars include elements of both urban and rural guerrilla warfare, and although the balance between the two may differ according to the circumstances they are normally mutually supporting.

Limited war is an international conflict conducted within limitations accepted by both sides and which falls short of general war. Limits accepted in recent conflicts have embraced the aims of the conflict, the geographical extent of military operations and the weapons used.

Above: A Mujahideen heavy machine gun crew prepares for action in the mountains above Puzhgur in the Panjshir valley, eastern Afghanistan. The Soviet Union's counter-revolutionary war in Afghanistan is representative of one of the four levels of combat.

Left: Consultations between the commander and gunner of a US Army M60 tank during one of the annual Reforger exercises in Germany. Such exercises, designed to practice the reinforcement of NATO armies in Germany, form an essential part of training.

Above right: Launch of a Canadair/Dornier CL-289 airborne surveillance drone, designated AN/USD-502 by NATO. Up-to-date battlefield intelligence is essential to modern field commanders, and RPVs are a useful means of providing it.

Right: Crew station of the US Army's cancelled Sgt York divisional air defence system. Despite a radar derived from that of the F-16 fighter and a tank chassis full of high-technology hardware, the system simply could not be made to work well enough.

General war is defined as a global conflict between the two superpowers, which might also include some or all of their allies as well as involving those with whom there had been no previous form of association. It is usually considered that such a conflict would start with a conventional phase in which the two sides would deliberately refrain from the use of nuclear weapons while trying to resolve the conflict through diplomatic means. The second and ultimate phase could involve the use of nuclear weapons, possibly escalating from tactical to strategic, though it is not beyond the bounds of possibility that strategic nuclear weapons could be used at any time if either side felt that were the only solution.

TECHNOLOGY AND LAND WARFARE

Compared with the naval and air forces, for whom the technological revolution was at the core of their development from 1914 onwards, land warfare technology developed relatively slowly until about 1942. In fact, until relatively recently the aphorism that whereas navies and air forces man equipment, armies equip the man, could

fairly be applied. Even at the start of World War II army equipment was very unsophisticated, and with the odd exception in the artillery arm, few, if any, pieces of army equipment represented the state of the art in any field of technology.

Starting in the middle of World War II, however, the technological revolution has gradually gathered pace in land warfare, and modern armies are every bit as technologically oriented as their counterparts in the naval and air environments. This revolution has affected every aspect of the conduct of land warfare, from weapon systems capability through command, control and communications systems to the infantryman's rifle and his means of moving about the battlefield. In fact, it was the infantryman who resisted this change the longest, but even he has finally succumbed, and the change over the last 25 years is quite extraordinary.

In 1960, almost without exception, infantry battalions in central Europe were foot-borne units equipped with rifles, light and medium machine guns and mortars. There were small numbers of anti-tank weapons — a few 3.5in recoilless rocket launchers in each company and perhaps a handful of 105mm or 120mm recoilless rifles under

battalion control — but surveillance equipment was limited to very basic items such as binoculars, trip-flares and even wires with tin cans. HF or VHF radio communications were provided down to platoon level, or in some armies down to section or squad level, but wire links were still used in defensive positions. Transport was limited to a small number of field cars for the more senior officers plus trucks for logistic support and some of the heavier support weapons. In effect, the battalion had changed little between 1945 and 1960, and a survivor of World War I would have found little but the use of radio to surprise him.

By the late 1970s the picture was totally different. For example, a Soviet motor rifle battalion comprised some 435 officers and men, every one mounted in a vehicle. Prime vehicle was the BMP-1, armed with a 76mm gun, a Sagger anti-tank launcher and a 7.62mm machine gun and equipped with a radio; the battalion had 33 BMP-1s together with a BRDM scout car for reconnaissance, eight GAZ-69 field cars and 25 ZIL trucks. The majority of the men were armed with automatic assault rifles and there were also 27 RPK light machine-guns. Nine SA-7 air defence missile launchers and four Sagger manpack launchers were totally new, though the six 120mm mortars were little different from 20 years previously, but there were also man-portable radars, laser target-markers and infra-red and, possibly, thermal imaging sights and surveillance devices, while radios were not only much more widespread but also much more sophisticated.

In Western infantry battalions the change had been very similar, though in some respects it had gone further — in communications, for

Below: US Army personnel carry out field maintenance on the engine of an M60 tank. Mechanisation may be the key to battlefield mobility, but it brings additional complications with the demands it places on overhaul and repair facilities, to say nothing of the enormous strain imposed on logistic and resupply systems.

Above: Computers are now reaching into every corner of the battlefield, as demonstrated here by a US Army airborne soldier using a portable comms terminal.

Below: Modern mobile air defence systems such as this West German Gepard must combine mobility, firepower and autonomous target detection capability.

example — and by the late 1980s the process was, if anything, accelerating. The new generation of IFVs are much more sophisticated than their predecessors, missile systems are increasingly complex, radios offer ever more facilities and surveillance devices have virtually eliminated the security formerly offered by darkness, when once a soldier could rest a little.

Elsewhere on the battlefield the change is every bit as marked: the tank, for example, has developed from a fairly simple and straightforward vehicle into one of the most complex items of modern defence technology, while all artillery designed for operation in central Europe is self-propelled on sophisticated tracked chassis. Military communications, which once were led by civil technology, are now at the very limits of the state of the art and are of such sophistication that they cost as much as major weapon systems. And computers are everywhere, their normal role being to speed up the handling of the vast amounts of data being fed into headquarters from the multiplicity of inputs now available.

Unfortunately, no technological advance is ever totally independent and without consequences elsewhere. For example, the greater rates of fire available with modern artillery have undoubted tactical advantages, but they naturally entail a great increase in the number of rounds needed at the gun positions, which means a greater number of resupply vehicles, more drivers, more space on the roads and more protection, especially from air attack. In addition, the greatly enhanced performance of the guns means that target acquisition needs to be more rapid and to reach further past the forward line of troops, which calls for more sophisticated systems such as remotely-piloted vehicles or stand-off piloted aircraft such as the British Castor. All these need better communications to tie them all together, to interchange information quickly and to respond to enemy moves in time to forestall them, and every form of communications in turn affects electronic warfare operations.

Some technological advances are remarkably transitory. Active infra-red for example, was hailed in the early 1960s for its ability to make it possible to see in the dark and weapon sights, surveillance devices and driving goggles using IR technology were rushed through development and into production. Unfortunately, it was then realised that it was all too easy to detect sources of active IR and development effort was switched to passive devices such as thermal imaging and image intensification.

There are other knock-on effects, which sometimes may not be too obvious. For example, the rapid spread of night vision devices means that no longer can forward troops safely use the hours of darkness for resupply, replacement of units, withdrawal of damaged equipment for repair or rest. And if the battle is to be fought round the clock troops are going to reach a state of exhaustion very quickly and need replacing more often.

The consequence of all this is that the land battle is becoming a complicated environment in which equipment in almost every area is operating at the limits of technology, and while low-intensity warfare using old-technology equipment in the traditional way is well understood, high-technology armies of the kind that would be involved in a NATO/Warsaw Pact confrontation in Central Europe have never been tested. Of course there are exercises and simulations, some of them on a large scale and of considerable complexity, but there is a world of difference between simulations and the kind of confusion that a real war might engender. For example, there is no knowing what would happen if all the military radios now in use in Central Europe were operated at the same time: modern technology may make better use of the frequency spectrum and enable different sets to work close to each other without interference, but their capabilities are only tested on a small scale in peacetime. Similarly, it is questionable whether the logistics systems on *either* side could meet the ammunition and fuel requirements.

Tank Design

The tank designer has to balance a number of competing factors in arriving at a design which will begin to meet the operational staff's requirement. At its simplest this is a trade-off involving protection, firepower and mobility, and a result can usually only be reached by compromise — so that the design may not meet all its criteria exactly but at least does approach each one — or by deliberately accepting limits in one in order to optimise another. Thus, for example, Western tanks of the early 1950s designed to beat the JS-3 (the British Conqueror, US M103 and French AMX-50) emphasised firepower because at that time a 120mm gun was needed for the task, and protection came second in priority with the result that the vehicles were large, very heavy and slow. Fortunately, technological advances have now come to the designer's rescue, and modern production methods and materials enable 120mm guns to be constructed with thinner barrels which therefore weigh much less than those of the 1950s, while engines are now more powerful and lighter for a given volume. The contemporary British Challenger, for example, has a combat weight of 59.1 tons (60,000kg), slightly less than that of the Conqueror of the 1950s, however, the former has an engine with a power output of 1,200bhp compared with the latter's 810bhp and is, as a result, very much more mobile.

There are, of course, compensations. Reduced protection will normally lead to a lighter tank, but this results in greater mobility, which makes it more difficult for an enemy to score a hit. Using this philosophy, the French AMX-30 of the 1960s was considerably lighter than its contemporaries such as Chieftain and M60, because the French Army was prepared to accept light armour in order to gain battlefield mobility, something which, in any case, was in keeping with the national penchant for dash and élan. Finally, the physical size of the MBT is constrained by a variety of factors, one of which is the standard loading gauge of the railway system.

THE THREAT

No single weapons system on the battlefield has to face such a plethora of threats as the MBT, which may be attacked from above (aircraft, indirect fire weapons and top-attack direct-fire weapons), from the front and sides (direct-fire weapons — particularly from other tanks — and helicopter- or ground-launched anti-tank guided weapons), and from beneath (mines). These threats are both long-range, such as unseen artillery firing laser-guided projectiles, and extremely short-range, for example infantrymen in foxholes only yards away. Furthermore, the nature of the threat extends from attack on the hull by high-velocity, high-density, 'punch-through' projectiles such as tungsten-carbide and depleted uranium APFSDS, through chemical

Tank ammunition energy volumes

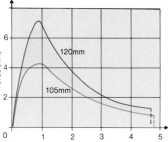

Above: The US M60 was one of many Western tanks to be fitted with the British L7 105mm main gun. This outstanding gun became the virtual standard in Western MBTs designed in the 1960s and 1970s.

Left: A comparison of the energy volumes of two APFSDS-T rounds, one of 105mm and the other of 120mm calibre, while travelling in the barrel. The 105mm gun remains in wide service in Western MBTs, but despite the weight of both round and gun the greater terminal effects and longer range of the 120mm make it increasingly popular.

Above: West German Leopard 2 armed with a Rheinmetall 120mm smoothbore main gun. Note the vertical faces of the turret, the wide, rubber-treaded tracks and carefully designed front.

Below: The French AMX-40, the latest development in the AMX-30 series, is designed specifically for export. The French Army's next main battle tank will be the totally new Leclerc.

attack using HESH and HEAT, to 'mobility kill' attacks aimed at the engine and running gear. In addition, the crew can be attacked through the use of nuclear and chemical weapons, and the mobility of the tank may be reduced by obstacles, either natural (e.g. rivers) or man-made (e.g. anti-tank ditches).

THE TANK GUN

The most critical item of the tank's equipment is its main gun, by means of which it seeks to impose its supremacy across the battlefield. The past 40 years have seen an unending competition between armoured protection and firepower, and with each advance in protection the gun or its ammunition have had to be improved, and vice versa. At the end of World War II the largest-calibre 'normal' tank gun was the Tiger II's 88mm weapon, but most tanks had guns of between 76mm and 85mm calibre, although the US M23 had a 90mm gun and the massive JS-2 a 123mm. Since then the Soviet Army has led the way to higher calibres, being the first to 100mm on T-54, to 115mm on T-62 and then to 125mm on T-64. In the West a brief early excursion in the USA and UK to 120mm was reversed by the outstanding British 105mm L7, which became, in effect, the standard tank gun outside the Warsaw Pact, the only major nation not to adopt it being France. The British themselves, however, then moved to 120mm with the rifled L11, to be followed later by the Germans with the Rheinmetall smoothbore and by France with the GIAT 120mm smoothbore.

A further increase in calibre, say to 152mm, is by no means impossible, but it seems unlikely at the moment. Such a gun would exert a very large recoil force and would need to be mounted on a large tank, although even then the shock might be too great for the crew's comfort, as tended to be the case on the US M551 Sheridan when firing the HEAT round. In addition, the rounds

Above: The OTO Melara OF-40 was developed after the company had produced the Leopard 1 for the Italian Army and, like the French AMX-32 and AMX-40, is intended solely for export.

would be of such a size that the number carried would inevitably be reduced and would be too heavy for manual loading; an autoloader would thus be essential. However, if the gun were to be externally mounted (as opposed to in a turret), and fitted with a muzzle-brake and a soft recoil system, then such an installation might be feasible. An increase in calibre would have further effect, principally on the logistics system, which would either be able to deliver fewer rounds with the same amount of transport lift, or, if the number of rounds had to remain constant, would require either larger vehicles or greater numbers of them.

Considerable advances have been made in propellant technology in order to achieve higher muzzle velocity for the projectile, reduce barrel fouling and make the round easier to handle. The French GIAT 120mm round, for example, has a combustible cartridge so that only a small stub casing is ejected after firing, thus doing away with the problem of disposing of the traditional large brass cartridge case. The British experimented in the 1960s with a liquid-propellant tank gun, which appeared to offer some advantages in handling and stowage within the tank. That particular project was eventually discontinued, but today Rheinmetall, among others, are carrying out further research in the same area.

The length of the barrel has a number of influences. A longer barrel increases the efficiency of the transfer of energy from the propellent charge to the round, and it leads to greater accuracy, but a point is eventually reached where the effects of barrel vibration, tank motion, barrel droop and thermal effects (for example, rain on a hot barrel) begin to outweigh these advantages. (Barrel droop is the result of mechanical effects where the weight of the barrel causes very slight bending; with modern high-velocity, flat-trajectory rounds, the slightest deviation from normal will result in a miss and droop thus becomes a significant factor.) These problems can, in their turn, be countered to a certain extent. For example, modern production techniques, allied to metallurgical advances, can produce stiffer barrels, thus countering vibration and the effects of motion, while muzzle reference systems can measure droop and make the necessary allowances. Finally thermal sleeves can ensure an even temperature over the entire length of the barrel.

Traditionally there have been two methods of mounting the main gun — in a rotating turret or in a fixed position on the glacis plate. The rotating turret has many advantages: it gives all-round traverse, allows the commander to view the battlefield from the highest part of the tank, and enables the gun to be loaded, aimed and fired on the move. The alternative, where the gun is mounted in the glacis plate, has been used in AFVs which are generally designated tank destroyers. Most such vehicles carry their main gun in a flexible mounting; that fitted to the German Jagdpanzer Kanone can traverse 15° left and right and elevate between —8° and +15°. The alternative is a fixed mounting, as in the Swedish S-tank, where aiming is achieved by using the tank's hydropneumatic suspension and steering system. Both these types of fixed mounting are lighter and less complicated and they make the use of an automatic loader much easier, but they cannot be used to fire on the move and they also involve exposing much more of the tank in a 'hull-down' firing position.

The recoil forces on the trunnion of a tank are very powerful. The average recoil force (F) is approximately calculated by the equation

$$F = \frac{(wp.vp + wc.vc)^2}{2.g.wg.L}$$

where wp = weight of projectile (lb), wc = weight of propellant (lb), wg = weight of recoiling mass of the gun (lb), vp = muzzle velocity of projectile (ft/sec), vc = escape velocity of propellant gases (ft/sec), L = length of recoil (ft) and g = acceleration due to gravity (32ft/sec²). Taking approximate values for

Left: The Swedish S-tank has more revolutionary features than any MBT before or since. Although never tested in battle, it has caused most designers to re-examine their design philosophies.

a typical 120mm gun, where wp = 50lb (22.68kg), vp = 3,500ft/sec (1,067m/sec), wc = 29.5lb (13.38kg), vc = 4,700ft/sec (1,433m/sec), wg = 6,400lb (2,903kg) and L = 1ft (0.30m), then

$$F = \frac{(50 \times 3,500 + 29.5 \times 4,700)^2}{2 \times 32 \times 6,400 \times 1} lb$$

$$= \frac{240,177}{2,240}$$

$$= 107.2 \text{ tons (108.9 tonnes)}$$

From this it will be seen that the recoil force is inversely proportional to both the mass of the gun and the length of the recoil, and hence the recoil force can be reduced by increasing the weight of the gun or by increasing the recoil length. The former leads to a heavier tank, while the latter has long been inhibited by the limited space available inside the turret.

It should be noted, however, that the recoil force must not exceed 1.5 times the weight of the vehicle, otherwise the latter becomes an unstable firing platform. This has not proved to be a problem with recent MBT designs, where the weight has comfortably exceeded this limit; indeed, the guns of these vehicles have not even required muzzle-brakes to reduce the recoil. But a recent development has been the 'soft recoil' system, which, by greatly reducing the trunnion pull, enables a much heavier gun to be mounted on a hull of given size than has previously been the case. This has been made possible by a combination of a muzzle brake, to give an initial reduction in trunnion pull, and a longer recoil stroke. It will be seen from the equation above that simply by doubling the length of recoil (L) from 1ft (0.31m) to 2ft (0.62m) the trunnion pull is halved to 53.6tons (54,461kg). But, in combination,

105mm recoil forces

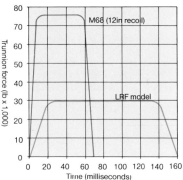

Above: The trunnion pull of a normal M68 105mm tank gun, US version of the British L7, compared with that of the Low-recoil Force version with muzzle brake. The dramatic reduction has made it possible to mount the powerful L7 gun in a much smaller chassis.

Right: The turret of a US Army M1 Abrams MBT on exercise in West Germany, with a weapon-firing simulator mounted on the M68 105mm gun barrel. Such simulators are now essential for training.

Above: A spent 105mm cartridge case is ejected from the turret bustle of an Austrian Army Jagdpanzer SK 105. The turret is an Austrian-built

these measures can lower the recoil force of a 105mm gun from some 37 tons to the region of 9 tons, and as a result APFSDS rounds can be fired with a muzzle velocity of some 4,920ft/sec (1,500m/sec). For example, until recently the lightest tank to mount the L7 (M68) 105mm gun was the Japanese Type 74, which had a combat weight of 37.4 tons (38,000kg). However, the use of a 'soft recoil' system on the L7/M68 105mm tank gun has enabled it to be mounted on a number of private-venture light tanks, including the Cadillac-Gage Commando Stingray (19.1 tons, 19,359kg), the Vickers Mk.5 (19.4 tons, 19,700kg) and the Teledyne Armored Gun System (18.75 tons, 19,050kg), a very low-

version of the French GL-12 oscillating turret and the gun is fed from two revolver-type magazines, one on each side, containing a total

profile AFV with an externally mounted 105mm M68, an autoloader, a front-mounted engine and a 3-man crew.

The turrets of Soviet tanks have tended to be much lower and squatter than those of Western tanks; some of them are virtually hemispherical in shape, which avoids shot traps but results in very cramped working spaces for the crew. Such turrets also limit the depression of the main armament to −4°, thus making it difficult to select hull-down positions, particularly on reverse slopes. As a comparison, the depression possible on British tanks is −10° on Chieftain and Challenger and was as much −15° on Centurion. It is, of course, arguable that the

of 12 rounds. Once emptied, the magazines must be reloaded manually from outside the tank an obvious tactical problem.

limited depression on their tank guns does not worry the Soviets, because they see the tank as a weapon system to be used in mass attacks, and the careful selection of fire positions is thus a matter of no more than academic concern to them. The West, on the other hand, sees the tank as much more of a weapon of defence, available in very limited numbers and, therefore, to be conserved with much greater care.

One method of reducing the size of the turret is the elimination of the loader. Once this has been done the commander and operator can be moved down within the hull and the gun can then be mounted in a very much smaller turret, in a split turret, on a telescopic mounting or on a

simple overhead mount. This subject is discussed below.

AMMUNITION

Although rounds such as high-explosive, white phosphor and canister exist for secondary tasks, it is the armour-attack round which enables the main gun to fulfil the tanks's primary mission, the destruction of other tanks. Today there are three major types of anti-tank round, sub-calibre, high-explosive anti-tank (HEAT) and high-explosive squash-head (HESH).

The mechanics of perforating armour plate are complex, but the process amounts to equating the kinetic energy of the projectile to the work done in penetrating and finally just perforating the plate. This can be expressed mathematically as

$$w.v^2 = k.d^3 \left(t/d\right)^n$$

where w = projectile weight (lb), v = projectile velocity (ft/sec), d = projectile diameter (in), t = thickness of armour plate which is only just perforated (in), k = constant, depending upon the projectile and armour plate (normally about 10^6) and n = index (normally 1.414). Armour-piercing capability can therefore be improved either by increasing muzzle velocity (v) or by increasing the diameter of the round (d), which was the pattern during World War II, when nations produced ever larger tank guns. This trend continued after the war, and in the 1950s the British were actively testing a 180mm gun which was to have been fitted in the FV215b, a heavy anti-tank SP based on the Conqueror chassis with a combat weight of some 75 tons (76,205kg)!

The sub-calibre round utilises kinetic energy to 'punch' its way through armour (i.e. maximising v in the equation above). It is held in the barrel by a sabot, which is discarded as the round leaves the barrel (hence the name Armour-Piercing Discarding Sabot, APDS). These rounds must be made of a high-density material and for many years have been constructed of tungsten carbide, although today a number of nations are considering the use of depleted uranium. To achieve maximum terminal effect the penetrator must have a slim nose and the overall diameter of the round must be kept to a minimum to reduce velocity losses along the trajectory, which results in a long, thin projectile. However, with spin-stabilisation the length-to-diameter ratio cannot exceed 5:1 or else control is lost. This has led to the development of the long rod penetrator, which has a length:diameter ratio of 12:1, but since spin-stabilisation is no longer possible the projectile must be fitted with fins to maintain stability — hence the Armour-Piercing Fin Stabilised Discarding Sabot (APFSDS) round. The Soviet Union, West Germany and France have solved the problem by using smoothbore guns, but the British and Americans have developed 105mm

Above: The Soviet Army demonstrates its T-72 MBT to a delegation of French Army officers; examples of the various types of ammunition are standing on the glacis plate. The long barrel of the 125mm smoothbore gun with its bore evacuator and full-length light alloy thermal sleeve are clearly shown, as is the excellent ballistic shape of the turret and the well-sloped glacis plate.

and 120mm rounds with slipping driving bands to make them compatible with existing rifled barrels.

When APDS was developed in World War II tungsten was the hardest known metal available in any quantity and at an affordable price. Tungsten has a density of 19.3gm/cm³, a figure exceeded only by the platinum group of metals; for comparison, steel has a density of 7.85gm/cm³. Tungsten's melting point is 3,410°C, the highest of all metals. The availability of tungsten is not a serious problem: it is the 26th most abundant element in the Earth's crust and there are large reserves; further, there is considerable scope for recycling,

and the USA currently produces some 20 per cent of its annual requirements in this way. For many years an alloy, tungsten carbide, was used in penetrators, but in recent years tungsten metal itself has most often been used.

Depleted uranium (DU) is a natural by-product of the uranium-enrichment process used in producing fuel for weapons-grade fissile material and for nuclear power stations. In such processes, for every kilogram of enriched uranium produced five kilograms of DU are also produced, and large quantities are available in countries with a nuclear industry. DU is also very cheap. However, it is difficult to use in the manufacturing process as it is

pyrophoric and chemically toxic, although its radioactivity level is very low. Penetrators made of DU are liable to stress-corrosion cracking if impurities are present. Maximum levels permitted are 50 parts per million of iron, 75ppm of oxygen and 1ppm of hydrogen. DU is also susceptible to atmospheric attack and must have a protective coating. In its raw state it is much cheaper than tungsten, but the complexities of the manufacturing process, coupled with problems of storage and use, suggest that tungsten will be more cost-effective in the longer term.

The second type of armour-defeating round is the High Explosive Anti-Tank (HEAT) projectile, also described as the

Left: The Noricum NP 105A2 105mm APFSDS round, manufactured in Austria, showing the three-element sabot and five-finned tungsten alloy penetrator.

Below: A 25mm APFSDS round leaves the barrel (right), whereupon the sabot breaks up (left), leaving the finned penetrator to continue on its way to the target.

Right: The effect of a Noricum 105A2 105mm APFSDS round on a 5in (125mm) sheet of HD 9 armour plate. This is the entry hole made at an impact angle of 73°.

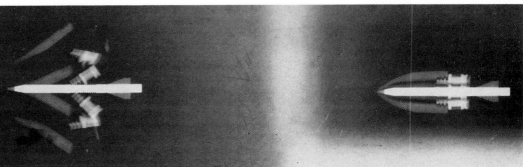

APFSDS ammunition effect

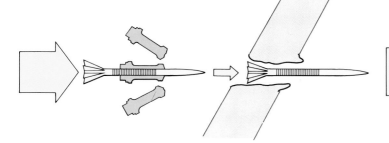

Above: The armour-piercing discarding sabot (APDS) round discards its sabot as it leaves the muzzle of the gun. The penetrator rod — usually fin-stabilised — then travels at high velocity to the target, where it punches its way through the armour plate and ricochets around the interior of the tank, doing severe damage to crew and equipment.

High-explosive anti-tank ammunition effect

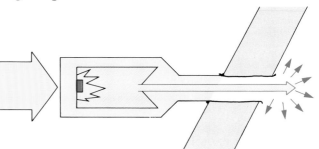

Above: HEAT rounds use the Monroe Effect, involving detonation of the high-explosive shell at a critical distance from the target. The conical hollow focusses the explosion into a high-speed jet which penetrates armour plate to a depth of about five times the warhead's diameter, leaving a hole about 10 times the jet's diameter.

HESH ammunition effect

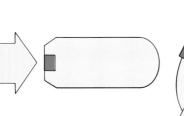

Above: A high-explosive squash-head (HESH) round consists of a large amount of HE with a base fuze in a thin steel case. On hitting the target the explosive spreads to form a cake and is then detonated. The shock generated is enough to knock a scab off the interior of the plate; the scab ricochets around the interior of the tank at high speed. The exterior explosion is also sufficiently powerful to do considerable damage to external fittings such as periscopes.

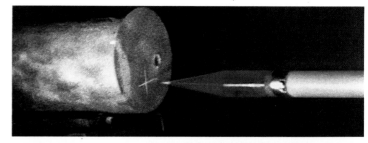

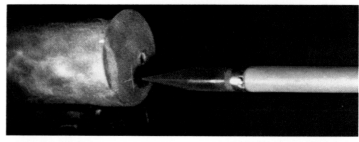

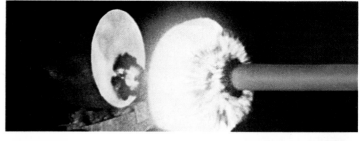

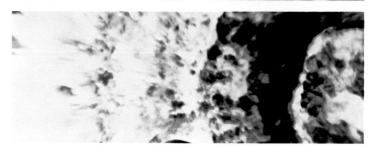

Hollow-Charge. In this round there is a conical cavity in the nose of the explosive filling, with a copper liner. This is exploded at an appropriate stand-off distance fom the armour, and a phenomenon known as the Monroe Effect results in the production of a thin, very high velocity jet (some 27,000ft/sec, 8,230m/sec) of molten metal, which pierces armour up to five times the warhead's diameter with a hole some eight to ten times the diameter of the jet itself. Inside the tank there is a lethal blast followed by a diverging spray of high-velocity metal particles. The performance of the HEAT round is degraded by the spin which is necessary to achieve accuracy, because the jet is dissipated by centrifugal force. The French have endeavoured to overcome this with their 105mm OBUS-A round, in which the HEAT element is mounted in ball races within an outer shell, so that it rotates only slowly (some 20-30rpm) during the flight to the target. The diameter of the charge is slightly reduced, but the French claim that the benefit of not dispersing the jet more than outweighs this. A penetration of 360mm of standard armour plate at 0° incidence is claimed.

The effect does not rely upon the velocity of the round, but is much more dependent upon its diameter and the distance from the armour plate at which it is detonated; it is thus widely used in anti-tank missile warheads as well as in tank guns. The effect is greatly diminished, if not totally defeated, by Chobham armour, but HEAT rounds are still of value in destroying older tanks and other armoured vehicles (e.g. SP guns and APCs). The jet is also dissipated by the Active Armour now being added to many tanks. Spaced armour and side skirts also cause the HEAT round to dissipate its energy on outer protection, thus leaving the inner armour unaffected.

The third major type of round is High-Explosive Squash-Head (HESH), known as High Explosive Plastic (HEP) in the USA. In this projectile the greater portion of the round is an explosive contained in a thin steel case and there is also a fuse with a slight time delay. On hitting the target the case fractures and the explosive filling spreads in a cake; it is then detonated, and the resulting explosion generates very powerful stress waves, as a result of which lethal metal scabs are thrown from the inside, travelling around the interior of the tank at considerable velocity and causing great damage as they do. The HESH round does not actually penetrate the tank at all and its effects are not degraded by spin. An added advantage is that the explosion on the outside of the tank can considerably damage external fittings such as sights, periscopes, searchlights and lasers. HESH shells can also be used against concrete, but they have been rendered ineffective for anti-tank purposes by spaced or sandwich armour.

Above: A sequence of high-speed photographs taken at 8,000 frames per second showing what happens (from top to bottom) when the hollow-charge warhead of an Oerlikon 80mm rocket is detonated against a steel rod target. The target was 15in (400mm) long and was completely penetrated by the high-velocity jet.

In the 1960s the USA developed the XM163 152mm gun/launcher system, in which the gun could fire either a guided missile or a conventional round of ammunition. Although the system achieved limited operational status in the M60A2 and the Sheridan light tank it was not a success and has been withdrawn. It has recently been disclosed however, that the 125mm gun on the Soviet T-64B and T-80 is a similar type of gun/launcher. Unless the Soviet Army has developed something totally new it must be assumed that the missile (NATO designation AT-8 Cobra) uses laser-homing and has a HEAT warhead, which will have only limited effect against such tanks as the Leopard 2, Challenger and M1, which are fitted with Chobham armour.

SECONDARY ARMAMENT

A tank requires a secondary armament to supplement its main gun, with the primary purpose of dealing with nearby infantry. Traditionally, such a secondary armament has been a combination of a coaxially-mounted machine-gun and a manually-controlled machine-gun on a flexible mounting on the commander's cupola. The coaxial machine-gun has usually been of 7.62mm calibre, while the turret-roof MG has again been normally 7.62mm although some vehicles have carried 12.7mm weapons.

Today's MBT, however, finds itself faced with threats not only from fixed-wing aircraft but also from helicopters, and thought is being given to dealing with these. The French, a particularly innovative nation, have fitted 20mm AAMG in all tanks since the AMX-30. Mounted to the left of the main gun, this weapon is intended for use against slow-flying aircraft and helicopters and can be elevated both in conjunction with and independently of the main gun up to a maximum elevation of 40°. Other nations, such as the British, use remotely-controlled MGs on the commander's cupola in the AA role. However, there is no doubt that a better answer has to be found, not only to enable crews inside the tank to acquire and identify aerial targets but also to defeat them before they can launch their ATGW. Some consideration has been given to

Above: As well as a coaxially mounted 7.62mm M240 machine gun, the secondary armament of the US M1 includes the two roof-mounted MGs seen here. A Browning M2HB 12.7mm heavy machine gun mounted at the commander's station has powered or manual traverse and manual elevation, while the loader has a hand-controlled 7.62mm M240.

using the main gun to fire a specialised AA round (an APDS round would simply go straight through), but no viable solution has yet been found.

AUTOLOADERS

Consideration is also increasingly being given to using autoloaders in tanks. The British showed some interest in autoloaders in the 1950s and 1960s but rejected them, while the Swedes introduced one in the 1960s in the S-tank and the USSR now has two different types in service in the T-64 and T-72. The S-tank autoloader, which is both simple and reliable, has a firing rate of some 25 rounds per minute. However, this is achieved because the gun is in a fixed mounting, which makes for mechanical simplicity but

Above: A US Army M601A main battle tank. There is an infra-red searchlight mounted above the M68 105mm main gun. The secondary armament includes a coaxially mounted M73 7.62mm MG and an M85 12.7mm MG in the commander's cupola on the turret roof. The M73 weapon is being replaced by the M240, US designation for the FN MAG.

imposes severe tactical limitations. Where the gun is mounted in a revolving turret, however, the complexities of transferring rounds from a fixed stowage to a rotating turret are somewhat daunting and have deterred many armies. The Soviets are known to have had considerable problems with the automatic loader in the T-64, while the apparently insoluble problem with the autoloader in the UK/FRG/Italian SP70 (which admittedly, is an SP gun rather than an MBT) was the main cause of the failure of that collaborative project.

An autoloader is required to select a projectile and a charge from their respective stowage areas, line them up with the open breech and then ram them home, but this simple statement conceals some very complicated requirements. The

majority of armies require their MBTs to fire, at the very least, two kinds of ammunition, of which one will be a penetrator (e.g. APDS) and the other an anti-tank/HE round (e.g. HESH/HEP). Many armies also require their tanks to carry a small number of smoke and possibly canister rounds as well. The Soviet T-72, for example, carries three types, 12 APFSDS, 22 HE-FRAG (FS) and six HEAT. The autoloader must be able to select any one required round from the variety carried and must also be able to extract and dispose of misfires as well as to download live rounds from the breech back to the autoloader, for example at the end of a shoot.

Moreover, if separate charges are used (as is almost inevitable with ammunition of 120mm calibre or greater) then the charge must be selected as well. Next, the projectile and charge must be moved from their stowage to the gun, which will introduce problems of alignment and, in some designs, of turning as well. The turning depends upon the stowage selected. Where the rounds are stowed vertically (as in the T-64) they must be lifted clear and then rotated before they can be offered up to the gun. In the T-72, however, the rounds are stowed horizontally in a carousel, which holds 40 boxes below the turret basket. The selection of rounds having been made, the carousel rotates and the box is lifted until it is level with the breech, whereupon a swinging arm comes forward and rams the projectile. The box is then lowered to enable the charge to be rammed. This method does away with the requirement for turning the round, but the gun must return to precisely the same position each time (in both azimuth and elevation) on each occasion for the round and charge to be rammed. This inevitably slows down the rate of fire.

The next French tank (the Engin Principal de Combat, or EPC) will be fitted with an autoloader of a somewhat different type, mounted in the turret bustle. A conveyor-type magazine will contain some 20 rounds, with the rounds being selected automatically by a sensor. The rounds will be stowed with the projectile forward and the selected type will be aligned with a hatch and then pushed forward from the rest by the rammer into the breech. A further

120mm-gunned Leopard 1 ammunition stowage

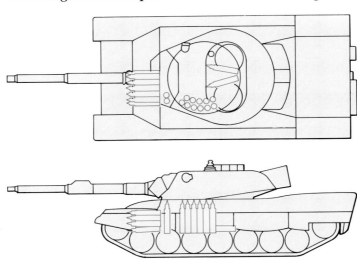

Above: Ammunition stowage is a problem for tank designers, who must take into account ease of loading and safety. Shown here is the new 120mm version of the West

German Leopard 1, which carries 29 rounds in the hull and 13 in the turret. The standard Leopard 1 accommodates 42 rounds of 105mm ammunition in the hull.

20 rounds will be stowed in the hull, and the magazine will be recharged manually when the situation permits.

The autoloader is inevitably heavy and complicated, and must take up a fairly large amount of space. It will also reduce the total number of rounds that can be carried. It may, furthermore, go wrong, in which case there must be a manual reversionary mode or the tank will have to withdraw to a place where the faults can be identified and repaired. However, the great advantages lie in doing away with the human loader, with all the savings in space, manpower and training costs that this implies.

AUTOMOTIVE SYSTEMS

The automotive system of a tank is required to fulfil a number of functions, many of which are generally similar to the requirements for any engine system, including that of a private car. It must be efficient and reliable, and it must provide the maximum power for the minimum size, weight, noise output and fuel consumption; it must also provide a quick response to the driver's demands for changes in output. There are, however, also a number of requirements which set the military engine apart, in particular that it must run constantly, even when stationary; furthermore, when the vehicle is moving the engine is almost invariably run at full power. Finally the power unit must be capable of rapid removal and replacement in the field.

Tank mobility depends on a combination of two factors, the power-to-weight ratio of the vehicle and its suspension system. 'Power' is frequently taken to be the specific output of the engine, but this is an inaccurate oversimplification; in fact, it is the power output at the drive sprocket, and thus the overall efficiency of the complete power-train, which is the critical factor (some 30 per cent of the power is used to drive cooling-fans, transmission, etc). This is, however, a very difficult figure to obtain, and

Above: US Army M60A1s, typical of the second generation of diesel-engined MBTs, have a ground pressure of 11.37lb/sq in (0.8kg/cm2)

and a track width of 28in (71cm). The tracks left by the vehicles show how differential steering enables them to manoeuvre.

the power-to-weight ratio, using specific power output in comparison with the combat weight of the MBT, is a useful measure of the tank's mobility, and certainly assists in comparing one tank with another. For example, the fact that the British Chieftain MBT had a power-to-weight ratio of 11.79hp/ton while the figure for the German Leopard 1 was 14.69 was a good indicator that, of these two contemporaneous tanks, the latter had far better cross-country mobility than the former.

Great advances have been made in diesel-engine design. For example, the 1960s US Teledyne-Continental 650hp 12-cylinder diesel engine (the power unit for, among others, the M60A1) had a power-to-weight ratio of 13hp/ton (9.9kW/tonne) and a

MTU MB-838 power

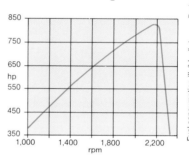

Above: Curve of output against rpm for the Leopard 1's 10-cylinder diesel engine shows how the power drops away dramatically above the optimum revolutions.

DD 8V-92TA performance

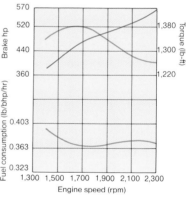

Above: The effect of engine speed (rpm) on brake horsepower, torque and specific fuel consumption of the Stingray light tank's eight-cylinder Detroit Diesel powerplant.

Above: The West German MTU MB-838 Ca-500 mechanically supercharged 10-cylinder diesel engine. With dry weight of 4,232lb (1,920kg), this engine has a

maximum power output of 830hp (610kW) at 2,300 rpm; the 10 cylinders are in a 90° configuration. This very reliable engine powers the widely used Leopard 1 MBT.

Above: The US Avco Lycoming AGT-1500 is the first mass-produced gas turbine used in an MBT. It has a twin-spool axial/centrifugal compressor and delivers

1,500shp (1,125kW) at 3,000rpm. High fuel consumption and very hot exhaust problems are being solved, but difficulties with static running have yet to be addressed.

road fuel consumption of 9mpg (312lit/100km), whereas today's 1,500hp 10-cylinder MTU diesel engine (which powers the Leopard 2) has a ratio of 27.6hp/ton (20kW/tonne) for a road fuel consumption of 12.84mpg (219lit/100km). Not only has the power output of engines increased, but it has outpaced the increase in the weight of the tank, resulting in improved power-to-weight ratios. Unfortunately, the extra power demanded by the operators has led to an increase in the volume and weight of the power-packs, although steps are now being taken to reduce these.

The only current competitor to the diesel is the gas-turbine, whose main advantages over the diesel are its lower weight and reduced maintenance requirements. It was first installed in the Swedish Strv-103 (S-tank), where a Boeing 490shp turbine is used in conjunction with a Rolls-Royce K60 240bhp diesel; the latter runs all the time while the gas-turbine is normally only brought into use in combat. A gas-turbine was first used as the sole motive power for a tank in the ill-fated US/FRG MBT70 (which never got beyond the prototype stage), and this experience was used in developing the installation for the M1, which has an Avco-Lycoming 1,500hp turbine. This particular engine has been the subject of some criticism for its high fuel consumption, especially when the tank is stationary, and its exhaust, which is so hot that no vehicle or man can approach the rear end of the tank too closely while the engine is running. However, the US Army considers M1 to be able to meet its goals of operating a 24hr combat day without refuelling and of travelling 275 miles (443km) at 25mph (40km/hr) on secondary roads. The Soviet T-80 is also powered by a gas-turbine.

For the future, it is essential that the size of the power-pack and fuel consumption both be reduced. Utilising technological advances in engine construction and improving the integration of ancillaries (such as the generator, gearbox and filters) into the power unit as a whole, the size of both diesels and gas-turbines is being brought down. For the diesel, consumption is being reduced further by design refinements, but, although the consumption of gas-turbines on the move can almost certainly be brought down to similar levels to that of the diesel, the problem of static running (where a turbine is inherently inefficient) is not likely to be solved quickly. The answer, therefore, would appear to be a mixed diesel/gas-turbine power plant, i.e. as pioneeered by the Strv-103 30 years ago!

SUSPENSION

Suspension and track systems are vital to the mobility of an MBT. The running gear is, in fact, the limiting factor in cross-country mobility since it is its effectiveness in reducing crew discomfort to tolerable levels which dictates the speed at which a tank can travel.

MTU MB-838 fuel consumption and torque

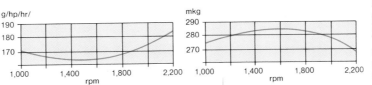

Above: Fuel consumption curve for a typical modern, high performance diesel engine. This graph should be compared with that for power output on the opposite page.

Above: Torque for the same engine: (maximum torque of 285mkg = 2,080 ftlb). MBT engines are fitted with torque converters to ensure high start-up momentum.

Above: The effectiveness of the S-tank's hydropneumatic suspension. At the top is its maximum elevation of +12° and below the normal running position; maximum depression is 10°.

Below: The Japanese Type 74 MBT also has hydropneumatic suspension, enabling it to be inclined 6° forward or backward and 9° left or right, and raised or lowered to vary ground clearance.

There has been much recent research on suspension and track systems, although the relatively cheap and well-understood torsion-bar system remains predominant. The US M1, for example, has seven road wheels on each side, with rotary shock absorbers at the first, second and seventh road wheel stations, but roadwheel travel has been increased from 162mm on the M60 to 381mm on M1. Leopard 2 also has torsion bar suspension with seven road wheels; maximum bump travel is just under 7in (325mm).

Hydropneumatic suspension with variable height was pioneered on the Swedish S-tank and was installed on the ill-fated MBT70, but the only conventional MBT to reach service status with such a system has been the Japanese Type 74. On this vehicle each of the ten roadwheels has its own unit, mounted inside the hull for protection, by means of which ground clearance can be adjusted from 200mm to 650mm, while the tank's attitude can be adjusted ±6° longitudinally and ±9° laterally. This last facility enables the effect of trunnion tilt to be eliminated on a sloping fire position. The only other MBT with such a suspension is the Brazilian Osorio, which has yet to enter service.

The British have developed the Horstmann suspension system over many years, although the helical springs of the earlier models have now given way to hydrogas units; the latest suspensions have twice the travel of that on Chieftain. It is noteworthy that the Israeli Army installed a system similar to that on Centurion on the early models of the Merkava MBT, although the Mk 3 is likely to have a hydropneumatic system.

For the future, there may be a wider adoption of the hydropneumatic system, although its cost, complexity, vulnerability and maintenance needs count against it. One possibility lies in mixed systems such as that on the Korean KT-1 which has torsion-bar suspension on the inner roadwheels but hydropneumatic suspension on the front and rear roadwheels.

Finally, the relatively unglamorous track is an item of great significance to MBT crews and is the subject of much research. Present tracks are not only heavy and noisy, but they can also cause much damage to roads and countryside, which may not be important in war but certainly is in peacetime. Track life varies considerably. Leopard 2's Diehl tracks have a life of 4,660 miles (7,500km); they are fitted with rubber-bushed pins and have rubber pads for road-running which can be replaced with snow grousers. M1's tracks, on the other hand, have failed to live up to their target life of 2,000 miles (3,220km) and have shown an average life of only 1,390 miles (2,240km), although this is due, to a certain extent, to the constraints of peacetime exercises.

AMPHIBIOUS CAPABILITY

Many armies require their tanks to have an amphibious capability, so that they can continue advancing without having to wait for cumbersome, slow-moving bridging equipment to be brought up to river-crossings. In order to float, a vehicle needs to have sufficient buoyancy, and some light vehicles (such as the Soviet PT-76 tracked reconnaissance vehicle) and a number of APCs can float without any further aid or preparation. MBTs, however, need flotation equipment, and collapsible canvas screens have been tested on the British Centurion and the Vickers 37-ton tank. These screens are effective in that they provide more than adequate flotation, but tactically they are of limited value since they require some time to erect, are very conspicuous and are vulnerable to hostile fire.

Most tanks are capable of submerged fording, many of them up to the tops of their turrets. This means, in effect, that rivers up to about 7ft (2.2m) deep can be crossed, provided careful reconnaissance has confirmed that the bottom will bear the load. Some Western tanks, such as Leopard 1 and AMX-30, also have extension tubes which can be fitted to the commander's cupola, which enable fording to a depth of about 13ft (4m) to be accomplished. Such tubes are wide enough for a man to climb up and thus serve for both ventilation and escape, although this capability is rarely practised and would probably not be used on any scale in time of war.

The Soviet Army, however, has a different approach, using a narrow schnorkel tube, mounted on a special fitting on the turret roof, which enables the tank to ford rivers up to 18ft (5.5m) deep. The sealing process prior to immersion takes some time and the system is not popular with crews; nevertheless, it is practised fairly often and would undoubtedly be used in war. As with all fording, detailed reconnaissance is essential and there is a possiblity of the tracks losing their grip, not only because of the slippery nature of the river bottoms but also because the tank is experiencing lift equal to the weight of the water it is displacing.

Above: Leopard 1s of the Belgian Army entering a river on a fording exercise. Most MBTs can ford rivers – in the case of Leopard 1 up to a depth of 7.4ft (2.25m) — without special preparation or equipment. Even so, careful reconnaissance of the entrance, exit and river-bed is necessary to ensure that the tanks do not come to grief. For greater depths special equipment such as snorkels becomes necessary.

Above: Soviet T-72s fully closed down and with snorkels mounted about to undertake a deep fording operation. The snorkel fits on a mounting on the gunner's hatch.

Left: A German Leopard 2 starts a deep fording crossing. Unlike Soviet models, the snorkel is wide and the commander controls the tank from its top, as shown here.

Right: The Soviets often come up with simple solutions to complex problems. Here large-scale decontamination of vehicles is carried out rapidly by washing them down with water sprayed from redundant aircraft gas turbines.

ARMOUR

Protection of an MBT is a function of the material used in construction, of design features and of size. For many years tanks have been constructed of steel armoured plate, usually nickel-chrome-molybdenum steel in the form of rolled plate or castings. The effectiveness of the armour is enhanced by good design, for example by sloping surfaces to increase the effective distance to be penetrated and by avoiding of shot-traps, or simply by using thicker plates, which means, of course, a heavier tank.

Sloping the armour gives an increased effectiveness against armour-piercing shot, presenting a higher actual thickness to be penetrated, but the effective ballistic thickness is greater still. Thus a plate 4in (101.6mm) thick and angled at 60° has an actual horizontal thickness of 7.9in (200mm) but provides ballistic protection equivalent to a 12in (300mm) vertical plate; because the effective thickness is greater, the actual thickness of the plate can be reduced and thus a useful saving in weight can be achieved.

Sloped armour is effective principally against armour-piercing shot, especially APDS/APFSDS. However, it is little more effective against HEAT warheads than vertical plates, and protection against such attack is better provided by some form of screen which will detonate the round outside the critical distance for the jet. Spaced armour is also very effective against HESH/HEP.

One way of optimising protection is to concentrate the armour in the areas of greatest threat. Thus hulls have the maximum thickness of armour protection on the glacis plate, nose and turret front, with reduced thicknesses on the upper and rear surfaces of the hull and turret, and least of all on the hull floor. The new range of 'top-attack' anti-tank weapons is designed to take advantage of this weakness, although clearly one counter by the tank designer would be to add more armour to such areas; this would increase the weight of MBTs, however, which are already at their limits.

Other protective measures include placing the engine in the

Above: A major recent development is reactive armour, seen here on an Israeli M48. Tailored for each type of MBT, it is fitted in small blocks,

front of the tank (as in the Israeli Merkava), using side-skirts to detonate HEAT rounds before they hit the suspension, and spaced armour. A major advance in the early 1970s was the British Chobham armour (named after the research establishment where it was designed). The nature of this armour is a closely guarded secret, but it is believed to consist of spaced layers of several different materials which can defeat both kinetic and chemical energy rounds. It is now used by the major Western tanks such as Challenger, M1 and Leopard 2 but does not appear to have been made available to Israel for the Merkava. Even with Chobham armour, sloping enhances its effectiveness, but a feature of the German Leopard 2 is that the turret has vertical sides, which suggests a total belief in the efficacy of the protection being provided; Challenger and M1 still use sloping plates on the turret. It is generally accepted that the latest Soviet tanks (T-64, T-72 and T-80) use a form of 'special' armour, but its

which do not interfere with the tank's weapons, optics or escape hatches. For an additional weight of under a ton it gives greatly enhanced

nature is not yet known publicly in the West.

An even more recent advance is 'active armour', which consists of a series of explosive plates covering vulnerable parts of the tank. These plates are built in different sizes and shapes to facilitate fitting them to the tank in a manner similar to the heat-dissipating tiles used on the Space Shuttle. They are basically explosive charges which detonate when hit, exploding outwards and dissipating the jet of a HEAT round, blowing off the explosive scab of a HESH round and, possibly, deflecting the penetrator of an APDS round. This new development first appeared on Israeli tanks (where it is known as Blazer armour) and is also now being seen on an increasing number of Soviet tanks.

NBC PROTECTION

Tanks are required to operate on the nuclear battlefield; indeed, they are considered to be one of the primary weapons systems to be used to

protection against hollow-charge warheads, but is not activated by small-arms fire, artillery fragments or the heat of fires.

exploit the situation following a nuclear strike. The thick armour on a tank does, in itself, provide a degree of nuclear protection, but recent Soviet tanks also have an interior lining of a synthetic material, containing lead, which provides enhanced protection against nuclear fallout, neutron radiation and electromagnetic pulse (EMP). Most modern tanks also incorporate an NBC protection system, which functions by maintaining a slight overpressure within the crew compartment, provided by air which has passed through various filters. This enables the crew to continue to operate without respirators in a contaminated environment.

SIZE

The physical dimensions of the tank are subject to numerous constraints, perhaps the most important of which is the total permissible weight, since size is directly proportional to weight. A major factor is the diameter of the turret-ring, which must be

sufficient to enable the breech to be lowered as the muzzle is raised to extend the range, and for the gun to be loaded and fired in any of these positions. As the size of the gun has increased, so has the turret-ring diameter; the Centurion turret-ring was 74in (1.88m) in diameter, while that of the M60 is 85in (2.16m). The total width of most tanks exceeds the turret-ring diameter by a considerable margin, but the difference can be reduced by bringing the turret-ring bearings over the tracks, as has been done, for example, with the Israeli Merkava.

The overall width of the tank is limited by the dimensions of rail and road transporters, bridges, ships, etc, but perhaps the chief constraint is the maximum permitted railway load width of 10ft 4in (3.125m). Some tanks exceed this but can still be transported by rail, either by removing such items as track-guards (where this is possible) or by using carefully selected routes.

Length is similarly limited by a variety of factors. For high speed movement across uneven surfaces, the greater the length of track on the ground the better, while the greater the area of track on the ground the less the ground pressure and thus the better the ability of the tank to move across soft terrain. However, the combination of tracks which are laterally rigid and the concomitant use of skid steering imposes limits on the configuration of the tank, because in order to be manoeuvrable the ratio of the length of track in contact with the ground to the distance between the track centrelines must lie between 1.1:1 and 1.8:1. Examples among modern tanks are: 1.12:1 for the Soviet T-72, 1.53:1 for the Israeli Merkava and 1.36:1 for the US M1.

The height of the tank again depends upon a number of factors. Adequate ground clearance is necessary to prevent 'bellying-

down' and is normally of the order of 18in (45.72cm). The primary factor in the distance between the floor and roof of the hull is the height of the seated driver, which is about 3.25ft (0.99m), while the distance between the hull floor and the turret roof is dictated by a combination of the height of a standing loader (say 5.5ft, 1.68m) and the depression required of the main gun.

Within all these areas there is scope for compromise. For example, the driver's seat can be reclined, as is the case in the British Chieftain and Challenger, thus saving a few inches in the height of the hull. The overall height of the tank can be further reduced by eliminating the need for the human loader, and it can be varied by the use of adjustable suspensions such as hydropneumatic systems; in the Japanese Type 74 this leads to a height variable between 8.14ft (2.48m) and 6.66ft (2.03m). The height can also be reduced by accepting a limit on the depression of the main gun, thus diminishing turret height. The Soviet Army is prepared to accept this (T-62's depression is —4°), but the British Army is not (Chieftain's depression is —10°).

The track problem has also been faced in various ways, none of them so far very successful. Laterally flexible tracks have been tested from time to time, but with little success, while the Swedish Army is currently testing an articulated tank destroyer (UDES XX20) in which two tracked bodies give the equivalent of a laterally flexible track, together with considerable length, without destroying manoeuvrability.

CREW

During World War II the great majority of MBTs were crewed by five men, the commander, loader, gunner, driver and bow machine-

Above: Tanks do not always travel on their own tracks and designers must ensure that they are able to be transported by ship, wheeled transporter and, as shown here, on railway flat cars.

Below: The US Army High Mobility Agility Test Rig (HIMAG) was built to determine tactical and technical values of mobility and agility. The programme should lead eventually to a new generation of MBTs.

Left: T-80, latest in a long line of successful Soviet MBTs. The Soviets were the first major army to develop a three-man tank with an autoloader replacing the loader to save weight and height.

Above: The tank crewman is obviously an essential element of the tank system. He is expensive to train and takes up a great deal of space, as well as adding to the height of the vehicle.

gunner. Then, as the tactical need for the bow machine-gun disappeared the crew was reduced to four (a move led by the USSR with the JS-3) and this was long considered to be the irreducible minimum. The argument for four men centres upon the multitude of tasks which must be performed apart from just fighting the tank, including guard duties, radio watch, tank maintenance, replenishment and cooking, and even then difficulties may arise if the commander is frequently called away, as in HQ tanks.

The first operational MBT to be fitted with an autoloader was the Swedish Strv-103 (S-tank), which enabled the crew to be reduced to three men. Like so many of the features of the S-tank, however, this was considered by some experts to be an aberration, a one-off experiement, and tanks like Leopard 1 and 2, Chieftain and Challenger, M60 and M1 continued to be designed for a crew of four. There was, therefore, considerable surprise when the Soviet T-64 appeared wih an autoloader and three-man crew, and with the subsequent unveiling of T-72 and T-80 it is clear that the Soviet Army has rejected the four-man crew for the foreseeable future.

In a four-man crew the driver sits at the front, usually centrally although where the engine is located at the front (as in the Israeli Merkava) he has to be moved to one side. The remaining three men are in the turret, the loader standing on one side and the commander and gunner seated on the other.

There are numerous advantages to the three-man crew. In the first place either one man can be reduced per tank in the fleet (which, in an era of manpower shortages and high training costs, is a major saving) or personnel can be redeployed to increase the number of tanks. Secondly, there is a major reduction in the space needed in the tank, which leads to savings in weight and gives the possibility of moving the remaining two turret crewmen below the turret-ring or of moving the driver back into the turret. This offers the very important tactical advantage of lowering the overall height of the tank.

ROBOTS

One possibility for the not-too-distant future is that of robot tanks. Some small robot tanks were produced in World War II, mainly for use in mine-clearing, while tracked robot vehicles are now often used in explosive ordnance disposal (EOD). The latter are cable-controlled by an operator within sight of the vehicle, but there is no practical reason (apart from the use of ECM) why radio control and remote TV could not be used, as is the case with, for example, airborne remotely-piloted vehicles (RPVs).

What is novel about the latest proposals is that they are for fighting robot tanks, capable of undertaking various tactical missions, including attacking enemy targets. Such a concept has many attractions, not only for the savings in manpower it

implies but also for the opportunities in undertaking high-risk missions it presents. The US Army has already begun the development of a number of these devices. The Robotic Obstacle Breaching Tank (ROBAT) is designed to breach minefields under fire and in conditions of daylight or darkness, and a number of private companies have designed various mobile devices to undertake sentry duties and investigate suspected minefields. The significant feature of these, however, is not only that they are armed, but that they are also capable of dealing autonomously with identified targets.

The US Army's AirLand Battle 2000 study gives serious consideration to the use of Remotely-Located Weaponry (RLW), which might include a static battle station armed with machine-guns and mortars and equipped with

Robot AFV concept

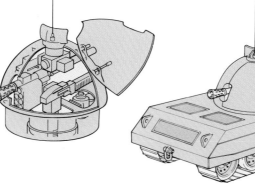

Above: One concept for a robot tank involves the turret shown here, with 40mm recoilless anti-tank weapon and machine gun, mounted on a remotely controlled tracked chassis.

Ikv-91 fire control system

1 Gunner's sight	rate sensor
2 Commander's sight with collimator	7 Elevation actuator 8 Elevation rate sensor
3 Mechanical linkage	9 Laser transmitter/ receiver
4 Gunner's control handle	10 Manual range input
5 Commander's control handle	11 Cant sensor 12 Sight servo motors with sensors
6 Traverse actuator and	

surveillance devices. Control of the RLW could be either exercised remotely from a command-post or delegated to the RLW's own control system. It is, of course, only a small step to mount the RLW turret on a tracked chassis.

FIRE CONTROL SYSTEMS

The primary mission of the MBT is to kill another MBT and therefore any one design's success or failure must be judged against its success in this area. This problem can be expressed in terms of the probability of a kill (P_K) against a hostile tank, which, in turn, depends upon a number of factors, primarily the probability of a hit (P_H), the probability of the round perforating the target (P_P), the probability of inflicting lethal damage (P_L) and the overall probability of the system functioning correctly (i.e. its reliability, P_R). The

Below: Elements of the 1kv-91's fire control system. Such sophistication is essential to ensure first-round accuracy and economic utilisation of resources.

probability of a kill is the product of these factors: $P_K = P_H \times P_P \times P_L \times P_R$.

For example, for a modern MBT, fitted with a fire-control system, firing a 105mm APDS round from a defensive position against a moving target, at a range of 1,640yd (1,500m), the values might be of the order of $P_H = 0.83$, $P_P = 0.85$, $P_L = 0.85$ and $P_R = 0.99$. So

$$P_K = P_H \times P_P \times P_L \times P_R$$
$$= 0.83 \times 0.85 \times 0.85 \times 0.99$$
$$= 0.59.$$

In other words, there is a 59 per cent chance of killing the hostile tank at a range of 1,640yd (1,500m). But, if the range is allowed to shorten to 1,093yd (1,000m) P_H rises from 0.83 to 0.94, and, assuming that the other values remain unaltered, P_K rises to 0.67, or 67 per cent.

It is clear from the above equation that P_P and P_L are functions of the ammunition, while P_R is a function of the overall design of the MBT. P_H, however, the delivery of the round to the precise point on the target where it will have the best chance of first penetrating and then inflicting lethal damage, is a function of fire-control. The round can fail to achieve such a hit because of either vertical or horizontal errors. A horizontal error is brought about by incorrect alignment of the gun with the target and, with modern sights, is relatively rare. A vertical error, however, is very important when modern, high-velocity, flat-trajectory ammunition is being used, and is normally the result of a miscalculation in the range to the target. The corollary of this, of course, is that when designing a tank to be difficult to hit, much greater benefit is gained from reducing its height than its width.

For many years range calculation was achieved by eye, but as battle ranges grew this clearly became unsatisfactory. The next development was the optical

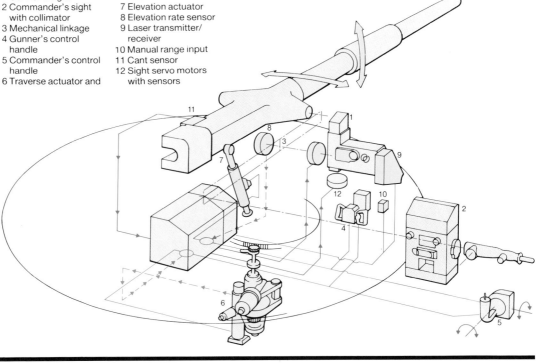

M1 Abrams fire control system

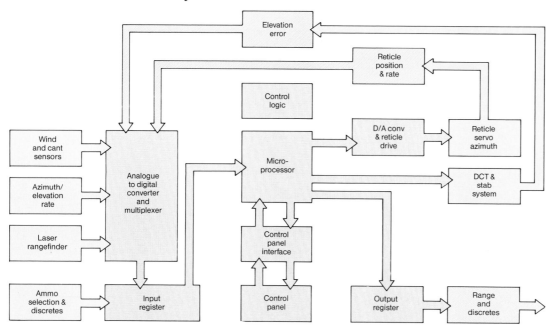

Above: The block diagram for the US Army's M1 fire control system. The system is fully automatic and accepts atmospheric, ballistic and orientation inputs from sensors, keyboard and computer systems. It then computes pointing data for the main gun and outputs the data by variety of sensors placed about the controlling gun/sight servos. Such sophisticated systems are rapidly becoming the most expensive single elements in modern MBTs.

rangefinder, of which two types were used, stereoscopic and coincidence. The former proved too complicated and difficult to operate, and the latter is much more generally used. Typically, such devices have a magnification of between ×8 and ×10 and feature split-image coincidence, as on many modern 35mm cameras. The British Army did not like optical rangefinders — the only one installed in a production tank was on the Conqueror — and instead used from the 1950s to the 1980s a 0.5in (12.7mm) ranging machine-gun, with a range of some 2,000yd (1,800m). This fired tracer ammunition, ballistically matched to the main gun's ammunition, and was very popular with the British Army as it was cheap, simple to use and reliable and took full account of wind and trunnion tilt, all of which are advantages compared with the optical rangefinder. However, its use was limited to 2,000yd (1,800m), whereas modern main guns are capable of firing out to some 3,500yd (3,200m); it tended to slow down the rate of engagement; and its use could give away the fact that an anti-tank round was about to be fired.

Optical devices and RMGs are now being replaced by laser rangefinders, which are virtually instantaneous in operation and extremely accurate; typical figures are a range bracket of 328 to 10,100yd (300-10,000m) with an accuracy of ±22yd (20m). They are detectable, however, and many MBTs are now being fitted with sensors to tell them when they are being 'lased'.

Obtaining the first-round hit with a high probability of success depends to a very large degree upon the integration of the various factors involved in an effective fire-control system (FCS), which normally consists of four sub-systems. The sensor sub-system comprises a

tank to provide continuous updates on such factors as wind direction and velocity, air temperature and pressure, altitude, trunnion tilt, angle of sight, charge temperature, barrel wear, target displacement and ammunition type. The sighting sub-system comprises the sights, laser rangefinders and wiring ellipse electronics. The data-handling sub-system integrates these inputs and consists of a computer, a commander's control and monitor unit and the firing handles, and this finally passes the appropriate control signals to the gun control sub-system, which provides the mechanisms to traverse and elevate the gun.

Fire-control systems are rapidly becoming the most expensive single pieces of apparatus in a modern

MBT. Their complexities and capabilities are best illustrated by a typical example, that of the Vickers Mk 7 Weapon Control System, which is installed in the Vickers Mk 7 MBT. In this MBT the complete weapons system is integrated by the Marconi Centaur 16-bit military micro-computer.

The gun control sub-system is electrically controlled and the gun can be 'slaved' either to the commander's gyro-stabilised day sight or to the gyro-stabilised thermal sight; alternatively, it can be stabilised in space using a two-axis gyroscope mounted under the breech. Maximum stabilised speeds are 700mils/sec in traverse and 150mils/sec in elevation. The gun control equipment provides power drives actuated by the gunner's controller, the commander having

overdrive facilities via his gyro-stabilised gun controls, and there is also emergency manual reversion.

The gun-control system is interfaced with the ballistic computer to give rapid reaction and accurate aiming. This data-handling sub-system, based on the 16-bit fire-control computer, operates in conjunction with the gunner's telescopic laser sight, the commander's gyro-stabilised panoramic laser sight, the thermal imaging system and the gun control equipment. The computer stores ballistic and other information. It receives target range from either the gunner's or the commander's laser rangefinders, while the target's angular rate is automatically fed in as the target is tracked.

The sighting sub-system comprises a number of devices, distributed between the gunner and the commander. The gunner's main sight is a telescopic monocular ×10 sight with a 7° field of view, mounted coaxially with the main armament to eliminate the errors associated with the earlier types of mechanical linkages. There is a laser rangefinder module, using a Neodynium-YAG (Nd-YAG) laser, which has an accuracy of less than 5.47yd (5m) over a range bracket of 437 to 10,936yd (400-10,000m) and is capable of carrying out measurements ('lasing') once per second. When the gunner acquires a target an aiming mark is injected into the sight, superimposed on the sight graticule. As he starts to track the target he initiates the first control sequence by pressing the laser button, which he releases after about three seconds when he is satisfied with the tracking, and the laser fires to take the range. The necessary corrections are then computed and the computer moves the aiming mark ahead of the target, simultaneously passing signals to the gun control sub-system causing the gun to traverse and elevate to bring the aiming mark back onto the target. The gunner makes any fine correction and fires when ready.

M1 Abrams turret power control system

1 Gunner's control box
2 Commander's control
3 Gunner's control
4 Traverse mechanism
5 Power supply
6 Main accumulator
7 Elevation mechanism
8 Recoil exerciser valve
9 Superelevating
   actuator

Right: The Cadillac Gage power control system for the M1, showing the gunner's position and the commander's control unit. This electrohydraulic system uses constant pressure power controls.

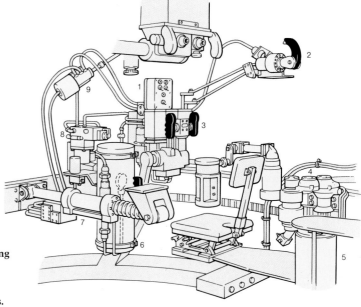

Helio tank periscope configuration

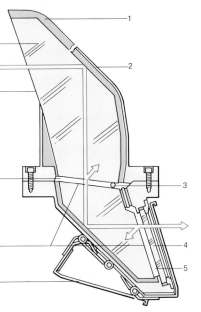

1 Polyurethane encapsulation or alloy cover for external installation
2 Shatter alloy, DMC or armour steel case for internal glass mounting
3 Dessicating valve
4 Polycarbonate anti-spall protection
5 Gas-filled desicated air gap
6 Folding blind
7 Coating or glass filter for laser protection
8 Gas-filled balistic air gap
9 Non-reflecting front face
10 Stabilised or crown glass

Above: Even such a relatively simple device as a tank periscope must be able to deal with new threats such as battlefield laser systems as they appear.

Right: Gunner's periscope, laser rangefinder and night sight eyepiece and controls from the sighting subsystem of the ELOP Matador tank fire control system.

In addition to his main sight the gunner is also provided with a periscopic sight mounted in the turret roof. This has ×1 magnification and a field of view of 30° horizontally and 10° vertically. It is used for surveillance and target acquisition.

The commander's main sight is an SFIM gyro-stabilised panoramic sight, with a 5° or 16° field of view, which allows him to see through a full 360° in azimuth and 70° in elevation without moving his head. Two degrees of magnification, ×3 and ×10.5, are provided. The gyro-stabilised head enables him to hold the sight accurately on target with an aiming error of less than 0.1mrad whilst his tank is moving. An Nd-NAG laser rangefinder (identical to that in the gunner's sight) is incorporated in the sight. Indicators

in the sight's right eyepiece show the position of the vehicle, sight and gun axes, while fire-control information from the computer and laser is displayed in the left eyepiece.

The tank commander is also provided with a ring of six fixed, wide-angle, non-reflecting head, ×1 magnification periscopes around his hatch to give all-round vision. When these are used in the surveillance mode he can rapidly align his main sight with any one of these six periscopes using a push-button mounted under each.

When firing on the move, the commander commences an engagement by pressing his laser fire button; the laser does not fire, but the computer is informed that a tracing sequence has started. He continues tracking the target with his thumb controller and after a few seconds,

when he is satisfied that he has a steady track, he releases the laser fire button; the laser then fires and gives the target range to the fire-control computer. The computer uses this input to calculate the required gun elevation, having already worked out the lead angle from the target tracing rate. This information is fed into the gun control equipment and the turret is slaved in traverse and elevated to the correct aiming point. When this is achieved a 'ready-to-fire' light is illuminated in the sight and the commander maintains his track. When the gun and sight are aligned a gun coincidence indicator is also illuminated in his sight and he can fire as long as this indicator remains illuminated and his tracking is on target.

In addition to the sighting systems described above, a gyro-stabilised,

panoramic, thermal-imaging sight is mounted in the turret roof. The thermal information received from the scene is converted into a CCIR video signal and is presented on two 625-line television monitors, one each for the commander and gunner. This device has a spectral range of 8 to 12 microns. A further sensor is a thermal pointer, normally stowed within the vehicle, which can be mounted on the head of the thermal sight and used to provide an auto-scanning capability, activating an audio alarm if the thermal picture changes and thus allowing the crew members to rest. The loader is provided with a simple periscope with 360° rotation. Its lower mirror can be folded up when not required,

Besides the devices described above, the sensor sub-system consists of a number of sensors elsewhere in the vehicle. Trunnion tilt (the tilt of the gun trunnion axis relative to the normal) is obtained from a sensor mounted in the gun. A muzzle reference system is built into the gunner's telescopic sight, which permits rapid compensation to be made for main gun barrel droop and bend at any angle of elevation. The information is input directly into the computer and a compensation factor fed into the panoramic sights. Ambient air temperature, altitude and crosswind rate and angle are sensed and fed in automatically. Other parameters, such as type of ammunition, barrel wear and charge temperature are set into the computer manually.

Left: This picture of the inside of an M1 turret gives an impression of calm and spaciousness, but on the battlefield, with the tank moving across country at high speed, generating noise and engine and cordite fumes, it will be anything but a pleasant environment.

Light Armoured Fighting Vehicles

As MBTs have become ever more sophisticated, heavy and expensive an increasing number of armies have started to look for something smaller, lighter, easier to crew and less difficult to maintain — and more affordable. There has, of course, always been a demand for light AFVs — tracked or wheeled vehicles with reasonable firepower, protection against at least small-arms fire, and a good degree of mobility — although the issue has sometimes been confused by designating them 'reconnaissance vehicles' (as were, for example, the US Sheridan and British Scorpion) or 'fire support vehicles'. They are used for airborne, reconnaissance and flank protection duties in general and high-level conventional war in support of MBTs, and are also used as tanks in their own right in operations where an MBT would be inappropriate or unavailable, for example against unsophisticated opponents and for policing operations. Such light AFVs would not be expected to operate against MBTs, nor, until recently, would they have been considered to be in competition with them.

In the 1950s and 1960s a number of light tank designs were brought into service, including the Soviet PT-76 (13.78 tons, 14,000kg, 76mm low-pressure gun); the US M24 (18.1 tons, 18,370kg, 75mm gun), M41 (23.1 tons, 23,495kg, 76mm gun) and M551 (15.56 tons, 15,830kg 152mm gun/launcher); and the French AMX-13 (14.76 tons 15,000kg, 90mm gun). These were followed in the 1970s by two excellent light tank designs, the Austrian Jagdpanzer SK-105 (17.2 tons, 17,500kg, 105mm gun) and the British Scorpion (7.94 tons, 8,073kg, 76mm gun), although the former is officially described as a tank-destroyer and the latter as a reconnaissance vehicle. All these are able to perform a vast range of duties: the Scorpions and Scimitars taken to the Falkland Islands by the British in the 1982 South Atlantic War were, for example, able to operate as tanks, as they had the necessary mobility and firepower and there was, surprisingly, no AFV opposition.

Today, however, a number of factors are together beginning to place greater emphasis and

Leopard 1 and derivative AFVs

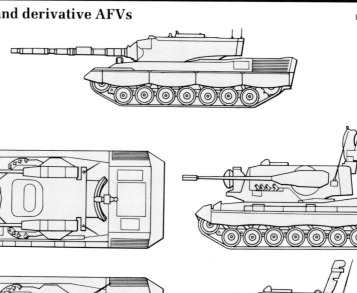
Leopard 1A3 main battle tank

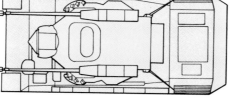

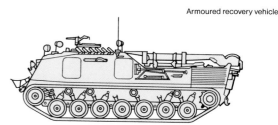
Gepard SP anti-aircraft gun

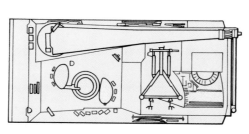
CA 1 SP anti-aircraft gun

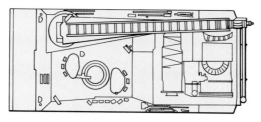
Armoured recovery vehicle

Armoured engineer vehicle

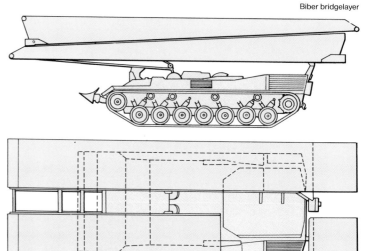
Biber bridgelayer

Below: The Belgian Cockerill 90mm gun has been installed on a wide variety of light AFV chassis, including that of the Alvis Scorpion shown here. The resulting Scorpion 90 has been sold to the armed forces of Malaysia and Nigeria.

Above: Tanks need to be supported by a whole range of other armoured vehicles, and successful chassis are frequently used as the basis for these. The Leopard 1 main battle tank has formed the basis for a series of derivative AFVs, shown here with the components of the original tank in blue and new parts in grey. The Gepard AA tank is in service with Germany and Belgium; the Netherlands Army's CA 1 has a Dutch radar but is otherwise similar to the Gepard.

importance on the light AFV. First is the increasing realisation that development of the MBT has gone as far as it can along the present lines of ever-larger, ever-heavier vehicles, mounting ever-bigger guns and, of course, costing ever-more money. The second is that technology is enabling designers to produce light AFVs with capabilites far beyond those considered feasible only a few years ago.

A 'soft recoil' system on the L7/ M68 105mm tank gun has enabled it to be mounted on a number of private-venture light tanks, including the Cadillac-Gage Commando Stingray (19.1 tons, 19,359kg), the Vickers Mk 5 (19.4 tons, 19,700 kg) and the Teledyne Armored Gun System (18.75 tons, 19,050kg), the last a very low-profile AFV with an externally mounted 105mm M68, an autoloader, a front-mounted engine and a 3-man crew. This breakthrough has been made possible by fitting a muzzle brake, which gives a lower trunnion pull, and which can then be further reduced by a longer recoil stroke, lowering the recoil force from some

37 tons to about 9 tons. As a result APFSDS rounds can be fired with a muzzle-velocity of some 1,500m/sec.

A second line of development has been the use of APC chassis to mount turreted heavy weapons. This enables a fairly standard, lightly armoured chassis to be used as the basis for a very useful fire support vehicle and has the added advantages that not only has development already been carried out and funded, but significant in-service logistics savings in stores, maintenance annd training costs are available. Thus, for example, the TAM tank consists of a 105mm gun turret mounted on the Marder chassis, while the GIAT CS90 gun has been mounted on the AMX-10 APC chassis to produce the AMX-10 PAC90. The M113 APC is used for a number of applications, including the IMI 60mm gun.

WHEELED AFVS

While there is no question of wheeled vehicles replacing or even competing with the current range of heavy (40 tons plus), tracked MBTs,

Above: The AMX-10RC reconnaissance vehicle, designed in the 1970s for French Army reconnaissance and cavalry regiments and mounting a 105mm

wheels are a much more attractive proposition in the field of light AFVs.

Compared to tracked AFVs, wheeled AFVs cost some 40-60 per cent less to produce and have 60-80 per cent less fuel consumption, much higher road speeds, a longer life span and much lower maintenance costs. They cause less crew fatigue and are also much quieter than their tracked counterparts. They cause much less damage to roads and, because they are lighter, can use bridges which are barred to tracked vehicles. Furthermore, they have less rolling resistance: typically, on roads the tracked vehicle has a rolling resistance equal to 4 per cent of its weight while for a wheeled vehicle with cross-country tyres the figure is just 2 per cent of its weight. To optimise their cross-country performance wheeled vehicles need multi-wheel drive and independent suspension, with a variable tyre-pressure system as a valuable bonus. It is a reasonable assessment that, with such systems, only 10 per cent of the terrain in Europe that is accessible to tracked vehicles is actually innaccessible to wheeled AFVs and in general terms, for combat weights below about 20 tons (20,321kg), a well-designed wheeled vehicle with good suspension and multi-wheel drive is only marginally less capable than a tracked vehicle. A 6×6 or 8×8 wheeled AFV also has a definite advantage over a tracked vehicle, since if the latter breaks or throws a track it is completely immobilised whereas the former can keep going with one, and in some cases two, wheels out of action.

The wheeled light AFV, whose history is actually longer than that of the tank, and which seemed to be on the verge of disappearance in the 1960s, is currently enjoying a revival. There are numerous designs in service or in development, for service either as reconnaissance vehicles or, in the case of the heavier types, as light fighting vehicles. They range in size and complexity from the Brazilian ENGESA EE-3 Jararaca, a 5.4-ton (5,500kg) scout car with a straightforward spring suspension and a pintle-mounted 12.7mm machine-gun, to the French AMX-

gun, uses the engine of the tracked AMX-10P but with a 6 × 6 hydropneumatic suspension that allows ground clearance to be adjusted to suit the terrain.

10RC, armed with a 105mm gun on a 6×6 variable-height, hydro-pneumatic suspension and weighing no less than 15.6 tons (15,800kg). This latter vehicle is of great interest since it is virtually a wheeled version of the tracked AMX-10 APC. While the French could have produced a reconnaissance vehicle based on the tracked chassis with a 105mm gun turret, they have, in fact, chosen to develop the -10RC, in which they consider the tactical advantages and life-cycle costs to have outweighed the costs of developing the wheeled chassis.

The need for independent suspension has long been recognised as essential for wheeled light AFVs, but the complexities of multi-wheel drive have until recently tended to defeat many designers. In consequence there are still many four-wheel light AFVs in use, which are the least effective of the breed.

The 4×4 vehicle does not have as large a ground contact area as it should have, and there is an inherent tendency for it to belly-down on transverse ridges or to bog-down when wheel-slip develops on one wheel. To overcome this problem a number of vehicles have been developed which are essentially 4×4s but have additional wheels. The Soviet VRDM series, for example, has a pair of small belly wheels on either side, between the front and rear wheels, which can be lowered by the driver when required to improve cross-country performance or to cross ditches. These wheels have smooth tyres and are chain driven from a power take-off controlled by the driver; the vehicle is normally only driven in first gear while they are in operation. The French Panhard ERC 6×6 is a hybrid in that it has six powered wheels, but on roads the central pair of wheels can be raised. Another French idea, successful in its day but now out of use, was the Panhard EBR. This had four large, pneumatically-tyred wheels with four metal-clad, intermediate wheels which could be lowered and used for cross-country work. On both the intermediate wheels still turned when raised off the ground.

Above: Wheeled AFVs are also capable of mounting relatively heavy weapons, and the Panhard ERC armoured car, seen here with its central wheels raised, has been fitted with Hispano-Suiza Lynx 90 turret.

Below: Alternative turrets fitted to the ERC include the GIAT TS 90, seen here during a firing demonstration, and the SAMM TTB 190, both with 90mm guns, as well as a whole range with machine guns and light cannon.

The problems with the 4×4 are largely solved in a 6×6 configuration. There is much greater draw-bar pull, increased ground contact area and thus less rolling resistance. The only problem with 6×6, other than its increased complexity compared to 4×4, is that under certain conditions there is a tendency to pitch. Generally, however, 6×6 solves most of the shortcomings of the 4×4 configuration and is lighter and cheaper than 8×8.

The largest number of wheels used on wheeled AFVs to date is eight. This configuration overcomes the tendency of the 6×6 to pitch and generally produces the best cross-country performance of any wheeled vehicle but the layout is, of course, more complicated and expensive than 6×6 or 4×4. Whatever the configuration, the wheels should be as large as possible to minimise ground pressure and rolling resistance, although there is an apparent tendency with 8×8 AFVs to reduce the wheel size. A distinct improvement in performance is gained through having a variable tyre pressure system which can be controlled by the driver whilst on the move; all Soviet wheeled AFVs have had such a device for years, but very few Western vehicles have this useful facility.

SUSPENSION

Independent suspension uses one of three systems, trailing arms, leading arms or double transverse links (wishbones). The last-mentioned have structural advantages but are complicated mechanically in that the drive shaft must change in length (thus needing sliding, splined joints) and has large angular movements; moreover, they need space in which to operate, which tends to restrict the width of the hull. Trailing and leading arms, however, move only vertically, enabling a wider hull to be used except over steered wheels.

A particularly interesting system is fitted to the Brazilian ENGESA EE-9 armoured car and EE-11 APC, both of which are 6×6 vehicles using the ENGESA Kangaroo walking-beam system. In this a rigid rear axle holding the two walking-beams is connected to the hull by double-leaf, semi-elliptical springs and double-action, telescopic dampers. The beams are able to rotate freely around the central hub with a maximum travel of 35.4in (0.9m), which ensures that all six wheels are in contact with the ground at all times. Power is taken from the drive shaft to all four rear wheels by gears within the walking beam.

Most vehicles use a mixture of leaf springs and telescopic dampers, which are cheap, simple and well-understood. The critical factor is the vertical travel permitted to the wheels, because, to a large extent, this governs the cross-country speed. With spring suspensions such travel is normally limited to between 5 and 8in (125-200mm), but this is increasing: the wheels on the Swiss Mowag Shark, for example, have a vertical travel of 16.5in (420mm).

Hydropneumatic suspension has a number of major advantages for light AFVs, the main one being that the ground clearance can be adjusted to suit the terrain. The Messier system, for example, used on the French AMX-10RC 6×6 reconnaissance vehicle, is capable of adjustment between 8.27in (210mm) minimum and 23.6in (600mm) maximum, with 13.8in (350mm) normal for road movement and 18.5in (470mm) the norm for cross-country. The vehicle's attitude can also be adjusted laterally by raising or lowering each side, enabling the vehicle to be levelled in firing positions. Torsion bars are also used in some wheeled vehicles, particularly with trailing arms.

DRIVES

The only light, wheeled AFVs without multi-wheel drive are a few types designed for internal security

Above: The Belgian SIBMAS 6 × 6 APC, shown here with Cockerill CM 90 turret as delivered to Malaysia, is typical of modern light AFVs in being fully amphibious, using its wheels to achieve 4km/h in water.

Below: The same turret is fitted to this variant of the Cadillac-Gage Commando V-150 4 × 4 armoured car, numerous examples of which have been sold to many Third World armed forces.

duties in an urban environment; all others now have multi-wheel drive. There are two types of transmission. The first is the conventional single line of transmission shafts running down the centre of the vehicle with differentials taking power via universally-jointed half-shafts to each set of wheels; the second is the H-drive, with a single central differential and shafts running fore and aft down each side of the vehicle.

The H-drive offers a number of advantages. It prevents wheel cross-spin and it allows the height of the hull to be reduced as the driver and engine can be placed between, rather than over, the transmission shafts. It also makes it possible to use skid-steering as on tanks, although so far this has been introduced only in the French AMX-10RC. The H-drive can, moreover, cope well with battle-damaged wheels or tyres: on a 6×6, for example, the vehicle can continue to move with any one wheel damaged, or with two damaged provided they are not both on the front, the back or the same side. (This is an attribute for which British Saladin and Saracen drivers have frequently been very grateful, where terrorist mines have blown off a wheel during internal security operations.) However, the H-drive suffers a number of disadvantages. On roads it is apt to suffer from transmission torque wind-up and tyre-scrub, although the use of limited slip differentials on each side (as in Panhard vehicles) solves this problem.

An unusual system has been adopted by the USSR for its very successful BTR series wheeled APCs, which have two rear-mounted engines. These are configured so that the right-hand engine drives the first and third axles and the left-hand engine the second and fourth. Torque is transmitted from each engine to the wheels through a

Left: Another 90mm-armed vehicle, the MOWAG Piranha 6 × 6 has a MECAR KEnerga weapon in a two-man turret. The front-wheel steering shown in action here gives a turning radius of 24ft (7.3m).

hydraulically-controlled, single-plate clutch with a 4-speed gearbox (with synchromesh on 3rd and 4th gears) and a 2-speed transfer box to the final drives of the two axles, with gearless differentials and four wheel reducers. Torque from the final drive to the reducers is transmitted through stub-axles and gimbal drive gears.

STEERING

Almost all wheeled AFVs use conventional steering, turning one or more sets of wheels to change direction; most, particularly the heavier vehicles, have the benefit of power assistance. Whilst steering is obviously an essential function, the disadvantage in a fighting vehicle lies in the fact that the steering wheels must be given room to turn, which leads to a much narrower internal hull compartment.

Below: The FL-12 turret with GIAT 105mm gun, developed for the AMX-13 light tank, is also used by the SK-105 and has been installed on this MOWAG Shark 8 × 8 weapons carrier for trials.

All 4×4 vehicles use front-wheel steering only. With 6×6 vehicles, however, a variety of steering systems has been adopted. Some simply use front-wheel steering, while others, like the Renault VBC-90, steer the front four wheels. The Spanish company ENASA has a system in which its 6×6 drive uses steering on the front and rear wheels, with only the two central wheels unsteered. Of the 8×8 vehicles, most have steering on the front four wheels, as in the Soviet BTR-60/70 and the US LAV, but the West German Spähpanzer can steer all eight wheels, although only the front four are steered on roads.

Uniquely, the French AMX-10RC has skid-steering and, since none of its wheels swivel, it can have a wide hull. However, as with tracked vehicles, it runs the risk of stalling when trying to turn on soft ground.

WEAPONS

For many years wheeled AFVs had only light weapons, such as machine-guns or 20 or 30mm cannon. The British Saladin of the 1960s, however, mounted a 76mm

Above: Steyr-Daimler-Puch has proposed many armament configurations for its Pandur 6 × 6, including this ARSV 4/250 variant with 25mm cannon.

gun and this led the way towards a much heavier armament. Thus 90mm cannon are now commonplace, being used on vehicles such as the ENGESA EE-9 (Brazil), Renault ERC-90 (France), Panhard AML (France) and Ratel FSV-90 (South Africa), and at least two contemporary vehicles, the AMX-10RC (France) and the MOWAG Shark (Switzerland), mount 105mm guns.

The problem has been that of recoil, but, as discussed in the section on tanks, the development of soft recoil systems is now making much larger weapons available to lighter vehicles. The 105mm gun fitted to the AMX-10RC, for example, has a muzzle brake and a 600mm recoil travel, and these reduce the recoil force to some 13 tonnes, which is well within the normally accepted limit of 1.5 times the vehicle's weight (which in this case would be 15.8 × 1.5 = 23.7 tonnes).

Anti-tank Warfare

The battle to combat the tank must be viewed as an entity if it is to be understood properly and if the way in which designers have sought to help solve tactical problems by technological means are to be placed in their proper context. When originally faced with tanks in World War I the Germans scoffed at 'this ridiculous weapon', but were then forced to start treating them seriously and to find some means of combating them. First to be used were ordinary field-guns in the direct-fire mode, and these accounted for no less than 98 per cent of all Allied tanks destroyed or seriously damaged in the war. However, after early tank losses to such artillery in 1916-17 the Allies doubled the thickness of tank armour from 0.5in (12mm) to 1in (24mm), increased the speed of the ponderous vehicles and revised their tactics. As a result tank losses due to artillery fire dropped from 54 per cent in the Battle of the Somme in 1916 to just 24 per cent at Amiens in 1918. German field gun losses to tank fire were equally serious, so they turned to the development of specialised anti-tank weapons and by the war's end were testing a 37mm anti-tank gun with a round capable of penetrating some 1.2 to 1.6in (30mm to 40mm) of armour.

The battle thus joined in 1916 has continued ever since, the balance of advantage swinging from one side to another as scientists and tacticians have combined their efforts to defeat the opposition. For tanks the measures have included thicker armour and bigger guns, until by the end of World War II the 'heavy' tanks had become so gross and unwieldy that, like the dinosaurs they resembled, they ensured their own demise. Designers have also tried to increase mobility at the expense of armour, so that the tank can cross ground with such rapidity and expose itself so fleetingly that anti-tank weapons are unable to engage it. Unfortunately for tank crews such designers' dreams can seldom be realised under combat conditions so they have had to compromise and produce tanks in which protection is achieved through a judicious balance between good (but not the best possible) mobility and good (but not the thickest and heaviest possible) armoured protection, together with a heavy (but perhaps not the largest) main gun.

The anti-tank forces have meanwhile had two simple goals: first, piercing the enemy's armour and second, having achieved that, incapacitating the crew or the tank, or both. For many years these objectives were reached by making bigger shells, to be fired from ever heavier and more bulky conventional guns. By the middle of World War II, however, the guns were, like the tanks, becoming so large that they were difficult to move and to site tactically. Designers sought an escape from this in three main directions. First, they looked for different types of ammunition which would increase the effectiveness of the conventional gun without adding to its weight; this led to such rounds as the sub-calibre

Armour Piercing Discarding Sabot (APDS), which penetrates due to its kinetic energy, and to chemical-energy rounds such as hollow-charge (High Explosive Anti-Tank, or HEAT) and High-Explosive Squash Head (HESH)/High Explosive Plastic (HEP). Second, the designers turned to much lighter weapons altogether by eliminating the recoil forces and producing large-calibre, recoilless guns which were effective against the most modern tanks but still capable of being manoeuvred around the battlefield by the infantry. Third, a completely new weapon, the guided missile, was adapted to the anti-tank role. No single one of these weapons, delivery systems or warheads has proved to be the complete answer, and the effectiveness of each has, of course, depended as much upon its tactical handling by the soldier-operators as upon its technical excellence.

One critical addition to the anti-tank armoury is the helicopter. Helicopters can carry a variety of payloads, have a series of very sophisticated on-board surveillance and target acquisition aids, and by their very nature are flexible, capable of rapid deployment from one part of the battlefield to another to meet changing threats. Their characteristics and use are outlined in a later chapter.

Physical obstacles to a tank's progress have been tried since 1916, and one of the basic design parameters for early tanks was its ability to cross an infantry front-line trench. Modern thought tends to concentrate on natural obstacles, reinforced by demolitions and minefields. Finally, nuclear weapons can be used to create anti-tank barriers, either through 'normal' nuclear explosions or by using an ER weapon to kill the crew.

Top and above: Copperhead is designed to give standard 155mm artillery weapons a true anti-tank capability and these pictures show the final moments in an engagement. After following a normal ballistic trajectory with fin stabilisation, the Copperhead round switches to laser homing during the final phases of its attack, deploying wings to enable it to reach the designated target and detonate its warhead.

Above: One of the most successful anti-tank weapons of its generation, the Hughes TOW system uses a tube launcher and the missile is controlled by signals passed down a wire. It has proved easy to use, highly accurate and effective. The major problem is that, like all other ATGWs, it uses a hollow-charge warhead, which is likely to be defeated by the latest types of armour.

The purpose of the defensive anti-tank battle is to render an aggressor's tank force ineffective through a combination of deception, delay and destruction. To achieve this the anti-tank plan must possess depth and flexibility, with all the elements being welded together into a cohesive entity. Anti-tank weapon delivery systems range from aircraft capable of attacking concentrations of armour deep inside enemy territory, through helicopters, artillery and anti-tank guns, to grenades launched from rifles. All these have their place in defeating tanks, but without an overall policy they will be ineffectively deployed and will almost certainly fail to stop an enemy's advance.

ATTACKING ARMOUR

For the aggressor the tank force is the mobile fighting arm which is designed to punch a way through the enemy's defences and then drive into the relatively weaker rear areas to capture the objectives which will ensure strategic victory. This was how the German panzers were used against Poland in 1939 and France in 1940, and it is how the USSR intends to use its forces against NATO in any future war in Europe. To resist such aggression and to prevent such a tank breakthrough the defensive forces must optimise their anti-tank capability, and this has happened to such an extent in NATO — a declared 'defensive' alliance — that the armies in Western Europe are virtually one great anti-tank system, with all other roles subordinated to this task. The Warsaw Pact armies also possess anti-tank forces, but their task is to destroy NATO armour in order to allow their tanks to break through, or to provide a quick defence against counter-attacks on a recently captured position. The Warsaw Pact is thus conducting an aggressive anti-tank battle, whereas NATO's task is to destroy Warsaw Pact armour in order to halt the advance — a great difference in emphasis. This leads NATO to consider such devices as the ER weapon, which is, of course, of no interest to the USSR.

Armoured forces can be rendered ineffective through neutralisation, immobilisation or destruction. Neutralisation is achieved by any means short of actual attack on the individual tanks and can be achieved by obstacles, which can be natural (rivers, canals, forests, mountains) or artificial (ADMs, minefields, urban areas); by electronic warfare, which can disrupt or totally prevent the effective command and control of groups of tanks as a cohesive military force; or by logistic warfare, in which the essential supplies to sustain the tank force are denied (e.g. vehicle fuel and ammunition). Such neutralisation can take place either on the battlefield or some distance from it, and by causing delay and disruption it renders the individual tanks open to destruction by long-range weapons launched from aircraft or from precision-guided munitions (PGM).

Direct attack on a tank can, in the first instance, result in the vehicle's immobilisation through the destruction of one or both tracks or of the power-pack, either by projectiles or by mines; in addition, the tank can be immobilised by killing or incapacitating the crew through nuclear radiation or by chemical weapons. The crew can also cease to be effective through less direct means, such as poor morale or exhaustion. An immobilised tank can, of course, be recovered and repaired, or have its crew replaced, but all of these place a strain upon the logistics system, which is itself a further factor in the overall anti-tank battle.

The actual destruction of a tank can be achieved by three means of attack, kinetic energy, chemical energy or the direct effects of nuclear weapons. Kinetic-energy rounds depend upon the hardness and mass of the projectile combined with the velocity of impact to punch a way through the target's armoured protection, whereas chemical-energy rounds depend upon the various effects of high explosive when detonated against armoured plate. In both cases success is the result of hitting the tank in the right place with the best type of projectile for the range annd armour protection involved. The chances of simple high explosive (for example, from an artillery shell) destroying a tank are remote, but the blast of a nuclear explosion will have a destructive effect upon a tank close to ground-zero (although at such a range the immediate radiation effects will have killed the crew anyway).

ANTI-TANK GUNS

During World War II the majority of anti-tank weapons were guns, firing a variety of armour-piercing rounds from a closed tube in the traditional way. Progress was rapid. The British, for example, started the war with the 2pdr gun capable of penetrating 2in (50mm) of armour plate at 1,000yd (914m) and ended with the 17pdr (76.2mm calibre) with an APDS round which could penetrate 8in (203mm) of armour at 1,000yd (914m). The heavy anti-tank guns available in 1945 were, however, becoming too cumbersome for

Above: Euromissile Hot Mephisto installation on a French VAB; four missiles are mounted on the electrically-actuated retractable launcher and a further eight are carried inside the vehicle. Hot has a range of 250ft (75m) to 2.5 miles (4km) and is a tube-launched, wire-guided system using automatic command-to-line-of-sight guidance.

Below: The Hot missile, shown in its tube (below left); with aerodynamic surfaces deployed (bottom left); as a cross-section through the guidance module (below); and in rear view.

Euromissile Hot

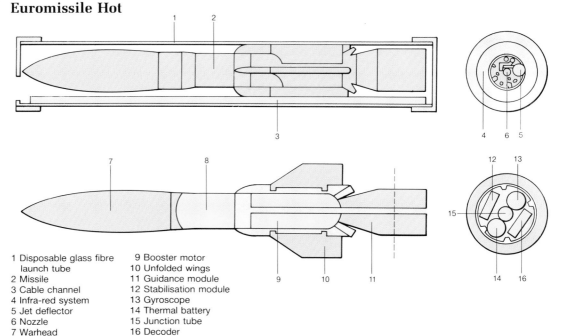

1 Disposable glass fibre launch tube	9 Booster motor
2 Missile	10 Unfolded wings
3 Cable channel	11 Guidance module
4 Infra-red system	12 Stabilisation module
5 Jet deflector	13 Gyroscope
6 Nozzle	14 Thermal battery
7 Warhead	15 Junction tube
8 Sustainer motor	16 Decoder

Above: The Swedish Bofors company has developed a new range of ammunition to restore the anti-armour capability of weapons such as the venerable 106mm BAT.

Right: The Bofors ammunition, especially the 3A-HEAT-T (lower), is claimed to overcome the protective capabilities of the new heavy and reactive armours.

infantry use and in most armies there was a rapid move away from them towards recoilless guns, rocket launchers and guided missiles. Nevertheless, anti-tank guns do remain in service with a number of armies, especially those in the Warsaw Pact. Most such weapons to have been deployed since 1945 have come from the Soviet Union, Belgium and Switzerland, but unless there is some totally new breakthrough in ammunition design it seems unlikely that there will be any further development, especially as new types of MBT are virtually invulnerable to such attack.

SP ANTI-TANK GUNS

Self-Propelled Anti-Tank guns (SPAT), also known as 'tank destroyers', enjoyed some popularity during World War II, the idea being to optimise firepower at the expense of either mobility or protection. Although some SPATs have rotating turrets, most have the main gun mounted in the upper glacis plate with very limited movement.

The SPAT lives on today with the Soviet SU-100 which is still in the reserve units of a number of armies, while the ASU-85 is in service with airborne units of the Soviet, East German and Polish Armies. The West German Army followed World War II practice when it produced the Jagdpanzer 4-5 in the 1960s; some 750 are in service with the Bundesheer and 80 with the Belgian Army. This vehicle has a 90mm gun with elevation limits of +15° and — 8° and a traverse of 15° left and right. Unlike these SPATs, the Austrian Jagdpanzer Kurassier has a fully traversing turret. This very neat design marries the French FL-12 oscillating turret and D-1504 105mm gun to a modified Saurer RK APC chassis. Finally, many authorities would argue that the Swedish S-tank is merely a sophisticated SPAT, especially as it cannot fire on the move. The Swedish Army also has a large number of Infanterikanonvagn 91 (Ikv-91) tank destroyers in service and also has a revolutionary articulated tank destroyer under development.

The SPAT is somewhat cheaper than the MBT, but it is tactically neither as effective nor as ubiquitous. It is, therefore, questionable as to whether it is a really worthwhile concept. Very few armies maintain any further interest in the weapon, especially as light tanks with soft recoil, large-calibre guns seem to provide a better solution.

RECOILLESS WEAPONS

The size and weight of the later anti-tank guns came about largely as a result of the need to absorb the ever-increasing recoil forces produced by larger rounds and greater muzzle velocities, and it was in an endeavour to escape from this trend that the recoilless gun was developed. This weapon simply utilises Newton's Law that 'action and reaction are equal and opposite'. The projectile is fired from a tube which is open at both ends, and as it moves forward it is counterbalanced by the rearward expulsion of a large volume of high-velocity gas.

The absence of recoil means that small weapons can be fired from a man's shoulder (for example, the 84mm Carl Gustaf and the 3.5in rocket launcher), while the heavier weapons such as the British 120mm Wombat and the Soviet B-11 107mm are fired from simple wheeled mounts. While these recoilless guns are light, uncomplicated and easily transported, they suffer from two major drawbacks. The sound of firing is both loud and easy to distinguish, and the back-blast from the rear of the tube is accompanied by both flash and a pall of smoke. It is thus virtually impossible to fire the weapons without giving their position away and this, together with their low muzzle velocity (and thus relatively long time of flight) imposes a tactical limitation on their use. The former problem has, however, been solved in an ingenious way by the German Armbrust, a 67mm recoilless gun in which the explosion is contained by two pistons, which means that the flash and smoke normally associated with such a weapon are eliminated.

The heavier versions of the recoilless gun are gradually losing favour, although they are still to be seen in great numbers in the Soviet-bloc armies and in the Third World. In contrast, the lighter, shoulder-fired recoilless guns are still very much in vogue. Although they suffer from the tactical limitations imposed by flash and blast they currently represent the best means of giving the infantry an effective close-range tank-killing capability. Weapons such as the Carl Gustaf are efficient, although the effectiveness of their

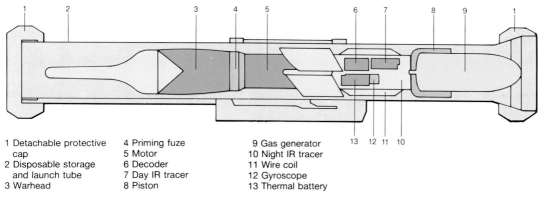

Above: Milan is a successful missile in wide-scale use. The spike on the nose is designed to ensure that the hollow-charge warhead is detonated at precisely the optimum stand-off distance from the target to ensure maximum effectiveness. Penetration of a standard armour plate is claimed to be more than 33in (850mm).

Below: Milan in its launch tube. The gas-generator drives the piston to impart an initial velocity of 250ft/sec (75m/sec) to the missile as it leaves the tube.

Euromissile Milan

1 Detachable protective cap	4 Priming fuze	9 Gas generator
2 Disposable storage and launch tube	5 Motor	10 Night IR tracer
3 Warhead	6 Decoder	11 Wire coil
	7 Day IR tracer	12 Gyroscope
	8 Piston	13 Thermal battery

tank mines is fired from a conventional 155mm gun (e.g. M109) to ranges up to 18,500yd (17,000m).

The primary task of an armoured force is to break through the enemy front-line and penetrate to the rear areas. It follows that although the artillery gun positions are set back from the forward infantry, the artillery units may nevertheless come under direct attack from tanks. Most field guns, particularly the Soviet models, are, therefore, supplied with anti-tank shells for use in a direct-fire engagement, although such an action should be the exception rather than the rule!

ANTI-TANK GUIDED WEAPONS

HEAT warhead against new types of armour is a question that remains to be resolved.

SP RECOILLESS GUNS

Recoilless guns have been mounted on vehicles: the British, for example, have mounted the 120mm BAT on the FV 432 APC, while the Americans have mounted their 106mm M40A1 both on the M113 APC and on various wheeled field cars. A specialised armoured vehicle used by the US Marines in the 1950s and 1960s was the M50 Ontos, comprising six 106mm RCLs mounted on a light tracked vehicle. The problem of back-blast and obfuscation remained, however, and the vehicle could not fire on the move. The only other country to show any interest in this concept has been Japan, who developed the Type 60, a tracked vehicle mounting two 106mm RCLs on an extendible arm; it is still in service but is unlikely to be replaced.

ARTILLERY

The ability of tube artillery to act effectively against tanks has been somewhat limited for many years, although a direct hit in the right spot —the probability of which is remote and which would require the expenditure of large amounts of ammunition — would certainly either immobilise the vehicle or

incapacitate the crew. The use of artillery to deliver shells well beyond the range of direct-fire weapons is of great tactical importance, and a major attempt to extend the range at which battlefield weapons can engage tanks is being made by the Americans in their Precision-Guided Munitions (PGM) programme.

The M-712 Copperhead system comprises a projectile fired from a conventional 155mm cannon against a target illuminated by a laser target marker (LTM), with a laser seeker and a guidance system mounted in the projectile to steer it onto the target. Targets outside the range of a forward observer located with front-line troops can be marked by LTMs mounted in helicopters, aircraft or RPVs. Intended primarily for attack on tanks, Copperhead proved to be a much more difficult

Above: The Chinese Norinco 40mm anti-tank launcher fires a 94mm diameter rocket out to a maximum range of 330yards (300m). Such weapons are unlikely to be effective against the new armours.

development programme than had originally been expected, and it is not being procured in the large quantities once forecast. One of the major problems has been the original underestimation of the extent to which a future battlefield is likely to be obscured by smoke, fire, dust and haze, thus severely limiting target acquisition, especially at longer ranges and from ground observers.

A second, indirect-fire contribution to the anti-tank battle is also being developed in the USA. This is the M718 Remote Anti-Armor Mine System (RAAMS), in which a 155mm projectile carrying nine anti-

Today, the most important anti-tank weapon, apart from an MBT's main gun, is the anti-tank guided weapon (ATGW), which has developed rapidly in the past 30 years. The apparent success of ATGWs in the 1973 Yom Kippur war led some commentators to the view that the effectiveness of such missiles had reached a level where the tank itself was no longer a valuable weapon of war. A more sober assessment showed that while the ATGWs scored early successes due to tactical surprise about the method in which they were used, they were, in fact, fairly easily countered and the

Below: The Bofors BILL is a unique top-attack weapon, with the hollow-charge warhead aimed downwards at an angle of 30°. This is designed to penetrate the more vulnerable upper surfaces of the tank.

Above: The British LAW 80 uses a built-in spotting rifle to ensure that the aim and range are correct before firing. The rifle is thrown away with the tube after firing.

majority of tank kills had been, as in the past, caused by the guns of other tanks.

All known ATGWs have shaped-charge (HEAT) warheads, and their main differences lie in the guidance systems, of which there are currently two types, Manual Command to Line-of-Sight (MCLOS) and Semi-Automatic Command to Line-of-Sight (SACLOS). In a MCLOS system the operator is required to direct the flight of the missile by observing both the target and the missile, transmitting corrections to the missile to keep it on track by means of a joy-stick and control box; the operator thus steers the missile throughout its flight. In a SACLOS system, however, the operator simply keeps the cross-hairs of his weapon sight on the target and a computer then calculates the difference between the missile flight-path and the line-of-sight to the target; it then transmits commands to the missile to bring it back onto the correct course. The controller does not have to concern himself with the missile and does not 'fly' it in the same sense as the MCLOS operator.

Arguments have raged for 20 years about the value of ATGWs and particularly about the two basic control methods currently available. MCLOS missile systems are criticised because of the time taken for an operator to acquire the necessary skills — an important consideration in a conscript army — although simulators are now available to alleviate this particular problem. It is of interest that all the Soviet ATGWs fired in the Yom Kippur war used MCLOS systems and, if the effectiveness of the Egyptian infantry was anything to go by, the training problem is not an insuperable one.

ATGWs are launched from either tubes or from zero-length launchers, which can be mounted on helicopters, on vehicles or on the ground. The main reason for the success of ATGW is that the HEAT warhead permits a considerable tank-killing capability to be combined with a light missile of minimal dimensions, sufficiently cheap to be purchased in large numbers, even by the smaller armies; further, the effect of the warhead is not dependent upon the range of the weapon nor its velocity of impact. ATGWs do have a number of disadvantages, however, particularly their relatively low speed, leading to long flight times at ranges over 1,000yd (914m) and their considerable minimum range, typically 200 to 300yd (183-274m).

The major problem for ATGWs in the immediate future is that recent technological developments in tank design are all designed primarily to degrade the performance of HEAT warheads. Such developments include the new 'special' armours now in service with both NATO and the Warsaw Pact (pictures and official diagrams released concerning the British Chobham armour suggest that the high-energy jet of current HEAT rounds cannot penetrate it at all), Israeli Blazer

Dynamit Nobel Panzerfaust 3 off-route mine

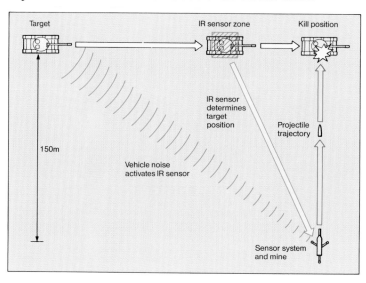

Above: Adding the SIRA IR sensor to the Panzerfaust 3 RCL launcher produces an unattended, sensor-operated off-route mine, fired automatically when a target is detected.

Below: The MBB PARM off-road anti-tank mine is triggered by a tank running over a fibre-optic cable laid in the direction of fire; like Panzerfaust, it has a shaped-charge warhead.

reactive armour and the appliqué armour now being fitted to tanks such as T-62 and Chieftain.

OBSTACLES

The elementary nature of most obstacles and the apparent ability of modern tanks to surmount them combine to give the misleading impression that anti-tank barriers are no longer of any great value. Nothing could be further from the truth, and obstacles, both natural and man-made, continue to be an essential part of any anti-tank plan. There are two fundamental requirements for any such obstacle: it must be part of an integrated plan, and it must be covered by controlled, observed fire.

Natural obstacles include rivers, canals, dense woods, lakes and buildings, but virtually all of these will require some form of artificial enhancement to optimise their anti-tank capability. The danger of complacency arising from the apparent impregnability of obstacles was illustrated yet again in the Yom Kippur war of 1973. The Israelis' western frontier lay on the Suez Canal, a natural barrier of considerable effectiveness. Not satisfied with this, however, they reinforced their side of the canal with a sand wall some 50 to 70ft (15-21m) high and of considerable width. The combination of the canal, the sand wall and the defences of the so-called Bar-Lev Line was impressive but unfortunately it impressed the Israelis more than it did the Egyptians. A junior lieutenant in the Egyptian Engineer Corps came up

Below: One of the major tasks of the British Combat Engineer Tractor is to help tanks overcome obstacles using such devices as this rocket-launched grapple.

FFV 028 anti-tank mine performance

A: 50mm armour plate;
exit hole diameter approximately 65mm

B: 10mm commercial iron plate;
exit hole diameter approximately 80mm

C: 10mm commercial iron plate;
exit hole diameter approximately 140mm

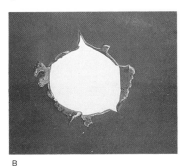
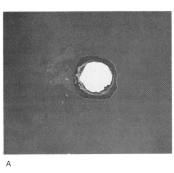

Above: The penetration effects of the Swedish FFV 028 anti-tank mine, with the mine placed 1.6ft (0.5m) below the plates. The 50mm plate, representing the tank's belly armour, is penetrated by the shaped-charge jet and the 10mm thick witness plates give an indication of the jet's effects on the tank's interior structure.

Dynamit Nobel AT-2 anti-tank mine configuration

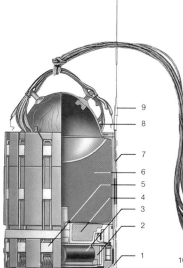

1 Safe and arm assembly housing
2 Sensors
3 Battery
4 Electronic and mechanical fuze assembly
5 Erection mechanism
6 Shaped charge
7 Warhead case
8 Cover
9 Target sensor
10 Parachute

Above: The Dynamit Nobel AT-2 is intended for aerial delivery by artillery shells or rocket systems. The mine's final descent is controlled by a parachute.

Right: The West German Army uses the Skorpion mine-launching system for the rapid deployment of dense anti-tank and anti-personnel minefields, using very few men.

with the answer: use the water of the canal and high pressure hoses to wash away the sand wall. The achievement of both strategic and tactical surprise, coupled with the Israelis' complacency, meant that the obstacle was not covered by fire at the critical time and the Egyptian infantry assault, together with the sappers' use of a 'low-tech' device in an imaginative way, soon cleared the way for the armoured divisions to sweep through into the Sinai Desert.

This episode illustrates the strengths and weaknesses of a 'barrier mentality', especially in the anti-tank battle. The right sort of barrier ought to be effective, but, as was shown by the Egyptians, none can be totally effective, and it must be watched and protected as any other defensive position. There may be areas in Western Europe now which are, according to NATO generals, 'impossible for tanks' and which, therefore, have had their defences reduced. The question must be whether the Soviet generals will agree with that assessment.

The creation of artificial obstacles as part of an anti-tank plan is a major preoccupation for all engineer corps, since even natural obstacles need some form of improvement to increase their effectiveness. The most rudimentary form of obstacle is the anti-tank ditch, but this seems so unsophisticated that many armies have long since rejected it as a weapon of modern war. The Israelis, however, used an anti-tank ditch to great effect on the Golan Heights in the Yom Kippur war. They had dug a ditch some 33 to 39ft (10-12m) wide and 13ft (4m) deep across the open plateau which stretches from Mount Hermon in the north to Rafid in the south, a distance of some 35 miles (55km). The spoil was piled on the Israeli side of the ditch. Although simple in concept, it was a major engineering undertaking, but it repaid the efforts one hundred fold, because when the Syrian tanks attacked they had to mount a special operation to cross the ditch using bridgelayers. Some 1,700 Syrian tanks attacked the Israeli regulars defending the Golan with 175 Centurions and M48s, and it was vital that these held the line until the arrival of the reserves. Despite the surprise attack the Israelis stood fast: the Syrians certainly crossed the ditch in many places, but the cost in tanks, crews and (possibly most important of all) time ultimately was devastating.

All engineer corps have a large range of plant and equipment to assist them in preparing obstacles. Such equipment includes armoured tractors (British Combat Engineer Tractor, Soviet IMR, etc), heavy-duty, large volume diggers (Soviet MDK-2, BAT and BTM) and many heavy vehicles drawn directly from the civil construction industry.

MINES

Considerable effort has been devoted over the past 20 years to improving the effectiveness and speed of laying of anti-tank mines. The minefield has the advantages of being able either to stop (or at least seriously deplete) an advance on one sector or to 'channel' the enemy into ground of the defenders' own choosing. As with other obstacles, minefields must be part of an overall plan and must be covered by fire.

The majority of anti-tank mines comprise a large explosive charge and a pressure-sensitive firing device, although some also have rods which react to lateral forces; others respond to magnetic or seismic disturbance. The force of the explosion will normally break a track and damage at least some of the roadwheels and suspension (resulting in a 'mobility' kill), although with luck the belly-plate may also be pierced. To make this more certain a number of mines constructed on the hollow-charge principle are now in servcice and these will penetrate belly-plates of up to 70mm thickness, doing considerable damage inside the tank. Other operational types include the British Barmine and the French Horizontal Action Anti-Tank Mine (MICAH), together with the various air- and artillery-delivered minelets with their effective HEAT charges.

The major modern development lies in the means of delivery and laying. The biggest practical problem with mines is that they cannot, in general, be laid in peacetime and need to be positioned very quickly one hostilities have started. Nowadays, the traditional methods are simply not quick enough and are too labour-intensive, and mechanical layers have been developed, together with minelaying helicopters, artillery shells and rockets.

Artillery

The artillery branches of the major armies emerged from World War II as fully mechanised forces using wheeled guns and tractors, except for a few instances where tracked vehicles had been adapted to carry guns and howitzers in open mounts; 155mm was the largest calibre in normal use, and most field and medium artillery pieces were of 130mm or less. The immediate needs were to increase mobility by putting the guns on tracked mounts, while other trends were the ever-increasing sophistication of the installations and a growth in calibre to provide more effective terminal effects at ever-greater ranges.

Soviet artillery divisions persevered with towed guns deployed in linear positions long after many other armies, especially those of NATO nations facing them in northwestern Europe, had converted to self-propelled weapons in dispersed positions, but once they had decided to convert to SPs the task was completed with quite extraordinary rapidity, and in the process Soviet gun designers managed to obtain greater projectile range than almost any of their Western counterparts.

The Soviet 152mm 2S5 is contemporary and generally similar in tactical concept, size and calibre to the US M109 yet the Soviet weapon has a 16 per cent greater muzzle velocity and a 64 per cent greater range, and similar differences in range have been demonstrated with other types of projectile, the Soviet weapon having the advantage in every case. Such differences are technically the result of a combination of barrel design and construction, pressure within the barrel and projectile design. The tactical implication is that the Soviet guns can be used in counter-battery fire against NATO weapons at ranges which the latter cannot match.

As for calibre, in the 1950s most Western nations saw 105mm as the standard for field artillery, with 155mm and 175mm for the heaviest requirements, but 155mm in the West and 152mm in the Eastern bloc are now standard, and the USSR has put a 203mm SP into service, while many NATO armies have long deployed small numbers of 8in (203mm) guns.

As calibres have increased so, too, have range and payload. The World War II Sexton, a standard SP gun in armoured divisions, was armed with a 3.45in (87.6mm) gun firing a 25lb (11.34kg) projectile to a maximum range of 13,397 yards (12,250m). Today's equivalent is the M109A1, a 155mm weapon firing a 94.6lb (42.91kg) projectile to a maximum range of 19,794 yards (18,100m), while the rocket-assisted projectiles available for certain guns have ranges of up to 33,800 yards (37,000m).

The payload of artillery shells has improved not only in quantity but also in variety and effectiveness, so that the traditional high explosive, armour-piercing, chemical, smoke and illuminating rounds are now supplemented by the nuclear shells that have been available for years, plus laser-guided shells such as Copperhead and top-attack anti-tank shells such as SADARM.

To optimise the utilisation of the available firepower, computerised command, control and peripheral systems are necessary to coordinate artillery fire support on a divisional and corps basis. Target acquisition methods have also had to be improved in order to give the guns timely and accurate information on enemy locations and to take advantage of the weapons' range capabilities.

AMMUNITION

An artillery projectile is essentially a means of transporting a payload from the gun to the enemy; most payloads are lethal, but there are also non-lethal types such as smoke, pyrotechnics, leaflets, sensors and ECM devices. The designer's task is to produce a shell which maximises payload, terminal effects, accuracy

Above: Soviet artillery units kept towed guns, which they deployed in lines in the open, long after other major armies had changed over to self-propelled weapons.

Below: First Soviet SP was the 2S3 152mm gun/howitzer, now in service in large numbers. Modern Soviet guns of 152mm calibre and above are nuclear-capable.

Above: The 203mm 2S7 SP gun can fire nuclear or conventional rounds to ranges of over 32,800 yards (30km). The canvas conceals breech and ammunition crane.

Below: Accuracy for rockets is very important. The Contraves Fieldguard system tracks a pilot rocket which self-destructs in the terminal flight phase. A computer

then produces weather-corrected fire commands derived from the difference between calculated and actual trajectories before the main battery opens fire.

Contraves Fieldguard fire control system operation

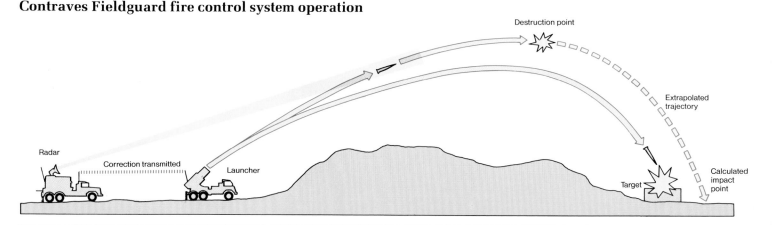

and range, while at the same time minimising barrel wear, and accommodating additional devices such as fuses, drogue parachutes, rocket motors or base-bleed gas generators. In addition, the shell must be capable of being stored for protracted periods — frequently in excess of 10 years — transported easily over rough terrain without damage, and then reaching predicted performance without preparation, on the one and only occasion it will be used.

The traditional projectile is a cylinder with a pointed front end and a slightly tapering boat-tail at the rear. In order to maintain stability it is spun in flight, the spin being imparted by rifling in the barrel to a fixed driving-band, normally mounted toward the rear of the body.

The design of the projectile is the inevitable compromise between a number of conflicting requirements: it must be able to carry a useful payload in a body which has good ballistic design, and which can withstand the exceptional pressures within the chamber, the shock of abrupt acceleration to high velocities and the spinning-up process as it moves through the rifling, all without distortion or catastrophic failure. The projectile in the Soviet 152mm D-30, for example, has been accelerated from rest to a velocity of 1,465mph (655m/sec) in a distance of 23.43ft (7.14m) by the time it leaves the muzzle.

The two principal factors affecting a projectile's performance are its initial thrust and drag. The thrust comes from the detonation of an explosive charge within the chamber, and it is standard practice to use charges of increasing size to achieve greater ranges. However, limits to the size of charge that can be used are imposed by the construction of the shell, the tube and the chamber, and the ability of the recoil system to absorb the shock of firing. Also, the barrel can be made longer, as in the case of the US 8in M110A1 and M110A2, whose barrels are 8ft (2.44m) longer than that of the original M110. Again there are limits, since long barrels can suffer from droop — a very small curvature in the barrel — and whip caused by stresses during firing, and both can affect accuracy.

One method of increasing thrust without affecting the recoil forces is to install in the base of the projectile a small rocket motor which fires once the projectile has left the barrel. Various countries have such rocket-assisted projectiles (RAPs) in production and there is no doubt that significant range increases are obtained. The US 8in M110A2, for example, fires its normal M106 HE round to a range of 23,300 yards (21,300m), whereas its rocket-assisted HE round has a maximum range of 31,800 yards (29,100m), an increase of 36 per cent.

Nothing is ever achieved without cost, however, and the addition of a rocket motor has two drawbacks. First, the rocket motor takes up space in the projectile and typically reduces the payload by about 30 per cent; alternatively, the projectile

Above: The increasing rates of fire and larger calibres of modern artillery weapons are placing severe loads on logistic systems. One response is specialised ammunition resupply vehicles such as this US Army M992 Field Artillery Ammunition Support Vehicle, which carries 90 rounds of 155mm or 48 rounds of 203mm.

Below: Like their Soviet counterparts, modern US heavy artillery weapons such as this 155mm M109 SP howitzer can fire nuclear projectiles.

Right: The Czech 152mm self-propelled howitzer on its wheeled chassis represents a realistic approach to the increasing complexity of SP systems.

must be made larger. Second, RAPs are inherently inaccurate, due primarily to variations in the timing in firing and cutting-off the motor. The motor in the US M650 203mm RAP, for example, ignites seven seconds after firing and burns for four seconds, and variations of microseconds in either period will seriously affect terminal accuracy.

Once a projectile has left the barrel its maximum range is a function of drag, or air resistance, during its ballistic trajectory. Drag comes in three principal forms, body drag, wave drag and base drag. Body drag is caused by the friction between the projectile body and the air it is

GIAT 155mm base bleed shell

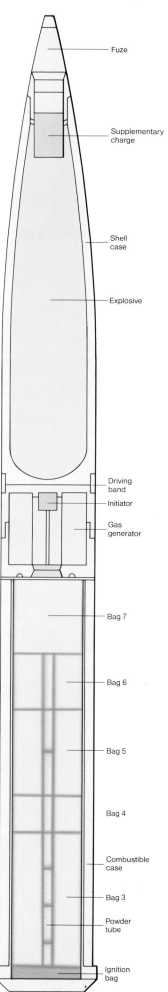

- Fuze
- Supplementary charge
- Shell case
- Explosive
- Driving band
- Initiator
- Gas generator
- Bag 7
- Bag 6
- Bag 5
- Bag 4
- Combustible case
- Bag 3
- Powder tube
- Ignition bag

passing through and is increased by the effects of rotation; wave drag is caused by the shape of the forebody — the profile between the tip and the driving band — and base drag results from the partial vacuum induced at the base of the projectile, and is a function of the shape of the rear end.

Various methods of increasing range have been tried. One, currently achieving some success, is to improve the ballistic shape of the projectile by adopting a longer, ogival shape, increasing in diameter from the pointed tip to the rear-mounted driving-band; such measures can decrease wave drag by up to 30 per cent. Range can also be enhanced by reducing the frontal area to produce a sub-calibre round held in place in the barrel by a discardable sabot; this reduces the mass of the projectile, but also reduces payload volume.

A further method of increasing range is base-bleed, in which a combustible (pyrophoric) compound is burned at the base of the projectile and emits a gas at a relatively low (subsonic) velocity. This creates a positive over-pressure in the immediate vicinity of the base, reducing base drag by up to 80 per cent, and because the gas is generated at low velocity it does not of itself act as a propellant and so does not increase the dispersion, as can happen with rocket-assisted projectiles.

A different method of increasing range has undergone examination

Left: Base bleed involves a gas generator in the base of the shell which expels gas at low pressure to reduce base drag and extend range without degrading accuracy. The

under the US Advanced Indirect Fire System (AIFS) programme: designed for use in the 8in M110A2, the AIFS projectile utilises a 5.97ft (1.82m) long projectile weighing 231lb (105kg) and with a claimed range of 43.5 miles (75km). The projectile, with a rear-mounted ramjet and trailing fins, is essentially a tube-launched missile. The original nose air intake limited the payload and later models have centrally mounted pop-out intakes, leaving the entire nose-section available for the payload, and the problems of producing missile components which can survive the very high pressures and the acceleration stresses in the barrel seem to have been achieved, but whether the project would reach production status was a question that had not been decided by early 1987.

PAYLOADS

Artillery projectiles can carry a whole host of payloads. The basic shell carries high explosive such as TNT, RDX or the newer Compound B, a mixture of 60 per cent RDX, 39 per cent TNT and one per cent desensitised wax. Other shells carry anti-tank and anti-personnel submunitions: the US M483A1 155mm shell, for example, carries 64 M42 shaped-charge anti-armour grenades and 24 M46 fragmentation grenades, making it effective against light armour, vehicles and personnel. The ballistically similar

GIAT 155mm H2 round, shown here in the form designed for the self-propelled GCT gun, provides a range increase of more than one third with the maximum charge.

M718 shell, a component of the Remote Anti-Armor System (RAAMS) carries nine of the much bigger magnetically activated M75 anti-armour minelets, each capable of stopping any known tank. Each minelet includes a self-destruct device, set in the factory for a time generally thought to be over 24 hours. A six-gun 155mm battery can lay an anti-armour minefield 330 yards (300m) deep by 273 yards (250m) wide with two salvos.

Anti-personnel minefields can also be laid. The US 155mm range includes the Area Denial Artillery Munition (ADAM), M692 and M731, each carries 36 M74 anti-personnel minelets, the difference being that the former self-destructs in over 24 hours and the latter in a shorter time. When the M74 submunition is activated, either by self-deploying trip-wires or by disturbance, a fragmentation unit is blown upwards and explodes, producing some 600 fragments with an initial velocity of around 3,000ft/sec (1,000m/sec).

One traditional use of artillery shells is to lay and develop smoke screens to cover friendly troops from hostile view. This is a notoriously difficult task, depending greatly upon conditions of rain and wind; for example, a head or tail wind relative to the desired direction of the screen can reduce the coverage given by one smoke canister by up to 80 per cent of its normal diameter in the case of white phosphorus and by

Below: The Chinese Type 74 rocket system delivers heavy anti-tank mines to a range of 1,640 yards (1,500m). Four fire units lay a 440yd (400m) square minefield.

Right: French 155mm GCT SP gun. The 40-calibre barrel elevates between +66° and −4° with full 360° traverse, and 42 rounds are carried.

around 30 per cent with hexchlorethane (HC), while the stronger the wind the more it thins out the screen.

To sustain a screen it is necessary to keep firing smoke shells; the Soviet army, for example, reckons on firing one HC 122mm or 130mm shell per minute under normal circumstances, but two or three per minute in adverse conditions. The US 155mm M825 shell carries 116 felt wedges, saturated in white phosphorus, which are scattered over the target area to generate a screen up to 273 yards (250m) long and lasting about 10 minutes. The Italian P5 155mm smoke shell carries 16.5lb (7.5kg) of smoke composition in four canisters, each of which is estimated to burn for two and a half minutes, producing a screen some 219 yards (200m) long, up to 50ft (15m) high and 164ft (50m) wide. Some such smoke shells now include an infra-red screening element, providing temporary protection against IR sensors as well as optical viewing.

A recently developed role for artillery shells is the delivery of expendable communications jammers. Currently limited to service with the US Army, their use may well spread for specific operations for carefully determined periods of time. In the US shell six jammers, known as pucks because of their resemblance to an ice-hockey puck, are dispensed by pre-set timers during flight; slowed down by de-spin fins and streamers, the pucks impact the ground at some 130ft/sec (40m/sec), penetrating, in typical soil, to a distance of between one and three inches (25-75mm). An antenna is then deployed and jamming transmissions begins almost immediately.

Shells are also used to deploy parachute-retarded flares to provide sustained battlefield illumination. A typical shell, the Italian Simmel P4, burns for a minimum of 65 seconds, descending at a speed of 16.5ft/sec (5m/sec), and has a maximum range of 26,250 yards (24,000m).

Artillery shells are used for other purposes. Nuclear and chemical shells are described in the appropriate sections elsewhere in this book, but another use is for distributing propaganda leaflets, especially to the enemy's forward troops. Some armies, especially those of the Warsaw Pact, also issue their artillery with anti-tank shells for use in the direct-fire mode in a last-ditch engagement.

SP ARTILLERY

The major armies now use SP artillery for general and major conventional wars, but towed guns continue to be developed to meet the needs of less demanding operational theatres. Indeed, there are even self-propelled mountings with wheeled chassis, the argument being that in

Above: US M109A1 155mm SP howitzer. Range is 19,800 yards (18,100m), or 26,250 yards (24,000m) for rocket-assisted projectiles.

Below: The tri-national SP-70 project failed in 1987 after 14 years in development. It was stated that the requirement had proved too ambitious.

areas with good roads and tracks, such as Europe, a wheeled chassis gives all the mobility that artillery actually needs in a cheaper and less complicated installation and one which is much easier to maintain.

Bigger calibres, heavier shells and demands for increased rates of fire have led to the use of autoloaders, with the result that the French 155mm GCT can fire at an average rate of eight rounds per minute, while the future US SP is intended to have a maximum sustained rate of fire of 12 rounds per minute. Of course, such high rates could not be sustained for long periods; not only do they impose heavy loads on crews and the mechanical and hydraulic systems in the vehicles, but they could easily exceed the capacity of the logistic system.

Two examples of comparable modern gun/howitzers will serve to illustrate the characteristics and trends in modern SPs. The Soviet 2S3 152mm SP gun/howitzer and the US 155mm M109A2 howitzer are similar in general appearance with tracked chassis and fully traversing turrets. The Soviet equipment uses the very successful 152mm D-20 towed gun/howitzer and a chassis derived from that used for the SA-4 Ganef SAM system. The normal HE shell weighs 95.9lb (43.5kg) and has a maximum range of 20,232 yards (18,500m), but there is also an extended range shell (HE/ER) with a range of 26,247 yards (24,000m) as well as a rocket-assisted projectile (RAP) with a reported range of 38,276 yards (35,000m). Other rounds include nuclear (2kt), chemical, HEAT, illuminating and smoke. Maximum rate of fire is between four and six rounds per minute and the sustained rate is two rounds per minute.

The M109 entered service in June 1963 and has been a particular success: around 2,000 are in service with 30 or so armies, and the latest version, the M109A2, is fitted with a new and much longer barrel, primarily in order to increase the range. It has a normal maximum range of 19,794 yards (18,100m) firing the standard HE shell and 26,247 yards (24,000m) with a rocket-assisted projectile and is capable of firing HE, chemical — CS,

VX or GB — 2kt nuclear and smoke shells, as well as transport shells carrying various submunition payloads. The normal rate of fire of one round per minute can be increased to three for short periods.

One consequence of the increases in projectile size and weight, rate of fire and mobility of modern SPs is that they have outstripped the capabilities of existing logistic systems, and both the US and Soviet armies have had to develop specialised artillery resupply vehicles. The US M992 Field Artillery Ammunition Support Vehicle (FAASV) uses the same chassis as M109 and carries 118 projectiles, 139 propellent charges and 176 fuses; ammunition is transferred mechanically to the SP at a rate of eight rounds per minute. A similar tracked vehicle is in use in the Soviet army, based upon the 2S7

chassis. The Soviets do, in fact, appear to have given themselves another problem with their new 152mm 2S5 and 203mm 2S7, which have their ordnance in open mounts, leaving no space on board for ammunition stowage and almost certainly obliging them to be accompanied by an ammunition vehicle at all times.

An indication of the complexity of modern SP guns is given by the recent cancellation of the 155mm SP-70, which was being developed jointly by West Germany, the UK and Italy. This very sophisticated weapon system combined many of the hull and automotive features of the Leopard 1 and 2 tanks with the ordnance from the successful FH-70 towed howitzer and a new, fully-traversing turret and autoloader. Development started in 1973 and prototypes were running by 1978, but the equipment was nowhere near production by early 1987 when it was finally cancelled. SP-70 fired all NATO and FH-70 ammunition; unassisted projectiles could be fired to a maximum range of 26,300 yards (24,000m) and the M549 RAP to 32,800 yards (30,000m).

WHEELED SP GUNS

Modern technology enables wheeled chassis to be used as SP mounts: leading example is the Czech 152mm SP howitzer, whose Tatra 815 truck chassis with its central tyre pressure regulation system and 8 × 8 drive provides fully adequate performance. The ordnance, derived from that used on the Soviet 2S3, is mounted in a split turret whose traverse is limited to the frontal arc only. The Czechs, whose armament industry has often provided ingenious solutions to old problems, appear to have produced a sensible, cheap and thoroughly practicable system, which other countries now seem to be following.

Second to appear was the South African G-6 155mm SP, which consists of a G-5 gun mounted in a revolving turret on a 6 × 6 wheeled chassis; combat weight is surprisingly heavy at some 35.9 tons (36,500kg). The design originated in Canada but substantial development work was done in South Africa.

The Chinese have also developed a wheeled SP 122mm howitzer using a lengthened 8 × 8 version of the six-wheeled infantry fighting vehicle and a 122mm gun mounted in a low turret at the rear of the vehicle with ±25° traverse and —3° to +70° elevation. It has a stated range of 22,965 yards (21,000m).

TOWED ARTILLERY

Despite its conventional appearance the SRC International GC 45 155mm towed howitzer is the only towed 155mm gun/howitzer to reach NATO's requirement for a maximum range of 32,810 yards (30,000m) without recourse to rocket assistance. Its principal ammunition is the base-bleed Extended Range Full-Bore (ERFB) round developed by the defunct Space Research Corporation in Canada and now manufactured in Belgium. This round has a range of 21,980 yards (20.1km) when fired from the US M109A1, 28,325 yards (25.9km) when fired from the US M198 155mm towed gun and 32,810 yards (30km) from the GC 45, and has regularly attained ranges of between 42,650 yards (39km) and 47,025 yards (43km) under certain conditions. The GC 45 is the basis for the G-5 on the South African G-6 wheeled SP, which has a claimed range of 32,810 yards (30km) with its HE round and considerably further with a base-bleed round.

The GC 45 and its associated ammunition demonstrate that modern technology can still provide simple — as opposed to increasingly complicated — solutions, and that good design allied to an imaginative approach and coupled with modern techniques can produce equipment that is better, cheaper and more effective.

ROCKET ARTILLERY

Rockets have improved dramatically since the inaccurate area bombardment weapons of World War II and Warsaw Pact armies place particular emphasis on the use of rockets, especially the modern BM-27. These systems are cheap and easy to produce, though the rockets

Above: Towed guns are lighter, simpler and cheaper than SPs, but they provide no protection for their crews, which would be a significant consideration in an NBC environment.

Below: The GIAT 155mm TR towed howitzer is in service with French motorised infantry divisions. The eight-man firing team can prepare the piece for action in as little as two minutes.

earned great respect from German troops, and the most modern system in service, the BM-27, mounts a 16-round launcher on an 8 × 8 ZIL-135 truck chassis. The vehicle uses stabilising jacks when firing, and its 220mm rockets have a range of 21.75-24.9 miles (35-40km) with payloads including high explosive, chemicals and minelets. A specialised resupply vehicle carries one complete reload of 16 rockets and reloading time is estimated at 15-20 minutes. Of the remaining Soviet systems, the most important is the 140mm RPU-14, which has 16 tubes mounted on a two-wheeled trailer chassis and is used by Soviet airborne forces.

The Czechs have taken the Soviet BM-21 launcher and mounted it on an armoured version of the Tatra 813 8 × 8 truck, which also has space for a full 40-round reload pack; reload time is only two or three minutes. The vehicle has a high-capacity winch and a dozer blade is mounted on the front.

Remembering World War II, the West German Army has developed the Light Artillery Rocket System-2 (LARS-2), which consists of a 36-barrel launcher mounted on a MAN 6 × 6 truck chassis. Payloads include parachute-retarded anti-tank minelets, smoke and high explosive. Minimum range is 6,561 yards (6,000m), maximum range is 15,310 yards (14,000m), and the rockets can be fired singly, semi-ripple or full ripple, the last launching the rockets at 0.5 second intervals; reloading takes 15 minutes.

Most NATO armies disposed of their World War II rocket systems in the late 1940s and did not replace them, but the tactical value of such systems gradually became apparent and in 1976 the USA formulated a staff requirement for a General Support Rocket System, since redesignated the Multiple-Launch Rocket System. The MLRS has the same battlefield mobility as armoured formations and consists of a tracked vehicle derived from the M2 IFV carrying a trainable, elevating 12-round launcher. Its missions include counter-battery fire against both field and air defence artillery sites, and it is a very significant addition to NATO's anti-tank capability.

Above: The AM General M923 5-ton truck seen here towing an M198 155mm howitzer has a centralised tyre pressure regulation system.

Left: An M198, with 32 rounds of ammunition and its 11-man crew, – a total lift of some 22,000lb (9,980kg) – can be transported by a single CH-47D Chinook.

themselves are more expensive than shells and reload times are longer, and rockets are ideal surprise weapons; the noise of a surprise rocket attack can have a marked effect on the morale of an enemy, and they are particularly effective as counter-battery weapons. They are also efficient delivery systems for smoke and chemical agents, and can create high concentrations much more rapidly than howitzers.

Modern rockets are more accurate than their predecessors: the Soviet 240mm BM-24, for example, has a circular error probable of 300ft (93m) at 8,000 yards (7.25km) and 387ft (118m) at its maximum range of 12,080 yards (11km). Nevertheless, they are not at all suitable for precision attacks against targets requiring pin-point accuracy.

The Soviet Union has developed rocket launchers since the early 1940s when the Katyusha rockets

Teruel 2 rocket trajectories

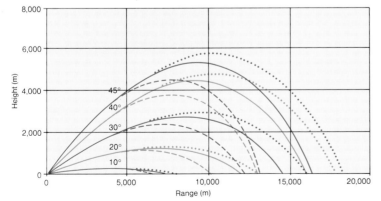

Above: The 140mm rockets fired by the Spanish Teruel 2 system are fitted with aerodynamic brakes allowing a choice of trajectories for each launch angle. Chart shows the effect of two brakes (solid line) or four (dashed), compared to none (dotted).

Above: The Chinese Type 81 107mm 12-tube rocket launcher has a maximum range of 8,750 yards (8,000m) and is intended for use against enemy infantry in the open or in lightly protected trenches, or in counter-battery tasks against artillery positions.

Surveillance and Target Acquisition

The intelligence requirements of a commander in the land battle are determined by his mission and by the level of command. Thus, at company level the battle is fought within the constraints of visual observation and direct-fire weapons, while at divisional level the extent of the battle is limited by the range of indirect-fire weapons with considerable ranges, such as rocket launchers and 155mm artillery. However, other factors are involved, and in practice military commanders divide the area beyond the Forward Line of Own Troops (FLOT) into two. The first, the *area of influence*, is that in which they are able to acquire and attack targets; the second (and larger) is the *area of interest*, which is that occupied by forces capable of affecting the commander's future operations. Thus, for example, in US Army doctrine, an army group commander's area of interest extends 620 miles (1,000km) beyond the FLOT, while his area of influence extends some 90 miles (150km), with corps, division and brigade areas being proportionally smaller. These areas determine the range at which surveillance and target-acquisition need to operate; whether they are achieved is, of course, dependent on other factors.

RADAR

Radar is a well-developed means of detecting targets and is in widespread use in most armies. It provides not just detection and tracking of aircraft, but is also able to detect artillery shells and mortar bombs in flight, analyse their trajectory and, by extrapolation, determine the launch point, which can then be engaged with counter-battery fire. Smaller, infantry radars are used to detect movement by people and vehicles in the forward areas. The US AN/PPS-5A, for example, can detect moving vehicles at distances up to 11,000 yards (10,000m), distinguishing between tracked and wheeled, and moving people up to about 6,500 yards

Above: This portable ground surveillance radar system is used by US infantry units to give either audible or visual warning of troop and vehicle movement out to a range of 6,560 yards (6,000m).

Below: Night vision devices such as this Sopelem TN2-1, operating in the near-IR band, can be used during the hours of darkness for surveillance, aiming weapons, operating equipment, or driving.

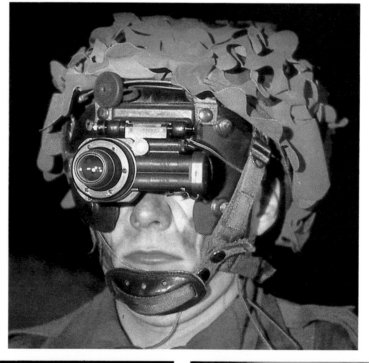

(6,000m). It is accurate to within 22ft (20m) and is man-portable. A comparable Soviet set, the GS-12, has a better performance against vehicles, out to 13,125 yards (12,000m), but is not so effective against people, at about 3,828 yards (3,500m). All such radars are, however, active emitters and can thus themselves be detected, located and attacked.

IMAGE INTENSIFIERS

Image intensification (II) uses electronic techniques to enhance the intensity of light reflected by very dimly illuminated objects. Enhancement can be of the order of 40,000 times, which enables objects to be 'seen' quite clearly, even on a very dark night when they are quite invisible to the naked eye. Like thermal imaging (TI), II is passive. The US AN/VVS-2, for example, is being installed on M1 and has a depth of focus from 13ft (4m) to infinity; specified image tube gain is at least 25,000.

THERMAL IMAGING

Thermal imaging systems use a pattern of heat sensors which can detect small differences in temperature, thus enabling the operator to look at a heat picture or a graphic representation of heat reflections. TI can see through rain, fog and smoke to some degree and can, except in the most extreme cases, produce an image adequate for identification. Since virtually every item of military equipment emits heat, TI can both be used for surveillance and can also be directly incorporated into weapons sights. TI devices are, of course, passive and therefore undetectable, but they are vulnerable to ECM and can be 'spoofed' by decoys or blinded by false signals.

REMOTE SENSORS

Information concerning events beyond the limit of visual systems can also be obtained by remote

Above: Active night vision devices are detectable and are being replaced by passive devices such as this Rafael MTIS thermal imaging system, which can detect tanks at 7,100 yards (6,500m).

Right: Thermal (upper) and normal images of a Leopard 1 MBT at a range of 623 yards (570m). The thermal image was taken when the tank was covered by smoke and the other a few seconds later.

Above: Since World War I battlefield surveillance has been performed by aircraft, a current example being this US Army OV-1D Mohawk. However, aircraft are now very vulnerable.

Below: One solution to the surveillance problem is to use drones, such as this Canadair CL-89, which can fly over hostile ground with relative impunity, being very difficult to detect.

Below: The Lockheed Altair is a small propeller-driven flying-wing configuredf RPV with a self-contained inertial navigation system. It is launched from a vehicle-mounted ramp and is provided with real time TV and data down-links.

ground sensors. Such devices originally came into widespread use during the Vietnam War, although there were problems at first as it was discovered that some could provide false information: for example, seismic devices recorded *every* ground tremor, including those from animals. Such problems have, however, been largely overcome, and modern types include seismic, acoustic, magnetic, electromagnetic and thermal devices. These sensors can be placed in position by hand, or, in the case of those beyond the FLOT, by aircraft or special artillery shell.

Seismic detection acts on vibrations carried through the ground. Modern sensors can detect an individual moving at distances up to 100ft (30m) and vehicles travelling about 1,000ft (300m) away, and skilled operators can distinguish between types of vehicles or estimate numbers of people. Acoustic devices are, in effect, sensitive microphones, and they are normally used in conjunction with seismic detectors; ranges are similar to that for the human ear. Magnetic sensors detect the movement of some types of ferrous metals up to about 13ft (4m) distant for personnel and about 80ft (25m) for vehicles.

MANNED AIRCRAFT

One of the major surveillance problems is being able to 'see over the hill' and, in particular, deep into the area of interest, but this can be overcome by using airborne platforms. Aircraft operate in support of the ground forces by carrying out reconnaissance missions, frequently deep into hostile territory, some ground forces having fixed-wing aircraft under their direct control. The US Army,

for example, uses the Grumman OV-1 Mohawk, a twin-turboprop aircraft capable of operating from rough forward airstrips. The standard version, the OV-1D, is equipped with cameras, IR surveillance equipment, sideways-looking airborne radar (SLAR) and an ECM pod, while the EV-1 is a dedicated ECM variant with specialised equipment.

In an effort to solve the problem of the real-time acquisition of both first- and second-echelon targets well beyond the FLOT, the British Army produced a requirement in the early 1980s for a system known as Castor (Corps Airborne Stand-Off Radar). There were two contending systems, one based on an RAF-operated Canberra aircraft using a synthetic aperture radar and the other on an Army-operated Pilatus Britten-Norman Islander with an MTI radar. The Canberra-based system is designed to fly at considerable heights but well back from the FLOT, while the Islander would obviously fly much lower, operating from rough strips, probably forward of the Corps rear boundary. The outcome of this project is not yet announced, although both contending aircraft have flown.

PILOTLESS AIRCRAFT

Aircraft operating near or beyond the FLOT are, of course, vulnerable to air defence weapons and in such high-risk areas most armies use pilotless aircraft, either with on-board computers set to follow a programmed flight-path (drones) or controlled by a distant ground-based operator (remotely-piloted vehicles, RPVs). A further advantage of drones and RPVs is that they can be very small and uncomplicated; some of them, indeed, seem to be no more than glorified model aircraft. The most recent of these aircraft can carry not only an impressive array of sensors but also have real-time down-links enabling them to pass information directly to their operating base so that it can be acted upon quickly, a point of special importance in target acquisition. A particular advantage of the RPV over the drone is that its flight-path can be changed during the mission so that it can, for example, be directed to adjust artillery fire or to illuminate a target by laser.

The Canadair AN/USD-501 reconnaissance drone is used by several armies. This winged body is launched from an inclined ramp using a rocket booster, but in sustained flight it is powered by a small turbojet; it is recovered by parachute. It carries cameras and IR linescan, although these must be returned to base for processing and analysis as there is no down-link. Normal operating speed is about 400kts (740km/hr) and maximum range is 100 miles (160km). Israel has had considerable success in using RPVs, the leading army type being the Tadiran Mastiff. The Mastiff Mk III carries a 30kg payload, which can include a TV camera with a real-time down-link, a TV camera with a panoramic film camera, or various ECM packages.

Lockheed Altair RPV internal arrangement

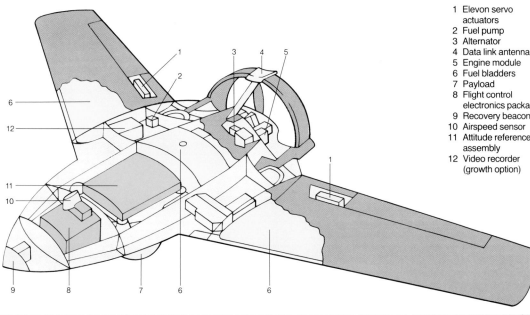

1 Elevon servo actuators
2 Fuel pump
3 Alternator
4 Data link antenna
5 Engine module
6 Fuel bladders
7 Payload
8 Flight control electronics package
9 Recovery beacon
10 Airspeed sensor
11 Attitude reference assembly
12 Video recorder (growth option)

Air Defence

The purpose of battlefield air defence is to protect ground forces and installations from air attack. The primary responsibility is that of the air forces, which must seek to destroy enemy aircraft by attacks on airfields and air-to-air combat; assuming that air forces cannot prevent all hostile aircraft from entering friendly airspace, it is the responsibility of the ground forces themselves to field surveillance, target acquisition and weapon systems which can provide both area and point air defence.

The consequences of losing air superiority were experienced by the German Army in northwest Europe from mid-1944 to the end of the conflict: they were harried at every turn from the air and the Allies were able to roam more or less at will. Unfortunately, in the postwar period the former Allies, who had experienced the benefits of this air supremacy, suffered from gross complacency lasting well into the 1960s, when the possibility of facing a situation of air inferiority was finally appreciated.

In the the mid-1960s NATO ground-based tactical air defences in Europe consisted of a belt of reasonably capable Hawks, supported by a few mobile missile systems and a small number of guns, almost all of World War II vintage. The process of making up for this deficiency has been a long and expensive one, and the trail is littered with abandoned projects. In the USSR, however, the Soviet Army had suffered badly under German air attack, especially in 1942 and 1943, and learned lessons which were not forgotten. As a result Soviet Army air defences have been kept up to date and many of the systems involved have been exported, enabling them to be tested in a number of wars.

The effectiveness of ground fire is all too frequently underestimated. For example, of the total of 1,000 US aircraft lost in the Korean War only 110 were shot down in air-to-air combat and 214 were lost in accidents and other causes, while the North Korean and Chinese ground defences accounted for no fewer than 676. Similarly, during the 1973 Middle East War the Israeli air force lost a total of 120 aircraft — six in air-to-air combat, 18 to other causes and

96 to Arab ground defences. Finally in the most recent conflict — the South Atlantic war of 1982 — the British lost nine Harriers and Sea Harriers, four in accidents and five to Argentinian ground defences.

THE THREAT

Hostile fixed-wing aircraft, helicopters, remotely-piloted vehicles (RPVs) and drones are unlikely to arrive over the combat zone at high level and the operational aim to which technology must find the answer is to force them ever lower. Thereafter time is of the essence: a low-level, head-on attacker first detected at a typical distance of two miles (3.2km) will be overhead 15.7 seconds later if it is travellling at 400 knots (204m/sec) and just 10.5 seconds later at 600 knots (306m/sec). In this very brief space of time the aircraft must be

A-10 gun attack profile

A-10 Maverick delivery profile

Above: The air threat to ground forces takes a number of forms. This Luftwaffe Panavia Tornado is coming in fast and low, and is in the process of dispensing its MW-1's 4,536 sub-munitions.

Left: Tactics used by the US Fairchild A-10 dictate that it spends most of its time at less than 100ft (30m) above the ground, popping up to a maximum of 500ft (150m) to destroy tanks with brief bursts of gunfire.

Below left: Terrain-masking and three-dimensional jinking are used in the run-up to low-level Maverick missile attacks from 500ft (150m); a cloud base of 1,000ft (300m) presents no problems to a Thunderbolt pilot.

Right: Helicopters are a growing threat to tanks, SP guns and APCs. This West German BO105, hovering behind trees armed with six Hot missiles while it waits for a target, would be very difficult for opposing AFV crews to detect.

Below: If USAF tactics are correct this photograph shows an enemy tank commander's first sight of an attacking A-10 as it appears suddenly above the trees — too late for effective countermeasures.

Typical airborne attack profiles

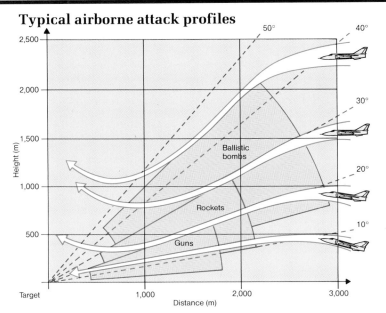

Above: Weapon characteristics dictate attack profiles. For an aircraft travelling at 450-560mph (200-250m/sec), engagement time for ground weapons would be between four and six seconds.

Below: Release zones for attack weapons. Only with dispensers can aircraft remain at 164ft (50m); with other weapons they must climb, for reasons of weapon effect and aircraft safety.

Airborne attack weapon release zones

identified, a decision on firing has to be taken and the weapons engagement must be completed.

The first element of the air threat comes from low-flying manned aircraft moving at high speed. Such aircraft are likely to be within the observation arc of ground-based sensors and the firing zone of ground-based weapons for very short periods, even in open terrain such as the Middle East, while in close, rolling terrain such as that found in northwestern Europe their exposure time will be even less. On the other hand, pilots travelling at very low levels cannot use the full speed capability of their aircraft and factors such as obstacle avoidance, turbulence, navigation and fuel consumption impose limits on their speed, generally keeping it well below Mach 1. In addition, the pilot is required to detect and confirm the target and then set up his aircraft for weapon delivery.

The most important fighter-bomber attack methods are the level and dive attacks. Level attacks are normally used to deliver napalm, armour-piercing HE and fragmentation bombs and are carried out at speeds of 400-600 knots (736-1,104 km/h) and at heights down to 60ft (19m). In the more normal dive attack the pilot climbs to altitude some 3.5-5 miles (5-8km) from the target in order to achieve a dive angle of 30-45° for bombs or 10-30° to deliver guided or unguided rockets or gunfire. The aircraft will only be vulnerable to AA fire from a weapon in the immediate vicinity of the target for an average period of some 15 seconds during the attack, though guns are seldom deployed singly and it may well be vulnerable to other guns for longer.

Most RPVs are fixed-wing aircraft, though a few models in development are rotary-winged; consequently their characteristics are similar to those of manned aircraft, except that they are much smaller and slower. Their construction of non-radar-reflective materials, such as glass-reinforced plastics and wood, means that they present very small radar signatures, while their low-power engines generate minimal infra-red signatures, so that even though they fly rather higher and slower than manned aircraft and follow less complicated flight-paths they are considerably more difficult to detect and their survival rate in conflicts such as Vietnam and the Middle East wars has been remarkably high.

Moving helicopters are not too difficult to detect, their fuselages and their main and tail rotor-discs giving good radar signatures, but modern anti-tank helicopters hovering behind cover pose new problems, since the vast majority of air defence radars are electronically configured to eliminate static targets and the two rotors, though still turning at high speed, are virtually end-on to the radar beam, thus presenting a minimal target.

Dealing with airborne threats involves three phases — detection, identification and engagement — which must be capable of execution under all conditions as aircraft all-weather performance continues to improve.

Below: NATO defences against sudden Warsaw Pact armoured thrusts in critical areas such as the Fulda Gap depend increasingly on attack helicopters like this US Army AH-64A Apache.

Above: The US Patriot SAM system uses the MPQ-53 radar, a multi-function phased-array device responsible for surveillance, IFF, target-tracking and missile guidance – functions which required nine separate systems for Nike Hercules and Hawk.

Above: The West German Siemens DR 151 is a mobile surveillance radar mounted on a 5-ton truck with the antenna on a 60ft (18m) extending mast. It has a range of 28 miles (45km).

Right: The Ericsson Giraffe AD radar's extending mast gives the antenna an effective height of 40ft (12m), providing a surveillance range of 25 miles (40km) and target designation to 12.5 miles (20km).

DETECTION

Surveillance of hostile airspace and the detection of approaching aircraft is carried out most effectively by radar, though since radar operates at the upper end of the radio frequency band where the waves are transmitted in straight lines and the majority of hostile sorties will be flown at very low level, the radar antenna needs to be sited on a high point to give it a useful range.

In general terms, an aircraft with a mean radar cross-section of $1m^2$ flying at a height of 750ft (230m) can be detected at a range of 37 miles (60km) — the height being significant because of the curvature of the earth. Aircraft designers have responsded to the threat of detection by trying to reduce the radar signature using stealth techniques, and by seeking to enable the aircraft to fly even lower and faster. Stealth measures include reducing the frontal and side areas of the aircraft,

using radar absorbent material on air intakes, raking twin fins, making the side elevation as nearly elliptical as possible, shrouding the nose electronics/avionics packages, careful design of the nose radar scanner, and so on.

Radar transmissions can also be detected by hostile ground- and air-based receivers, enabling the enemy to take action to destroy the radar installation by means of artillery, rockets or air-launched anti-radar missiles. In addition, the effectiveness of radars can be limited, if not totally defeated, for limited periods using electronic countermeasures.

The prinicpal electronic means of avoiding jamming is frequency hopping, which involves the transmitter changing frequencies in a sequence known only to itself and the associated receiver and which will appear totally random to any ECM devices. A less sophisticated method is to switch the radar transmitter on and off, transmitting only when absolutely essential for target acquisition and engagement. It is vital to switch the radar off if an incoming anti-radar missile is detected, a move which could completely disrupt early SAM systems, since guidance and control was lost over any missile in flight at the moment of shut-down: the missiles then went ballistic and eventually crashed.

As well as reflecting radar waves, aircraft and their engines are heat sources and are at a different temperature from that of the surrounding air: with current technology this characteristic cannot be used for detection from the ground but it is of great value as a homing system for missiles. The temperature of the fuselage itself rises only to about 50°C, even at Mach 0.9, in typical central European conditions, and is of much less significance than the engine and the exhaust plume. The hot engine parts, such as the combustion chambers, turbine blades, after-

burner, jet-pipe and nozzle produce a lot of radiation at a constant intensity, and while the exhaust plume is cooled by mixing with the surrounding air and is of lower intensity than the engine it is still significant for tail-chasing missiles, which respond strongly to it at close ranges.

Aircraft designers are endeavouring to reduce vulnerability to IR-seeking missiles by passive measures such as fitting tail-cones and ensuring that a missile attacking from ahead cannot see the compressor, and cooling air is being used to reduce temperatures of swivelling nozzles in V/STOL aircraft. Helicopters also have IR radiation suppressors fitted on their engine exhausts, a measure which, combined with engine screening, reduces the IR signature substantially.

Visual detection remains an important element of ground-based air defence, and is facilitated by the fact that the aircraft is moving and frequently leaving a smoke trail, and is normally of substantial size. However, its effectiveness can be reduced by weather factors, which are especially significant in northwestern Europe, by the use of camouflage and by the terrain. Noise, except in the case of very slow-moving aircraft, is not a factor.

IDENTIFICATION

The identification of an aircraft, prior to the decision by ground forces on whether or not to fire, is crucial. The problem is that the interval between acquiring a target and the latest moment at which firing is feasible is very short, and experience shows that ground troops who have once undergone air attack tend to shoot

Left: The warning and fire control station of the French Mygale short-range AD system. The radar's range is 8.7 miles (14km) for aircraft or 4.7 miles (7.5km) for hovering helicopter targets.

first and identify afterwards, a tendency which causes some concern to friendly aircrew.

To ground troops a friendly aircraft returning home across the FLOT after a strike against hostile forces may be indistinguishable from a hostile aircraft on its outward leg to attack friendly ground troops, and in every combat since World War I with a significant air threat there have been stories — frequently true — of what are euphemistically described as 'own goals' or 'blue-on-blue engagements', in which ground troops have shot down friendly aircraft. The same, incidentally, has often happened at sea, where the problem is very similar. An additional modern hazard is that such engagements can take place not just because of mistaken visual identification but also as a result of incorrect electronic interrogation or faulty equipment.

On the modern battlefield, the speed and low height of the target, especially if it is approaching head-on, give little time for visual identification. An electrical system of identification is therefore required, but this has to be thoroughly reliable, efficient, capable of dealing with numerous targets simultaneously, resistant to ECM and in universal use by all aircraft of all allied nations likely to use the same airspace. As is so often the case with defence equipment what appears to be a simple requirement is actually very difficult to meet. At first sight a direct 'question-and-answer' system is all that is required, transmitting a coded signal at an aircraft which is equipped with a transponder and recognising the coded answers.

However, this does not cover a host of possible ambiguities. The

Below: Operator's console in a Control and Reporting Centre (CRC) for the Siemens SILLACS AD system. CRCs contain all necessary data processing and communications equipment.

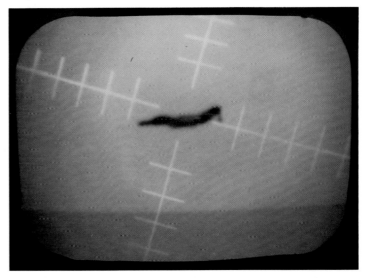

Above: The Chinese Type 408-C long-range air warning radar system operates in the 150-180MHz and 100-120MHz bands. Built-in ECCM resistance enables it to operate in an EW environment.

Below: Video display in a US Red Flag exercise, showing an F-4 Phantom about to be 'hit' by a missile. Such exercises train US aircrew in countering the very considerable ground threat.

absence of a response could, of course, indicate an enemy aircraft, but it could also mean a faulty or inoperative transponder in friendly aircraft damaged by enemy fire, a transponder masked by trees or terrain at the critical moment (always possible in close country and at low heights), or, quite simply (and by no means impossibly), a signal sent in the wrong code. Methods of overcoming such problems are being investigated, one of which is to use very advanced electronic techniques to measure, with extreme rapidity, certain crucial parameters of a target to enable the shape of the aircraft to be compared with stored data. Another is a means of identifying the aircraft by analysing the radar returns given out by the engine, rather than the aircraft itself, since these are just as

Above: A display of Soviet SAMs used by the Egyptian Army in the early 1970s. In the foreground are SA-4s on tracked launchers; behind them are SA-3 (left) and SA-2 (right) ground launchers.

identifiable. These analyses would then be added to the information from the IFF returns to provide a more positive identification.

IFF interrogators are integrated into most ground-based air defence radars. On detection of a target by the radar an IFF signal is transmitted on a fixed frequency, using a very narrow beam to ensure that only the aircraft being tracked responds. In the current NATO system the ground transmission frequency is 1,030MHz and beam widths are less than 5°, and the signal is encoded using settings that are changed daily. Aircraft transponders analyse the signal and if appropriate, reply, using (in NATO's case) a fixed frequency of 1,090MHz. Of course, such a system has its drawbacks not the least of which is that a hostile aircraft needs only a very simple detector to indicate when it is being interrogated by an IFF system and where the signal is coming from; jamming or other ECM action is then relatively straightforward.

Having detected the aircraft and identified it as hostile, the next step is to engage it with an effective weapon a system which can conduct the engagement in sufficient time and with adequate terminal effects.

SURFACE-TO-AIR MISSILES

The first major SAM system to be tested in a ground-based gun/missile air defence (AD) system was the Soviet SA-2, used in the Second Indo-China War by the North Vietnamese Army (NVA) and providing an AA defence denser than that used in Germany at the height of World War II. The SA-2 was a first-generation SAM designed to operate against targets flying at heights in excess of 9,843ft (3,000m). At first it was relatively successful but when adequate ECM and avoidance tactics had been developed, the missiles' success rated diminished.

The first SA-2 kill occurred on July 24, 1965, when a USAF aircraft was shot down, and from then until the end of the US air war in 1972 9,058

Below: The truck-mounted, fully autonomous FlakRakRad Roland II system has been developed for air-base defence missions for the West German Air Force and Navy and USAF bases in Europe.

Roland operational principle

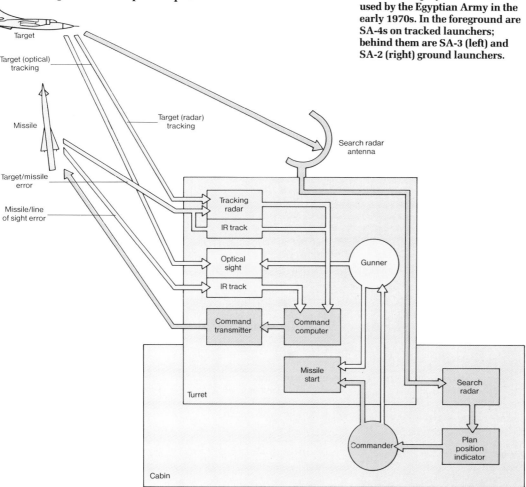

Above: Roland tracks targets optically or by radar. The missile is followed by an IR localizer which computes the deviation and gives commands to bring the missile back on course.

Below: A Roland scores a hit in a live firing demonstration against a target drone. The warhead contains 14.3lb (6.5kg) of high explosive and is fitted with both proximity and impact fuzes.

recorded SA-2 launchings (of which no fewer than 4,244 were made during the short Linebacker II operation in 1972) resulted in 150 aircraft destroyed. The success rate of the SA-2 indicates the effectiveness of the countermeasures —5.7 per cent in 1965, 2.8 per cent in 1966, 1.75 per cent in 1967 and 0.9 per cent in 1968, ending with a slight rise to 1.5 per cent in 1972. But even if the missiles were not all that effective in themselves, they did force US aircraft down into the range of the very dense AD gun systems, which brought down some 15 times more aircraft than the missiles. Between August 4, 1964, and October 29, 1969, the USA lost 919 aircraft over North Vietnam 92 (10 per cent) to fighter aircraft, 64 (7 per cent) to SAMs and no fewer than 763 (83 per cent) to AD gunfire; the balance were lost in the brief bombing campaign in 1972. These losses included eighteen B-52s, fifteen of them in Linebacker II in December 1972.

The NVA AD system comprised some 5,000 to 6,000 sites and the US was forced to devote some 25 per cent of its missions to the suppression of enemy air defences (SEAD) role, which, coupled with an equal number of ECM and ECCM tasks, left only 50 per cent of the missions to operational sorties. Such a reduction in the number of aircraft devoted to strike missions is termed 'virtual attrition', as opposed to 'actual attrition', which is the shooting down of aircraft.

In the 1973 Yom Kippur war, total Israeli losses were 120 aircraft, of which no less than 80 per cent were lost to ground AD systems, 5 per cent in air-to-air engagements and 15 per cent to other causes. SA-6s averaged approximately one aircraft kill per 50-60 missiles fired, but they nevertheless were responsible not only for the destruction of some 70 aircraft but also for forcing the Israelis to fly ever lower, thus bringing them into the zone of the ZSU-23-4, which accounted for a further 48 aircraft. The vast numbers of shoulder-launched SA-7 SAMs destroyed just two aircraft; they damaged some thirty more, but all survived to fight another day. The Arab air defences again exerted a 'virtual attrition' effect upon the Israeli Air force, since so many aircraft had to be diverted from attacking combat units on the ground to SEAD missions.

Numerous short-range SAM systems have been developed, offering the advantages of light weight and protection for infantry units and small, isolated detachments. In order to remove the problem of the operators needing to guide the missile throughout its flight many early systems used IR-homing guidance, so that all the operator had to do was point the launcher in the general direction of the target, await a signal the target was in range, and fire. Unfortunately, the missiles could be launched only after the aircraft had carried out its attack. Nevertheless, systems such as the US Stinger and the Soviet SA-7 have proved to be reasonably

effective, even though countermeasures have been devised against them. The first countermeasure against SA-7 and the similar SA-9, for example, was for the target to fire flares which decoyed the IR head away from the aircraft, but this was combated by setting the head to home on the second hottest heat source it acquired. On discovering this, the next defensive counter was to drop groups of flares of differing heat intensities. This in turn has been countered by firing missiles in salvos, with the seeker heads set to different heat intensities.

Right: The Swedish RBS-70 VLM is the man-portable RBS-70 mounted on a special stand which is fixed to the platform of a suitable vehicle.

Above: The operator of a British Tracked Rapier SAM. The Rapier system has proved itself in several conflicts, including the South Atlantic War of 1982.

Below: The Matra Mistrale man-portable SAM is one of the latest designs to give ground troops a local air defence capability. The effectiveness of such weapons has

been demonstrated in Afghanistan, where Blowpipe and Stinger missiles have caused many casualties among Soviet and Afghan aircraft and helicopters.

Above: To create the ZSU-23-4 the Soviets took a well developed quadruple 23mm cannon mount – the ZU-23 – and located it with a radar in a simple turret on the SA-6 SAM tracked chassis. The result was one of the world's most effective air defence systems.

Above: The updated Super-Fledermaus anti-aircraft fire control system used by the Danish Army uses a monopulse radar for target acquisition and tracking.

Below: Anti-aircraft gun performance against attacking aircraft as seen by the guns' manufacturers. Breda predict that an aircraft flying at 670 mph (300m/sec) will be detected at 5,900 yards (5.4km), and under fire between the 3,280 yard (3.0km) and 1,640 yards (1.5km) points. In the centre a Gepard engages an aircraft attacking in a dive at 570 mph (200m/sec), while in the bottom example a target flying at 570mph (200m/sec) is engaged at a range of 2,700 yards (2.5km).

Breda Twin 40L70 aircraft engagement

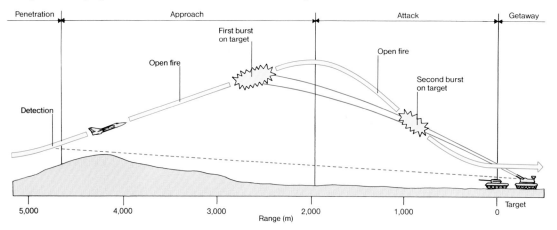

Gepard engagement of attack aircraft: dive profile

Gepard engagement of attack aircraft: low-level profile

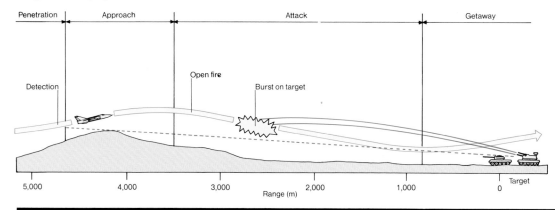

In contrast, command-guidance missiles are capable of intercepting aircraft whatever the phase of attack, and, most importantly, prior to weapons release. Early such missiles used command to line-of-sight (CLOS) guidance, which required the operator to steer the missile all the way to the target using a thumb-stick to keep the missile on a collision course with the target. This proved effective on missiles such as the British Blowpipe, but required a well-trained and steady operator. The latest generation of missiles uses semi-automatic command to line-of-sight (SACLOS) guidance, in which all the operator has to do is keep the sight on the target while a TV camera in the aiming unit tracks a flare on the missile; computers compare the difference and then transmit signals to the missile to bring it back on course. Development efforts are now tending to concentrate on producing much higher missile speeds to reduce the flight time, on improving the 'gather time' and thus reduce the minimum range, and on developing an all-weather and night-time capability.

GUN SYSTEMS

Guns have certain advantages over missiles in the AD role in that they have very short response and flight times. They cannot, however, adjust their flight once fired, and modern AD guns are confined to the low-level role, relying on missiles to bring targets down to a height at which the relatively small calibre guns can deal with them. Most armies now use AD guns in multiple installations with calibres of between 20mm and 40mm, larger calibres having been abandoned except for a few World War II types still serving with some armies. Smaller calibres such as 12.7mm are also used, but only in the point-defence role.

Some very sophisticated gun systems have been produced, such as the West German Gepard and the

Above: The West German Gepard is armed with twin Oerlikon 35mm KDA cannon; each has a cyclic rate of 550 rounds per minute and is provided with 310 rounds of anti- aircraft and 20 rounds of armour-piercing ammunition. Engagements normally open when the target is 3,300-4,400 yards (3-4,000m) distant.

elderly but still highly respected Soviet ZSU-23-4, while the attempted US answer, the Sergeant York DIVAD, has recently suffered a spectacular and humiliating cancellation. Such systems typically combine a surveillance radar, a tracking and engagement radar, a multiple (two or four) gun installation, and a computerised fire-control system on a tracked mounting. All this is inevitably expensive, and it has been calculated that, if produced today, each Gepard would cost in excess of £3 million.

Detection must be achieved as early as possible, although the radar's theoretical maximum range, typically about 10 miles (16km), is likely to be limited by terrain to about 3 miles (4.8km). The engagement itself must be carefully controlled, in order to achieve the maximum probability of a kill to ensure that ammunition is not wasted (the rate of fire is extremely high: Gepard, for example, could expend its complete load of 660 rounds in 36 seconds) and to minimise barrel wear. The aircraft's attack profile must therefore be very rapidly estimated so that the engagement is conducted during a straight-line portion of its course as the chances of obtaining a hit on a manoeuvring target are small. Finally, a nice balance is required to achieve the optimum length of burst: enough rounds should be put into any one target to cause it to crash, but no target should be pursued by fire for so long that other aircraft on the mission escape.

COMMAND AND CONTROL

Ground-based air defence elements are normally integrated to provide a layered and interlocking defence system. Radar-directed SAMs provide the outer cover against medium- and low-level attack from ground-attack fighters and interdictors, supplemented by short-range SAMs and air defence gun systems for medium cover, and final close-in defence is provided by very short-range (usually hand-held) SAMs and machine-guns. Indeed, there is now such a plethora of weapons systems that their control, particularly in relation to the safety of friendly aircraft, is becoming a major problem. Further, dealing with such defences has become such a major task for air forces that the 'suppression of enemy air defences' (SEAD) has become a mission in its own right.

ANTI-HELICOPTER DEFENCE

A subject causing growing concern to many armies is defence against anti-tank helicopters, which are becoming an increasing threat to tanks, high-value SP guns and APC/IFVs. Armour specialists regard with some scepticism the claims that fighter helicopters will be able to penetrate sufficiently far over the FLOT to deal with anti-tank helicopters; it therefore behoves tanks and APC/IFVs to have some capability in this field themselves. Some experts claim that the tank's main gun can be used in this role, and certainly the Israelis have tried this on occasion, although in the only known case where they actually shot down a helicopter it was unfortunately one of their own.

The Soviet AT-8 Cobra missile, fired by T-80 and T-64B, is reported to have an anti-helicopter role, using laser guidance, while many of the 20mm and 30mm cannon mounted on APC/IFVs can clearly also be used for the same purpose. The major limitation on tanks and APC/IFVs engaging helicopters, however, is not the gun, but rather the target-acquisition capability of the crew, their response time having acquired the target, and the tracking capability of the turret control systems, all of which are optimised for dealing with relatively slow-moving ground targets rather than aircraft.

Above: A great variety of automatic medium-calibre anti-aircraft cannon is available. This French GIAT 25 M811 fires the full range of NATO 25mm ammunition which is used in the anti-aircraft, fire support and anti-armour roles. Rates of fire can be varied between 125 and 650 rds/min with instantaneous selection.

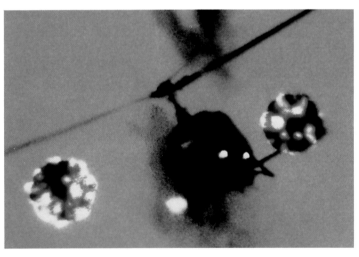

Above: A helicopter target is engaged by a 40mm cannon firing Bofors proximity-fuzed PFHE Mk 2 ammunition. Anti-helicopter defence is an urgent priority for ground troops.

Below: The interior of a Thomson-CSF anti-aircraft command centre. In an operational environment countering the anticipated threat, the situation would hardly be as relaxed as it appears here.

Infantry Warfare

The fundamental role of the infantryman has changed little over recent centuries; his tasks are still to seize and hold ground, to dominate and control close country, and, finally, to carry out close surveillance. The first of these is the ultimate measure of success in a campaign — the final evidence of victory in the Vietnam War in 1975 came when the North Vietnamese infantry marched into the President's Palace in Saigon — and while the brunt of the fighting continues to be borne by the infantryman, there have been tremendous changes in the way he fights. Perhaps the most significant of these are in his technological environment, and scientific advances have had a geat impact. For example, in a major war it would be extremely unusual for modern infantryman to go into battle on foot, armoured personnel carriers and helicopters being the more usual means of transport, with the result that the speed of action has increased dramatically.

MOBILITY

Perhaps the best illustration of the dilemma posed by technological advance is the development of the armoured personnel carrier. Obviously, an armoured vehicle gives protection and mobility, easing two of the age-old problems of the infantry. However, what started off as a very simple armoured box on tracks has become increasingly sophisticated. Early APCs were armed with simple pintle-mounted machine guns, usually of around 7.62mm calibre, but nowadays complicated turrets are fitted and 20mm and 30mm cannon are common, while increasing amounts of weaponry and equipment are carried. The result is that the number of infantrymen who can deploy from the vehicle has decreased with each successive design.

A particular example of how technology and operational requirements can go astray is the story of the infantry weapons in the US Army's M2 infantry fighting vehicle. The apparently simple requirement was for the occupants to be able to use their personal weapons from inside the vehicle, the tacit assumption being that the soldiers would insert the muzzles of their M16s through slits or balls, but the outcome is that each member of the six-strong squad has a firing port in which a ball-mounted M231 — a specially developed version of the M16 — is permanently fitted.

Although the fundamental mission of the infantry may not have changed, passionate arguments have raged over how that mission is to be achieved for the past 40 years, as the balance has been seen to swing from armoured forces supporting the

infantry to infantry supporting armour in a combined-arms battle. The basic problem for foot soldiers in general war is their inherent vulnerability and relative lack of mobility, and World War II saw the appearance first of troop-carrying trucks and later of tracked armoured personnel carriers. Mobile infantry units were seen for some years as having a specialised role and the majority of battalions remained unchanged, but by the late 1950s the conversion to APCs was gathering momentum and today the infantry are as mobile and vehicle-dependent as the armoured forces. Two subsidiary disputes have concerned whether the vehicle should be a simple personnel carrier or a fighting vehicle in its own right, described variously as a mechanised infantry combat vehicle (MICV) or infantry fighting vehicle (IFV), and whether it should be tracked or wheeled.

INFANTRY FIGHTING VEHICLE DESIGN

Early doctrine favoured the battle-taxi concept of an armoured box to deliver the infantry to the area of the start-line, where they dismounted, and gave rise to vehicles such as the US M113, Soviet BTR-50 and British FV432; later came the concept of a heavily armed MICV from inside which the infantry were able to fire while on the move, only debussing when on the objective. The latter, owing much to German experience on the Eastern Front in World War II and leading to vehicles such as the Soviet BMP-1 and West German Marder, was put to the test in the 1973 Middle East War, when the Egyptians used their BMP-1s exactly as taught in the Soviet tactical textbooks with results frequently verging on the disastrous.

The demonstration beyond doubt that the idea of a MICV charging onto the objective with all weapons

Above: A key feature in IFV/APC design is rapid and easy egress for the infantry. The US Army's M2 Bradley IFV features a large rear door, hinged at the bottom, which forms an ideal exit.

Below: Interior of the Bradley M2 IFV. Six men are accommodated in the space shown here, and when they are mounted with all their weapons and personal equipment there is little room to spare.

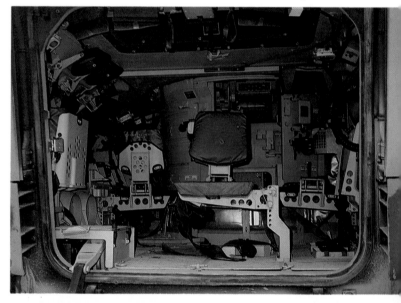

Right: An Israeli M113 displays its Toga add-on armour, which consists of lightweight carbon sheets bolted to the main structure. TOGA prevents rounds up to 14.5mm calibre from even reaching the vehicle's bodywork.

Right: Standard M113 of the Norwegian Army. This successful US-designed vehicle is in service in vast numbers and is the archetypical 'battle taxi' APC, a type now being superseded by the Infantry Fighting Vehicle.

blazing away was unworkable led to a very open discussion in Soviet military journals, one which was followed with fascination in the West, and as a result the concept for the use of BMP-1 was totally revised. It is now generally accepted that the proper use of such vehicles involves the infantry dismounting some 200-300m short of the objective and completing the final phase of the attack on foot, covered by fire from artillery, tanks and APCs.

One of the major continuing problems is that ever more equipment, especially weaponry, is being packed into the vehicles so that what started as a straightforward desire to utilise spare carrying capacity and to give the infantry more firepower in the forward areas has resulted in the infantry squad being squeezed out of its own vehicle. Armament has increased from a pintle-mounted machine-gun in the 1960s to sophisticated turrets mounting 20mm cannon in the 1970s and, on the Swedish APC90, 40mm cannon in the 1990s, frequently supplemented by guided anti-tank weapons. The Soviets even managed to squeeze a 73mm low-pressure gun into the BMP-1. The consequence has been that the dismounting infantry squad has reduced in numbers — from 11 in the US M113 to seven in the M2, from 10 in the French AMX-VCI to eight in the AMX-10 and from no fewer than 20 in the Soviet BTR-50 to only seven in the BMP-2.

The prototype of the most important and influential design of its generation, the US M113 APC, ran in 1958 and production started in 1960; since then over 70,000 have been produced. The archetypical battle taxi, the M113 is a tracked, diesel-engined aluminium box with a crew of two and a dismounting squad of 11. The vehicle has been updated — current version is the M113A3 — and has been used as the basis for many specialist vehicles; like the Jeep, it is relatively cheap to manufacture, easy to maintain and, within certain well recognised limitations, effective in use.

The orginator of the MICV concept, the West German army, has pursued a consistent policy, having developed the heavily armed and sophisticated Marder in the 1960s and stuck with it ever since. Marder weighs 27.75 tons (28,200kg), considerably more than any other MICV or APC, and has a vehicle crew of four and a dismounting section of six. The armament fit comprises a forward turret with an externally

Right: The Soviet MT-LB was developed and produced in parallel with the BMP and there are several variants. The infantry carrier shown here has a crew of two and carries a maximum of 11 infantrymen.

BMP infantry deployment

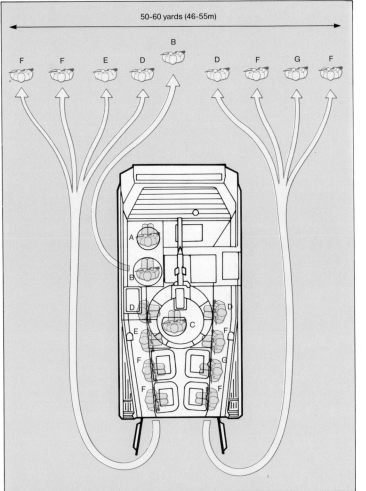

50-60 yards (46-55m)

mounted 20mm automatic cannon with a coaxial 7.62 machine gun and a rear turret with a remotely controlled 7.62mm machine gun, while four of the riflemen are provided with firing ports. The 20mm cannon is to be replaced by a 25mm cannon in the late 1980s, but the Germans have decided not to fit an ATGW, preferring to use a specialist vehicle.

Soviet IFV designers show considerable ingenuity, frequently finding sensible, inexpensive solutions to problems where Western designers tend too often to go for complicated and expensive answers. For example, on BMP-1 and BMP-2 part of the fuel is carried in tanks built into the rear doors: although a fire hazard, this fuel is always used first and can be jettisoned quickly on going into action; alternatively, the empty tanks become buoyancy aids for amphibious operations. Again, the cramped crew conditions are alleviated by roof hatches, which are left open except when in actual combat. And since the upper glacis plate of BMP-1 and BMP-2 is set at a highly oblique angle for protection against armour-piercing rounds which means that small arms fire may ricochet into the sensitive optical equipment on and in front of the turret, ribs are fitted across the upper glacis plate to deflect such bullets; these ribs also help to stiffen the glacis plate itself.

Several Soviet World War II open-topped wheeled APC designs were produced well into the 1950s, but they were followed by two of the best APCs of their generation, the tracked BMP-1 and the wheeled BTR-60, which have been developed into the BMP-2 and BTR-70 respectively. They also produce a second tracked APC, the MT-LB. ·

When it was first seen in 1967 BMP-1 was thought to be exactly what the West's armies wanted; a

Left: In Soviet battle drills the driver (A) and gunner (C) stand fast, the remainder debussing as shown: squad commander (B), PKT MG team (D), RPG-7 gunner (E), riflemen (F) and SA-7 missileman (H). Once in line the men are some 6-8 yards (5.5-7m) apart, covering a frontage of 50-60 yards (46-55m), while the BMP follows some 300 yards (275m) behind.

true MICV, significantly smaller than western APCs, but with much greater firepower. The eight troops have multiple periscopes and can, at least in theory, fire on the move, and there is a vehicle crew of three: the commander, who also commands the dismounted section, plus a driver and a gunner. Both crew and passengers have NBC protection in the pressurised hull and air filters are fitted as standard. The 73mm smooth-bore, low-pressure gun fires fin-stabilised HEAT rounds, the automatic loader giving a firing rate of eight rounds per minute, and above the gun is an AT-3 launcher with one round on the rail and three more inside the vehicle. In addition, one man in the section carries an SA-7 Grail SAM launcher.

BMP-2, the long-awaited successor to BMP-1, appeared in 1982 and followed the same tactical concept as its predecessor. Major differences are that the new vehicle has a two-man turret equipped with a long-barrelled 30mm cannon, 7.62mm machine-gun and AT-5 Spandrel ATGW launcher and that the dismounting section has been reduced to seven.

One of the success stories in the infantry vehicle field, a superb example of an alternative, simpler technological approach and one which is much cheaper in the long run, is the FMC Armored Infantry Fighting Vehicle (AIFV), which was developed from M113 by way of the Product-Improved M113 and, while not adopted by the US Army, is now in service with a number of armies, including those of Belgium and the Netherlands. The vehicle is constructed of welded aluminium armour, with an additional layer of bolt-on, spaced, laminated armour; closed-cell polyurethane foam is incorporated within the armour system to aid buoyancy in amphibious operations.

Above: The Soviet BMP-1 was for many years the standard by which other nations judged their IFVs. In a small package the designers included a crew of two, nine infantrymen and good armament.

The basic vehicle is normally armed with a turret-mounted Oerlikon 25mm KBA-BO2 cannon, with a coaxial 7.62mm machine-gun, but there are many other weapon fits for different roles. There is a crew of three (commander, driver, gunner) and a dismounting section of seven, for whom there are five firing ports. With a combat weight of 13.47 tons (13,687kg) and a power:weight ratio of 19.6hp/ton the AIFV is a straightforward and cost-effective fighting vehicle. It also shows what can be done when ambitions are kept within reasonable bounds, and how logical and careful development based on a successful foundation frequently provides a better solution than a radically new design.

Below: The Luchs reconnaissance vehicle used by the West German Army has excellent cross-country performance from its 8 × 8 drive; it is also very quiet in operation.

Fully amphibious, it has propellers mounted under the rear of the hull, and it can be driven in either direction, front and rear drivers' positions being provided.

Above: The West German Transportpanzer 1 Fuchs is used in various roles, including APC. The 6 × 6 wheeled drive gives good cross-country performance.

WHEELED APCS

Wheeled vehicles provide less expensive, simpler and quieter battlefield mobility, and while they are unlikely to equal the cross-country performance of a tracked vehicle modern 6 × 6 and 8 × 8 drive systems coupled with increasingly efficient tyre design and variable pressure systems are proving to be viable alternatives.

Early wheeled APCs, such as the Soviet BTR-152 (6 × 6) and the British Humber 1-ton (4 × 4) — the famous 'armoured pig' — were based on existing truck chassis, but it was rapidly appreciated that a specially designed vehicle was needed. The British led the way with the Saracen, a 6 × 6 APC version of the Saladin armoured car, while the Soviets designed the 8 × 8 BTR-60 and its replacement the BTR-70. Many designs are available, mainly intended for use in low-intensity warfare like the US Marine Corps, LAV-25, though the British Army's

AT-105 Saxon, a relatively simple and cheap 4 × 4 vehicle, is being procured for use in certain parts of the Central Front.

As in other fields, however, wheeled IFVs are becoming bigger, more complicated and more expensive, and the latest wheeled APCs, such as the South African Ratel, West German Transportpanzer 1 and US LAV-25, weigh more than the tracked M113.

RIFLES

During World War II infantry rifles were generally of 0.30in (7.62mm), 0.303in (7.7mm) or 0.312in (7.92mm) calibre. Such rounds were considered necessary to provide the required range and stopping power, but not only was the ammunition heavy, the weapons themselves were big and heavy and had a relatively heavy recoil. Most were single-shot bolt-action designs, though some self-loading rifles did enter service during the course of the war.

Since World War II there have been three major trends in rifle development: a general reduction in the maximum tactical range required, the acceptance of the need for a fully automatic or semi-automatic action, and a move toward standardisation within alliances which, in conjunction with smaller calibres, has led to a reduction in weight.

The British led the way in the early 1950s with the 0.28in (7.11mm) EM-2, which unfortunately appeared at a time when the USA was successfully pressuring NATO to adopt 7.62mm as the standard calibre. During the Vietnam War the 5.56mm M16 rifle was rushed into production in the USA and the latest standardisation proposal has resulted in NATO agreement on 5.56mm — the Warsaw Pact has opted for 5.45mm —but with the Belgian SS 109 round

Above: The US Marine Corps has adopted a wheeled APC and is procuring the Swiss-designed 8 × 8 LAV-25 in large numbers. It is armed with a 25mm Hughes M-242 Bushmaster cannon and a 7.62mm M240 coaxial MG, giving commonality with the M2/M3.

Above: The US Army has tested this Fast Attack Vehicle (FAV) for its Light Infantry Divisions. It may be very exciting to drive but the operational concept remains to be proven in combat.

Below: Armies need field cars in vast numbers and the US Army is at last replacing the famous series of Jeep designs with the Hummer High Mobility Multi-purpose Wheeled Vehicle (HMMWV).

rather than the US M193. The SS 109 is dimensionally identical to the M193 but differs in design and weight, having a brass jacket surrounding a lead core, but with a steel nose which increases penetrating power, and a greater mass which gives it higher kinetic energy at all ranges than that of the M193.

The latest assault rifles are all highly effective at the ranges expected to be encountered on the modern battlefield, which is agreed by most armies to be some 330-440 yards (300-400m). It has also been concluded that much smaller rounds have enough range and accuracy over such distances as well as being lighter, which in turn leads to lighter rifles and to easier training. Modern rifles are only about half the weight of their 7.62mm predecessors, use magazines with capacities of 20 to 30 rounds and, if set to full automatic, can fire some 30 rounds in about three seconds.

Current service rifles are clearly identifiable as products of a long chain of development, but the next generation of weapons is likely to be quite different. All firearm development revolves around ammunition and for many years rifle ammunition has consisted of bullets fitted into brass cartridge cases, but there is an increasing probability that caseless rounds will achieve production status in the 1990s.

The West German armaments firm of Heckler & Koch, for example, now has prototypes of its G11 rifle under test at various Bundesheer establishments: the ammunition for this rifle consists of a bullet surrounded by the propellant to form a single block, 0.3in (8mm) square and 1.28in (32.5mm) long, which has a neck behind the front end to ensure that it cannot be loaded the wrong way round. The new propellant leaves far less fouling than previous types and there is no empty case to be ejected, and the rifle itself weighs only 8lb (3.65kg) and does need to be stripped; only the bore and chamber need cleaning.

While all seem now to be moving to a lighter round for the general-purpose assault rifle, most armies are retaining 7.62mm weapons for snipers: the US Army, for example, uses an adapted version of the M14 fitted with a telescopic sight and a flash suppressor and firing three types of ammunition, while the British Army uses the well tried L42A1 rifle with a telescopic sight and the Soviet Army uses the 7.62mm Dragunov, the only known semi-automatic sniper weapon. Some commercial firms now offer 0.5in sniping rifles.

SUB-MACHINE GUNS

In the years since 1945 sub-machine guns have been used by troops who needed a firearm smaller and lighter than the standard rifle. Such weapons as the British 9mm Sterling and the US 9mm M3A1 have only short effective ranges and relatively poor stopping-power, and it was thought at one time that the new assault rifles were so light and easy to use that there was little need for sub-machine guns, particularly since they use ammunition of different calibres, but the new lightweight 5.56mm bullets do not have sufficient effect at very short ranges, especially if fired from a short barrel. Sub-machine gun designers are, therefore, concentrating on wresting better performance from the traditional 9mm Parabellum round. Indeed, a number of manufacturers have produced 5.56mm assault rifle designs converted to take 9mm ammunition.

LIGHT MACHINE GUNS

The light machine gun is a section or squad weapon which is required to combine a good rate of sustained fire and a reasonable range with light weight and relative simplicity. The British have opted for a variant of their new assault rifle with a slightly more robust barrel and a bipod, but the US Army has recently taken into service a new SAW (squad automatic weapon) on a scale of one per fire team — that is, two per squad. The M249, developed from the Belgian FN Minimi, is a 5.56mm weapon which, complete with 200 rounds, sling and cleaning kit, weighs just 22lb (9.97kg) — its predecessor, the 7.62mm MM60, weighs 23lb without any ammunition — and has an effective range of 1,300m and a rate of fire of 750rds/min.

GRENADES

The infantryman has long carried grenades. Very useful as personal artillery, their capability was limited for years by the man's throwing ability and various devices have

Above: The British Light Support Weapon is similar to the new 5.56mm Individual Weapon System, but has a longer barrel, a bipod and a pistol grip to give increased range and accuracy.

Below: This FN rifle grenade has a telescopic extension and can be launched with any type of ball ammunition; the 5.56mm version has a range of 328 yards (300m) and a lethal radius of 11 yards.

Below: The last line of anti-tank defence is represented by hand-held weapons such as this Italian Folgore 80mm recoilless cannon.

All use hollow-charge warheads, whose effectiveness against the latest types of armour is open to question.

been introduced to increase their range. Grenade launchers which fit onto the muzzle of the rifle and use ballistite cartridges are still found, but the US Army's M203 launcher clips underneath the M16 rifle and throws a 40mm grenade out to a maximum of 380 yards (350m).

The next stage is to automate the process, but that can only be achieved at the cost of weight and complexity. The Soviet Army uses the 20mm AGS-17 Plamya automatic grenade launcher, which fires three types of round — HEAT, anti-personnel and phosphorus — to a maximum range of 875 yards (800m) at a rate of 100rds/min, while the similar US Mk 19 Mod 3 40mm grenade launcher fires dual-purpose anti-personnel/anti-armour 12oz (340gm) grenades to a range of 1,800 yards (1,650m). Both weapons are heavy and require vehicles for mobility.

INFANTRY ANTI-TANK WEAPONS

Perhaps the infantryman's greatest problem is close-range defence against tanks: after all other weapons have failed to stop the advance of enemy armour, he must, in the last resort, defend himself. And not just in a major war, where there would be layers of anti-tank defence out to about 5,000m: in minor wars in underdeveloped areas modern tanks are just as likely to be found. A bewildering variety of weapon systems are available, but all fall into three general categories: long-range missile systems, medium-range missile and gun systems, and last-ditch systems.

However, the development of new tank armours such as the British Chobham and Israeli active types has posed new problems. For many years the technological answer to tank armour has been the hollow-charge warhead, whose penetrating power is directly proportional to its diameter and which can penetrate to a maximum depth of eight times its diameter. However, if the high-velocity molten jet formed when the warhead detonates is going to be deflected by the new armours the size of the warhead is of limited relevance. The difficulty is compounded by the fact that the majority of infantry anti-tank engagements, and particularly those at ranges of under 500m, will involve tanks heading straight toward them, so their weapons must be used against the thickest part of the tank's armour.

The weakest area of a tank's armour is the top surface, and among the devices produced to attack this particular area is the Swedish Bofors RBS-56 Bill. This top-attack missile is designed to fly approximately 3ft (1m) above the operator's line-of-sight and fire a shaped-charge warhead when immmediately above the tank turret. The tank designers' immediate response to this and other top attack weapons has been to install reactive armour on the turret roof, and no doubt next-generation MBTs will have thicker roof armour to overcome the new threat.

Meanwhile, most infantry rely on long-range vehicle-mounted missiles such as the very successful and effective US Tow, the British Swingfire, the Franco-German Hot and the Soviet AT-5 Spandrel, which have ranges of up to 4,380 yards (4,000m). Medium-range missiles — that is those with ranges of up to about 2,200 yards (2,000m) — include the Franco-German Milan, the Soviet AT-3 Sagger and AT-4 Spigot and the US Dragon, all of which are man-portable and fired from ground launchers and most of which use SACLOS guidance. For short-range engagements most armies use lightweight, tube-launched, man-portable rocket systems, such as the British LAW 80, Swedish Carl Gustav, Italian Folgore and French ACL STRIM. Finally, there are a number of last-ditch devices such as anti-tank grenades fired from rifle muzzles — for example, the Belgian Energa — while the Soviet Army still trains its infantrymen to attach anti-tank mines to enemy tanks passing over their foxholes.

MORTARS

The simple tube mortar, described as the infantryman's own artillery, is a very effective method of bringing heavy fire to bear both rapidly and accurately, while its light weight, simplicity of operation and rugged construction makes it ideal for infantry use. Mortars have not changed in their principles of operation since World War I, but they have been progressively refined to obtain increases in range, greater effectiveness in their terminal effects and reductions in weight. For example, the US M29A1 81mm mortar weighs 115lb (52.5kg) and has a maximum range of 5,140 yards (4,700m) while its replacement, the British L16, weighs 78lb (35kg) complete — a reduction of 32 per cent - and has a range of 6,189 yards (5,600m), an increase of 20 per cent.

Infantry formations in most armies have man-portable lightweight mortars, usually of 60mm calibre, and medium vehicle-mounted mortars, usually of 81mm calibre. A few armies, such as the Soviet, still have infantry-operated 120mm mortars, but anything bigger is operated by artillery units. One new hazard is the use of mortar-locating radars which can rapidly locate mortar base-plate positions and thus enable counter-battery fire to be brought to bear within a very short space of time.

AIR DEFENCE

As with anti-tank defence, the infantry rely in the first instance for air defence on specialised long-range weapons systems, operated by air defence regiments, but as in the anti-tank battle they need their own short-range systems for last-ditch defence and once again missile technology has come to their aid. Many armies now use shoulder-launched missiles such as the British Blowpipe and Javelin, the US Stinger and the Soviet SA-7 Grail, which have typical

ranges of up to 3.7 miles (6km) and use either SACLOS guidance or IR homing. Their operation is not without difficulty, however: SACLOS guidance enables aircraft targets to be engaged during their approach, but needs very rapid response and a much higher standard of operator training, while IR homing requires much less training but can only be used to engage departing targets. Further, while the prospect of a dense carpet of lightweight anti-aircraft weapons over the forward areas of the battlefield may deter hostile aircraft, it is of almost equal concern to a friendly pilot, and the control of such weapons has become a major concern, especially to the pilots of friendly aircraft.

PERSONAL EQUIPMENT

After many years without change, modern technology is starting to have a major impact on the infantryman himself and a spin-off effect on virtually every other soldier on the battlefield. Packs, pouches and belts are being made of materials such as cordura and nylon with fasteners of nylon or light alloy, buttons are being replaced by zips or velcro, combat uniforms are being made of camouflaged material and Goretex capes may at last keep the rain out, while Kevlar helmets provide much better protection at a fraction of the weight of the old steel helmet.

For many years, too, the wearing of body armour, or flak jackets, was considered somewhat effete, particularly by infantry and artillery troops, but the availability of much stronger and lighter jackets, combined with a change in attitude, has resulted in a marked increase in their use.

Above: To provide mobility and protection mortars are often mounted in APCs. This British 81mm mortar is being fired through the roof hatch of an FV432. Note crew's NBC clothing.

Below: The infantryman's load never reduces; equipment and ammunition may get lighter, but he is simply given more to carry, a point made by this US soldier's festoons of grenades.

Battlefield Helicopters

The helicopter arrived on the battlefield in the 1940s as a very useful tool for casualty evacuation, with the additional ability to transport small numbers of troops (especially senior officers) around and, on occasion, move small quantities of essential stores. It was also useful for reconnaissance. These roles were carried out on a very limited scale but with increasing efficiency in the various colonial campaigns in the late 1940s and early 1950s in countries such as Malaya and Vietnam. The Korean War saw the first widespread use of helicopters, while the abortive Anglo-French operation at Suez was the occasion for the first major amphibious landing in which the most critical ship-to-shore transport was the helicopter. The French then extended the use of the helicopter in the Algerian War, but it was the Americans' use of helicopters in Vietnam which represents the real 'coming of age' of this new system.

A detailed assessment of modern helicopter technology is given in a companion volume in this series, *Modern Combat Helicopters,* published by Salamander Books in 1986, to which the reader should turn for in-depth study; what follows is a general survey of the helicopter's role in the land battle.

TRANSPORTS

The performance of helicopters improved rapidly during the 1960s and 1970s, as did their reliability. As far as most armies were concerned, the primary use to which helicopters should be put was transport, and at this they excelled. They proved to be capable of transporting troops, stores, equipment (including some very awkward loads), guns and even light tanks, and placing them precisely where they were required. Western 'heavy lift' types such as the Sikorsky CH-53 and Boeing-Vertol CH-47, with a troop load of 37 and 44 respectively, have given a new meaning to the phrase 'battlefield mobility', but even their payloads pale beside those of the Soviet giants, the Mil Mi-6 (Hook) and Mil Mi-26 (Halo), which can carry 90 and 100 troops. Such figures should be treated with some caution since payload can vary with temperature, range, safety considerations, etc — for example, in the South Atlantic War of 1982 an RAF Boeing CH-47 flew with 73 armed troops on board because the operational situation dictated it — but they serve as a means of comparing one type with another. There is nothing technologically clever about the Soviet helicopters — they are just bigger.

Below the heavy-lifters come a series of medium-lift helicopters, capable of carrying between 10 and 20 men. Aircraft such as the Anglo-French Puma, US Sikorsky UH-60A, Soviet Mil Mi-8 and British Westland Commando carry a minimum of a complete squad or section with its weapons over a radius of about 150 miles (240km).

Finally, there are the small two-or three-man helicopters, of which

there are a vast number of types. Once designated 'liaison' and 'reconnaisance' helicopters, they are now usually described as 'multirole', and are capable of carrying a variety of weapons, particularly machine-guns and lightweight anti-tank guided weapons.

GUNSHIPS

The development of transport helicopters continued, and great numbers are now in service with virtually every army. However, just as infantrymen could not resist the temptation to mount weapons on APCs — why waste such a valuable gun platform? — so, too, did people start to hang weapons on helicopters. The consequence, again as with APCs, is that there is now a whole breed of these specialised attack aircraft.

There have, however, been two marked changes in the role for which these machines are intended. Initially, gunships were designed primarily to attack troops on the ground, with a secondary capability against light armoured targets — basically, a fire-suppression role in support of troop-carrying helicopters. Then it was realised that with modern weapons and avionics, and with new concepts of tactical deployment, these gunships could

Above left: The carrying capacity of helicopters such as this RAF Chinook is so great that ground units have their hands full to generate enough loads for them.

Left: Soviet transport helicopters such as this Egyptian Mi-8 carry weapons to suppress ground defences as they come into hostile landing zones.

Below: Among the most successful West European helicopters are the Aérospatiale 332B Puma and Super Puma. Many armies use them to move mobile reserves.

become very effective anti-tank weapons platforms and make an invaluable contribution to dealing with the ever-increasing numbers of tanks.

This then gave rise, in turn, to the problem of how to keep such dangerous aircraft in check and ensure that the tanks got through. Ground-based guns and missiles were part of the answer, and it was hoped that fixed-wing aircraft could also help, but trials showed that a skilfully flown helicopter could evade a fixed-wing aircraft at low level with comparative ease. So, just as it is generally accepted that the best method of dealing with a submarine is another submarine and that the best anti-tank weapon is another tank, it became apparent that the only effective weapon to deal with a helicopter was another helicopter: this has given rise to the concept of a fighter helicopter, of which the first example is the Soviet Hokum.

Occasionally during the Algerian War the French had installed a machine-gun on an *ad hoc* mounting in the door of a Sikorsky S-55 to force terrorists to keep their heads down during the approach to a landing zone. It was, however, in Vietnam that matters went beyond the question of simple self-defence and reached the point where helicopters were deliberately designed as weapons carriers, i.e. gunships. First, there were simple conversions of the UH-1 (Huey), in which the weapons systems — machine guns, Gatlings, rocket launchers, missile launchers, etc — were strapped on to the fuselage sides and undercarriage of an otherwise standard helicopter. But then the inevitable specially-designed versions appeared, with slim fuselages, higher-performance rotors, uprated engines and increasingly sophisticated weapons systems. An adaptation of the UH-1, the AH-1 HueyCobra appeared in 1965, was quickly ordered into production as an interim gunship, and is still in production 22 years later. The aircraft which was supposed to be the definitive gunship was the Lockheed AH-56 Cheyenne, a large, complex machine which was eventually cancelled in 1972 after a very troubled history.

While the US tried to sort out the mess it had got itself into, the USSR produced another of those designs (like the BMP APC) which Western experts wished they could have produced themselves. This aircraft, the Mil Mi-24 (Hind) gunship, is heavily armed and well-protected, has an excellent performance and has proved capable of being continuously updated; it entered production in 1972 and is still manufactured. It took the USA· over 10 years to get their next gunship, the McDonnell Douglas AH-64 Apache, into production and it is now, at last, in service. Other nations are following the same route as the USSR and the USA; gunships in production or under development include the Italian Agusta Mangusta, the European collaborative Eurocopter and the Romanian IAR-317 Airfox.

Above: One of the most significant developments of recent years has been the appearance of armed helicopters for the anti-tank role. Small aircraft are remarkably difficult to detect, especially in wooded and hilly terrain, and promise to be highly effective in countering the massive Warsaw Pact tank threat.

Below: After a protracted development programme the US Army at last has a specialised attack helicopter in service – the AH-64A Apache.

Right: The Soviets have developed both attack helicopters such as Havoc (lower right) and the Hokum (foreground), optimised for anti-helicopter missions.

Meanwhile the USSR has put yet another type, the Mil Mi-28 (Havoc), into production. Currently the only air-superiority helicopter fighter, the Soviet Hokum is designed by the Kamov design bureau, and has that concern's characteristic twin co-axial contra-rotating rotors. It has a very streamlined shape and is credited with an estimated top speed of 217mph (350km/hr) and a radius of action of 155 miles (250km). It is twin-engined, with an armament that includes a very large cannon in a chin turret.

Command, Control and Communications

Battlefield command, control and communications (C³) have become ever more important as the complexity, geographical spread, response speed and capability of land forces have increased. C³ has also become important as a way of seeking to optimise the use of scarce resources, i.e. as a 'force multiplier'. It is an indication of the importance placed upon C³ that in an era of tighter defence budgets few, if any, Western armies are reducing their expenditure on C³; instead, they are maintaining existing levels, or, in some cases, actually increasing them. As an example, among the numerous C³ systems currently being procured by the US Army are the Maneuvre Control System (MCS), an automated command and control system; the Mobile Subscriber Equipment (MSE), a tactical communications sytem; and SINCGARS-V, a new combat net radio family. Procurement funding for these three systems alone over the years FY85 to FY88 (both inclusive) will be $US 3,288 million at FY86 prices — a very considerable sum by any standard.

The exercise of command and control is becoming increasingly complicated and time-urgent, and all armies are finding that the old-fashioned methods of organising, manning and operating headquarters no longer meet today's requirements. As a result, all are introducing automated data processing (ADP) systems (computers) to assist in handling information, in processing intelligence and in preparing inputs upon which decision-making can be based. In the more advanced systems the computers are linked together over the tactical communications network to enable them to keep each other up to date and, where permitted, to interrogate each other's data banks. A particular application of such systems is in the artillery world, where automated systems have become essential to co-ordinate, control and resupply the gun systems now available.

The third element of C³, communications, is critical to the exercise of the other two. Perhaps the greatest recent change in communications philosophy is that whereas new items of equipment used to be fielded in piecemeal fashion they are now being deployed as complete systems, for example Ptarmigan and RITA. This has the advantage of lower unit price through the purchase of larger quantities and also ensures a higher degree of interoperability between sub-systems than was the case in the past. It also, however, means that systems take longer to develop and are more susceptible to technical problems, and thus become more expensive.

SOVIET C³

All Soviet field headquarters are organised in a similar manner, varying only in size. Control is exercised through a series of command posts (komandnyy punkt); at divisional level, for

Above: Ground troops use vast numbers of radios for command and control, but whether such means will be available in a hostile EW environment is questionable.

example, there are four command posts. The commander is at the Forward Command Post, some 3 miles (5km) from the line of contact, controlling the first-echelon troops in combat. The Main Command Post is set up on the main axis some 3-10 miles (5-15km) from the line of combat and is run by the chief-of-staff. The Alternative Command Post is set up a similar distance from the line of combat but sufficiently far from the main CP to survive a medium-yield nuclear weapon and with sufficient staff to take over and ensure continuity of control. Main and Alternate CPs move about three times in every 24hr period, leap-frogging with each other. Finally, there is a Rear Services Control Point some 3-10 miles (5-15km) further back from the Main CP, responsible for logistic control.

Soviet tactical HQs move very frequently, thus posing not only a problem for enemy intercept/DF but also a considerable challenge to their own communicators. At higher levels (divisional and rearwards) more reliance is placed on microwave (radio-relay) and civilian trunk systems, but it would appear that, in general terms, they are less complex than their Western counterparts and thus probably more reliable and survivable.

The majority of Soviet military electronic equipment still uses valve technology, making it rugged (and survivable in an EMP environment), although heavier and less reliable than modern Western equipment.

A further factor is that the Soviet Army's concept of command is based on 'top-down' control, which means that only limited flexibility and initiative is allowed at the lower echelons. This reduces the number

RITA communications system

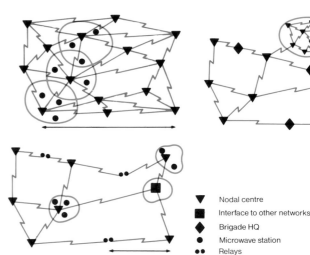

▼ Nodal centre
■ Interface to other networks
◆ Brigade HQ
● Microwave station
●● Relays

Above: The French RITA is a fully integrated and automatic tactical communications system. It provides direct dialling; voice, data and telegraph circuits; and net radio access; all are fully secure.

Below: Interior of a vehicle in the French RITA system. Modern area systems are sophisticated and expensive, but promise a new era in tactical command, control and communications (C³).

of radio nets and also cuts down on the amount of traffic actually passed; thus on a tank company net, for example, it will be comparatively rare for an individual tank to transmit as well as listen. The communications systems reflect this philosophy, while also taking into account the enemy's ability to interrupt and intercept electronic transmissions. Further, the Soviet Army still encourages the use of hand, flag and light signals, a truly low-tech solution but no less effective for that!

US C³

The US Army currently uses tactical radio systems based on traditional radio nets using the high-frequency (HF) and very high-frequency (VHF) bands, with some specialised users (e.g. ground-to-air) operating on even higher bands. Two major systems are in use, the AN/VRC-12 vehicle-borne family and the AN/PRC-77 man-portable family. A major programme is now under way for the Single Channel Ground and Airborne Radio Subsystem - VHF (SINCGARS-V), which will provide the next generation of sets. These will be light in weight and secure, and will use the most modern microprocessor techniques. They will be capable not only of totally secure voice transmissions, but also of passing data, an ever-increasing requirement on today's battlefield. The most interesting aspect, however, is that 'frequency hopping' will be used to provide a major degree of electronic counter-countermeasure (ECCM) protection, which means that the set transmits on any one frequency for only a micro-second at a time. For an enemy, therefore, the intercept problem becomes very acute, although the technique is not without its difficulties at the transmitting end as well. Unfortunately, by mid-1986 SINCGARS had run into both

technical and production difficulties and its future was uncertain.

At higher tactical levels the US Army is procuring a version of the French RITA trunk system, known as Mobile Subscriber Equipment (MSE). This is a radio-based communications system designed to provide mobile and stationary tactical users in corps and divisional areas with an automatic, fully secure, digital telephone service similar to that described for the British Ptarmigan below, which was a competitor with RITA for the MSE contract.

As with other armies the US Army is putting a major effort into developing a Maneuver Control System (MCS) to provide a field commander and his staff with automated assistance in controlling the battle. The long-term system will be known as Sigma and is likely to be very sophisticated indeed. Currentlly in service are a microcomputer called the Tactical Computer Terminal (TCT) and a rather more powerful device, the Tactical Computer System (TCS).

One particular system under development would put the entire battlefield map into the data base, which would not only give a picture similar to that on a current paper map, but would also give a 3-D image from any point on the map in any requested direction.

BRITISH C³

The British Army is in the process of fielding Ptarmigan, one of the most comprehensive and advanced military trunk communications systems in the world. This system is based on a network of trunk nodes interconnected by microwave radio links, which are spaced around the tactical area in such a way that they provide a communications grid, which 'illuminate' as much of the area as possible. Headquarters and other units requiring to communicate can then move about and when stationary can connect with two of the nearest trunk nodes, using microwave 'up-the-hill' links. Trunk nodes are moved by the signals commander to adjust the coverage of the grid to keep pace with

the battle, and, because of Ptarmigan's design, this can be done without affecting any of the users.

A further facility is single channel radio access (SCRA), which enables suitably equipped mobile users to access the trunk system, in a manner analogous to that now being provided by cellphone systems for civilian users; it can also be used to enable isolated users to have access to the main system. There are still a large number of users of combat net radio (CNR), the present range in use being designated 'Clansman'.

As with other armies the British army is fielding an automated battlefield C² ADP system. The first system, designated Wavell 1, has been entirely replaced by a totally new system, Wavell 2, which is, in effect, a second-generation system and not simply an updated Wavell 1. Wavell 2 assists commanders and staff at corps, division and brigade levels by giving them an up-to-date, accurate picture of the battlefield, with both own troops and enemy forces deployments, thus enabling more rapid appreciations and plans to be made.

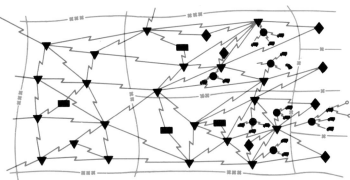

Left: British C50 mobile UHF radio relay set mounted in an FV439. Radio relay provides the majority of the bearer circuits in the RITA and Ptarmigan systems.

Below: Command and control for the British Army and RAF in Germany has been revolutionised by the new Ptarmigan system. Trunk nodes form a highly survivable and flexible grid.

Ptarmigan

Above: A British radio operator mans a mobile subscriber terminal in the Single Channel Radio Access (SCRA) element of the Ptarmigan trunk system.

- Corps
- Division
- Brigade
- ▼ Trunk node
- ▬ Headquarters/Access node
- ● Single-channel radio access
- ◆ Brigade HQ
- Mobile radio subscriber

Electronic Warfare

Electronic warfare (EW) is a modern, largely hidden battlefield, where vicious and merciless combat is fought daily, even in peacetime. It is a highly classified area, and in any event an esoteric, difficult-to-understand subject. Only occasionally do EW matters enter the public domain, and when an event occurs like the sinking of the British destroyer HMS *Sheffield,* which was essentially an ECM/ECCM engagement, it causes a major shock. Nevertheless, almost every modern military weapons system has a mass of on-board electronic equipment, virtually all of which is susceptible to some form of counter-measure.

The spread of electronics has been very rapid and now reaches into areas way beyond those of the traditional electronics fields of, say, radios and computers. For example, the MBT of the 1950s was equipped with only two major items of electronics, a radio and a simple gun stabilising system, whereas today's MBT has a mass of electronic devices, including laser rangefinders, an integrated fire control system, a gun stabilising system, thermal-imaging devices, image intensifiers, laser detectors, infra-red detectors, environmental control units and, last but by no means least, radios. Even an infantry section may have a mass of electronic devices, including short-range radars, various sighting and observation systems such as thermal imagers, image intensifiers and infra-red, remote sensors, laser target-markers and range-takers and, again, radios.

The short career of active infra-red (IR) is an object lesson in ECM. Active IR came into vogue in the late 1950s for use in surveillance and in devices such as night-vision goggles for vehicle drivers. Many pieces of equipment appeared over a period of a few years, until it was realised that it was extremely simple to detect active IR transmitters; in fact nothing more than a pair of IR goggles was needed — a very elementary ECM system. Active IR disappeared almost as rapidly as it had appeared, to be succeeded by passive IR which, in its turn, was overtaken by image intensifiers before today's thermal imaging arrived on the scene. However, countermeasures to thermal imaging are now being devised and so the ECM/ECCM cycle continues.

THE ELECTROMAGNETIC SPECTRUM

The EW battleground is the electromagnetic spectrum, which is one of the fundamental components of the universe and encompasses a whole host of everyday phenomena from speech through radios and televisions to infra-red cookers and lasers in compact disc players. Position in the elctromagnetic spectrum is expressed in terms of either *frequency* or *wavelength*. Frequency measures the rate of vibration and is expressed in terms of Herz (Hz), where 1Hz equals one cycle per second; thus 1MHz (one million Herz) equals one million cycles per second. Wavelength measures the distance between one point in an electromagnetic wave and the same point in the following wave, and is normally expressed in metric form; hence in a '10cm wave' the distance between two identical points on the wave is 10cm. The two are inversely related, that is, as the frequency rises the wavelength shortens and the path becomes more of a straight line. A further characteristic is that the higher the frequency the greater the amount of information that can be carried.

The military as a whole use virtually the entire spectrum, but land forces' usage tends to be confined to the area bounded by the high-frequency (HF) band at the lower end and by visible light at the upper. HF (3-30MHz) signals can travel very long distances by reflection off the ionosphere (sky-wave) and also comparatively long distances along the surface of the Earth (ground-wave); HF is still used a great deal, but has been superseded in some of its applications, for example by satellites for long-range strategic communications and by

Above: The US Army monitoring station at Fort Huachuca, Arizona, carries on the ceaseless task of monitoring the radio frequency band for transmissions originating from any part of the world.

Below: The electromagnetic spectrum is as real a potential battleground as anywhere in Central Europe, even though the combat may be unseen by most people. All parts of the spectrum are used in land warfare, from the very low frequency band at the bottom of the scale right up to the visible end of the spectrum, and the whole area is becoming increasingly crowded with signals.

The electromagnetic spectrum

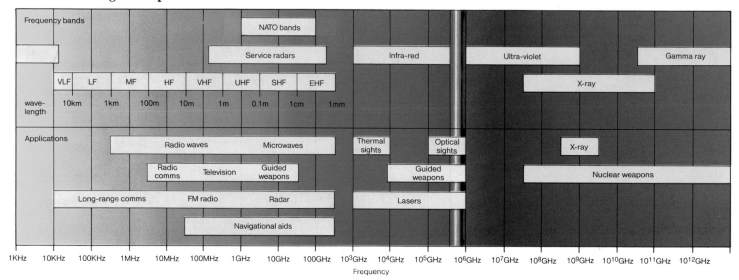

HF and VHF interception

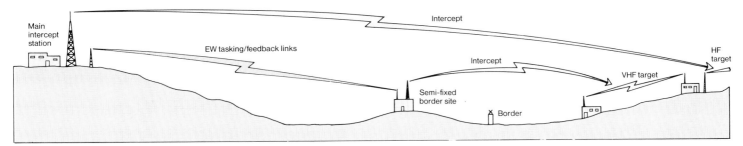

VHF for mobile battlefield communications. The two main problems with HF are its susceptibility to atmospheric variations (although this is diminishing with the latest technology) and the ease with which it can be intercepted by distant monitoring stations.

The very high frequency (VHF) band spans the frequencies 30-150MHz and ultra high-frequency (UHF) 150-400MHz. VHF has replaced HF for short-range battlefield communications and is also used for IFF (identification friend or foe), tacan (tactical air navigation) and some long-range search radars. Army use of UHF is confined mainly to ground-to-air communications and to tactical radio-relay (microwave) links. Because their waves do not 'bend' in the way that HF's do and tend rather to follow straight lines, VHF and UHF signals are more difficult to intercept at a distant ground station than HF, but they can still be monitored with ease by satellites or aircraft.

Radars operate in the 1-20GHz (1 Gigaherz = one million million cycles per second) range, which for convenience is subdivided into bands designated by the letters D through to M. Super-high frequency (SHF, 3-30GHz) is used for uplinks to satellites and for some types of short-range radio-relay communications on the ground.

Further up the spectrum yet is the infra-red (IR) band. All objects radiate IR energy; the hotter they are the greater the energy transmitted and the shorter the wavelength. Not all the infra-red spectrum is

Above: Because high-frequency radio signals travel for long distances, land-based intercept and direction-finding stations (left) can be targeted on transmitters deep in hostile territory. VHF transmissions, on the other hand, travel much shorter distances and intercept stations must be situated much closer to the links being intercepted to have any hope of success.

Left: The US Army's MLQ-34 is a mobile jammer designed to disrupt enemy radio nets. Jamming must be controlled to ensure there is no disruption of own communications.

Above: Emerson's MSQ-103A Teampack Dragoon ESM system is intended for use at divisional level in the US Army. Its receiving systems monitor the radio spectrum from 500MHz to 400Hz, covering the SHF and UHF bands. Any transmissions intercepted must be passed back to a central point for analysis.

militarily useful, as water vapour, carbon dioxide and other atmospheric constituents absorb the energy; there are, however, two usable 'windows' in the spectrum. Lasers are also used by ground forces; these operate in the band 10^3-10^6GHz.

All active electromagnetic transmissions can be detected and then either monitored or interfered with, and this is the essence of EW. EW is divided into three principal elements. Electronic support measures (ESM) are the actions taken to search for, intercept, locate, record and analyse radiated electromagnetic energy for the purpose of exploitation in support of military operations; electronic countermeaures (ECM) are the actions taken to prevent the enemy's effective use of the electromagnetic spectrum; and electronic counter-countermeasures (ECCM) are the actions taken to ensure the friendly use of the electromagnetic spectrum against EW, despite the enemy's use of ECM. Thus ESM comprise the essential preliminary activities of finding out what the enemy (or potential enemy) is doing and where. This enables EW planners to decide whether it is worth taking ECM action, which might include steps such as jamming, disruption or deception. Many ECCM, the protection against ECM, are essentially passive, such as the use of on-line security devices, changing operating schedules and call-signs, the use of skip-echelon communications, and ensuring that there is intervening high ground between radio-relay terminals and the enemy's monitoring stations. Others may, however, be active, for example the physical destruction of an enemy jamming station.

In the land battle, intelligence and reconnaissance assets are used to find, identify and locate enemy electronic emissions (ESM-elint). Once this has been done, however, the commander is faced with three possible courses of action. First, he can continue to intercept and monitor the emissions, which may in the longer term give him more information. Second, he could use his resources in an ESM mode, i.e. by jamming or by transmitting deceptive signals to confuse the enemy based on information gathered from monitoring the original signals. Third, since he knows the location of the emitters, he could physically attack and destroy them.

Military history contains many examples of the application of the first course, of which the most famous is, perhaps, the Ultra operation. The British had obtained a German Enigma machine and broken the code early in World War II and they decided that, if they took exceptional steps to protect this fact, they should be able to go on monitoring and gaining information for a considerable time. This is what happened, and, protected by Ultra, the most invaluable information was obtained throughout the war, the Germans apparently never guessing that this was happening. Some hard choices had to be made on occasion, however, when countermeasures to plans Germany had revealed through Ultra could not be taken, since to have done so could have compromised the entire operation.

Jamming is not the panacea it was once thought to be, although it still has a place in EW. Broad-band jamming is a really heavy-handed solution and is as likely to disrupt friendly communications as it is the enemy's; spot jamming, i.e. jamming on a particular frequency, is likely to be more productive.

ESM

It is well known that strategic ESM is taking place every day in peacetime. NATO and the Warsaw Pact, as well as many other organisations, have strategic electronic monitoring arrangements of varying degrees of

Above: The US Army's principal airborne ESM platform for battlefield use is the Sikorsky EH-60A mounting the Quick Fix II ECM system. Primary equipment is the ALQ-151, which provides direction-finding intercept and jamming facilities .

Below: The advantage of drones is that they are small, difficult to detect, able to fly over hostile territory with relative impunity and avoid risking expensive aircrew who are difficult to replace. This is the Mazlat Mastiff Mk III produced in Israel.

Above: Thermal imagers are able to detect the infra-red signature given off by heat sources through conventional smoke screens, making AFVs vulnerable to enemy detection. The British Army now uses the Visual and Infra-Red Screening Smoke system to guard against this threat. VIRSS utilises a special substance to provide an emissive IR 'hot spot' as well as having significant absorbitive secondary effects. It is effective against thermal imaging systems operating in the 3-5 and 8-14 micron bands.

sophistication. These monitor potential enemies' electronic emissions with a view to establishing orders of battle, operational methods and other information, but, above all, to give early warning of any hostile intent.

Most armies also have tactical ESM units. The Soviet Army, for example, has a Signal Intercept Regiment in each Front. This comprises a Radio Intercept Battalion, a Radio Direction-Finding Battalion and a Radar Intercept and Direction-Finding Battalion. The tasks of the unit are to detect and locate enemy radar positions, command posts, communications centres and nuclear delivery systems, to monitor clear-text radio transmissions, and to provide direction-finding information for targeting. There may also be a similarly structured but smaller Signal Intercept Battalion at Army level.

The Soviets have, in fact, developed their EW capability into an integrated system which they term Radio-Electronic Combat (REC). This is intended to combine signal intelligence, direction-finding, jamming, deception and offensive action (by aircraft, artillery, Spetsnaz, etc) to attack enemy organisations and systems by neutralising their means of control. REC is not, however, seen as a bludgeon, attacking massively and at random, but rather as a rapier, selecting with precision the most critical links in the various chains and the optimum times in the enemy planning process for the electronic attack in order to cause the maximum confusion — not least by achieving surprise.

EQUIPMENT

Many armies employ ESM/ECM aircraft. The Soviet Army uses the Mil Mi-4 (Hound-C), which carries powerful tactical jammers, sensors and direction-finding equipment. The antennas for the VHF jammers protrude either side of the fuselage and are presumably aimed at NATO combat radio nets. The US equivalent is the Sikorsky EH-60A, an ECM version of the UH-60 Blackhawk which mounts the Quick Fix II ECM system. Primary equipment is the ALQ-151 EW system which provides DF, intercept and jamming facilities in the 2-76MHz frequency range. There are two operators who can interface, via secure links, with any other suitably equipped US Army aircraft, both to exchange information and to combine DF efforts. There is also a secure, real-time data downlink to a divisional tactical operations centre.

Also part of the US Army EW inventory is the Beech Super King Air RC-12D, a twin-engined, fixed-wing aircraft. This is the airborne component of the Guardrail V system, which is designed to intercept, locate and if necessary to jam hostile electronic emitters, particularly those associated with SAMs. It is fitted with a CW (continuous-wave) jammer intended to defeat missiles such as

the Soviet SA-6, and an I/J-band jammer to counter the radars on equipment such as ZSU-23-4 and SA-9. Another aircraft type, the RU-21J, is fitted with tactical ESM sets for use against Soviet multichannel microwave links, for which task an airborne platform is essential.

Another way of performing at least some of these tasks is with an RPV, of which the Israeli Tadiran Mastiff is an excellent example. This platform has a wingspan of 14ft 1¼in (4.3m) and a length of 9ft 11¾in (3.04m) and weighs some 254lb (115kg); its 22hp engine gives it a maximum speed of some 80mph (130km/hr) and an endurance of up to 6 hours. Missions include real-time reconnaissance, remote-control photography, decoy manoeuvres, EW jamming and 'other uses'. The potential for ESM and ECM tasks with this vehicle is clearly considerable.

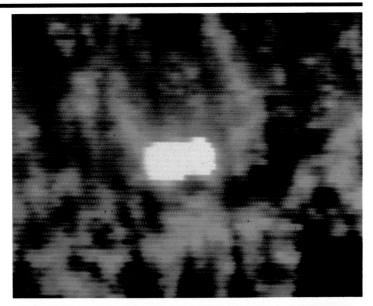

Top, above and below: Camouflage can overcome thermal reconnaissance systems which are otherwise able to detect the radiation of hot objects (top). This system, made by Diab-Barracuda of Sweden, involves covering the object to be concealed with a thermal blanket to screen its radiation, allowing only undetectable warm air to escape. A thermal net over the top (above) is then used to create a thermal signature compatible with the background radiation (below).

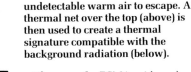

The scope for ECM is wide and extends far beyond the more obvious electronic devices such as radios and radars. For example, modern technology is now making possible the creation of smoke which will blind IR and possibly laser systems. Such smoke devices are fired from grenade-type launchers on tanks and, in addition to acting as an IR and optical smokescreen, should also offer protection from SACLOS ATGW (e.g. Tow, Milan, HOT, AT-4) as well as fire-and-forget homing missiles such as Maverick and Hellfire. The British are developing a series of devices to protect AFVs in this manner. These include the Schermuly Multi-Band Screen system firing a vertical fountain of hot particles from a series of cartridges, and the Wallop Guard decoy system using 57mm rockets which launch IR candles.

Tactical Nuclear Warfare

The advent of nuclear weapons and the prospect of their use has permeated every aspect of general war planning in the major armies. There is clearly a possibility that the use of tactical nuclear weapons could accomplish either, at one end of the scale, the total elimination of large numbers of hostile ground forces, or, at the other, the destruction of such critical point targets as airfield runways, headquarters, communications centres and logistic bases. The unavoidable dilemma, however, is that were these weapons to be used, their apparent military advantages might also be accompanied by numerous problems which might well counterbalance any possible gain.

Nuclear weapons can cause major losses to personnel annd matériel, and may change the tempo and direction of the battle. They have only been used twice in anger since their development — at Hiroshima and Nagasaki — in the closing days of World War II, giving some knowledge of the effects of nuclear weapons upon cities and their civil populations. But they have never been used against troops in battle. Tests and assessments can give some indication of the probable effects on equipment and of the medical effects upon people, and there is no knowing how large bodies of soldiers might behave under both the immediate threat and the actuality of tactical nuclear warfare.

The immediate effects of nuclear weapons are blast, thermal radiation, electromagnetic pulse (EMP) and initial nuclear radiation, their magnitude being dependent upon the height of the burst above the ground and its explosive power, or yield. The yield is a measure of the amount of explosive energy the nuclear weapon produces and is usually stated in terms of the quantity of conventional explosive (TNT) which would generate the same amount of energy. The bombs dropped on Japan, for example, had a yield of 20 kilotons (20kt), i.e. 20,000 tons of TNT, while the largest known bomb test was of a 70Mt weapon, a yield equivalent to 70 million tons of TNT.

In general terms, the energy produced by a nuclear explosion can be divided into three categories: kinetic energy, that is, the energy of motion of electrons, molecules and atoms as a whole; the internal energy of these particles; and thermal radiation energy. For a nuclear explosion in the atmosphere below an altitude of about 100,000ft (30,480m), some 35 to 45 per cent of the explosive energy is received as thermal energy in the visible and infra-red portions of the spectrum. In addition, below an altitude of about 40,000ft (12,000m), about 50 per cent of the energy is used in the production of air shock. A further 35 per cent produces thermal radiation.

The thermal effects are caused by the extreme intensity of the flash of the explosion and its heat — over 1,000,000°C. The effects of the flash are a function of the yield of the weapon and of the ambient conditions (whether the explosion occurs at day or night, its duration, the weather conditions and the general terrain). The physical effects of heat and light on men and equipment outside the immediate area of the explosion are predictable from tables derived from actual nuclear tests.

Radiation has both immediate and residual effects. With smaller devices (up to about 20kt airburst) only about 15 per cent of the overall casualties would be caused by radiation, although repeated exposure to radiation has a cumulative effect. Residual radiation results mainly from fallout, the dust cloud spreading after the explosion; militarily, it can deny to an enemy transit through, or the use of, a contaminated area.

There has been considerable controversy over the 'enhanced radiation' weapon, popularly described as the neutron bomb. This is a thermonuclear device designed to maximise the lethal effects of high energy neutrons and to reduce the blast effect. The result is that, for given yield, a lethal dose of nuclear radiation is delivered at a somewhat greater distance than for a fission bomb, with the consequence that people suffer the radiation effects but the physical damage to buildings and vehicles is reduced. It should be noted, however that ER weapons are of 1kt yield or less, since it is only in such small yields that the radiation-kill radius exceeds the destructive effects due to blast.

The principal electromagnetic effect resulting from a nuclear explosion is the electromagnetic pulse (EMP), which can damage electronic and electrical equipment having insufficient protection against sudden and massive (albeit very short-lived) pulses of electromagnetic energy. EMP can effect telecommunications equipment and long cabling, such as overhead telephone wires and power cables, as well as disrupting radio links, although the actual effects depend to a great extent on the height and yield of the nuclear explosion and on the design and nature of the electronic equipment. A well-authenticated example of EMP effents occurred during tests in 1962 when thirty 'strings' (series-connected loops) of street lights at various locations on the Hawaiian island of Oahu failed simultaneously as a result of a high-altitude airburst over Johnson Island some 800 miles away. On the battlefield, in the worst case, much equipment coild be degraded, if not actually destroyed, making command, control and communications very difficult if not impossible.

Nuclear weapons have had several major effects upon doctrine, tactics and plans for the land battle. The first occurred soon after the fielding of tactical nuclear weapons, when there were, not surprisingly, many theories about how the nuclear battlefield might work, but knowledge was limited and experience non-existent. Historically, one of the fundamental principles of war has been that of the concentration of force, but on the nuclear battlefield this woulld simply invite retaliation. Doctrine

Above: Nobody knows what a modern nuclear war might really be like; but scenes such as this photograph of Hiroshima in the aftermath of the August 1945 atomic bombing give some idea.

Below: As a result of US-Soviet arms limitation talks in late 1987 intermediate range nuclear weapons such as these Pershings should progressively disappear from the scene in Europe.

and tactics were therefore developed to emphasise dispersion, units only being concentrated when they could close quickly with the enemy in such a way that the latter would then only be able to use his nuclear weapons at the risk of hitting some of his own troops. This requirement for rapid movement from dispersed positions to concentration and then back again, coupled with the need for protection against the effects of the weapons themselves, has resulted in the development of a vast array of special vehicles.

NUCLEAR WEAPONS

Nuclear weapons which could affect the land battle would be delivered by aircraft, battlefield rockets, artillery and mortars; a US attempt in the 1950s, ludicrous but true, to develop a nuclear hand-grenade ended when it was realised that even the strongest thrower would inevitably be within the lethal radius of his own weapon! Nuclear-capable aircraft and their operation are described in a companion Salamander volume, *Modern Air Combat*, so the following survey considers land-based weapons only.

Taking US weapons as an example, the smallest tactical nuclear device available to the land battle commander is the W48 warhead for the 155mm M109 SP, which has an estimated yield of 0.1kt (i.e. 100 tons of TNT) and is in use with at least eight NATO nations; slightly higher on the scale is the M110 203mm (8in) SP, which uses the W33 warhead with a yield in the 5-10kt range. Both these artillery shells can be delivered with a high degree of precision, as with any artillery shell. The W79 warhead for the M110 had one version with an enhanced radiation 'neutron bomb' warhead, with a yield option of 50 per cent fusion and 50 per cent fission, but this was not, in the event, deployed. The standard version of W79 has, however, been procured (at a cost of $1 million per round) with a maximum 10kt yield, packed in an elaborate container fitted with special security and disable-on-command devices that prevent unauthorised use and ensure that they cannot be captured by terrorists in an operable condition.

The Lance battlefield missile system has a variety of nuclear warheads, varying in yield from about 1kt to 100kt and including enhanced radiation warheads with a yield of about 1kt and producing about 40 per cent fission and 60 per cent fusion. At the upper end of the battlefield nuclear weapons is the MGM-31 Pershing II. This missile is exceptionally accurate because of its Radar Area Correlation Guidance (RADAG) system located in the nose, in which a small active radar scans the ground at 120rpm and correlates the returns with stored target imagery. Circular area probability (cep) is of the order of 120ft (36m), and in combination with the W85 15kt warhead this gives exceptional terminal effects. Pershing II is reportedly also fitted with an earth-penetrator device, which enables the

Pershing II guidance system

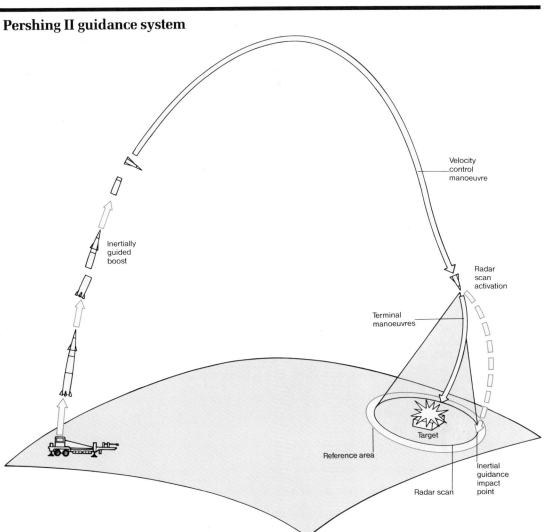

Velocity control manoeuvre

Inertially guided boost

Radar scan activation

Terminal manoeuvres

Target

Reference area

Radar scan

Inertial guidance impact point

Above: The US Pershing missile has an extremely accurate guidance system, using area correlation techniques to compare live radar returns from the target with a stored radar image.

Below: Short-range missiles such as this French Pluton were not covered by the 1987 arms talks, and France was apparently adamant in its refusal to abandon nuclear weapons.

warhead to burrow deep before exploding, a capability clearly intended for use against underground HQs and communications centres. This two-stage, mobile ballistic missile was the centre of a major political controversy when it was deployed in the early 1980s, due primarily to its accuracy, which, coupled with its deployment in West Germany and range of some 460 miles (740km), put part of western European USSR within its target area.

The USSR, too, has a whole family of battlefield nuclear weapons. Nuclear-capable guns are the 2S5 152mm SP and its towed M-1976 version, together with the 2S3 152mm SP and its towed D-20 version; in addition, the 240mm M-1975 SP mortar has a nuclear capability. The Frog-7 battlefield rocket has a 200kt warhead, but this system is now being replaced by SS-21 with a 100kt warhead. The long-serving SS-1c Scud-B with its 1kt warhead is also in the process of being replaced, in this case by the SS-23, which also has a 100kt warhead. Finally, SS-12 Mod 1 (previously known as SS-22) has a 1Mt warhead.

The only other battlefield nuclear missile is the French Pluton. Mounted on an AMX-30 chassis, the missile has inertial guidance and can be fitted with two warheads. One, of 25kt yield, is a development of the AN-52 free-fall weapon used by Mirage IIIs and Jaguars, and the second is a 15kt weapon.

Chemical Warfare

Chemical warfare (CW) is an emotive subject, but chemical weapons have certainly been used many times since the end of World War II. Known occasions include the Egyptian campaign in the Yemen in the late 1950s (blister agents) and the Second Indo-China War (defoliants and incapacitating agents), while CW weapons are being used today by the Soviet and Afghan armies in the campaign in Afghanistan (blister and choking agents), by the South Africans (who are reported to be using defoliants along their borders) and in the Iran-Iraq war (where blister and nerve agents have been in use for the past four years). These military examples appear almost mild, however, when compared to the effects of the industrial accidents at Seveso in Italy, at the Union Carbide factory at Bhopal in India in 1984 and the Swiss spillage into the Rhine in 1986, where the devastating effects on the unprotected civilian communities adjacent to the plants showed only too clearly the appalling potential of CW.

A further worrying factor on the military scene is that the number of nations with a CW capability has increased from about five in 1977 to some fifteen today, the latest being North Korea, which had recently received Sarin (GB) from the USSR for use in its new multiple launch rocket systems. The number of countries with their own CW production capability is also increasing, and it was recently revealed that Syria now has two factories, one near Damascus and the other in Homs, producing chemical weapons including nerve agents.

The pressure to end the use of chemical agents has been strong since just after they were first deployed, and the Geneva Protocol of 1925 did, in fact, forbid their use. This was ignored, although, despite the existence of very large stocks on both sides, CW never actually took place in World War II. The UK stopped manufacturing its own stocks some thirty years ago and the USA, the only Western country with a stockpile, stopped in 1969 but is now seeking to restart production in order to replace increasingly aged and unreliable stocks. Meanwhile, the Soviet Union has carried on with the production of chemical agents and is developing new ones; its current stockpile is assessed to be around 300,000 tons of chemical agents of all types.

Of late there has been some progress in the discussions on CW at the 40-nation Geneva Conference on Disarmament, and the major remaining problems appear to revolve around the issue of verification. If an agreement is reached it will take some three years before it can be ratified, following which there would be a 10-year period in which stocks and production facilities would be

Right: The US Army M687 155mm binary chemical projectile contains two substances which are stored separately and harmlessly, but when brought together they form a highly potent weapon.

destroyed. Thus, at the very best, the means to wage CW will remain in existence until the year 2000. Both the USA and France have stated that if the conference fails to make substantial progress they would re-start the production of chemical agents in order to deter CW attack upon their own forces.

CHEMICAL AGENTS

Military chemical agents currently known to exist fall into seven groups. The modern agents are toxins, defoliants, nerve agents, incapacitating agents and psychological agents, but older substances such as blister and choking agents are still available (and are used), although there is no known effort to develop them further.

Toxins are chemical compounds derived from bacteriological

Above: Soviet chemical troops conduct a decontamination exercise. The USSR has a more extensive chemical warfare capability than any other nation.

Below: A Dutch Army gun crew decontaminating their M110. Such drills are becoming increasingly important as the threat of offensive chemical weapons grows.

US XM687E1 155mm binary chemical projectile

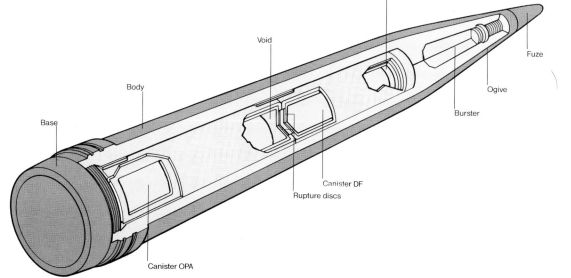

organisms (e.g. clostridium botulinum, popularly known as 'botulin'). Some are fatal to humans but do not induce epidemics since they are chemical compounds rather than organic substances. Other toxins have the same effect as psychological agents, being used, for example, to create acute terror symptoms.

The defoliants destroy plant life, either by causing unnaturally rapid growth (as with many widely available weedkillers) or by killing leaves and shoots. Whilst having an application in some limited war situations, these are unlikely to have any major application in general war.

The original nerve agents were Tebun (GA), Sarin (GB) and Soman (GD), and some of these older agents may still be stocked in some countries. The Americans have stockpiles of a later substance known as VX, but they are now starting production of a new agent designated GB2. The earlier nerve agents were persistent, with consequential tactical problems, but the newer agents are non-persistent.

The main incapacitating agents are CN (now little used by the military) and the well-known CS gas. The major application of such agents is in anti-terrorist and anti-riot operations, although they could have a limited application in general war as well. They are normally disseminated in smoke form and have an immediate effect, although recovery, once casualties are removed from the gas, is rapid.

Psychological agents have been used by various armies. These derive their potency from psycho-chemicals such as the hallucinogen known as lysergic acid (LSD). The USA is known to have developed another substance, BZ, which causes massive hallucinations and is ten times more powerful than LSD. Such agents appear to hold out the possibility of so disorienting groups of soldiers that their positions could be taken over without a fight, but there is a strong body of opinion which considers that the effects against trained soldiers have been overestimated, and, in any case, an antidote has been developed.

THE CURRENT SITUATION

Chemical agents are stockpiled in liquid, gaseous or powder form and can be disseminated by aircraft, using bombs or sprays, artillery shells, rockets, grenades or mines. Dissemination of these agents is not an easy or precise art and in the case of gaseous delivery is obviously very sensitive to wind conditions.

The USSR has long devoted considerable resources to CW and has continued production for many years, as a result of which there is a huge stockpile of assorted chemical weapons. In the USA, however, political pressures prevented the production of any chemical munitions from 1969, and as a result the stockpile of some 700,000 artillery shells, rockets and bombs has reached a stage where it is on average well over 25 years old and

substantially of limited value, with the exception of some 1,000 Weteye bombs. There are a number of 105mm chemical shells, but since few NATO armies retain 105mm artillery, these are obviously of little practical use. Further, these current stocks are filled with the previous generation of chemical agents, which are unitary in constitution and persistent in nature.

Meanwhile, production plans and facilities for a new range of chemical munitions exist in the USA, but were held in abeyance for some years pending Congressional authorisation. This was eventually given in 1986, with the stipulation that production was not to start until October 1987, to give the Geneva Conference time to reach agreement. The payload of these new-technology 'binary' shells and bombs is two chemical substances, difluoro and isopropyl alcohol

Above: Exercise Team Spirit 85, and a US Army soldier escorts a simulated casualty who apparently neglected to wear his protective rubber gloves, a deadly omission.

Below: Danish soldiers in NBC protective outfits. Well designed as such clothing may be, it is uncomfortable to wear for protracted periods.

Above: A British soldier with a chemical agent detection instrument. No part of his body is exposed and eating, drinking and bodily functions become major problems in such a situation.

Above: The Dutch Oldelft ACAL chemical agent detection and alarm system can be used in a stand-alone mode or as part of an interconnected detection network using field cable.

amine, which while separated are non-lethal (albeit toxic) but on being mixed form the deadly, non-persistent nerve agent GB2. As manufactured, each shell or bomb contains only difluoro, capped with a cardboard filler, and the isopropyl alcohol amine is stored separately. The second chemical is only inserted into the shell or bomb immediately prior to loading and, even then, the two chemicals are in separate compartments, not coming into contact with each other until the nose-fuse sets off an explosive charge, driving back a pusher plate which fractures the membrane between the two components and allows them to mix. Because it is non-persistent this chemical breaks down after a period of time, thus making decontamination of an affected area by friendly troops unnecessary.

PASSIVE CW DEFENCE

After very considerable effort and finnancial expenditure virtually all NATO and Warsaw Pact land forces are now fitted out with protective clothing (hood, suit, gloves and boots made of a special material) and respirators for use in a CW environment. Virtually all AFVs and many buildings are proofed against chemical agents usually by sealing the compartments and creating an overpressure, while much effort has been devoted to producing equipment to decontaminate the exteriors of vehicles and aircraft.

It is generally agreed that protracted operations under such conditions will be extremely taxing, especially for the individual soldier who will suffer from heat stress, restricted movement, impaired vision, limited communications and complications in eating, drinking and exercising bodily functions. Training exercises have shown that CW clothing and respirators reduce the effectiveness of the wearer by some 40 per cent after a fairly short time, with a further and more marked deterioration after a few days. Tasks of a sedentary nature, such as operating equipment, driving vehicles, staff work etc may not be too hard to continue for reasonable periods while wearing CW suits and respirators, but tasks that are physically demanding even under normal conditions, for example repairing runways, constructing bridges, loading ammunition manually in tanks and SPs, and rescuing and treating casualties, will be very difficult, and become progressively more so with time. There seems little that technology can provide in the short-term to overcome this problem, once it is accepted that some form of covering for the entire body, coupled with an air filtration system, is essential for survival in a CW environment.

A consideration frequently overlooked is that no attempt has been made on either side of the Iron Curtain to supply NBC clothing to the civilian population at large, which would be inescapably affected by the use of CW weapons in a conflict in Central Europe.

Low-Intensity Warfare

Of the fifty-plus military campaigns that have been fought since World War II, all have qualified for the term 'limited war'. Even the Second Indo-China War, which involved the USA as a direct participant on one side, opposing a North Vietnam supported (albeit indirectly) by the USSR and China on the other, never approached the scale of general war, nor did it ever show serious signs of expanding beyond the implicitly accepted confines of the three Indo-Chinese states of Vietnam, Laos and Cambodia.

It is certainly true that during the course of the Vietnam War the USA used virtually every weapon system available to it, even to the extent of using Iowa class battleships for shore bombardment and B-52 strategic bombers to devastate areas of North Vietnam, but it never took the war beyond the geographical limits of Indo-China. It is also the case that in Afghanistan the Soviet Union appears to be using the weapons normally available to their tank and motor rifle divisions for a conflict in Central Europe, but, again, they are tacitly accepting certain limitations.

It is now becoming apparent, however, that although it may seem to be desirable to see expensive military equipment used, there is still a good case for developing and producing at least some weapons especially for this type of warfare. Few of these would be radical examples of modern technology (for example, green laser communications to submerged submarines) but rather of the concerted application of technology to produce equipment which is lighter, more effective, longer-ranged and more mobile than before.

Low-intensity warfare predominantly involves ground battle, and it is not therefore

Above: Designed specifically for low-intensity operations, the M551 Sheridan mounted a 152mm gun/missile launcher but proved to be an expensive failure.

Below: The British CVR(T) series of tracked light armoured vehicles has been a great success and various versions exist armed with 76mm and 90mm guns, 30mm

cannon and missiles. Designed primarily for low-intensity warfare, they have repeatedly proved their value in operations such as the 1982 Falklands War.

surprising that most dedicated systems have been for use by armies, as opposed to navies and air forces. The various threats to ground troops on the potential nuclear battlefield have resulted in ever more sophisticated, heavier and complex weapons systems, which means that many of them are unsuitable for use in low-intensity warfare. The design of self-propelled artillery, for example, has led to weapons such as the SP-70, with a 155mm gun and a combat weight of 43 tons (43,525kg) — a mammoth piece of equipment and one difficult to maintain and deploy in unsophisticated

Unconventional Warfare

The preceding sections have described the current technology used by land forces intended to fight in either a general war on a global scale or in a limited war. There has not been a general war since 1945, but, despite a theoretical state of peace, there has been an apparently endless series of limited wars, some major and many minor, which have kept armies very busy; in addition to these there have been 'police actions', 'operations in aid of the civil power', 'anti-terrorist operations' and 'anti-riot operations'. The equipment and technology for 'higher' forms of warfare have sometimes sufficed, but special equipment has had to be devised to help armies conduct these exacting and frequently unpleasant missions.

SPECIAL FORCES

The past twenty years have witnessed an unprecedented increase in the number of 'special forces', raised mainly to conduct peacetime operations which are

Left: US Navy SEAL (Sea-Air-Land) team members on an exercise, armed with 5.56mm Colt Commando assault rifle. Such special forces are proliferating in order to deal with new threats.

(usually for political reasons) beyond the means of, or unsuited for, police forces or the conventional military establishment. They have proved to be of special value in the battle against terrorists and in anti-siege and anti-hijacking operations. Such forces exist both as autonomous units in their own right, for example, the US Delta, and as élite sub-groups of a larger body, as in the case of the British Special Boat Service (SBS), which is a part of the Royal Marines.

These forces require highly specialised field equipment and tend to use technology in a unique way. They need to observe, usually at very close ranges and without themselves being seen, to communicate reliably, securely and using the minimum time on the air, environments. Similarly, contemporary main battle tanks, most of which weigh over 50 tons (50,800kg), are just too large and too heavy for such an environment.

TANKS

The United States has twice tried to apply its massive technological resources to designing a tank for low-intensity warfare. The first was the M551 Sheridan, which was intended to be a reconnaissance vehicle — small, well-armoured and agile, but nevertheless with a powerful armament. This led to the M551 multi-purpose 152mm gun/launcher, which despite vast expenditure could never be made to work. Next came the RDF/LT (Rapid Deployment Force/Light Tank), based on the High Survivability Test Vehicle (Lightweight). Weighing just 13.2 tons (13,425kg) and highly mobile, the RDF/LT had a 75mm ARES cannon and a crew of three. The gun was mounted in a turret of novel design fed by an automatic magazine containing 60 rounds of mixed APFSDS and multi-purpose ammunition. Eight RDF/LTs could be accommodated in a C-5 Galaxy and two in a C-141 Starlifter or C-130 Hercules, and one could be carried under a CH-53E helicopter. The other AFV in this programme was the Light Armored Vehicle (LAV), an eight-wheeled vehicle based on the Swiss Mowag Piranha and armed with a 25mm Bushmaster cannon.

Both these US Army programmes were cancelled, although the US Marine Corps has gone ahead with the LAV-25. Meanwhile the British Scorpion/Scimitar light tanks have repeatedly proved their value in low-intensity operations, most recently in the South Atlantic War, when they once again showed their ability to travel over very rough and marshy

Right: The Soviet Army has designed numerous AFVs for its special forces. This is the BMD airborne mechanised infantry combat vehicle operated by the parachute troops. It carries six troops and is armed with a 73mm gun, an MG and an ATGW.

terrain. The Soviets, too, have some excellent very light fire-support vehicles, the main current example being the ASU-85.

ARTILLERY

Self-propelled artillery has become so large and heavy that it is no longer air-portable, nor, indeed, is it readily mobile in some Third World environments. Further, the firing conditions differ: for example, a number of SP guns designed to operate in European conditions do not have sufficient elevation to fire out of jungle clearings. Most nations, therefore, still use towed artillery for such conditions, and a surprising number of projects are under way, particularly at 155mm calibre. Nevertheless, many 105mm calibre guns remain in service, including the very successful British Light Gun.

The aim, in virtually every case, is to produce a more readily air-portable gun (especially by helicopter), with greater range and a more effective shell. In many of these programmes the advanced technology is as much to do with the manufacturing processes as it is with the actual gun or the ballistics. In the British 155mm FH-70, for example, very considerable attention has been paid to the trail and barrel to ensure that they are very strong yet as light as possible. Several of the weapons can now fire rocket-assisted projectiles (RAP), which can increase the range considerably — 25 per cent in the case of FH-70.

Above: The US Army Rangers are one of several units in the special forces category which are now part of the US order of battle. They have taken part in the Grenada operation of 1982 as well as a number of other recent but less publicised activities.

and to fight close-quarter battles in confined spaces. To a large extent, and for very understandable reasons, their equipment is very highly classified, and like the personnel themselves, very seldom seen in public. It was, for example, only when the Iranian Embassy siege took place in the centre of London and under the full glare of media attention that the all-black fighting rig of the British Special Air Service (SAS) and their use of the Heckler und Koch MP5 sub-machine gun became known.

TERRORISTS' USE OF TECHNOLOGY

Terrorists rarely employ sophisticated equipment developed specifically for their own use but rather are they normally forced to adapt what is available. Thus, for example, the Provisional Wing of the Irish Republican Army (PIRA) carried out a mortar attack on 28 February 1985 against the police station at Newry, County Down,

using a mortar constructed from nine steel pipes secured by wires to a girder and mounted on an angle-iron frame fitted to a lorry. The projectiles were made from oxygen cylinders fitted with rudimentary fins and packed with some 44lb (20kg) of explosive. With everything prepared the lorry was driven to a disused site some 220 yards (200m) from the target and, the terrorists having made their escape, the mortars were fired by an electronically-operated delay device.

Of the nine bombs fired, three were duds, two blew up in mid-air, three overshot the target by a considerable distance, but the ninth, falling far shorter than the others, went through the roof of the police canteen, killing nine off-duty police officers. All the components, apart from the explosives, were commercially available in Northern Ireland, and the use of such an extemporary device meant that the PIRA had not needed to take the risk of smuggling military mortars and bombs across the border.

In somewhat similar but even more bloody incidents, Lebanese terrorists attacked and killed large numbers of US Marines and French soldiers in Beirut in 1983. They used devices of exceptional power, in which large charges were strapped around steel cylinders of explosive gas. The resulting implosions and explosions, applied at the critical point inside the buildings, were sufficient to collapse the entire structures, with horrific death tolls including, in both cases, the drivers of the 'kamikaze' lorries which had rammed their way into the ground floor of the buildings.

Other items of equipment such as small, readily hidden weapons and optical and electronic surveillance devices are all available to terrorists if they know the right sources — and they have shown that, all too often, they do.

COUNTER-TERRORIST SURVEILLANCE

The counter-terrorist response has been, to a large degree, to use high technology. Some devices are used overtly, for example electronic baggage surveillance which has become a familiar and accepted feature of every journey by air; others, widely known about, are nonetheless usually unseen by the general public, including electro-optical equipment for examining mail, electronic sniffers for detecting explosives and electronic bugs for listening to telephone and radio conversations.

Information on other equipment is now becoming public. For example, fibre-optic technology has enabled many advances to be made in surveillance, especially in siege operations. Fibre-optic borescopes enable security forces to see 'through' walls and doors; a very small hole is drilled by a special bit to accept a borescope, and viewing can then be done by the naked eye or with a TV monitor. Such devices that enable troops to learn about the layout and contents of houses and rooms prior to carrying out a rescue operation, and similar technology can be used to look into suspect devices such as barrels and vehicles' petrol tanks, to check for explosives or contraband.

PROTECTION

Special security cars abound, protected by steel armour plate or kevlar, and body protection devices are readily available. One US company even markets a 'safe haven', a bomb- and bullet-proof cabinet fitted with communications and air-conditioning; the more expensive models even have a gun-port.

One application of technology in the fight against terrorism is the remotely-controlled robot for locating, defusing or destroying explosive devices. The line originated with the British Wheelbarrow which was developed in response to increasingly sophisticated PIRA bombs and the escalating toll of bomb-disposal experts. Most such robots run on tracks, which enables them to surmount small obstacles as well as giving the operator very precise control over their movement. A Canadian model runs on six wheels.

Most of these robots are connected to their control-box by cable, although some have appeared with

Above: Technology is one of the weapons used in the counter-terrorist battle. This BAe Condor system detects explosives and drugs hidden in aircraft cargo by analysing air samples.

radio control: cable is more awkward but has the advantage of being unjammable. The robots are equipped with extendible arms with interchangeable handling mechanisms, guns, TV cameras and various types of detectors. These relatively inexpensive machines — the Wheelbarrow is reported to sell for about £60,000 — have already saved many lives and will continue to do so; indeed, their roles seem likely to be extended — there seems to be no reason, for example, why such robots could not be used in certain circumstances by military and police forces.

Above: Another tool used to combat terrorist tactics is the remotely controlled robot designed to deal with explosive devices planted in cars or other similar containers. This is the Belgian ACEC Andros, with a tracked drive, cable control and a variety of specialised fittings to deal with different situations.

Right: The line between armed police and the military has become increasingly difficult to define. This is a West German Border Guards anti-riot squad.

Above: A weapon widely used by police and military in anti-terrorist operations is the Heckler and Koch MP5 9mm sub-machine gun, which is available in several versions with many accessories.

NON-LETHAL WEAPONRY

Another field for anti-terrorist equipment is non-lethal weaponry. The stun-grenade, for example, has been developed to disorientate the target for a brief but critical period, such as the moment rescuers enter an aircraft, as in the assault by the West German anti-terrorist squad GSG-9 on the hijacked Lufthansa airliner at Mogadishu in October 1977. The British XFS grenade has a cardboard body and gives off a very loud report — approximately 180dB at a distance of 3ft (1m) — and a peak

light intensity of 50 million candelas. In order to minimise fatalities among hostages a small preliminary charge is used to blow off the metal firing mechanism and aluminium cup one second before the main charge is detonated.

While terrorists have developed the use of explosives to produce bombs capable of killing large numbers of people at little or no cost to themselves, the security forces have also developed explosives, but in a somewhat different manner. When the SAS blasted their way into the Iranian Embassy in London they used specially-shaped charges to blow in windows and doors with the greatest of precision. Similarly, explosive charges have been developed for use in gaining entry to aircraft, ships or trains with the maximum speed and minimum warning to the terrorists.

Above: A weapon with obvious applications in the anti-terrorist role is the new British 5.56mm assault rifle, which is light, extremely accurate and very easy to use, and can be fitted with night sights such as the model installed on this example.

The plastic anti-riot round (widely and inaccurately known as the 'rubber bullet') has also been developed as a non-lethal weapon with the purpose of inflicting at worst, severe bruising and shock. Controversy has been generated over these rounds, but the search continues for weapons which can be used at such a distance from the rioters as to prevent physical contact between the two, which will not seriously harm a target, and yet which will still be sufficiently effective to deter troublemakers and make them disperse.

Gas has been used for many years in an anti-riot and anti-terrorist role. The old CN (tear gas) has now been almost universally superseded by CS, an irritant agent. The gas is delivered primarily by grenades, either thrown by hand or fired from guns and special projectors. In some disturbances in the late 1960s rioters quickly discovered that they could either kick or throw the grenades back into the squads of police or soldiers, and new devices have had to be designed which make this more difficult. The Brazilians have produced a grenade in which the gas-emission slots are canted outwards to make the grenade spin on the ground, while others simply have a much shorter time-delay fuse.

The British Royal Small Arms Factory at Enfield has developed a

special anti-riot gun, the 37mm ARWEN 37. This semi-automatic, multi-shot system can fire a variety of baton and CS rounds out to a maximum range of 110 yards (100m) and weighs only 8.3lb (3.8kg) when loaded with five rounds.

DRESS

Considerable thought and R&D effort has been put into some of the more esoteric areas of anti-riot operations. The dress of some modern police forces and paramilitary units on anti-riot duties is meant primarily to protect the wearer, but there can be no doubt that it is also intended, quite deliberately, to be intimidating. The large helmets with their clear plastic visors, the protective clothing (which naturally makes the wearer look larger), the heavy boots, the riot shield, the long truncheon and, not infrequently, the wearing of a respirator all combine to make the policeman or soldier look very menacing. Fairly crude psychological techniques are also used by some police and military forces to further heighten such an impression: these can include the rhythmic beating of truncheons on shields, the liberal spreading of smoke to create a murky environment and the use of specially-devised 'dazzle' beams to create confusion and disorientation.

Weapons

Below: US Army infantrymen pose as Soviets, deploying a cross-section of the weapons, from rifle to missile launchers, available to today's soldier.

Introduction

The weapon systems illustrated and described in the following pages give an indication of the state of the art in modern military hardware design, covering a representative selection of the most important tanks, reconnaissance vehicles, armoured personnel carriers, combat helicopters, self-propelled and towed artillery weapons, battlefield missiles and rockets, air defence and anti-tank weapons, small arms and mortars in current service.

Nearly half the 100 or so equipments included originate with one of the two super-powers, and another third from the United Kingdom, France or West Germany; almost all the remainder are the products of other European countries, with Argentina, China and Israel the only non-European suppliers, and even the Argentinian TAM tank was actually developed in West Germany to Argentinian specifications. And only a handful of the weapons are the result of international programmes: whatever the ostensible attractions of collaborative ventures, conflicting national requirements in various areas have effectively terminated several such projects.

On the other hand, a majority of the systems illustrated have been exported, some of them extremely widely, and without the revenue from export customers the developed nations would have difficulty funding the development of high-technology armaments. Even so, American and West European research budgets are coming under increasing pressure, and the level of technology deemed necessary to deal with the perceived threat on NATO's Central Front is resulting in weapon systems which few Third World nations could afford even if they had a requirement for such sophistication. Meanwhile, China is emerging as an increasingly significant supplier of arms, as its armaments industry develops new systems to succeed the copies of Soviet weapons manufactured in the country for the past few decades.

One area where there is a degree of cross-fertilisation of weapon system development is that of AFV armament. The British 105mm L7 — designated M68 in its US-produced version — was the standard Western tank gun for many years and is fitted to the M1, M60, Leopard 1 and Merkava MBTs, among others, while the Rheinmetall 120mm smooth-bore gun mounted by the Leopard 2 is also being installed on the current M1A1 version of the Abrams. Similarly, the Mauser MK 30 anti-aircraft gun is used on both the German Wildcat and the Greek Artemis systems, and the Bofors 40mm/L70 appears in these pages both on its standard mount and as part of the Breda Twin 4OL70 field mounting.

Of course, there are many other applications for these weapons, and many other guns are available, some of which are illustrated in the chapters of the preceding section dealing with MBTs and light AFVs. The Soviet Union, in contrast, has standardised a limited range of ordnance for its fighting vehicles, so that both the T-64 and the T-72 use the same 125mm smooth-bore gun, the BMP-1 and BMD have the 73mm 2A28 and the only medium-calibre gun used on an AFV is the 30mm 2A42 fitted to the BMP-2.

On the other hand, the Soviet army does deploy a wide range of rockets and missiles, and the widespread use of such weapons by modern ground forces is reflected in the fact that they appear in a majority of the categories included in this section, either as weapon systems in their own right or as one of the armaments carried by fighting vehicles.

A notable consequence of the application of missile technology is the range of weapons now deployed by infantry units, so that a modern APC, typically armed with a heavy machine gun or light cannon and carrying up to a dozen men with their own individual weapons, will normally also carry light anti-tank missile launchers. In the case of the US Army's M2 Bradley, an integral Tow heavy anti-tank missile system, 25mm Bushmaster cannon and coaxial 7.62mm machine gun are supplemented by six custom-designed 5.56mm M231 rifles able to be fired from inside the vehicle and three M72 anti-tank rocket launchers are stowed ready for deployment by the six-man infantry squad on dismounting.

Man-portable air defence systems are also widely used and have proved their worth in recent conflicts, though the difficulties experienced by the US Army in its attempts to procure a divisional air defence system — the Sgt York system was abandoned in 1985 after several years of expensive development and an off-the-shelf replacement was being sought as part of the new programme for a five-tier forward area air defence system — underline the problems involved in dealing with fast-moving, low-level airborne threats.

The air threat has been compounded in recent years by the helicopter's new capabilities in the anti-armour role. There is space here for only a small selection of the current range of battlefield helicopters, but those illustrated give a fair indication of the range of weapons and capabilities available. Here again, it is lightweight rocket and missile systems that have enabled the helicopter to emerge as a front-line weapon in its own right.

The payload/range performance possible with larger missiles is also highlighted in this section, but systems such as MLRS will continue to be outnumbered by artillery weapons, still the primary means of bringing concentrated and accurate heavy firepower to bear on the battlefield. The weapons illustrated are shown with representative selections of the rounds available where possible, and the accompanying table includes explanations of the abbreviations used to designate them.

Abbreviations
APDS Armour-piercing discarding saabot
APDS-T Armour-piercing discarding sabot tracer
APERS Anti-personnel
APFSDS Armour-piercing fin stabilised discarding sabot
APFSDS-T Armour-piercing fin stabilised discarding sabot tracer
APHE Armour-piercing high explosive
API-T Armour-piercing incendiary tracer
AP-T Armour-piercing tracer
FRAG-HE Fragmentation high explosive
HE High explosive
HEAT High explosive anti-tank
HEAT-FS High explosive anti-tank fin stabilised
HEAT-MP High explosive anti-tank multi-purpose
HEAT-MP-T High explosive anti-tank multi-purpose tracer
HE-FRAG High explosive fragmentation
HEI High explosive incendiary
HEI-SD-T High explosive incendiary self-destruct tracer
HEI-T High explosive incendiary tracer
HEP High explosive plastic
HESH High explosive squash head
MPT Multi-purpose tracer
PF-HE-T Pre-fragmented high explosive tracer
PF-TP-T Pre-fragmented target practice tracer
PRAC-T Practice tracer
SAPHEI-T Semi-armour-piercing high explosive incendiary tracer
TP Target practice
WP-T White phosphorus tracer

Left: Launch of a BGM-71 Tow 2 anti-tank missile from a US Army M2 Bradley infantry fighting vehicle, an example of the firepower available to modern mechanised infantry units.

Above: The six-round fire vehicle of a Shahine air defence system is trailed by its target acquisition unit over desert terrain. Both vehicles are based on the chassis of the AMX-30 MBT.

Below: An M110A2 8in howitzer from A Battery of the 6/37th Field Artillery, US Army, prepares for a fire mission near the South Han River during the joint US-South Korean Team Spirit 86 exercises.

The M110A2 and MLRS multiple launch rocket system are being integrated into combine battalions, each consisting of two six-howitzer M110 batteries and a single battery of nine MLRS.

M1 and M60

M1 ABRAMS

Origin: USA
Crew: 4
Armament: One 105mm gun; one 7.62mm machine gun coaxial with main armament; one 7.62mm machine gun at loader's station; one 12.7mm machine gun at commander's station; six smoke dischargers each side of turret
Armour: Classified
Dimensions: Length including main armament 32ft 0in (9.766m); hull length 26ft 0in (7.918m); width 12ft 0in (3.653m); height 9ft 6in (2.885m)
Combat weight: 120,250lb (54,545kg)
Ground pressure: 13.7psi (0.96kg/cm²)
Engine: Avco Lycoming AGT-1500 gas turbine developing 1,500hp (1,118kW) at 3,000rpm
Performance: Road speed 45mph (72.421km/h); range 310 miles (498km); vertical obstacle 4ft 1in (1.244m); trench 9ft 0in (2.743m); gradient 60 per cent
History: Developed from early 1970s with first production vehicles being completed in 1980; in service only with United States Army, for which 7,467 M1/M1A1s are to be built by the early 1990s

Background: Following the demise of the MBT-70, a joint development between West Germany and the United States, and the austere version for the US Army called the XM803, it was decided to build a new tank from scratch and competitive contracts were awarded to both Chrysler and General Motors for a new MBT under the designation XM1. After trials with both vehicles the Chrysler XM1 was selected for further development and was later placed in production as the M1 Abrams at two plants, one in Lima, Ohio, and the other in Detroit, Michigan.

The M1 Abrams was a revolutionary design, incorporating new composite armour and powered by a gas turbine engine which gives it a high power-to-weight ratio and good speed both on roads and across country. The main armament is the 105mm M68 installed in the older M60 but it has a new computerised fire control system incorporating a laser rangefinder which enables the tank to hit stationary and moving targets while itself moving at speed. The composite armour gives a high degree of protection against both chemical and kinetic energy attack; for enhanced survivability an explosion and fire suppression system is installed, and ammunition in the turret bustle is separated from the crew compartment by special sliding doors.

The original M1 has been replaced in production by the M1A1 which has many improvements, the most significant being the 120mm smooth-bore gun which is also installed in the West German Leopard 2 and improved armour protection. Further improvements in the area of fire control are already under way.

The introduction of the turbine-powered M1 has not been without problems and many still believe that turbines have no place on the battlefield, but the fact is that the M1 is more reliable than the diesel-engined M60 which has been in service with the US Army for some 25 years, and its speed and mobility has forced the US Army to develop new tactics.

M60

Origin: USA
Crew: 4
Armament: One 105mm gun; one 7.62mm machine gun coaxial with main armament; one 12.7mm anti-aircraft machine gun; six smoke dischargers each side of turret
Armour: Classified
Dimensions: Length including main armament 30ft 6in (9.309m); hull length 22ft 9in (6.946m); width 11ft 11in (3.631m); height 10ft 6in (3.213m)
Combat weight: 109,600lb (49,714kg)
Ground pressure: 11.37lb/sq in (0.80kg/cm²)
Engine: Teledyne Continental AVDS-1790-2A 12-cylinder air-cooled diesel developing 750bhp (560kW) at 2,400rpm
Performance: Road speed 30mph (48.28km/h); range 310 miles (500km); vertical obstacle 3ft 0in (0.914m); trench 8ft 6in (2.59m); gradient 60 per cent
History: Entered production at Detroit Arsenal Tank Plant in 1960 and still in production for export market; in service with Austria, Bahrain, Egypt, Iran, Israel, Italy, also built under licence by OTO Melara), Jordan, Oman, Saudi Arabia, Singapore (AVLB and CEV only), Spain (AVLB only), Sudan, Tunisia, United States (Army and Marines) and North Yemen

Background: The M60 series is a further development of the earlier M48 MBT but has the diesel engine fitted in late production M48s and a British-designed 105mm rifled tank

Below: The M1 is the latest MBT to enter service with the US Army. Its ammunition load includes smoke grenades (1), APFSDS-T (2), APDS-T (3), HESH (4), HEAT (5), HEP (6), APERS-T (7) and Canister (8) rounds plus belts of 7.62mm (9) and 12.7mm (10) machine gun ammunition. The actual mix of 105mm ammunition for the gun depends on the tactical situation and types of target to be engaged but the main tank-killing round is the APFSDS-T.

gun. The first model, the M60, was followed by the M60A1 with a new and improved turret; the M60A2 had a 152mm gun/missile launcher but has been phased out of service; and the current production model is the M60A3, whose many improvements include a computerised fire control system, a laser rangefinder and thermal night vision equipment. Further developments are planned for the future including reactive armour which will defeat anti-tank guided weapons with their HEAT warheads.

Turret traverse and weapon elevation is hydraulic, a feature which did not prove very popular with Israeli tank crews in the last Middle East conflict. A total of 63 rounds of 105mm, 5,950 rounds of 7.62mm and 900 rounds of 12.7mm ammunition are carried.

Variants include a scissors type armoured vehicle launched bridge, the M728 Combat Engineer Vehicle armed with a 165mm demolition gun and fitted with dozer blade and A frame, and a Robotic Breaching Assault Tank which has been designed to breach enemy minefields.

M60 series tanks have been used in combat by the Israeli Army, but they did not prove as survivable as the British supplied Centurion MBTs. All Israeli M60s have now been fitted with the Blazer reactive armour first revealed during the invasion of the Lebanon.

Above: A US Army M60A3 on excercise in Germany uses a main armament firing simulator mounted on the barrel to add realism to the proceedings. The device produces a combination of smoke, noise and flash similar to that of the 105mm gun firing.

Above: Although the M1 and M1A1 are entering service in increasing numbers, the M60A1 and M60A3 will remain in service with the US Army well into the next decade and a number of improvement programmes have already been started with still more to come. The 105mm gun of the M60 series is identical to that of the M1 and fires the same ammunition, including APFSDS-T (1), APDS-T (2), APERS-T (3), HEAT (4) and smoke (5) rounds. The smoke grenades (6) are fired from the dischargers each side of the turret, while the 7.62mm (7) and 12.7mm (8) machine gun ammunition comes in belts.

T-64, T-72 and T-80

T-64

Origin: USSR
Crew: 3
Armament: One 125mm gun; one 7.62mm machine gun coaxial with main armament; one 12.7mm anti-aircraft machine gun
Armour: Classified
Dimensions: Length including main armament 29ft 10in (9.10m); hull length 21ft 0in (6.40m); width 11ft 1in (3.38m); height 7ft 6in (2.3m)
Combat weight: 83,775lb (38,000kg)
Ground pressure: 14.3lb/sq in (1.09kg/cm²)
Engine: 5-cylinder opposed liquid-cooled diesel developing 700/750hp (522/560kW)
Performance: Road speed 43.5mph (70km/h); range 280 miles (450km); vertical obstacle 3ft 0in (0.915m); trench 8ft 11in (2.72m); gradient 60 per cent
History: Developed in early 1960s; in production from 1966 until 1981, by which time about 8,000 vehicles had been built. In service only with the USSR.
Background: The T-64 has always been something of an enigma, in that it has never appeared in any of the Red Square military parades and has never been exported, even to member nations of the Warsaw Pact. From most accounts there were many problems with early

Right: As the T-64B tank has not been seen in public there are still conflicting views on its employment and weapons fit. Its 125mm smooth bore-gun can fire the same ammunition as the T-72 as well as the AT-8 Songster missile, of which two versions are believed to be in service, one anti-tank with a HEAT warhead and the other anti-helicopter. The T-64 has never been exported.

production vehicles but these were subsequently overcome. The basic version is designated T-64 and is fitted with a two-man turret mounting a 125mm smooth-bore gun fed by an automatic loader, which enables a rate of fire of eight rounds per minute to be achieved. Types of ammunition fired include APFSDS, HEAT-FRAG and HE-FRAG (FS), and a total of 40 separate-loading rounds are carried, along with 3,000 rounds for the 7.62mm coaxial machine gun and 500 rounds for the cupola-mounted 12.7mm anti-aircraft machine gun.

The turret is believed to be of conventional cast armour with a glacis plate of laminate armour. T-64, T-72 and T-80 MBTs have been observed fitted with reactive armour to defeat NATO ATGWs which rely on HEAT warheads for penetration. The T-64B is fitted with a 125mm gun which fires the standard ammunition or an AT-8 Songster ATGW and, probably, an anti-helicopter round.

T-72

Origin: USSR
Crew: 3
Armament: One 125mm gun; one 7.62mm machine gun coaxial with main armament; one 12.7mm anti-aircraft machine gun
Armour: Classified

Dimensions: Length including main armament 30ft 4in (9.24m) hull length 22ft 10in (5.80m); width 11ft 10in (6.95m); height 7ft 9in (2.37m)
Combat weight: 90,388lb (41,000kg)
Ground pressure: 11.80lb/sq in (0.83kg/cm²)
Engine: Model W-46 V-12 diesel developing 780hp (581kW) at 2,000rpm
Performance: Road speed 37.2mph (60km/h); range 300 miles (480km); vertical obstacle 2ft 10in (0.85m); trench 9ft 2in (2.80m); gradient 60 per cent
History: Entered production in 1971 and subsequently built in large numbers for both home and export markets. In service with Algeria, Bulgaria, Cuba, Czechoslovakia (local manufacture), Finland, East Germany, Hungary (licensed production), Iraq, Libya, Poland (licensed production), Romania, Syria, USSR and Yugoslavia (licensed production).

Background: The T-72 MBT entered production some years after the T-64 but incorporated many features of the earlier vehicle, especially the main armament and fire control system. Like its predecessor, the T-72 has a 125mm smooth-bore gun fed by an automatic loader on the turret floor that holds 24 rounds of separate-loading ammunition. A 7.62mm machine gun is mounted coaxially with the main armament and there is a 12.7mm machine gun on the commander's cupola.

Like the T-62 and other Soviet tanks, the T-72 can lay its own smoke screen by injecting diesel fuel into the exhaust outlet on the left side of the hull. It is fitted with an NBC system and night vision equipment and can be fitted with a snorkel for deep fording; and to extend its operational range supplementary fuel tanks can be mounted at the rear. Recent versions of the T-72 have a laser rangefinder to increase first-round hit probability, smoke dischargers either side of the main armament and cladding on the turret roof which is believed to give increased protection against either sub-munitions or neutron radiation. The T-72 has seen combat with the Iraqi and Syrian armies in the Middle East, where Israeli 105mm-armed Merkava tanks have experienced no difficulty in penetrating frontal armour with APFSDS rounds.

T-80

Origin: USSR
Armament: One 125mm gun; one 7.62mm machine gun coaxial with main armament; one 12.7mm anti-aircraft machine gun
Armour: Classified
Dimensions: Length including main armament 32ft 6in (9.9m); hull length 24ft 3in (7.4m); width 11ft 2in (3.4m); height 7ft 3in (2.2m)
Combat weight: 94,798lb (43,000kg)
Ground pressure: 11.80lb/sq in (0.83kg/cm²)
Engine: Gas turbine developing 985hp (735kW)
Performance: Road speed 46.6mph (75km/h); range 248 miles (400km); vertical obstacle 3ft 0in (0.9m); trench 8ft 10in (2.7m); gradient 60 per cent
History: Details of the development of the T-80 are obscure and like the T-64 it had not appeared in public by mid-1987. It is estimated that more than 8,000 T-80s are deployed with the Soviet Army, but none has been

Above: The T-80, like the T-64, has been fitted with reactive armour to give a massive increase in protection against NATO ATGWs, which rely on HEAT warheads to penetrate armour.

exported, even to other members of the Warsaw Pact.

Background: Although the T-80 has some resemblance to the earlier T-64 it features several improvements, including additional armour protection, and like the US M1 Abrams is powered by a gas turbine for high speed and improved power-to-weight ratio. Main armament is similar to that of the T-64B and includes a 125mm gun which can fire the AT-8 Songster anti-tank missile, an anti-helicopter missile or HE-FRAG (FS), HEAT-FRAG or APFSDS rounds. While NATO MBTs such as the M1A1, Leopard 2 and Challenger are at least equal to the T-80, it is the Soviet tank's high degree of protection against such NATO anti-tank weapons as Hot, Tow and Milan which is causing most concern.

Left: The latest Soviet MBT is the T-80, which has features of both the T-64 and the T-72 and is armed with a 125mm gun firing separate loading ammunition. Instead of the normal diesel engine the T-80 is powered by a gas turbine, and this is the first time such an engine has been fitted in an operational Soviet tank.

Right: The T-72 is in service with the Soviet Army on a large scale and has also been exported. It has a three-man crew and an automatic loader, its ammunition being of the separate loading type consisting of the charge (1) and projectile. Rounds available include the AT-8 Songster missile (artist's impression 2), APFSDS projectile without sabot (3) and with sabot (4), HEAT-FS (5) and HE-FRAG (FS) (6). It also carries smoke grenades (7), plus 12.7mm (8) and 7.62mm (9) machine gun ammunition in ready-use belts.

Chieftain and Challenger

CHIEFTAIN

Origin: United Kingdom
Crew: 4
Armament: One 120mm gun; one 7.62mm machine gun coaxial with main armament; one 7.62mm machine gun on commander's cupola; six smoke dischargers each side of turret
Armour: Classified
Dimensions: Length including main armament 35ft 5in (10.795m); hull length 24ft 8in (7.518m); width 11ft 6in (3.504m); height 9ft 6in (2.895m)
Combat weight: 121,253lb (55,000kg)
Engine: Leyland L60 two-stroke, compression ignition, 6-cylinder (12 opposed pistons) multi-fuel developing 750bhp (559kW) at 2,100rpm
Ground pressure: 12.8lb/sq in (0.9kg/cm²)
Performance: Road speed 30mph (48km/h); range 250-310 miles (400-500km); vertical obstacle 3ft 0in (0.914m); trench 10ft 4in (3.149m); gradient 60 per cent
History: Developed in late 1950s with first prototype being completed

in 1961 and production (now complete) being undertaken by Royal Ordnance Leeds and Vickers at Elswick from mid-1960s; in service with Iran, Iraq, Jordan (ARV only), Kuwait, Oman and United Kingdom

Background: Between 1945 and 1962 more than 4,400 Centurion tanks were built for the home and export markets, the type being the standard tank of the British Army in the postwar period, and large numbers remain in service with Denmark, Israel, Jordan, South Africa, Sweden and Switzerland. When requirements for Centurion's replacement were drawn up emphasis was placed first on armour protection, second on firepower and third on mobility. The end result was the Chieftain which entered service with the British Army in the mid-1960s and has been continuously modified to meet changing operational requirements. Compared with the French AMX-30 and West German Leopard 1 the Chieftain has much greater armour protection and a heavier main armament; on the other hand it is

slower and more restricted in operating range.

Main armament consists of a rifled 120mm gun which fires separately loaded ammunition (projectile and charge), with a 7.62mm machine gun being mounted coaxially with the main armament and a similar weapon being mounted on the commander's cupola. When the Chieftain was first introduced the 120mm gun was aimed using a ranging machine gun, but this was subsequently replaced by a laser rangefinder and then a computerised fire control system was added. Even in the late 1980s Chieftain forms the backbone of the Royal Armoured Corps, though the Challenger is being introduced in increasing numbers. More recent improvements include the installation of a Thermal Observation and Gunnery System (TOGS) and appliqué armour to the turret front and sides. Variants of the Chieftain include an armoured vehicle launched bridge, an armoured recovery vehicle and, more recently, a specialised engineer vehicle designed to handle Challenger powerpacks.

CHALLENGER

Origin: United Kingdom
Crew: 4
Armament: One 120mm gun; one 7.62mm machine gun coaxial with main armament; one 7.62mm machine gun on commander's cupola; one bank of six smoke dischargers each side of turret
Armour: Classified
Dimensions: Length including main armament 37ft 11in (11.56m); hull length 27ft 4in (8.327m); width 11ft 6in (3.518m); height 9ft 8in (2.95m)
Combat weight: 136,685lb (62,000kg)
Ground pressure: 13.79lb/sq in (0.97kg/cm²)
Engine: Rolls-Royce Condor CV-12 12-cylinder diesel developing 1,200bhp (895kW) at 2,300rpm
Performance: Road speed 35mph (56km/h); range (estimate) 373 miles (600km); vertical obstacle 3ft 0in (0.9m); trench 9ft 2in (2.8m); gradient 60 per cent
History: Following the cancellation of the MBT-80 project further development of the Shir 2, originally developed for Iran, was carried out;

Left: In terms of numbers, Chieftain is still the most important tank in the British Army and it is now being improved with additional armour protection and the Thermal Observation and Gunnery System (TOGS). In the future the current L11 series gun will be replaced by a new high pressure gun firing new ammunition.

Below: Chieftain and Challenger ammunition includes 7.62mm (1) belts, APFSDS (2), APDS (3), APDS Practice (4) and HESH (5) rounds, charges (6,7,8 and 9), HESH practice (10), and Smoke (11) rounds, plus electric vent tube to ignite main charge (12), 66mm smoke grenades (13) and projectiles (14) for the VIRSS screening system, which is not yet in service with the British Army. All charges are stowed below the turret to enhance the tanks' survivability.

Above: The Challenger is the latest MBT to enter service with the British Army and by the end of the 1980s half the tank regiments in BAOR will be equipped with the tank. Its fire control system and gun are virtually identical to those of the Chieftain, but a new high pressure gun is to be installed.

the end result was the Challenger, which was accepted for service by the British Army in 1982 with first production vehicles being handed over by Royal Ordnance Leeds (now owned by Vickers Defence Systems) in 1983. It is expected that by the late 1980s about half the armoured regiments in British Army of the Rhine will be equipped with the Challenger MBT

Background: Main overseas customer for the Chieftain was Iran, which ordered more than 700 vehicles, and further development resulted in the Shir 1, essentially a Chieftain with a new powerpack consisting of a 1,200bhp (895kW) engine and new transmission. The Iranian revolution occurred before these tanks could be delivered, though production was already underway, and in the end Jordan took delivery of 274 slightly modified Shir 1s under the name Khalid from 1981.

The Shir 2, subsequently renamed Challenger, has the same powerpack, armament and fire control system as the Shir 1 but with a hull and turret of Chobham armour which gives a very high degree of protection against both kinetic and chemical attack over the frontal arc. The tank also has a hydropneumatic suspension system which gives an improved ride across country as well as a more stable firing platform.

Main armament of the Challenger is identical to that of the Chieftain, consisting of a 120mm rifled gun firing separate loading ammunition, and all the propellent charges are stowed below the turret for increased survivability. A total of 64 projectiles and charges are carried, along with 4,000 rounds of 7.62mm machine gun ammunition. The computerised fire control system includes a laser rangefinder for the gunner, and TOGS is being installed in current production vehicles. In the future a new high pressure gun will be installed in both Challenger and Chieftain and this will also fire a new APFSDS round with increased armour penetrating characteristics. An armoured recovery/repair version of Challenger will soon enter service with the British Army as the current Chieftain ARV cannot recover a Challenger under all circumstances.

Above: In mid-1987 the Challenger was one of four tanks—the others being the EE-T1 Osorio, M1A1 and AMX-40—that were being trialled by the Saudi Arabian Army. MBT's such as Challenger and M1A1 are so heavy they need their own special recovery vehicles.

AMX-30 and AMX-40

AMX-30

Origin: France
Crew: 4
Armament: One 105mm gun; one 12.7mm machine gun or one 20mm cannon coaxial with main armament; one 7.62mm anti-aircraft machine gun; two smoke dischargers each side of turret
Armour: Classified
Dimensions: Length including main armament 31ft 1in (9.48m); hull length 21ft 7in (6.59m); width 10ft 2in (3.10m); height 9ft 5in (2.86m)
Combat weight: 79,366lb (36,000kg)
Engine: Hispano-Suiza HS 110 12-cylinder water-cooled super-charged multi-fuel developing 720hp (537kW) at 2,000rpm
Ground pressure: 10.95lb/sq in (0.77kg/cm²)
Performance: Road speed 40mph (65km/h); range 310-372 miles (500-600km); vertical obstacle 3ft 1in (0.93m); trench 9ft 6in (2.9m); gradient 60 per cent
History: Developed at the same time as Leopard 2 with first prototypes being completed 1960 and first production vehicles delivered by the Atelier de Construction Roanne in 1966. Current production model is AMX-30 B2. In service with Chile, France, Greece, Iraq (variants only), Qatar, Saudi Arabia, Spain (was made under licence), United Arab Emirates and Venezuela

Background: In the immediate postwar period the French Army took delivery of a large number of M47 tanks from the United States and these formed the backbone of French medium tank battalions until the introduction of the AMX-30 in the late 1960s. Although some 2,000 AMX-30 series MBTs have been built for the home and export markets, the vehicle is not liked by all operators as it has no stabilisation system for the main armament and the powerpack has been a constant source of trouble.

Main armament comprises a 105mm gun with a 12.7mm machine gun or 20mm cannon mounted coaxially to the left, the latter being unusual in that independent elevation allows it to engage slow-flying helicopters. A 7.62mm machine gun mounted on the commander's cupola can be aimed and fired from within the vehicle. A total of 47 rounds of 105mm ammunition can be carried, including the recently developed APFSDS, as well as 480 rounds of 20mm and 2,070 rounds of 7.62mm.

French Army AMX-30s are being upgraded to the AMX-30 B2 standard, which includes a fire control system with a laser rangefinder and an LLLTV system for commander and gunner. In the future additional armour protection will probably be fitted to the turret as the basic AMX-30 has very thin steel armour.

The chassis of the AMX-30 is used for a wide range of specialised vehicles including a bridgelayer, GCT 155mm self-propelled gun (also used by Iraq and Saudi Arabia), Roland surface-to-air missile system, AMX-30D armoured recovery vehicle, EBG combat engineer vehicle, twin 30mm self-propelled anti-aircraft gun system (for Saudi Arabia) and the Shahine surface-to-air missile system (also for Saudi Arabia).

The AMX-30 and AMX-30 B2 will start to be replaced in French Army service from the early 1990s by the new Leclerc MBT, which has a three-man crew and is fitted with a 120mm gun fed by an automatic loader.

AMX-40

Origin: France
Armament: One 120mm gun; one 20mm cannon co-axial with main armament; one 7.62mm anti-aircraft machine gun; two smoke grenade launchers or six-round GIAT/Lacroix system mounted each side of turret
Armour: Classified
Dimensions: Length including main armament 32ft 11in (10.04m); hull

Above: The AMX-30 will start to be replaced by the new Leclerc MBT in the early 1990s and to enable it to remain effective until then a major improvement programme is now underway. This includes the addition of a new COTAC fire control system that features a laser rangefinder and low-light-level TV system and automotive improvements to upgrade it to AMX-30 B2 standard.

Right: The AMX-30 and AMX-30 B2 MBTs fire the same 105mm fixed ammunition which includes (above) APFSDS (1), HEAT (2), HE (3), Smoke (4) and illuminating (5) rounds. In addition there are 80mm smoke grenades (6), 20mm ammunition for the coaxial cannon (7) and 7.62mm MG ammunition in belts (8). Types of ammunition carried by the AMX-40 (right) include APFSDS (1), APFSDS practice (2), HEAT-MP-T (3) and HEAT-MP-T practice (4). The AMX-40 also carries belts of 20mm (5) and 7.62mm (6) ammunition plus Galix grenades (7).

Above: GIAT urgently needs export orders for its private-venture AMX-40 MBT in order to bridge the production gap between the end of AMX-30 B2 deliveries and the start of Leclerc production. The latter will be the most advanced tank in NATO when it enters service.

length 22ft 4in (6.8m); width 11ft 0in (3.36m); height 10ft 2in (3.10m)
Combat weight: 94,800lb (43,000kg)
Ground pressure: 12.65lb/sq in (0.89kg/cm²)
Engine: Poyaud V12X 12-cylinder diesel developing 1,100hp (820kW) at 2,500rpm
Performance: Road speed 34mph (55km/h); range 373 miles (600km); vertical obstacle 3ft 3in (1m); trench 10ft 6in (3.2m); gradient 60 per cent
History: The AMX-40 has been developed by the Atelier de Construction d'Issy-les-Moulineaux (AMX) specifically for the export market, the first prototype being completed in 1983. Not in production or service by mid-1987

Background: The French Army's present fleet of AMX-30s is being brought up to the new AMX-30 B2 standard pending the introduction of the new Leclerc MBT in the 1990s. There will, however, be a gap on the production lines at Roanne bewteen the ending of production of the AMX-30 B2 and the start of Leclerc production, and even when the Leclerc is in production priority will be given to the French Army and for some overseas markets the new tank may well be too expensive and too sophisticated.

As a result GIAT decided to develop a new export tank. The initial AMX-32, which was originally offered with either a 120mm or a 105mm gun, was not

considered to be a sufficient improvement over the AMX-30, so the new AMX-40 was designed from scratch, though incorporating some existing components, including the COTAC computerised fire control system of AMX-30 B2 and AMX-32 which allows the tank to engage targets under both day and night conditions.

Main armament comprises a 120mm smooth-bore gun firing APFSDS or HEAT rounds with a 20mm cannon mounted coaxially to the left with independent elevation and a 7.62mm machine gun on the commander's cupola. A total of 38 rounds of 120mm, 480 rounds of 20mm and 2,170 rounds of 7.62mm ammunition are carried.

The forward part of the hull and turret are protected by a new laminate armour that is a substantial improvement over that fitted to the AMX-30 and AMX-32 and the vehicle can also be fitted with the six GIAT/Lacroix projectors either side of the turret which can fire not only smoke and illuminating grenades but also fragmentation grenades against a massed infantry attack or a new grenade to decoy ATGWs with an infra-red system.

The AMX-40 has already been demonstrated in several countries and in mid-1987 was shipped to Saudi Arabia for comparative trials alongside the Brazilian ENGESA EE-T1 Osorio, British Challenger and US M1A1.

Above: The AMX-40 MBT has been designed by AMX/GIAT specifically for the export market and has substantial improvements in the key areas of armour, mobility and firepower. Main armament comprises a 120mm smooth bore gun firing APFSDS or HEAT rounds while frontal armour is of the laminate type for improved battlefield survivability. The diesel engine gives a high power-to-weight ratio and greater cross-country mobility.

Leopard 1 and Leopard 2

LEOPARD 1

Origin: West Germany
Crew: 4
Armament: One 105mm gun; one 7.62mm machine gun coaxial with main armament; one 7.62mm anti-aircraft machine gun; four smoke dischargers each side of turret
Armour: 0.39-2.75in (10-70mm)
Dimensions: Length including main armament 31ft 4in (9.543m); hull length 23ft 3in (7.09m); width 10ft 8in (3.25m); height 8ft 7in (2.613m)
Combat weight: 88,184lb (40,000kg)
Ground pressure: 12.23lb/sq in (0.86kg/cm²)
Engine: MTU MB 838 Ca M500 10-cylinder multi-fuel developing 830hp (619kW) at 2,200rpm
Performance: Road speed 40mph (65km/h); road range 373 miles (600km); vertical obstacle 3ft 9in (1.15m); trench 9ft 10in (3m); gradient 60 per cent
History: Developed to meet requirements of West German Army with first production vehicles being completed in 1965. In service with Australia, Belgium, Canada, Denmark, West Germany, Greece, Italy, the Netherlands, Norway and Turkey. Production is now complete but could be resumed if further orders were placed

Background: When the West German Army was re-formed the United States supplied large numbers of M47 and, later, M48

tanks, both armed with 90mm guns. These were only considered an interim solution until a new MBT could be designed and built, and since France also needed to replace a large fleet of M47 tanks in 1956 the two countries agreed on an outline specification for a new MBT. In West Germany two teams were formed to design and build prototype vehicles while in France there was just one design team.

After a relatively short period West Germany decided to concentrate its resources on just one of the two designs, which was eventually accepted for service as the Leopard 1, while the French vehicle became the AMX-30. Prime contractor for the Leopard 1 was Krauss-Maffei of Munich, while the specialised variants such as the recovery vehicle, bridgelayer and engineer vehicle were designed and built by Krupp-MaK of Kiel. By the time production was completed in 1984 some 4,744 gun tanks had been built in West Germany or under licence in Italy by OTO Melara, as well as large numbers of variants including the Biber armoured vehicle launched bridge, armoured recovery, armoured engineer, and training vehicles, and finally the Gepard twin

35mm self-propelled anti-aircraft gun system.

The first gunned version, Leopard 1, was followed by the 1A2, 1A3 and 1A4, and over the years the tank has constantly been upgraded with additional armour protection, a new fire control system and passive night vision devices. Leopard 1 has proved to be a tough and reliable tank although it has never been tested in combat. Main armament comprises the combat-proven British 105mm L7 series gun with a coaxial 7.62mm machine gun and another 7.62mm machine gun on the roof for air defence. A total of 60 rounds of 105mm and 5,500 rounds of 7.62mm ammunition are carried.

LEOPARD 2

Origin: West Germany
Armament: One 120mm gun; one 7.62mm machine gun coaxial with main armament; one 7.62mm anti-aircraft machine gun; eight smoke dischargers each side of turret
Armour: Classified
Dimensions: Length including main armament 31ft 9in (9.668m); hull length 25ft 4in (7.722m); width 12ft 2in (3.70m); height 9ft 3in (2.807m)
Combat weight: 121,583lb (55,150kg)
Ground pressure: 11.80lb/sq in (0.83kg/cm²)
Engine: MTU MB 873 KA 501 4-stroke 12-cylinder multi-fuel developing 1,500hp (1,119kW) at 2,600rpm

Performance: Road speed 45mph (72km/h); range 342 miles (550km); vertical obstacle 3ft 7in (1.1m); trench 9ft 10in (3m); gradient 60 per cent
History: Developed to meet requirements of West German Army with first production vehicles being completed in 1979. In service with West Germany, the Netherlands and Switzerland. Still in production

Background: Following the demise of the US/West German MBT-70 programme West Germany pushed ahead with a new MBT which was eventually accepted for service as the Leopard 2, production being shared by Krauss-Maffei of Munich and Krupp-MaK of Kiel on a 55/45 basis.

The Leopard 2 has significant advantages in the three key areas of tank design, armour, mobility and firepower. The hull and turret front and sides incorporate Chobham armour, which provides a high degree of protection against both chemical (HEAT) and kinetic energy attack, and the vehicle is fitted with an explosion detection and suppression system in the crew compartment; an NBC system is also fitted as standard. The Leopard 2 has a higher power-to-weight ratio and higher speed than the Leopard 1 MBT despite being some 15 tonnes heavier. Main armament is a Rheinmetall-developed 120mm smooth-bore gun — also installed in new-production US Army M1A1 MBTs — which fires APFSDS and

Above: The Leopard 1 has been, in commercial terms, the most successful European tank with sales, including licence production and variants, totalling over 6,500 vehicles. Many countries are now upgrading their Leopard 1s with additional armour protection.

Right: The ammunition fired by Leopard 2 has a semi-combustible cartridge case and all that remains after firing is the stub. Types of ammunition fired are an APFSDS-T round and its training version (1 and 2) and HEAT operational and training versions (4 and 3). This ammunition can also be fired by the US M1A1 Abrams.

1   2   3   4

HEAT-MP rounds; the rounds are unusual in having combustible cartridge cases. A 7.62mm machine gun is mounted coaxially with the main armament and there is a sim lar weapon on the turret roof for anti-aircraft defence. The 120mm gun is fully stabilised in both elevation and traverse and the computerised fire control system, which includes a laser rangefinder, allows moving targets to be engaged successfully when the tank is itself moving at speed across country.

The West German Army has ordered 2,050 Leopard 2s, of which most had been delivered by mid-1987, while the Netherlands has taken delivery of 445 vehicles; Switzerland has ordered 380 vehicles, the first 35 direct from Krauss-Maffei and the remainder built under licence at Thun in Switzerland.

An armoured recovery version of the Leopard 2 is under development by Krupp-MaK and a driver training version is in service.

Left: Leopard 2 (left) compared to Leopard 1. Although the Leopard 2 is much heavier than the earlier tank it has greater cross-country mobility as well as improved armour and firepower.

Left: The Leopard 2, now in service with the West German, Netherlands and Swiss armies, was the first of the so-called second-generation MBTs to enter service. It has a 120mm gun and computerised fire control system that enables it to engage and hit targets under virtually all battlefield conditions, both day and night.

OF-40 and TAM

OF-40

Origin: Italy
Crew: 4
Armament: One 105mm gun; one 7.62mm machine gun coaxial with main armament; one 7.62mm or 12.7mm anti-aircraft machine gun; four smoke dischargers each side of turret
Armour: Classified
Dimensions: Length including armament 30ft 3in (9.222m); hull length 22ft 7in (6.893m); width 11ft 6in (3.51m); height 9ft 1in (2.76m)
Combat weight: 100,309lb (45,500kg)
Ground pressure: 13.08lb/sq in (0.92kg/cm²)
Engine: MTU 10-cylinder super-charged multi-fuel developing 830hp (619kW) at 2,200rpm
Performance: Road speed 37.2mph (60km/h); range 373 miles (600km); vertical obstacle 3ft 7in (1.1m); trench 9ft 10in (3m); gradient 60 per cent
History: Designed by OTO Melara specifically for the export market with first prototype being completed in 1980 and first production vehicles following in 1981. In service only with the United Arab Emirates

Background: Between 1974 and 1983 OTO Melara built 720 Leopard 1 MBTs under licence from West

Above: Although the OF-40 has been produced very recently, in the key areas of armour, mobility and firepower it is only a slight improvement over the Leopard 1, introduced more than 20 years ago. In fact, some of the automotive components are identical to those used in Leopard 1. In 1987 OTO Melara and FIAT completed the first prototype of the new C1 MBT, which is armed with a 120mm gun, for the Italian Army.

Right: The OF-40 MBT has been sold to the United Arab Emirates, which purchased 36 tanks and three armoured recovery vehicles. Types of ammunition fired by the 105mm gun are APFSDS (1), APDS (2), APDS practice (3), HEAT-MP-T (4), HESH (5), WP-T Smoke (6) and canister (7). Also carried are smoke grenades for the turret grenade launchers (8), plus 12.7mm (9) and 7.62mm (10) ammunition in belts for commander's and coaxial MGs.

Germany for the Italian Army after an initial batch of 200 vehicles had been purchased direct from Krauss-Maffei. In addition, OTO Melara built 160 specialised versions of the Leopard 1 including 64 bridgelayers, 68 armoured recovery vehicles and 28 armoured engineer vehicles. For obvious reasons the Leopard 1 could not be exported, so a new export tank was developed under the designation OF-40, the O standing for OTO Melara, the F for FIAT, which is responsible for the powerpack, and 40 for the original design weight. The OF-40 uses some automotive components of the Leopard 1, but has a new hull and turret of all-welded steel armour and a different fire control system incorporating a laser rangefinder and a stabilised sight for the tank commander.

The United Arab Emirates placed an order for 18 OF-40 Mk 1 MBTs, which were delivered in 1981, and followed with another order for 18 Mk 2 MBTs and three armoured recovery vehicles. The original Mk 1s were then brought up to the Mk 2 standard, which involves a more advanced fire control system including a stabilisation system for the main armament. The latter consists of a 105mm gun mounted in a power-operated turret with elevation from −9° to +20°; a total of 57 rounds of 105mm ammunition

are carried, including APDS and HEAT rounds. A 7.62mm machine gun is mounted coaxially with the main armament, and a similar weapon is mounted on the roof for local and anti-aircraft defence; 5,700 rounds of 7.62mm ammunition are carried. The computerised fire control system incorporates a laser rangefinder for the gunner and a stabilised sight for the tank commander. Standard equipment includes an NBC system and night vision equipment.

Early in 1987 OTO Melara completed the first prototype of the new C1 MBT for the Italian Army. The C1 is armed with a 120mm gun and has laminate armour protection, and it is anticipated that between 200 and 300 vehicles will be built to enable Italy's remaining M47 tanks to be replaced.

TAM

Origin: West Germany
Crew: 4
Armament: One 105mm gun, one 7.62mm machine gun coaxial with main armament; one 7.62mm anti-aircraft machine gun; four smoke dischargers each side of turret
Armour: Classified
Dimensions: Length including armament 27ft 0in (8.23m); hull length 22ft 3in (6.775m); width 10ft 3in (3.12m); height 7ft 11in (2.42m)

Combat weight: 67,240lb (30,500kg)
Ground pressure: 11.23lb/sq in (0.79kg/cm²)
Engine: MTU MB 883 Ka 500 6-cylinder supercharged diesel developing 720hp (537kW) at 2,200rpm
Performance: Road speed 46.6mph (75km/h); range 342 miles (550km); vertical obstacle 2ft 11in (0.90m); trench 9ft 6in (2.9m); gradient 60 per cent
History: The TAM was designed to meet the requirements of the Argentinian Army by Thyssen Henschel of West Germany, with first prototypes being completed in 1976 and production starting in Argentina several years later

Background: In the early 1970s Argentina awarded a contract for the design and development of a new MBT called the TAM (Tanque Argentino Mediano) and the VCI (Vehiculo Combate Infanteria) infantry combat vehicle to the West German company of Thyssen Henschel. To reduce development times and costs proven components were used wherever possible, and following trials with prototype vehicles production was initiated in Argentina, though some key components such as the engine and transmission are supplied by West Germany. The original intention was to build 512 TAMs and VCIs but

production stopped in the early 1980s after about 350 had been built, a consequence of the economic situation in Argentina.

In many respects the chassis of the TAM is similar to that of the West German Army's Marder MICV, with the driver front left, the engine compartment to his right and a three-man power operated turret at the rear armed with a 105mm gun with an elevation of +17° and a depression of −7°. A 7.62mm machine gun is mounted coaxially with the main armament and a similar weapon is mounted on the turret roof for anti-aircraft defence, and a total of 50 rounds of 105mm and 6,000 rounds of 7.62mm machine gun ammunition are carried. Standard equipment includes NBC and fire extinguishing systems, and to extend the operational range of the tank long-range fuel tanks can be fitted at the rear.

Further development of the vehicle by Thyssen Henschel has resulted in the TH 301, which has recently been tested in Thailand. The TH 301 has a number of improvements including a more powerful engine and a computerised fire control system which incorporates a laser rangefinder and LLLTV (low-light-level television) system for commander and gunner. Main armament is a 105mm Rheinmetall Rh 105-30 gun.

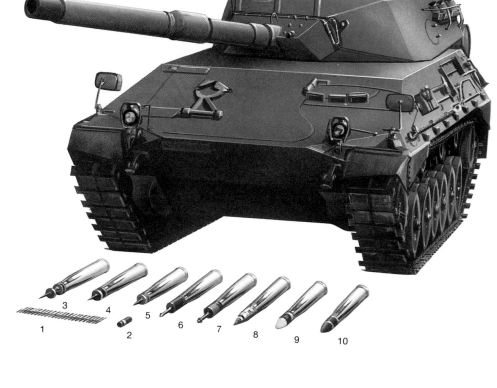

Right: The TAM was designed by the West German company of Thyssen Henschel to meet the requirements of the Argentinian Army. Ammunition types carried are 7.62mm MG (1), smoke grenades (2), APFSDS (3), APDS (4), APDS practice (5), HEAT-MP-T (6), HEAT-MP practice (7), WP-T Smoke (8) HESH (9) and HEP (10), the last being the US version of the British HESH (High Explosive Squash Head) for use against various targets.

Merkava

Origin: Israel
Crew: 4
Armament: One 105mm gun; one 7.62mm machine gun coaxial with main armament; one 7.62mm machine gun at commander's station; one 7.62mm machine gun at loader's station; one 60mm mortar
Armour: Classified
Dimensions: Length including main armament 28ft 4in (8.63m); hull length 24ft 5in (7.45m); width 12ft 2in (3.7m); height 9ft 0in (2.75m)
Combat weight: 132,276lb (60,000kg)
Ground pressure: 12.8lb/sq in (0.90kg/cm²)
Engine: Teledyne Continental AVDS-1790-6A V-12 diesel developing 900hp (671kw)
Performance: Road speed 28.53mph (46km/h); range 248 miles (400km); vertical obstacle 3ft 1in (0.95m); trench 9ft 10in (3m); gradient 60 per cent
History: Developed from late 1960s and first revealed in 1977, used in combat for first time during the invasion of the Lebanon in 1982. Still in production and used only by Israeli Army

Background: For many years Israel obtained its tanks from the United Kingdom (Centurions) or the United States (M48s and M60s), but political considerations made it unlikely that the United Kingdom would continue to provide MBTs and the Arabs could also put pressure on the United

States. The Israelis therefore decided to go ahead and develop their own new MBT in Israel. To reduce development time and costs proven components were used wherever possible, so the gun is the standard 105mm rifled gun as used in every Israeli MBT, while the engine and transmission are further developments of those used in Israeli Centurion and M48/M60 tanks.

What makes the Merkava unique is its design. Whereas the trend in some countries has been to make the MBT lighter and faster, the Merkava is, apart from the British Challenger, the heaviest MBT in the world.

Israeli combat experience has shown that speed is no substitute for armour protection.

The Merkava's unconventional layout, with the driver toward the front on the left, the powerpack on his right and the turret mounted toward the rear, has allowed the maximum possible armour protection over the frontal arc. The armour is believed to be a combination of spaced and laminate types rather than an additional reactive layer as fitted to Israeli M48/M60 and Centurion tanks.

The turret is also an unusual shape and when the Merkava is hull down

Above: The Merkava Mk 2 MBT has now been replaced in production by the Mk 3, which features a number of improvements, including the replacement of the 105mm rifled gun by a 120mm gun. The design emphasised survivability.

presents a small target compared with other tank turrets. Main armament comprises a 105mm rifled tank gun which is fitted with a thermal sleeve and a fume extractor. The thermal sleeve helps stop the barrel getting too hot; otherwise it would bend slightly and accuracy

Left: One unusual feature of the Merkava is that the crew can enter and leave via a door in the hull rear which can also be used for ammunition resupply. It also allows a few troops to be carried, though this is not the door's primary function.

Right: Whereas many tanks rely on their speed for battlefield survivability, Merkava relies on its armour protection, which is enhanced by placing the engine at the front of the vehicle rather than in the customary rear position.

Right: Ammunition for coaxial and roof mounted 7.62mm MGs (1), plus 12.7mm ammunition for the MG over the main gun (2). Ammunition for the 105mm gun is APFSDS-T (3), APDS (4), HEAT (5), canister (6), HESH (7), Smoke (8) and Phosphorus (9). This ammunition is also used in Israeli M48, M60 and Centurion tanks.

would be degraded. A 7.62mm machine gun is mounted coaxially with the main armament and similar weapons are mounted on the roof at the commander's and loader's positions. These are used both for anti-aircraft fire and for laying down suppressive fire against infantry and anti-tank defences.

The 105mm gun's main tank-killing round, an APFSDS projectile developed in Israel by Israel Military Industries, has a long-rod penetrator and has such excellent penetration characteristics that it has also been adopted by many other countries, including Switzerland, Sweden and West Germany. During the 1982 invasion of the Lebanon the 105mm APFSDS round proved capable of penetrating and knocking out Syria's Soviet supplied T-72s.

The normal ammunition load is 62 rounds of 105mm and 10,000 rounds of 7.62mm machine gun ammunition, but the former can be increased. Another unusual feature of the Merkava is that it has a roof-mounted 60mm mortar, for which 30 high explosive or smoke bombs are carried.

The Merkava does not rely on its armour alone for its survival. Current production tanks have been fitted with an explosion and fire detection and suppression system which detects and extinguishes fires in the crew compartment caused by HEAT projectiles in the blink of an eye. A computerised fire control system enables the Merkava to engage stationary or moving targets whether the tank itself is stationary or moving designated Matador Mk1, it is made by Elbit.

In most tanks the only means of entry and exit for the crew, apart from the driver, are the turret hatches, and combat experience by the Israeli Army has shown that many tank crews have been killed or wounded as they tried to get out of the turret. New ammunition has also to be loaded through the turret hatches which is a very tiring and time consuming process. Merkava has three hatch covers in the rear of the hull, the left-hand one giving access to the batteries, the centre one being a two-part door hinged at top and bottom and the right-hand one giving access to the NBC pack.

The centre hatch can be used to resupply the Merkava with ammunition or to allow the crew to leave the vehicle in comparative safety. There is sufficient space for additional ammunition to be carried — up to 85 rounds — or several infantrymen, but the prime role of the Merkava is not to act as an APC.

By early 1987 it was estimated that about 600 vehicles had been built with production running at between 80 and 100 vehicles a year. The Mk 1 was succeeded in production by the Mk 2 which has an improved fire control system, better armour protection and increased operating range. The Mk 3, which has subsequently replaced the Mk 2, as well as yet more improvements in armour protection will have an improved power-to-weight ratio and a 120mm gun, and which should give the Israeli Armoured Corps the edge on its Arab neighbours for the foreseeable future.

Type 63, SK 105 and Ikv-91

TYPE 63

Origin: China
Armament: One 85mm gun; one 7.62mm coaxial machine gun and one 12.7mm anti-aircraft machine gun
Armour: 0.55in (14mm) maximum
Dimensions: Length including main armament 27ft 8in (8.437m); hull length 23ft 6in (7.15m); width 10ft 6in (3.2m); height 10ft 3in (3.122m)
Combat weight: 41,226lb (18,700kg)
Ground pressure: Not available
Engine: Model 12150-L 12-cylinder water-cooled diesel developing 400hp (298kW) at 2,000rpm
Performance: Road speed 40mph (64km/h); range 230 miles (370km); vertical obstacle 2ft 10in (0.87m); trench 9ft 6in (2.9m); gradient 60 per cent
History: Developed by China North Industries Corporation to meet requirements of Chinese Army; in service with China and exported to North Korea, Pakistan, Sudan and Vietnam

Background: China received most of its original military equipment from the Soviet Union including quantities of PT-76 light amphibious tanks. The Chinese then not only reverse-engineered this vehicle but also carried out many improvements, including installing a new turret with a more powerful 85mm gun — the PT-76 has a 76mm gun — and fitting a more powerful diesel engine, which increased both its road speed and its power-to-weight ratio.

The Type 63 is fully amphibious with the only preparation required being to switch on the bilge pumps and erect the trim vane at the front of the hull. When afloat it is propelled in the water by two water jets, one either side of the hull, at a speed of 7.45mph (12.5km/h). The Type 63 has seen combat with Chinese, Pakistani and Vietnamese forces.

Above: The Type 63 light tank is fully amphibious, being propelled in the water by two water-jets mounted at the rear of the hull. It shares many components with the Type 77 amphibious armoured personnel carrier, also in service with the Chinese army.

Above: The Type 63 is the Chinese equivalent of the Soviet PT-76 and its 85mm gun fires fixed ammunition including APHE (1), HE (2) and HVAP (3) rounds. Ammunition for the 12.7mm machine gun is in belts (4), as is that for the 7.62mm co-axial MG (5). The vehicle is fully amphibious with little preparation.

Right: The SK 105/A2 is the latest version of the Kurassier light tank and is armed with a 7.62mm belt-fed MG (1) while the 105mm gun fires fixed rounds including HEAT (2), HE (3), APFSDS (4) and practice (5) varieties. The smoke grenade launchers use standard grenades (6). The turret of the SK 105 is unusual in that it is in two parts, upper and lower, with the 105mm gun fixed in the upper part that pivots on the lower part. The gun is fed by two revolver type magazines, each of which holds six rounds: this arrangement enables a high rate of fire to be achieved until ammunition is exhausted.

SK 105

Origin: Austria
Armament: One 105mm gun; one 7.62mm machine gun coaxial with main armament; two smoke dischargers each side of turret
Armour: 0.31-1.57in (8-40mm)
Dimensions: Length including main armament 25ft 6in (7.763m); hull length 18ft 4in (5.582m); width 8ft (2.5m); height 9ft 6in (2.88m)
Combat weight: 38,580lb (17,500kg)
Ground pressure: 9.67lb/sq in (0.68kg/cm²)
Engine: Steyr 7FA 6-cylinder liquid-cooled 4-stroke turbo-charged diesel developing 238kw (320hp) at 2,300rpm
Performance: Road speed 40mph (65.34km/h); range 323 miles (520km); vertical obstacle 2ft 8in (0.8m); trench 7ft 11in (2.41m); gradient 60 per cent
History: Developed by Saurer-Werk (now Steyr-Daimler-Puch); first prototype completed in 1967 and first production vehicles delivered in 1971. In service with Austria, Argentina, Bolivia, Morocco and Tunisia

Background: Although classed as a tank destroyer by the Austrian Army the SK 105, often called the Kurassier, is usually referred to as a light tank. Many of the automotive components of the SK 105 are identical to those used in the Steyr range of armoured personnel carriers, enabling users to field a complete family of vehicles based on similar parts, which makes for easier training and logistics.

The turret of the SK 105 is a modified version of the French Fives-Cail Babcock FL-12 oscillating turret: the 105mm gun is fixed in the upper part, which pivots on the lower part. In the turret bustle are two revolver type magazines, each of which holds six rounds of ammunition, enabling one round to be fired every five seconds until the 12 ready rounds have been expended; the empty cartridge cases are ejected automatically through a door in the rear.

The SK 105 has an NBC system and night vision equipment and variants include the Greif armoured recovery vehicle, Pionier vehicle/engineer vehicle and driver training vehicle.

IKV-91

Origin: Sweden
Crew: 4
Armament: One 90mm gun; one 7.62mm machine gun coaxial with main armament; one 7.62mm anti-aircraft machine gun; six smoke dischargers each side of turret
Armour: Classified
Dimensions: Length including main armament 29ft 0in (8.84m); hull length 21ft 0in (6.41m); width 9ft 10in (3.0m); height 7ft 7in (2.32m)
Combat weight: 35,935lb (16,300kg)
Ground pressure: 6.96lb/sq in (0.49kg/cm²)
Engine: Volvo-Penta TD 120 A 4-stroke 6-cylinder turbo-charged diesel developing 223kW (330hp) at 2,200rpm
Performance: Road speed 40mph (65km/h); range 310 miles (500km); vertical obstacle 2ft 8in (0.8m); trench 2.8m (9ft 2in); gradient 60 per cent
History: Developed by Hagglund and Soner to meet requirements of Swedish Army; first prototype completed in 1969; in production between 1975 and 1978

Background: The Infanterikanonvagn 91 (Ikv-91) was developed to meet the unique requirements of the Swedish Army for a highly mobile tank destroyer with a low ground pressure to allow it to operate in the snow and an amphibious capability with little preparation. These requirements meant that the vehicle would have to rely on its manoeuvrability and size to avoid detection as the defined weight limits did not allow for substantial armour protection to be included as an aid to battlefield survivability.

The Ikv-91 is armed with a Bofors 90mm gun that fires fin-stabilised HE and HEAT rounds and its computerised fire control system includes a laser rangefinder. The advent of reactive armour has led to the development of a new HEAT round which is claimed to be effective against such armour. A total of 59 rounds of 90mm and 4,250 rounds of 7.62mm ammunition are carried. For the export market Hagglund and Soner have developed the Ikv-91 105mm, which has improved armour as well as a 105mm gun.

5
4
3
2
1

Left: The SK 105 was originally developed by Steyr-Daimler-Puch to meet the requirements of the Austrian Army. It has also been exported to Argentina, Bolivia, Morocco and Tunisia and shares many common components with the Steyr range of light armoured vehicles.

Above: Hägglunds and Söner produced the Ikv-91 tank destroyer for the Swedish Army between 1975 and 1978. Main armament comprises a 90mm gun that fires HE (1) and HEAT (2) projectiles. The latter projectile is fin stabilised (3) to allow for greater accuracy and more recently new ammunition for the 90mm gun has been developed.

Mounted on each side of the turret is a bank of six smoke grenade launchers that fire standard grenades (4). Two 7.62mm MGs are fitted, one coaxial with the main armament and one on the roof, and both are belt-fed (5). More recently a 105mm version of the Ikv has been developed for export; this also features better armour.

Scorpion and Stingray

SCORPION

Origin: United Kingdom
Armament: One 76mm gun; one 7.62mm machine-gun coaxial with main armament; four smoke dischargers on each side of turret
Armour: Classified
Dimensions: Length 15ft 9in (4.794m); width 7ft 4in (2.235m); height 6ft 11in (2.102m)
Combat weight: 17,797lb (8,073kg)
Ground pressure: 5.12lb/sq in (0.36kg/cm²)
Engine: Jaguar J60 petrol developing 190hp (142kW) at 4,750rpm
Performance: Road speed 50mph (80.5km/h); range 400 miles (644km); vertical obstacle 1ft 8in (0.5m); trench 6ft 9in (2.057m); gradient 60 per cent
History: First production vehicles completed in 1972; now in service with Belgium, Brunei, Honduras, Iran, Ireland, Kuwait, Malaysia, New Zealand, Nigeria, Oman, Spain, Tanzania, Thailand, Togo, Philippines, United Arab Emirates and the United Kingdom (Army and Air Force)

Background: The Alvis Scorpion Combat Vehicle Reconnaissance (Tracked) was developed as the replacement for the Alvis Saladin 6 × 6 armoured car with the requirement being for a smaller and

Above: An Alvis Scorpion of the Honduran Army during exercises with US Army troops in March 1985. The low ground pressure of the Scorpion allows it to operate in terrain which is unsuitable for other tracked and wheeled armoured vehicles. This example is fitted with a 76mm gun, though the Scorpion is also available with a 90mm gun and a wide range of other equipment.

Below: By mid-1987 over 3,500 members of the Scorpion family had been built for home and export markets. 7.62mm ammunition for the co-axial MG is in belts (1), while the 76mm gun fires fixed canister (2), smoke (3), HESH (4), high explosive (5) and practice rounds (6 and 7). Mounted on each side of the turret is a bank of four electrically operated smoke grenade launchers which fire smoke grenades (8 and 9). When fitted with a flotation screen the Scorpion is fully amphibious.

lighter vehicle but with a similar armament and greater cross-country mobility. To save weight the hull and turret of the Scorpion are of all-welded aluminium with the wide tracks giving a low ground pressure to enable it to operate in soft terrain such as that encountered in the Falklands; it is equally at home in the desert.

Main armament of the basic Scorpion is a 76mm gun, a further development of that installed in the Saladin, which fires canister, HESH, HE, smoke and illuminating projectiles, with 40 rounds of 76mm ammunition being carried. A 7.62mm machine gun is mounted coaxially with the main armament, and 3,000 rounds are carried for this.

A full range of night vision equipment is installed, as is an NBC system, and with the aid of a flotation screen the Scorpion is fully amphibious. To meet different user requirements a wide range of options are available, including a diesel engine and 90mm gun.

So far some 3,500 Scorpions have been built for the home and export markets and the basic chassis has been developed into a complete family of vehicles, including the Striker anti-tank vehicle with Swingfire missiles, Spartan APC, Samaritan ambulance, Sultan command post vehicle, Samson armoured recovery vehicle, Scimitar

reconnaissance vehicle and Streaker high-mobility load-carrier. Further development has resulted in the Stormer APC which has recently been adopted by the British Army to mount the Shorts Starstreak High Velocity Missile (HVM) system.

STINGRAY

Origin: United States
Crew: 4
Armament: One 105mm gun; one 7.62mm machine gun coaxial with main armament; one 12.7mm machine gun on roof; four smoke dischargers each side of turret
Armour: Classified
Dimensions: Length (including main armament) 30ft 8in (9.35m); hull length 20ft 5in (6.229m); width 8ft 10½in (2.71m); height 8ft 4in (2.55m)
Combat weight: 42,500lb (19,278kg)
Ground pressure: 9.81lb/sq in (0.69kg/cm²)
Engine: Detroit Diesel Model 8V-92 TA developing 535hp (400kW) at 2,300rpm
Performance: Road speed 41.63mph (67km/h); range 300 miles (483km); vertical obstacle 2ft 6in (0.76m); trench 7ft 0in (2.13m); gradient 60 per cent
History: Developed as private venture; first prototype completed in 1984; ready to enter production on receipt of orders

Background: Since the early 1960s the Cadillac Gage Company has built well over 3,000 of its Commando range of 4 × 4 multi-role vehicles, and in the early 1980s the company realised that there was a requirement for a light tank which had the firepower and mobility of vehicles such as the Leopard 1 and M60 but was much cheaper to purchase, operate and maintain.

Obviously the Stingray does not have the same level of armour protection as the Leopard 1 and M60 but its hull and turret have been designed so that reactive or other armour can be added.

Main armament comprises the British Royal Ordnance 105mm Low Recoil Force gun, which has a

muzzle brake and special recoil system to allow it to be fired from a light vehicle. The gun can fire standard 105mm ammunition including APFSDS and HEAT rounds. A total of 36 rounds of 105mm ammunition are carried along with 2,400 rounds for the coaxial 7.62mm machine-gun and 1,100 rounds for the roof-mounted 12.7mm machine-gun.

The fire control system is the British Marconi Command and Control Systems Digital Fire Control System, with commander and gunner both having a day/night sight. The main armament is stabilised in both planes and targets can be engaged while the Stingray is stationary or moving.

Above: The Cadillac Gage Stingray light tank has the same mobility and fire power as Leopard 1 but is much lighter, relying for survivability on speed and manoeuvrability.

Below: The Stingray light tank has been developed as a private venture by Cadillac Gage and early in 1987 the first prototype was undergoing extensive trials in the Far East. The Royal Ordnance 105mm L7 gun fires all standard tank ammunition

including HESH (1), Smoke (2), APDS (3) and APFSDS (4). Mounted coaxially with the main armament is a 7.62mm belt-fed (5) MG while a belt-fed (6) 12.7mm MG is mounted on the roof at the commander's station for anti-aircraft and local defence.

AMX-10 and Fox

AMX-10RC

Origin: France
Crew: 4
Armament: One 105mm gun; one 7.62mm machine gun coaxial with main armament; two smoke dischargers each side of turret
Armour: Classified
Dimensions: Length including main armament 30ft 0in (9.15m); hull length 20ft 10in (6.357m); width 9ft 8in (2.95m); height 8ft 9in (2.68m)
Combat weight: 35,000lb (15,880kg)
Ground pressure: Not available
Engine: Hispano-Suiza HS-115 supercharged water-cooled 8-cylinder diesel developing 260hp (194kW) at 3,000rpm
Performance: Road speed 52.8mph (85km/h); range 621 miles (1,000km); vertical obstacle 2ft 4in (0.7m); trench 3ft 9in (1.15m); gradient 60 per cent
History: Developed by Atelier de Construction d'Issy-les-Moulineaux to meet requirements of French Army; first prototype completed 1971; first production vehicles completed by the Atelier de Construction Roanne in 1978; in service with France and Morocco

Background: From 1950 the Panhard EBR 75 (8 × 8) vehicle was the standard long range armoured car of the French Army but by the late 1960s it was apparent that a new design would be needed for the 1970s and after studying designs from GIAT and Panhard the former's was selected.

The resulting AMX-10RC (6 × 6) reconnaissance vehicle has a number of unique features of which its suspension is probably the most interesting. All six wheels are powered and the suspension is of the hydropneumatic type which allows the driver to adjust the ground clearance to suit the terrain being crossed; for example, when travelling across rough country the suspension is lowered to give maximum possible ground clearance. The driver can also raise or lower the suspension on just one side or the front or rear. Most wheeled vehicles have conventional steering on the front wheels but the AMX-10RC has skid steering. Many of the automotive components of the AMX-10RC are also used in the full tracked AMX-10P infantry fighting vehicle.

The 105mm gun fires HEAT, HE or APFSDS rounds and a total of 38 are carried. A 7.62mm machine gun is mounted coaxially with the main armament and 4,000 rounds are carried for it. The computerised fire control system includes a laser rangefinder and LLLTV system with displays for both commander and gunner, and the vehicle is fitted with night vision equipment and an NBC system. It is fully amphibious, being propelled in the water by two waterjets, mounted one either side at the hull rear, at a maximum speed of 4.47mph (7.2km/h).

The AMX-10RC is normally deployed at Corps level with each Corps having one regiment of 36 vehicles; the French Force d'Action Rapide (FAR) also has two regiments each with 36 vehicles and some of the latter have been deployed recently to Chad. The French Army did intend to purchase 525 vehicles but procurement was subsequently reduced to around 300 for financial reasons and Panhard ERC 90 F4 Sagaie (6 × 6) armoured cars were ordered instead.

Above: The smoke grenades (1 and 2) are fired by the launchers at rear of the hull. Types of ammunition fired by 90mm gun include HE (3) and APFSDS (4) and their respective training rounds (5 and 6). In addition canister, HEAT, smoke and long-range HE are available, all of which have fixed brass cartridge cases.

Left: The 30mm RARDEN cannon of the Fox fires three-round clips of APDS-T (1), APSE-T (2), HEI-T (3) or PRAC-T (4) which are made in the UK. The four-round smoke dischargers each side of turret fire a variety of grenades while the 7.62mm MG co-axial with the RARDEN is belt-fed (7).

Above: Although the Fox armoured car was designed by Daimler production was undertaken by Royal Ordnance Leeds. In addition to being used by the British Army the vehicle has been exported in small numbers.

Above: The Fox Combat Vehicle Reconnaissance (Wheeled) was designed at the same time as the Scorpion Combat Vehicle Reconnaissance (Tracked) and it has the same 30mm RARDEN cannon as the Scimitar.

FOX

Origin: United Kingdom
Crew: 3
Armament: One 30mm cannon; one 7.62mm machine gun coaxial with main armament; four smoke dischargers each side of turret
Armour: Classified
Dimensions: Length including main armament 16ft 8in (5.08m); hull length 13ft 8in (4.166m); width 7ft 0in (2.134m); height 7ft 3in (2.2m)
Combat weight: 13,492lb (6,120kg)
Ground pressure: Not available
Engine: Jaguar XK 4.2 litre 6-cylinder petrol developing 190bhp (142kW) at 4,500rpm
Performance: Road speed 64mph (104km/h); range 270 miles (434km); vertical obstacle 1ft 8in (0.5m); trench 4ft 0in (1.22m) with channels; gradient 58 per cent
History: The Fox Combat Vehicle Reconnaissance (Wheeled) was developed at the same time as the Alvis Scorpion Combat Vehicle Reconnaissance (Tracked). Prototypes of the Fox were built by Daimler but production of the vehicle was undertaken by Royal Ordnance Leeds (now owned by Vickers Defence Systems) with the first production vehicle being completed in 1973. In service with Malawi, Nigeria and the United Kingdom

Background: The Fox 4 × 4 light armoured car is a further development of the Daimler Ferret but with a new hull and turret of welded aluminium, more powerful engine and a heavier armament. Compared with the Daimler Ferret, of which more than 4,000 were built, the Fox has been built in very small numbers with the majority of the British Army's vehicles being used by the Territorial Army.

Main armament comprises the 30mm RARDEN cannon also installed in the Scimitar and Warrior vehicles with a coaxial 7.62mm machine gun. A total of 99 rounds of 30mm and 2,600 rounds of 7.62mm ammunition are carried.

The 30mm RARDEN cannon fires an APSE, an HEI and more recently an APDS round; the last will penetrate some 40mm of armour. The main role of light armoured cars such as the Fox is to report enemy movements back through the command link rather than get engaged in a fire fight. However, its 30mm cannon does enable it to defeat many of the light armoured vehicles on today's battlefield and its APDS round will also penetrate the sides and rear of most MBTs.

Several variants of the Fox have been developed as private ventures, including the Panga scout car with MG turret, Fox Milan with two Milan anti-tank missiles in ready-to-launch position, Fox/25mm Chain Gun and Fox/Scout, but by mid-1987 none had entered production.

When originally built the Fox was fitted with a flotation screen which, when erected, enabled the vehicle to swim across rivers and streams, being propelled by its wheels at a speed of 3.2mph (5.23km/h). This has now been removed from British Army vehicles.

Left: The AMX-10 PAC 90 Marine was developed by GIAT specifically for the export market and is essentially an AMX-10P IFV fitted with the GIAT TS-90 90mm turret.

Right: By 1986 the GIAT AMX-10RC (6 x 6) heavy amoured car had replaced the old Panhard EBR 75 (8 x 8) armoured car in the French Army and a quantity has also been sold to Morocco.

Luchs and BRDM-2

LUCHS

Origin: West Germany
Crew: 4
Armament: One 20mm cannon; one 7.62mm anti-aircraft machine gun on roof; four smoke dischargers each side of turret
Armour: Classified
Dimensions: Length 25ft 5in (7.743m); width 9ft 10in (2.98m); height 9ft 6in (2.905m)
Combat weight: 49,990lb (19,500kg)
Power-to-weight ratio: 20hp/tonne (14.91kW/tonne)
Engine: Daimler-Benz OM 403 A 10-cylinder diesel developing 390hp (290kW) at 2,500rpm
Performance: Road speed 56mph (90km/h); maximum range 497 miles (800km); vertical obstacle 2ft 0in (0.6m); trench 6ft 3in (1.9m); gradient 60 per cent
History: Developed to meet requirements of West German Army with a total of 408 vehicles being built by Thyssen Henschel between 1975 and 1978. In service only with West German Army

Background: When the West German Army was re-formed in the 1950s US M41 light tanks and French Hotchkiss carriers were procured for use in the reconnaissance role. These were only an interim solution and in the early 1960s plans were drawn up for a complete family of trucks and wheeled armoured vehicles that would all use common automotive components to reduce both procurement and operating costs. One of the armoured vehicles was an 8 × 8 armoured car which eventually became the Luchs. Prototypes were built by Daimler-Benz and the so-called Joint Project Office (JPO)

which was a consortium of West German automotive manufacturers. As a result of extensive trials the Daimler-Benz model was selected for production with Thyssen Henschel, then known as Rheinstahl Wehrtechnic, being awarded the production contract with production finally getting under way in 1974.

In many respects the Spähpanzer Luchs carries on the traditions of the famous German 8 × 8 armoured cars of World War II. It has a high road speed of 56mph (90km/h) which can be achieved in both directions and in addition to the driver at the front of the vehicle there is a second driver facing the back. It is fully amphibious with virtually no preparation, being propelled in the water by two propellers mounted at the rear of the hull. To reduce driver fatigue steering is powered on all eight wheels.

Standard equipment includes infra-red night vision equipment and an NBC system, though the former is rapidly being replaced by a thermal night vision system which shares many common components with those being installed in other armoured vehicles of the West German Army.

As the prime role of a vehicle such as the Luchs is reconnaissance it is only lightly armed and armoured. Main armament comprises the same model of 20mm cannon as that installed in the Marder MICV, and a 7.62mm machine gun is mounted on the roof for air defence. In the future it is possible that the 20mm cannon will be replaced by a 25mm cannon with greater armour piercing capabilities to cope with the increased threat from vehicles such as the BMP-2.

BRDM-2

Origin: USSR
Crew: 4
Armour: 0.55in (14mm)
Dimensions: Length 18ft 10in (5.75m); width 7ft 9in (2.35m); height 7ft 7in (2.31m)
Power-to-weight ratio: 20 hp/tonne (14.91kW/tonne)
Engine: GAZ-41 V-8 water-cooled petrol developing 140hp (104kw) at 3,400rpm
Performance: Road speed 62mph (100km/h); range 466 miles (750km); vertical obstacle 1ft 4in (0.4m); trench 4ft 1in (1.25m); gradient 60 per cent
History: Developed in early 1960s

and first seen in public in 1966. Currently used by Algeria, Angola, Benin, Botswana, Bulgaria, Cape Verde Islands, Central African Republic, Chad, Congo, Cuba, Djibouti, Equatorial Guinea, Ethiopia, East Germany, Guinea, Guinea-Bissau, Hungary, India, Iraq, Israel, Libya, Madagascar, Malawi, Mali, Mauritania, Mongolia, Morocco, Mozambique, Nicaragua, Peru, Poland, Romania, São-Tomé Principe, Seychelles, Somalia, Sudan, Syria, Tanzania, USSR, Vietnam, North and South Yemen, Yugoslavia, Zambia and Zimbabwe

Background: In the 1950s the Soviet Union introduced the BRDM-1 4 × 4 amphibious scout car as the

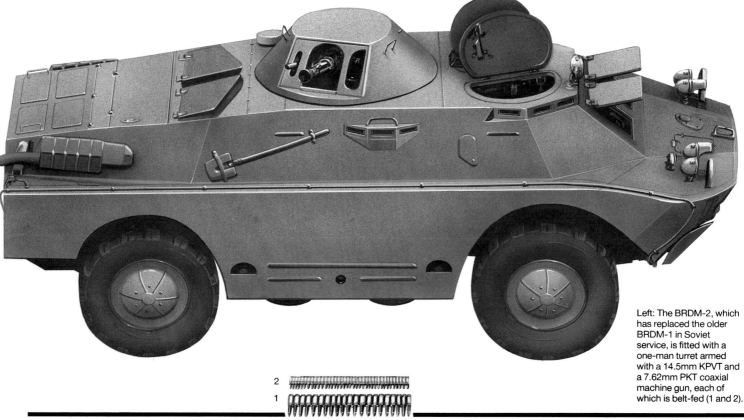

Left: The BRDM-2, which has replaced the older BRDM-1 in Soviet service, is fitted with a one-man turret armed with a 14.5mm KPVT and a 7.62mm PKT coaxial machine gun, each of which is belt-fed (1 and 2).

Left: The lightly armed Luchs relies on its speed and manoeuvrability for its survival. All eight wheels are powered, with steering on all wheels, and it can be driven at the same speed in both directions as it has a driver at each end.

replacement for the BA-64 used during World War II. Although the BRDM-1 was a significant improvement, it still had a number of drawbacks, and in the early 1960s a new vehicle was developed. Subsequently called the BRDM-2, this had many improvements including a one-man turret armed with 14.5mm and 7.62mm machine guns and a more powerful rear-mounted engine which gave improved land and water speeds.

The BRDM-2 is fully amphibious, being propelled in the water by a single water jet mounted at the rear of the hull, and to improve its cross-country mobility a pair of belly wheels can be lowered either side between the front and rear wheels. Standard equipment includes infra-red night vision devices, a central tyre pressure regulation system and an NBC system.

The BRDM-2 is widely used by the Warsaw Pact and has been exported in considerable numbers all over the world. The basic chassis has also been adopted to meet a large number of other roles, including command vehicle, chemical reconnaissance vehicle with lane-marking equipment installed at the rear, and both air defence and anti-tank carrier. The air defence variant is known as the SA-9 Gaskin and carries four missiles in the ready-to-launch position, while the latest of at least three anti-tank versions is the BRDM-3, whose Spandrel anti-tank guided missile system comprises five missiles carried in the ready-to-launch position with additional missiles carried inside ready for manual loading.

Although the BRDM-2 has limited capabilities on the Central European Front its simple controls and ease of handling make it popular in the Third World a fact evidenced by the long list of customers — currently standing at a total of 35 nations — which have taken delivery of the vehicle.

Right: The Spähpanzer Luchs (8 x 8) armoured car is fitted with a two-man power-operated turret armed with a 20mm cannon and a 7.62mm coaxial MG. The 20mm cannon fires API-T (3), HEI-T (4) and practice (5) rounds while 7.62mm ammunition (6) is in belts. The grenade launchers fire DM35 (1) or DM15 (2) smoke grenades. The 20mm MK 20 RH 202 Rheinmetall cannon mounted by Luchs is installed in the Marder infantry vehicle.

M113

Origin: USA
Crew: 2 + 11
Armament: One 12.7mm machine gun
Armour: 0.47-1.49in (12-38mm)
Dimensions: Length 16ft 0in (4.863m); width 8ft 10in (2.686m); height 8ft 2in (2.50m)
Combat weight: 24,595lb (11,156kg)
Ground pressure: 7.82lb/sq in (0.55kg/cm²)
Engine: General Motors Detroit Diesel Model 6V-53 6-cylinder water-cooled diesel developing 215bhp (160kW) at 2,800rpm
Performance: Road speed 42mph (67.59km/h); range 300 miles (483km); vertical obstacle 2ft 0in (0.61m); trench 5ft 6in (1.68m); gradient 60 per cent
History: Developed in late 1950s with first production M113 being completed by FMC Corporation in 1960; Current production model is M113A2. In service with Argentina, Australia, Belgium, Bolivia, Brazil, Canada, Chile, Costa Rica, Denmark, Ecuador, Egypt, El Salvador, Ethiopia, West Germany, Greece, Guatemala, Haiti, Iran, Israel, Italy, Jordan, Kampuchea, Libya, Morocco, Netherlands, New Zealand, Norway, Pakistan, Peru, Philippines, Portugal, Saudi Arabia, Singapore, Somalia, Spain, Sudan, Switzerland, Taiwan, Thailand, Turkey, USA, Uruguay, Vietnam, North Yemen and Zaïre — a total of 45 nations.

Background: In the mid-1950s the development of a new fully tracked armoured personnel carrier began with prototypes being built in both steel and aluminium. The latter was eventually accepted for service with the US Army as the M113 and first production vehicles were completed by the FMC Corporation in 1960. Since then the vehicle has been continuously modified and improved and by 1987 more than 73,000 had been built for the home and export markets, including some 4,500 built under licence in Italy by OTO Melara. The M113 has the distinction of being the most widely used armoured vehicle in the world and has formed the basis for the world's largest family of armoured vehicles, with new variants being added yearly.

The hull of the M113 is of all-welded aluminium armour to save weight and provides the crew with protection from small arms fire and shell splinters. The driver is seated front left with the engine compartment to his right and the whole of the rear being kept clear for the troop compartment. The troops are seated on bench seats that run down either side of the hull and enter and leave via a large power operated ramp in the rear. There is also a roof hatch above the troop compartment and a cupola with an externally mounted 0.5in M2 HB machine gun which can be used for local and anti-aircraft defence, though no protection whatsoever is provided for the gunner.

The original M113 was powered by a Chrysler petrol engine, but this model was replaced on the production lines in late 1964 by the diesel-engined M113A1, which has a much larger radius of action as the engine is more fuel-efficient; there is also a reduced risk of fire. The M113A1 was replaced in turn by the M113A2, whose many improvements include a tougher suspension.

To meet different user requirements many kits have been developed for the M113 series including an NBC system, smoke dischargers, additional armour protection, night vision equipment, a dozer blade, self-recovery gear and so on, while many countries have modified the vehicle to meet their own specific requirements. For example, many Swiss vehicles have been fitted with a Swedish Hägglund and Söner turret armed with a 20mm cannon, while many Israeli Army vehicles have additional armour protection to their fronts and sides to give protection against RPG-7 anti-tank grenades with their HEAT warheads.

The basic M113 is fully amphibious, being propelled in the water by its tracks; all that is required in the way of preparation is to switch on the bilge pumps and erect the trim vane at the front of the hull. It should be stressed that the M113 is amphibious only under almost ideal conditions and cannot swim in the open sea.

The vehicle has seen combat in many parts of the world including the Middle East — with both Israel; and Lebanese forces — and in South-East Asia, especially Vietnam, where it was the workhorse in the ground war. In the latter campaign it proved very vulnerable to mines and many troops preferred to take their chances on top of the vehicle rather than inside. Although the M2 Bradley Infantry Fighting Vehicle is entering US Army service in increasing numbers, the M113 will remain in US service for many years to come, as the Bradley is not replacing the M113 on a one-for-one basis.

The M113 has proved to be reliable and easy to maintain and has been produced in such large numbers that by today's standards it is cheap. There are literally hundreds of variants, but the more common ones are: M125 81mm and M106 107mm mortar carriers — in both cases the mortars can also be dismounted for use in the ground role; M163 20mm Vulcan clear-weather air defence system; the M577 command post vehicle, which has a higher roof and is fitted with extensive communications equipment; recovery vehicles; the M901 Improved Tow Vehicle, which has

Below: The basic M113 APC is armed with a single 12.7mm M2 HB Browning machine gun, but many countries have modified the vehicle to meet their own requirements. This Israeli M113 has extensive external stowage, fuel tanks repositioned on each side of the rear ramp and an additional pair of 7.62mm machine guns mounted on the hull roof. Many Israeli M113s now have additional armour protection on hull front, sides and rear. The ammunition (1) and (2) for the 12.7mm and 7.62mm machine guns is carried in the familiar belts which are stowed in boxes.

an elevating arm with two Tow anti-tank missiles in the ready-to-launch position; and the M981 Fire Support Team vehicle, which designates targets for the field artillery.

Another derivative, the M548 unarmoured tracked cargo carrier, itself has formed the basis for another complete family of vehicles. These include the launchers and loaders for the Lance surface-to-surface missile system; the Chaparral surface-to-air missile system; the British Army's Tracked Rapier air defence system; various electronic warfare systems carriers; ammunition resupply vehicles for self-propelled artillery such as the M107, M109 and M110; and a mine-carrying vehicle.

Further development of the M113 series by the FMC Corporation resulted in the Armoured Infantry Fighting Vehicle, which is much cheaper than the M2 Bradley Infantry Fighting Vehicle and is armed with a turret-mounted 25mm cannon and has firing ports for the infantry but retains its amphibious capability. The AIFV is in service with Belgium, the Netherlands and the Philippines and has itself spawned a large family of vehicles. The M113 family is often seen as the Army equivalent of the Douglas DC-3 Dakota: many countries have tried to design a replacement, but it will probably still be in production 30 years after the first ones came off the line in 1960.

Above: Over 73,000 M113 series vehicles have been built and examples are in use all over the world. The M2 Bradley is now supplementing the M113 in US Army service.

Below: The M901 ITV (Improved Tow Vehicle) is one of the latest members of the M113 family of vehicles and more than 2,500 have already been built for the home and export markets. The M901 has an elevating arm carrying long-range Tow launchers which are aimed and fired from within the vehicle. The missile is shown in its launch tube (1) and in post-launch configuration (2) along with smoke grenades (3) and 7.62mm ammunition (4).

LAV-25 and M2/M3 Bradley

LAV-25

Origin: Canada
Crew: 3 + 6
Armament: One 25mm cannon; one 7.62mm machine gun coaxial with main armament; one 7.62mm or 12.7mm anti-aircraft machine gun (optional); four smoke dischargers each side of turret
Combat weight: 28,400lb (12,882kg)
Engine: General Motors Detroit Diesel Model 6V-53T 6-cylinder diesel developing 275hp (205kW) at 2,800rpm
Performance: Road speed 62mph (100km/h); range 415 miles (668km); vertical obstacle 1ft 8in (0.5m); trench 6ft 9in (2.057m); gradient 60 per cent
History: To meet the requirements of the US Army and Marine Corps for a new Light Armored Vehicle (LAV) that could be rapidly transported by air, prototypes were submitted by Alvis of the UK, Cadillac Gage of the USA and General Motors of Canada, the last being based on the 8 × 8 version of the MOWAG Piranha built under licence in Canada. In the end the MOWAG Piranha was accepted with the intention that 680 would be procured for the US Army and 289 for the Marine Corps. In the event the US Army pulled out and the Marine Corps purchased a total of 758 vehicles, all of which were scheduled to have been delivered by late 1987

The Marine Corps has six versions of the LAV in service: the LAV-25 with 25mm cannon; LAV logistics with crane; LAV mortar carrier with 81mm mortar; LAV anti-tank with twin launcher for Hughes Tow missiles; LAV maintenance and recovery; and command and control vehicle. Other variants under development or expected to be procured in the future include anti-aircraft, assault gun and mobile electronic warfare vehicles.

The basic LAV 25 has a three-man crew (commander, gunner and driver) and carries six Marines in the rear, three each side facing outward, each of whom has a firing port with associated periscope. The two-man power-operated turret is armed with the same 25mm cannon as that installed in the M2 Bradley, with a 7.62mm machine gun mounted coaxially, and either a similar weapon or a 12.7mm machine gun can be mounted on the roof for anti-aircraft defence. A total of 210 rounds of 25mm and 420 rounds of 7.62mm ammunition are carried. The LAV is fully amphibious, being propelled in the water by two propellers mounted at the rear; steering is power-assisted on the front four wheels; and a full range of night vision equipment is fitted as standard.

The main advantage of the LAV-25 over the M2 Bradley IFV is that the former is not only much cheaper to procure, operate and maintain but being a wheeled vehicle it also has greater mobility on roads and can therefore be deployed from one part of the country to another faster than a tracked vehicle. The US Air Force is expected to procure a large number of LAVs in the 8 × 8 configuration under the designation of the Mobile Armored Reconnaissance Vehicle/Standoff Munition Device (MARV/SMUD) which will be used in the EOD (Explosive Ordnance Disposal) role on airfields following air attacks.

M2/M3 BRADLEY

Origin: USA
Crew: 3 + 7
Armament: One 25mm cannon; one 7.62mm machine gun coaxial with main armament; twin launcher for Tow anti-tank missiles; four smoke dischargers each side of turret
Armour: Classified
Dimensions: Length 21ft 2in (6.45m); width 10ft 6in (3.2m); height 9ft 9in (2.97m)
Combat weight: 49,802lb (22,590kg)
Ground pressure: 7.53lb/sq in (0.53kg/cm²)
Engine: Cummins VTA-903T turbocharged 8-cylinder diesel developing 500hp (372k) at 2,600rpm
Performance: Road speed 41mph (66km/h); range 300 miles (483km); vertical obstacle 3ft 0in (0.914m); trench 8ft 4in (2.54m); gradient 60 per cent
History: Developed by FMC

Corporation to meet requirements of US Army with first production vehicles completed in 1981 and first unit equipped in 1983. A total of 6,882 M2 IFV and M3 CFV vehicles will be procured by the US Army by the early 1990s

Background: The US Army has had a requirement for an IFV since the early 1960s but for a variety of reasons development was protracted and in the end one vehicle was designed for the infantry - the XM2 IFV - while the very similar XM3 Cavalry Fighting Vehicle was designed for the cavalry. These were accepted for service late in 1979 and type-classified as the M2 and M3. Production of both vehicles is undertaken by FMC Corporation at San Jose in California, and although the vehicle has been demonstrated to a number of potential customers, so far no firm export order had been placed by mid-1987.

The M2 is supplementing the M113 in the US Army, providing improved armour, mobility and firepower. The basic hull and turret is aluminium armour with an additional layer of spaced laminate armour for increased protection. The two-man power-operated turret is mounted in the centre of the hull and is armed with a stabilised 25mm cannon with a 7.62mm machine gun mounted coaxially to the right and a twin launcher for the Hughes Tow anti-tank missile on the left. A total of

Below: The LAV-25 is one of a complete family of 8×8 light armoured vehicles now in service with the United States Marine Corps. The LAV-25 has a three-man crew and can carry six fully equipped Marines, but there are also specialised versions ranging from mortar carriers to anti-tank vehicles with long-range Tow missiles.

Right: US infantry dismount from an M2 Bradley IFV. They are provided with special versions of the M16 rifle called the M231 for use from the firing ports.

900 rounds of 25mm and 1,340 rounds of 7.62mm ammunition are carried, along with seven Tow missiles.

The infantry enter and leave the vehicle via a large power-operated ramp in the rear and each man is provided with a firing port and associated periscope to enable him to use a special version of the M16 series 5.56mm rifle called the M231. The 25mm cannon is used to engage light armoured vehicles with APDS-T rounds and other targets with HEI-T, tanks being engaged with the Tow missiles. The M2 Bradley has a full range of night vision devices and an NBC system and is fully amphibious with its flotation screen erected.

The Fighting Vehicle Systems Carrier chassis uses many components of the Bradley, with the first application being the Multiple Launch Rocket System (MLRS) which has been adopted by five European countries. In the future additional improvements will be incorporated into the Bradley, and reactive armour will be added, as there has been considerable debate in the US about the vulnerability of the Bradley to many battlefield threats, especially missiles with their HEAT warheads.

Above: The FMC Corporation has built more than 3,000 M2 Bradley Infantry Fighting Vehicles for the US Army. The two-man power operated turret is armed with a 25mm cannon, 7.62mm coaxial MG and a twin Tow ATGW launcher on the left side: (1 and 3) 25mm ammunition; (2) smoke grenades; (4) LAW rocket; (5) LAW launcher; (6) Tow ATGW; (7) Tow launcher tube. The Bradley is fully amphibious.

BMP-1 and BMP-2

BMP-1

Origin: USSR
Crew: 3 + 8
Armament: One 73mm gun; one 7.62mm machine gun coaxial with main armament; one launcher over 73mm gun for AT-3 Sagger anti-tank missile
Armour: 1.29in (33mm) max
Dimensions: Length 22ft 2in (6.74m); width 9ft 8in (2.94m); height 7ft 1in (2.15m)
Combat weight: 29,762lb (13,500kg)
Ground pressure: 8.3lb/sq in (0.60kg/cm²)
Engine: Type 5D20 6-cylinder in-line water-cooled diesel developing 300hp (224kW) at 2,000rpm
Performance: Road speed 50mph (80km/h); range 310 miles (500km); vertical obstacle 2ft 8in (0.80m); trench 7ft 3in (2.2m); gradient 60 per cent
History: Developed in the early 1960s and first seen in public in 1967. In service with Afghanistan, Algeria, Bulgaria, Cuba, Czechoslovakia, Egypt, Ethiopia, Finland, East Germany, Hungary, India, Iraq, Iran, North Korea, Libya, Mongolia, Poland, Syria, USSR, North Yemen and Yugoslavia. Also built in China as the Type WZ 501

Background: Until the introduction of the BMP-1 in the mid-1960s Soviet infantry were transported as near as possible to their objective before dismounting and attacking the objective on foot. This meant that the whole momentum of the battle was slowed down. The introduction of

Right: Being the first infantry fighting vehicle to enter service with any Army, the BMP-1 had a number of shortcomings, such as the position of the commander.

Right: The introduction of the BMP-1 brought a new level of firepower to infantry vehicles. Its power operated turret is armed with a 73mm gun, 7.62mm coaxial machine gun and an AT-3 Sagger ATGW over the main armament, and it is fully amphibious and equipped with an NBC system.

the BMP, however, allowed the infantry to fight from within the vehicle, since each of the eight men carried is provided with a firing port for his rifle or machine gun and an observation periscope, and the vehicle was fitted with a more powerful armament system. (Early Soviet APCs such as the BTR-50P and BTR-152 had open tops, so the infantry were not protected from the elements, overhead shell splinters or NBC attack, and armament normally comprised one or two 7.62mm machine guns in unprotected mounts.)

The BMP-1 has the driver seated front left, with the vehicle commander to his rear and the engine compartment to his right. In the centre of the vehicle is a large one-man power-operated turret armed with a 73mm gun fed by an automatic loader and firing HEAT or HE-FRAG rounds; a total of 40 rounds of 73mm ammunition is carried. A 7.62mm machine gun is mounted coaxially with the main armament and 2,000

rounds are carried for this weapon. Over the 73mm gun is a launcher for the AT-3 Sagger wire guided anti-tank missile, and in addition to the single round in the ready-to-launch position a further four missiles are carried in reserve. The eight infantry are seated in the rear, four on each side facing outward, and enter via two doors in the hull rear.

The BMP-1 is fully amphibious, being propelled in the water by its tracks, and is fitted with an NBC system and a full range of night

vision equipment for commander, gunner and driver. Specialised versions of the BMP-1 include a command post vehicle, a mobile training centre, the BMP-R reconnaissance vehicle and the BRM-1, which is fitted with a Small Fred radar.

BMP-2

Origin: USSR
Crew: 3 + 7
Armament: One 30mm cannon; one 7.62mm machine gun coaxial with main armament; one launcher for AT-5 Spandrel anti-tank missiles; three smoke dischargers each side of turret
Armour: 1.29in (33mm) max
Dimensions: Length 22ft 0in (6.71m); width 10ft 2in (3.09m); height 6ft 9in (2.06m)
Combat weight: 32,187lb (14,600kg)
Ground pressure: 9.1lb/sq in (0.64kg/cm²)
Engine: 6-cylinder super charged diesel developing 400hp (298kW)
Performance: Road speed 40mph (65km/h); range 372 miles (600km); vertical obstacle 2ft 3in (0.7m); trench 8ft 2in (2.5m); gradient 60 per cent
History: Developed in the late 1970s and first seen in public in 1982. Still in production and known to be in service with Czechoslovakia, East Germany and the USSR

Background: While the BMP-1 was a giant step forward the vehicle did have two main disadvantages: the commander, being seated to the rear of the driver, had restricted vision, and the 73mm gun was inaccurate. The BMP-2 is designed to remedy these deficiencies. Slightly larger than BMP-1, it seats the driver front left with one infantryman to his rear and the engine compartment to his right. In the centre is a two-man (commander and gunner) powered turret armed with a 30mm cannon that fires AP-T or HE-T rounds and a coaxial 7.62mm machine gun.

Mounted on the turret roof is a launcher for the AT-5 Spandrel anti-tank missile; additional missiles are carried inside for manual reloading, and some vehicles have been observed fitted with the shorter-range AT-4 Spigot. Both the AT-5 and the AT-4 are second-generation missiles and all the gunner has to do to ensure a hit is to keep his cross-hairs on the target. Mounted on each side of the turret there is a bank of three electrically operated smoke dischargers, though both the BMP-1 and the BMP-2 can also lay their own smoke screens by injecting diesel fuel into the exhaust outlet on the left side of the hull.

As the turret of BMP-2 is much bigger than that of the BMP-1 there is only space for six infantrymen at the rear; these are seated three on each side facing outward. There are four firing ports in the left side of hull, three in the right side and one in the left rear door, which also contains some diesel fuel. Like the BMP-1, the BMP-2 is fully amphibious and has a full range of night vision equipment and an NBC system. While there is much debate on the role of the IFV on the high-intensity battlefield it is interesting to note that the USSR was the first country to field a vehicle of this type: the US Army did not field its own infantry fighting vehicle, the M2 Bradley, until 1983.

Above: Commander and crew of a BMP-1 armoured personnel carrier at attention during a Moscow military parade; the driver's and gunner's hatches are also open. In the later BMP-2 the commander shares the two-man turret with the gunner and his place is taken by an infantryman, while only six men are carried in the aft troop compartment. The chassis of the two vehicles are almost identical, though the later model probably has increased armour protection for the crew.

Left: The BMP-2 is the replacement for the BMP-1 and has a new two-man power operated turret armed with a 30mm cannon, 7.62mm co axial machine gun and an AT-5 Spandrel ATGW launcher on the turret roof. The 30mm cannon can also be used against low-flying helicopters.

FV432 and Warrior

FV432

Origin: United Kingdom
Crew: 2 + 10
Armament: One 7.62mm machine gun; three smoke dischargers on each side of hull front
Armour: 0.32-0.47in (6-12mm)
Dimensions: Length 17ft 3in (5.25m); width 9ft 2in (2.8m); height 7ft 6in (2.87m)
Combat weight: 33,686lb (15,280kg)
Ground pressure: 11.09lb/sq in (0.78kg/cm²)
Engine: Rolls-Royce K60 No 4 Mk 4F 2-stroke, 6-cylinder multi-fuel developing 240bhp (179kW) at 3,750rpm
Performance: Road speed 32mph (52.2km/h); range 300 miles (480km); vertical obstacle 2ft 0in (0.609m); trench 6ft 9in (2.05m); gradient 60 per cent
History: Developed by GKN Sankey (now GKN Defence Operations) to meet requirements of British Army; in production (approximately 3,000 built) from 1963 to 1971; only in service with British Army

Background: In the 1950s various prototypes of fully tracked armoured personnel carriers were designed and built by the Fighting Vehicles Research and Development Establishment, but it was not until the early 1960s that one of these, the FV432, entered production as the replacement for the Alvis Saracen (6 × 6) vehicle.

In many respects the FV432 is very similar to the US M113 family of vehicles developed at the same time, the major difference being that the FV432 is of welded steel whereas the M113 is of welded aluminium and therefore not only lighter but also fully amphibious with virtually no preparation.

The FV432 has night vision equipment and, unlike many other vehicles developed in the 1960s, is fitted with an overpressure NBC system. When originally introduced into service FV432 was fitted with a flotation screen which gave the vehicle an amphibious capability, but these have been removed.

The FV432 is normally armed with a pintle-mounted 7.62mm GPMG, though some vehicles have a 7.62mm Bren LMG while others have a turret mounted over the rear of the hull roof armed with a 7.62mm GPMG and smoke dischargers.

In addition to being used as a troop carrier the FV432 is used in a wide range of other roles including towing Bar minelayer with a Ranger anti-personnel mine system installed on the roof, command post vehicle, signals vehicle with additional aerials, ambulance, 81mm mortar carrier, maintenance vehicle, recovery vehicle and carrier for a ZB298 surveillance radar or Cymbeline mortar locating radar. The FV433 Abbot 105mm self-propelled gun uses many automotive components of the FV432.

From 1987 the FV432 will be supplemented by the GKN Defence Operations Warrior mechanised combat vehicle, but as only 1,048 of the latter have been ordered the FV432 will remain in service with the British Army well into the next decade and will probably be upgraded.

WARRIOR

Origin: United Kingdom
Crew: 3 + 7
Armament: One 30mm RARDEN cannon; one 7.62mm machine gun coaxial with main armament; four smoke dischargers each side of turret
Armour: Classified
Dimensions: Length 20ft 10in (6.34m); width 9ft 11in (3.03m); height 9ft 0in (2.73m)
Combat weight: 49,603lb (22,500kg)
Ground pressure: 9.24lb/sq in (0.65kg/cm²)
Engine: Rolls-Royce CV8 TCA V-8 diesel developing 550hp (410kW) at 2,300rpm
Performance: Road speed 46.6mph (75km/h); range 310 miles (500km); vertical obstacle 2ft 6in (0.75m); trench 8ft 2in (2.5m); gradient 60 per cent
History: Developed by GKN Defence Operations to meet requirements of British Army; first production vehicle completed in December 1986

Below: Since the mid-1960s the FV432 APC has been the workhorse of mechanised infantry battalions serving with the British Army of the Rhine. Even with the introduction of the Warrior MCV large numbers will remain in service in many roles, including mortar carrier, command post, APC and specialised support vehicle. Standard armament is a 7.62mm GPMG (right) with 1,600 rounds of belted ammunition (bottom).

Above: Warrior mechanised combat vehicle moving at speed with a Challenger MBT in West Germany. In combined arms operations all vehicles must have comparable mobility and speed.

Background: The British Army started to study its requirements for a mechanised combat vehicle while the FV432 was still in production but for a variety of reasons progress was slow and it was not until the late 1970s that the first prototype was built. At one time serious consideration was being given by the British MoD to manufacturing the US FMC M2 Bradley Infantry Fighting Vehicle under licence but in the end it was decided to continue with the MCV-80.

Following extensive trials with prototypes the MCV-80 was accepted for service with the British Army in 1984 and named Warrior. A total of 1,048 Warriors are to be built for the British Army at a rate of about 130 vehicles a year.

The infantry carried in the Warrior would normally dismount and fight on foot as there is no provision for them to use their rifles from inside the vehicle, whereas the M2 and Soviet BMP-1/BMP-2 are provided with firing ports and vision devices.

The armament of the Warrior is the Royal Ordnance 30mm RARDEN cannon, already installed in the Scimitar and Fox reconnaissance vehicles. This highly accurate weapon fires APSE-T, HEI-T and the new APDS round which will penetrate 1.57in (40mm) of armour. A McDonnell Douglas Helicopters 7.62mm Chain Gun, manufactured under licence by Royal Ordnance, is mounted coaxially with the 30mm cannon. Warrior represents a substantial improvement in armour, mobility and firepower compared with the FV432 and gives the British infantry a capability it has never before possessed.

Variants of the Warrior under development for the British Army include command post vehicle, mechanised repair and recovery vehicle, mortar carrier, engineer vehicle and artillery observation vehicle. The vehicle has already been demonstrated in Kuwait, Saudi Arabia and Turkey and GKN Defence Operations is proposing a wide range of variants, including a light tank armed with 105mm gun and anti-tank and anti-aircraft missile carriers, for the export market.

Below: The first Warrior mechanised combat vehicle was handed over to the Grenadier Guards in mid-1987 and a total of 1,048 are to be delivered. The Warrior has greater armour protection, firepower and mobility than the FV432 which it is replacing in many units, and the 30mm RARDEN cannon, already installed in the Fox and Scimitar, will defeat light armoured vehicles such as the Soviet BMP-2. Ammunition carried includes smoke grenades (1 and 2), 30mm ammunition (3,4, 5 and 6) for the RARDEN and 7.62mm machine gun ammunition in belts (7).

BTR-70, MT-LB and BMD

BTR-70

Origin: USSR
Crew: 2 + 9
Armament: One 14.5mm machine gun; one 7.62mm machine gun coaxial with main armament
Armour: 0.35in (9mm) max
Dimensions: Length 24ft 9in; (7.54m) width 9ft 2in (2.80m); height 7ft 7in (2.32m)
Combat weight: 25,353lb (11,500kg)
Engines: 2 × ZMZ-4905 6-cylinder petrol developing 115hp (86kW) each
Performance: Road speed 49.7mph (80km/h); range 372 miles (600km); vertical obstacle 1ft 8in (0.5m); trench 6ft 7in (2.0m); gradient 60 per cent
History: Developed in late 1970s and first seen in 1980; known to be in service with East Germany

Background: The BTR-70 is a further development of the BTR-60 (8 × 8) armoured personnel carrier which first entered service with the Soviet Army in 1960. Main improvements of the BTR-70 over the BTR-60PB include better protection over the frontal arc, more powerful engines for an improved power-to-weight ratio and a small entry hatch between the second and third road wheels. The manual turret of the BTR-70 is identical to that installed on the BTR-60PB and has 14.5mm and 7.62mm machine guns which can be elevated from −5° to +30°; turret traverse is a full 360°. A total of 500 rounds of 14.5mm and 2,000 rounds of 7.62mm ammunition are carried.

The BTR-70 is fully amphibious, being propelled in the water by a single water jet at the rear, and is fitted with an NBC system and night vision equipment. An unusual feature of the BTR-60, BTR-70 and later BTR-80 is that they are powered by two engines at the back, one of which drives four wheels on one side of the vehicle. The latest 8 × 8 APC, the BTR-80, which has already seen combat in Afghanistan, has a single 260hp (193kW) diesel, six smoke dischargers on the turret rear, guns that can be elevated to +60° and improved means of entry and exit for the troops.

MT-LB

Origin: USSR
Crew: 2 + 11
Armament: One 7.62mm machine gun
Armour: 0.27-0.55in (7-14mm)
Dimensions: Length 21ft 2in (6.45m); width 9ft 4in (2.85m); height 6ft 1in (1.86m)
Combat weight: 26,234lb (11,900kg)
Ground pressure: 6.54lb/sq in (0.46kg/cm²)
Engine: YaMZ 238 V V-8 diesel developing 240hp (179kW) at 2,100rpm

Above: MT-LB multi-purpose armoured vehicle of the East German Army towing a 100mm anti-tank gun. To lower the ground **pressure for use in snow and swampy ground the MT-LB can be fitted with wider tracks. The vehicle is fully amphibious.**

Below: The BTR-70 8×8 APC is a further development of the older BTR-60 vehicle and has the same turret as the BTR-60PB. It is used in large numbers by the Soviet motorised rifle divisions and has seen extensive use in Afghanistan. Like all Soviet wheeled AFVs it is fitted with a central tyre pressure regulation system.

Performance: Road speed 38mph (61.5km/h); range 310 miles (500km); vertical obstacle 2ft 4in (0.7m); trench 8ft 10in (2.7m); gradient 60 per cent

History: The MT-LB multi-purpose armoured vehicle was developed to meet a wide range of roles within the Soviet Army, including towing anti-tank guns carrying specialised communications equipment and acting as an armoured personnel carrier, especially in snow and swamp-covered terrain where its low ground pressure gives it a number of advantages over the more heavily armed and armoured BMP-1 and BMP-2. In service with Bulgaria, Czechoslovakia, Finland, East Germany, Hungary, Poland, the USSR and Yugoslavia. Still in production

Background: The MT-LB is one of the most versatile vehicles in service with the Soviet Army, although its original role was to replace the old AT-P armoured tracked artillery tractor. For example, infantry units on the Norwegian border use the MT-LB in place of other vehicles since it has a very low ground pressure and can be fitted with special wide tracks for use in snow conditions. The

vehicle is armoured only against small arms fire and shell splinters, and armament is limited to a manually operated turret with a 7.62mm machine gun mounted on the forward right side of the hull roof. Troops enter and leave via two doors in the hull rear.

The MT-LB is fully amphibious, being propelled by its tracks at a speed of 3.1-3.7mph (5-6km/h) and is fitted with night vision equipment and an NBC system. Specialised versions include the MT-LBU command vehicle, MTP-LB repair vehicle, ambulance, engineer vehicle, radar carrier with both Pork Trough and Big Fred radars, and it forms a basis for the SA-13 Gopher SAM system.

BMD

Origin: USSR
Crew: 7
Armament: One 73mm gun; one 7.62mm machine gun coaxial with main armament; one Sagger anti-tank missile over 73mm gun; two bow-mounted 7.62mm machine guns
Armour: 0.905in (23mm) max
Dimensions: Length 17ft 9in (5.4m); width 8ft 8in (2.63m); height 6ft 6in (1.97m)
Combat weight: 14,770lb (6,700kg)
Ground pressure: 8.67lb/sq in (0.61kg/cm²)
Engine: Type 5D-20 V-6 liquid-cooled diesel developing 240hp (179kW)
Performance: Road speed 43.5mph (70km/h); range 200 miles (320km); vertical obstacle 2ft 8in (0.8m);

trench 5ft 3in (1.6m); gradient 60 per cent

History: The BMD airborne combat vehicle was developed to improve the firepower and mobility of Soviet airborne divisions; until the introduction of the new vehicle they used light trucks. First seen in November 1973 although it entered service in 1970

Background: The introduction of the BMD into the restructured Soviet air assault divisions has given these units the ability to deploy quickly from their landing zones to wherever they are required, and BMD-equipped units spearheaded the Soviet invasion of Afghanistan.

The BMD has an unusual layout, with the driver front and centre, the vehicle commander to his left and on his right the bow machine gunner, who operates two 7.62mm machine guns, one mounted in the corner of each side of the hull firing forward. The gunner is in a one-man turret identical to that installed on the BMP-1. The other three crew members are seated in the small troop compartment to the rear of the turret with the engine compartment right aft. The BMD is fully amphibious, being propelled in the water by two water jets at the rear of the hull, and is fitted with an NBC system and night fighting equipment. More recently some vehicles have had the Sagger removed and an AT-4 Spigot mounted on the roof. There are many variants of the BMD, including a version with six road wheels a and 120mm assault weapon.

Left: The MT-LB is used for a wide variety of roles on the battlefield ranging from towing anti-tank guns, carrying radars and specialised electronic equipment to use as an APC in marginal terrain.

Below: The BMD airborne combat vehicle was designed specifically for use by the Soviet Air Assault Divisions and spearheaded the Soviet invasion of Afghanistan in 1979. The BMD has the same turret as the BMP-1 infantry fighting vehicle and has a crew of seven men. Like most Soviet light AFVs it is fully amphibious.

Marder and Fuchs

MARDER

Origin: West Germany
Crew: 9
Armament: One 20mm cannon; one 7.62mm machine gun coaxial with main armament; one remotely controlled 7.62mm machine gun at rear; six smoke dischargers
Armour: Classified
Dimensions: Length 22ft 3in (6.79m); width 10ft 8in (3.24m); height 9ft 10in (2.98m)
Combat weight: 64,374lb (29,200kg)
Ground pressure: 11.66lb/sq in (0.82kg/cm²)
Engine: MTU MB 833 Ea-500 6-cylinder liquid-cooled diesel developing 600hp (447kW) at 2,200rpm
Performance: Road speed 46.6mph (75km/h); range 323 miles (520km); vertical obstacle 3ft 3in (1m); trench 8ft 2in (2.5m); gradient 60 per cent
History: Developed to meet the requirements of West German Army with production being undertaken by Thyssen-Henschel and Krupp MaK between 1970 and 1975

Background: Before World War II the German Army pioneered close cooperation between tanks and other units, especially armoured infantry. This philosophy continued in the postwar period with a whole family of fully tracked armoured vehicles being developed. The first ones to enter service were the Jagdpanzer Kanone armed with a 90mm gun and the Jagdpanzer Rakete armed with SS-11 anti-tank missiles. Development of the MICV, which eventually entered service as the Marder, was protracted, with no fewer than three series of prototypes being built, each an improvement over the earlier model.

The end result was the Marder, which entered service with the West German Army in 1971 and until the

Below: The Marder's two-man turret is armed with a Rheinmetall 20mm co axial machine gun. The 20mm cannon fires HEI-T (1) and API-T (2) rounds and the grenade launchers on forward part of the turret fire various grenades (3 and 4) while 7.62mm ammunition is in belts (5). Many Marders now have a Milan ATGW on the turret.

Above: The Marder was the first infantry fighting vehicle to enter service in the West and further improvements are planned to extend its operational life into the next decade.

introduction of the US Bradley in the early 1980s was the only vehicle of its type in the West, though the Soviets had earlier fielded the BMP-1.

The Marder is well armoured and is fitted with a two-man power-operated turret armed with an externally mounted 20mm cannon and 7.62mm machine gun, the former capable of knocking out light armoured vehicles and penetrating the sides and rear armour of MBTs. Many Marders have been fitted with the Euromissile Milan second-generation wide-guided anti-tank missile to engage enemy tanks out to a range of 2,187 yards (2,000m). When the vehicle originally entered service a 7.62mm machine gun was mounted over the rear troop compartment but this has been removed from many vehicles.

The six infantrymen enter and leave via a large power-operated ramp in the rear, and a spherical firing port with a periscope above in each side of the hull allows the infantry to aim and fire their weapons from within the vehicle if required by the tactical situation. The Marder is fitted with an NBC system and a full range of night vision equipment, now being upgraded with passive devices.

Although there were many projected variants, some of which were even built at prototypes, the only vehicle in service is the Radarpanzer TUR which has a radar mounted on a hydraulic arm. The chassis is also used as the basis for the Roland SAM system and the Argentinian TAM tank.

FUCHS

Origin: West Germany
Armament: One 7.62mm machine gun; six smoke dischargers
Armour: Classified
Dimensions: Length 22ft 2in (6.76m); width 9ft 9in (2.98m); height 7ft 7in (2.3m)
Combat weight: 37,478lb (17,000kg)
Power-to-weight ratio: 18.82hp/tonne (14kW/tonne)
Engine: Mercedes-Benz OM 402A V-8 liquid-cooled diesel developing 320hp at 2,500rpm
Performance: Road speed 65mph (105km/h); range 500 miles (800km); vertical obstacle not available; trench not available; gradient 70 per cent
History: Developed from mid-1960s with a total of 996 production vehicles being built by Thyssen-Henschel for West German Army between 1979 and 1986 and 10 supplied to Venezuela

Background: The Transportpanzer 1 (Fuchs) armoured personnel carrier was developed at the same time as

the Spähpanzer Luchs (8 × 8) reconnaissance vehicle and shares a number of common components. The vehicle is fully amphibious, being propelled in the water by two propellers mounted at the rear of the hull; before entering the water a trim vane is erected at the front of the hull and the bilge pumps are switched on. Standard equipment includes night vision devices and an NBC system.

The basic Transportpanzer is fitted with a 7.62mm machine gun though other weapons such as a 20mm cannon can also be installed. The Transportpanzer 1 can carry up to 14 fully equipped troops but in the West German Army it is normally used for specialised roles, including battlefield surveillance with the RASIT radar on an elevating mount, command and communications, carrying combat engineers and their specialised equipment, NBC reconnaissance with special equipment for taking soil samples for analysis inside the vehicle, electronic warfare equipment carrier and supply carrier.

A whole series of vehicles was projected for the export market but despite extensive overseas demonstrations only Venezuela placed firm orders for the Transportpanzer 1 with two roof-mounted machine guns. An 8 × 8 version was built in prototype form for the Netherlands Army but never entered production. Automotive components of the Transportpanzer were also used in the Krauss-Maffei Wildcat twin 30mm air defence weapon, yet to enter production, and a 4 × 4 version called the Transportpanzer 2 did not progress past the prototype stage.

West Germany has very strict export controls on military equipment and so far this has virtually limited sales of armoured vehicles and similar equipment to NATO countries.

Above: The Transportpanzer Fuchs has full 6 x 6 drive and is fully amphibious, being propelled in the water by two propellers mounted under rear of the hull. Compared to many other vehicles on the world market, however, it is expensive and complicated, so export sales have been very limited, though Venezuela has 10.

Below: A total of 996 Transportpanzer 1 Fuchs vehicles have been delivered to the West German Army, which uses them for a wide range of specialised roles. This Fuchs 6 x 6 vehicle has a 7.62mm MG3 machine gun above the commander's hatch and a bank of Wegmann smoke discharges on the left side of the hull. The latter fire various grenades (1 and 2), such as smoke or fragmentation, while 7.62mm ammunition is in belts (3) for ready use.

AH-64 Apache

Origin: USA
Engines: Two 1,696shp General Electric T700-701 turboshafts
Dimensions: Main rotor diameter 48ft 0in (14.63m; length over tail rotor ignoring main rotor 48ft 2in (14.68m); height overall to tip of air-data sensor 16ft 9.5in (5.12m)
Weights: Empty 11,015lb (4,996kg); primary mission gross weight 14,694lb (6,665kg); maximum take-off 17,650lb (8,006kg).
Performance: Maximum level speed 186mph (300km/h); max cruise 182mph (293km/h); max sea level vertical rate of climb 2,500ft (762m)/min; OGE hover ceiling 10,200ft (3,109m); max range on internal fuel 428 miles (689km)

Background: The US Army recognised the potential and the need for a dedicated armed helicopter in the early 1960s, but it was not until 1976 that the Hughes YAH-64 was selected for production ahead of the rival Bell YAH-63. Subsequent development was protracted, hundreds of small and large changes being introduced before production was authorised in March 1982. Apart from the rotors, most of each Apache is made by Teledyne Ryan, and Hughes — since 1984 a subsidiary of McDonnell Douglas — assembles the helicopters at a new plant at Mesa, Arizona.

Compared with the prototype AH-56 Cheyenne of 20 years earlier, the Apache is roughly the same size, rather less powerful (though it has two engines instead of one) and somewhat slower. Avionics are in many ways similar, and in fact in some respects the earlier machine was more versatile. The biggest advances are in survivability, the Apache having IR-suppressed engines, comprehensive electronic warfare installations and, above all, an airframe and systems designed to survive strikes from fire of up to 12.7 and 23mm calibre.

In general the whole helicopter is conventional, with an all-metal semi-monocoque fuselage and stainless- steel/glassfibre rotor blades. Main blades are attached by multi-laminate straps with quickly removed pins for folding. The hub is articulated, with offset flapping hinges and elastomeric lead/lag dampers. As in the AH-1 Cobra the pilot sits above and behind the copilot/gunner and non-retracting tailwheel gear with long-stroke main units are designed to cushion crash descents. The tailplane is a powered control surface.

The Apache's eyes are its TADS/PNVS (target acquisition/designation sight and pilot's night vision sensor). Though independent the two systems are physically linked and work in parallel. TADS comprises direct-view optics with wide-field 18° and magnified 4° fields of view, a TV camera (0.9° and 4° FOVs), a laser spot tracker and an International Laser Systems laser rangefinder/designator. These are all mounted in a turret able to rotate ±120° in azimuth, +30° up and −60° down and there are extensive fuselage boxes, as well as a primary display for the copilot/gunner. The

TADS can also be swithed to provide the back-up night vision to the pilot in the event of PNVS failure.

The PNVS is simply a FLIR, gyrostabilised and mounted in its own turret above the nose (±90° in azimuth, +20°/−45° vertically). The FLIR has narrow, medium and wide FOV, respectively 3.1°, 10.1° and 50.0°. The FLIR infomation is normally presented on a monocular IHADSS (integrated helmet and display sighting system) on which is superimposed key flight data such as airspeed, radar altitude and heading. In emergency either crew-member can receive video from either the TADS or the PNVS, and both wear IHADSS.

Weapons comprise a remotely aimed gun and stores carried under fixed wings. The gun, contracted for along with the helicopter, is the Hughes 30mm M230A1 Chain Gun, a unique single-barrel weapon with external power and a rotating bolt driven by a chain which permits a simplified cycle. In the Apache it is normally controlled to 625rds/min, the magazine capacity being 1,200 rounds. Lear Siegler provide the electronic control system, with aiming possible anywhere in the area covered by the sighting systems. In a crash the complete gun mount collapses upwards between the cockpits.

The weapon wings, of 17ft 2in (5.23m) span, can carry four pylons each supporting either a quadruple group of Hellfire anti-tank missiles (maximum 16) or a 19-tube 2.75in rocket launcher (maximum 76 rockets); or up to four 192 gal (871 lit) external fuel tanks. The accompanying illustration also shows the armament proposed for the naval version, which would carry air-to-air missiles (initially AIM-9L Sidewinders) on the wingtips, and various attack missiles up to the size of the AGM-84 Harpoon anti-ship cruise missile.

The Apache production programme has fluctuated in size but since 1984 has stabilised at a planned 675 for the US Army alone, notwithstanding a price much more than double the original celing figure (a rise caused mainly by inflation).

Left: An AH-64 Apache fires a salvo of Hydra 70 rockets at the US Army's Yuma proving ground. The rockets are launched from 7-round or 19-round pods, are provided with a comprehensive range of warheads and have a maximum range of 9,600 yards (8,800m).

Below: The Apache was designed as a dedicated tank-killer, and its normal operational weapons load is restricted to the built-in 30mm Chain Gun (7 and 8) plus a maximum of four quad Hellfire missile launchers (6), each of which can be replaced by a seven-round (2) or 19 round (3) rocket pod. Quad Tow launchers (9) are the AH-1 Cobra's standard anti-tank missile. The 5in Zuni rocket (4) is an option for US Marine Corps AH-1 SeaCobra helicopters and could be carried by naval Apaches, which might also use Harpoon

(5) or Penguin (10) anti-ship missiles. Self-defence missiles could include Stinger (12) or Sidewinder (13), and the anti-radar Sidearm (11) derivative of the latter is available for defence suppression. Additional fuel can be carried in tanks (1) for ferry missions and standard countermeasures equipment includes the M130 chaff dispensers (14) and ALQ-144 IR jammer (15).

Mi-24 Hind

Origin: Soviet Union
Engines: Two 2,200shp Isotov TV3-117 turboshafts
Dimensions: (estimated) Diameter of five-blade main rotor 55ft 9in (17.0m); length with rotors turning 68ft 11in (21m); fuselage length 60ft 8in (18.5m); height with rotors turning 21ft 4in (6.5m)
Weights: (estimated) Empty 16,534lb (7,500kg) — official Western estimate is 18,250lb (8,400kg); normal loaded 24,250lb (11,000kg)
Performance: Maximum level speed in service about 199mph (320km/h), but A-10 (the Mil design bureau designation) helicopters of the Hind-C type, without modification, have set speed records at up to 228.9mph (368.4km/h); cruising speed (full weapon load) 183mph (295km/h); maximum rate of climb 2,953ft (900m)/min; hovering ceiling OGE 7,218ft (2,200m); official Western estimate of combat radius is 99 miles (160km), but an A-10 has set a record at full throttle round a 621-mile (1,000km) course.

Background: The Soviet Union has always shown itself willing to finance totally new weapons to meet specific requirements, even when it would be simpler and cheaper to modify an existing design. This family of helicopters was regarded as so important that it is based on a completely new design, despite the fact that it bears a very close resemblance to the Mi-8. Compared with the earlier model the Mi-24 is slightly smaller, and has a much smaller main rotor and it was originally sized to carry a unique mixture of eight troops in a cabin as well as heavy loads of attack weapons, including missiles. New versions introduced greater power, new rotors and a new tandem-seat forward fuselage. For ten years production at two plants, at Arsenyev and Rostov, has exceeded 15 per month, and more than 300 have been exported outside the Warsaw Pact.

No other helicopter combines the weapons, sensors, armour and flight performance of this family, to say nothing of adding a cabin for eight troops, or four stretcher casualties, or urgent front-line cargo, including reloads for the helicopter's own weapon launchers. The main rotor has a fully articulated hub of machined steel, with the usual hydraulic lead/lag dampers, and retains the blades by unusually short coupling links. These are bolted to the extruded multiple spars of titanium alloy, around which are bonded the honeycomb-filled glassfibre skins. The leading edge of each blade has an anti-erosion strip and electrothermal de-icing, and a balance tab is fitted to the outer trailing edge. The tail rotor has three alumunium-alloy blades and except for the first Mi-24 version is on the left of the fin, a modification which substantially reduced rotor 'slap' and tail-rotor noise.

The metal fuselage is not of the pod-and-boom form but is quite streamlined, and the tricycle landing gears are fully retractable. The main

Right: Missing its wingtip AT-2 Swatter anti-tank missiles but mounting the standard rocket pods, an example of the Mi-24 Hind-A, which paved the way for the much more heavily armed Hind-D and Hind-E gunship variants.

gears fold straight back, up and in to stow the wheels transversely, while the twin-wheel nose unit is longer in current versions to provide ground clearance for the chin-mounted sensors. The large wings, which are always fitted, are set at a high angle of incidence and provide about a quarter of the lift in cruising flight, thereby unloading the rotor and increasing attainable speeds. They also have pronounced anhedral, which enables rockets and missiles to be loaded easily from ground level.

The engines are close together ahead of the gearbox, and usually have hemispherical inlet protectors to deflect ice and other matter. Above and between the engines is the oil cooler, and aft of the rotor is an APU mounted transversely.

The first production versions, called Hind-A, -B and -C, had a large four-seat cockpit (pilot, copilot, navigator/gunner and forward observer) with access via the two giant left-side windows, the forward one hinging up and the bulged rear one sliding aft. The main cabin has a large door on each side whih opens above and below, the lower section having integral steps. Current Hind-D and -E — export versions of the latter are designated Mi-25 — have a flight crew of only two, the weapon operator in front having a canopy hinged to the right and the pilot, above and behind, having a door on the right. All versions have extensive armour.

All versions also have extremely comprehensive electronic flight-control and engine-management systems, communications and all-weather navaids including a projected map display. The long nose probe is a sensitive low-airspeed system. Most versions have an electro-optical (LLTV) sensor on the tip of the left wing or, in the case of Hind-A, in the top of the left inboard pylon. Under the nose on Hind-A is an optical gunsight. Hind-D and -E have an impressive group of sensors including radar and LLTV and, since 1982, a FLIR. All feed the integrated front cockpit sight system. Outstandingly comprehensive electronic and infra-red warning and jamming systems are installed.

Hind-A carries a manually aimed 0.5in (12.7mm) nose gun and six pylons, usually loaded with four UV-16-57s and two pairs of AT-2 Swatters. Many other stores can be carried up to an external weight of 3,307lb (1,500kg). Hind-D has a four-barrel 12.7mm gun turret under the nose, but Hind-E replaces this with a GSh-23L cannon fixed on the right side, and can fire AT-6 Spiral laser-homing missiles instead of AT-3s.

Despite the appearance of the Mi-28 Havoc the versatile Mi-24/25 remains in full-scale production for Warsaw Pact forces and for export, and is almost certainly being continually developed and updated.

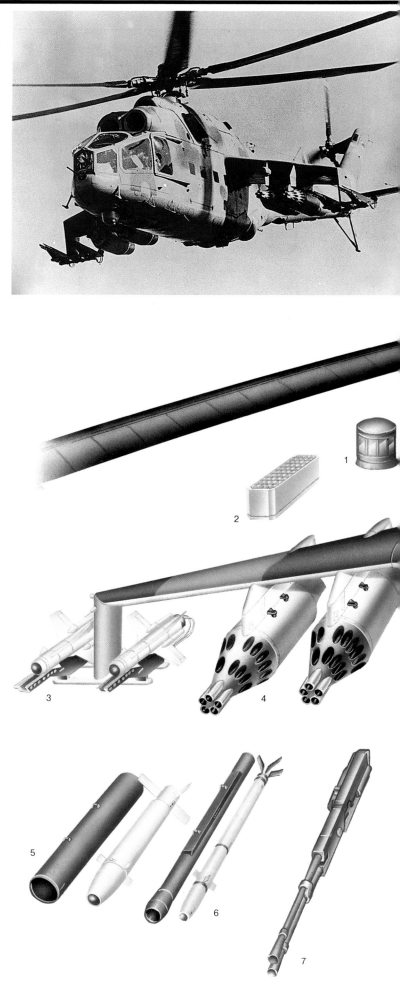

Below: The Hind-D, with its unique combination of weapons, sensors and accommodation for combat troops, is an integral component of Soviet tactical formations. Like any helicopter which expects to survive on a modern battlefield it carries countermeasures in the form of an infra-red jammer (1) and chaff/flare dispenser (2), while standard offensive weapons include twin launch rails (3) for AT-2 Swatter (15) or AT-3 Sagger (14) anti-tank missiles on each wingtip (3), UV-16-57 16-round or UV-32-57 32-round rocket launchers (4) for 57mm rockets (13) and a four-barrel 12.7mm chain gun (8). The Hind-E variant replaces the 12.7mm gun with a 23mm twin-barrel cannon (7) and has AT-6 Spiral missiles (5). Other armament options depicted here include tube-launched SA-7 Grail anti-aircraft missiles (6), 240mm (9), 210mm (10) and 160mm (11) rockets and FAB-250 bombs (12). This example of the Hind is shown with an IR-suppressive shroud fitted over the port engine exhaust.

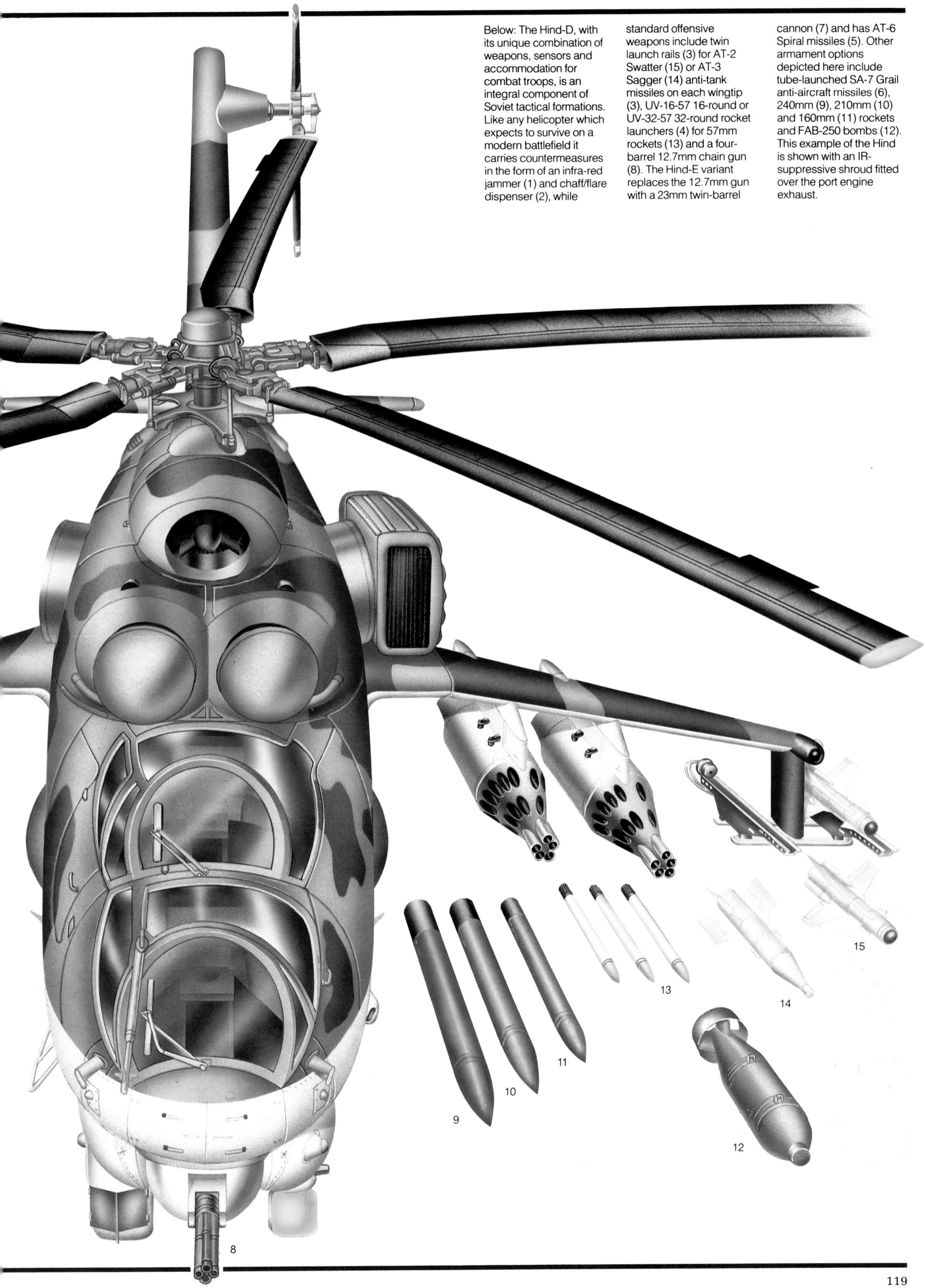

Mangusta

Origin: Italy

Engines: Two 952shp (708kW) Rolls-Royce Gem 2 Mk 1004D turboshaft engines

Dimensions: Diameter of four-blade main rotor 39ft 0.5in (11.9m); length with rotors turning 46ft 10.6in (14.29m); height over tail rotor 10ft 10.5in (3.315m)

Weights: Empty equipped 5,575lb (2,529kg); maximum loaded 9,093lb (4,100kg)

Performance: Maximum speed at sea level 16 mph (259km/h); max rate of climb 2,090ft (637m)/min; OGE hover ceiling 7,840ft (2,390m); basic mission with full weapon load is fly 62 miles (100km) to battle area, loiter for 90 min including 45min hover, and return to base with 20min reserve

Background; Like the A 109A, of which it was originally a derivative, this anti-armour helicopter underwent several changes of configuration, weight and power. Originally it was similar to the A 109 in weight, with C20 engines of 420shp, but continued growth in 1978-80 resulted in a switch to engines of more than double the power. The Mangusta (Mongoose) was designed to meet the requirements of the Italian army (Esercito), and its all-round capability is such that it obviously meets the needs of almost all other modern armies. The current plan is to equip two squadrons each of 30, with another six for training, deliveries starting in early 1987. It would be strange if many other orders did not follow.

Though originally based on the A 109A, the A 129 soon became a totally new helicopter, with dynamic parts of wholly new design marking a great upgrading in power and capability. The main rotor is larger than that of the A 109A and has composite blades with a glassfibre spar, composite skins, Nomex honeycomb cores and stainless-steel leading edge, while the sheath tip, which will be frangible, may be of BERP (British Experimental Rotor Programme) type in the production helicopter. All parts of the main and composite tail rotor and transmission are designed to have ballistic tolerance against hits by 12.7mm projectiles, and to have 'considerable tolerance' against 23mm. All bearings in the articulated main hub are elastomeric, requiring no maintenance, and all parts of the helicopter are designed for easy access and minimal maintenance requirements.

The fuselage makes extensive use of composites and metal honeycomb panels. All parts are designed to withstand 12.7mm fire, and the A 129 meets the stringent crash demands of MIL-STD-1290. External paint is IR absorbing and has a low optical signature. The nose gunner and backseat pilot both have Martin-Baker HACS 1 (helicopter armoured crashworthy seat) seats, flat-plate canopies with hinged doors and explosively jettisoned side panels.

Typical of the advanced damage-resistant design features is the use of three separate hydraulic systems for flight control, one of them driven off the tail-rotor gearbox, and two further systems for rotor and wheel braking. The tailwheel type landing gears are designed for ground impacts at vertical velocities up to 15ft (4.6m)/sec. Left and right fuel systems, with crossfeed, have particularly advanced protection systems and digital control. The engine installations are designed for minimum noise and exhaust IR signature. Dual Dowty Boulton Paul/Nardi hydraulic power units drive multilaminate glassfibre rotor swashplates, the flight control system being mechanical with dual fly-by-wire backup for the main rotor and FBW for the tail rotor with mechanical backup.

The A 129 has been designed to fly by day or night in any weather. All operative items are linked by a Harris IMS (integral multiplex system), an advanced digital data bus which controls FBW flight manoeuvres, engines, navigation, communications, flight director, autopilot, full condition monitoring for engines/fuel/transmission/electrics/hydraulics, flight performance/caution/warning systems, and weapons fire control. The IMS computer can store ten complex flight plans or 100 waypoints, and works in conjunction with doppler and radar altimeter for NOE control.

In the cockpit are MFDs giving complete displays of all navigation, performance, radio, weapon and warning information, with synthetic maps showing targets and hostile defences. The main nose sensor — likely to be moved to a mast — is a PNVS (pilot's night vision sensor), with FLIR information presented through an IHADSS (integrated helmet and display sighting system) worn by both crew members. Other devices include a GEC Avionics omni-air-data system and comprehensive radar and laser warning receivers and various radar jammers, IR jammers and chaff/flare dispensers.

Inner armament stations are stressed to 661lb (300kg) and outers to 441lb (200kg); all can be elevated 3° and depressed 12°. Initial basic armament of eight Tow on the outers can be supplemented by various gun or rocket pods on the inners, alternatives to Tow includinng eight Hot or six Hellfire. Other weapons include self-defence air-to-air missiles, such as Sidewinder or Stinger.

In April 1985 Agusta signed an agreement with Westland for an A 129 Mk 2, probably powered by a 2,308shp (1721kW) RTM 322 engine, to meet a remarkably tardy requirement for the UK.

Above: An Italian Army A 129 Mangusta in standard anti-armour configuration, with quadruple launchers for Tow anti-tank missiles on the wingtip armament stations and seven-round launchers for 70mm rockets inboard. Guns can replace the rocket pods.

Below: The A 129 Mangusta could carry most Western attack helicopter stores. Standard anti-tank weapons are quad launchers (6) for Tow missiles (7), and a typical complement would be 19-round, 12-round or 7-round rocket launchers (3) or pods for twin 7.62mm machine guns (2), a single 12.7mm machine gun (10) or three-barrel 20mm cannon (21) or flexible mounts for a 7.62mm six-barrel Minigun (11) or 12.7mm heavy machine gun (13). Triple Hellfire rails (18) or quad launchers (8) for Hot anti-tank missiles (9) could replace Tow on the wingtip stations, while the 68mm SNEB rocket pod (15) could replace the standard HL-7-70 (14) or HL-19-70 (17) 70mm rocket pods, and a proposed naval variant could carry Sea Skua (16) or Marte (19) anti-ship missiles. As well as chaff/flare dispensers (5) and IR jammers such as the ALQ-144 (22), the Mangusta could employ Stinger (1), Sidewinder (4) or Matra Mistral (20) air-to-air missiles for self defence, and external fuel tanks can be carried on the inboard underwing stations (12).

Lynx

Origin: Great Britain
Engines: Two Rolls-Royce Gem turboshafts; (most) 900shp Gem 2, (AH.5,7) 1,120shp Gem 41-1; (Lynx-3) 1,346shp Gem 60
Dimensions: Diameter of four-blade main rotor 42ft 0in (12.8m); length, rotors turning (most) 49ft 9in (15.16m), (-3) 50ft 9in (15.47m); length, main blades folded (most) 43ft 2.3in (13.16m), (-3) 45ft 3in (13.79m); height over rotors (most) 12ft 0in (3.66m), (-3, MMS not fitted) 10ft 10in (3.3m)
Weights: Empty (AH.1) 5,683lb (2,578kg), (-3, estimate) 7,114lb (3,227kg); maximum takeoff (1) 10,000lb (4,536kg), (-3) 13,000lb (5,897kg)
Performance: (maximum weight) Maximum speed at sea level 190mph (306km/h); cruising speed (1) 161mph (259km/h), (-3) 172mph (277km/h); maximum rate of climb (1) 2,480ft (756m)/min; hovering ceiling OGE (1) 10,600ft (3,231m); typical range with troops, 20min reserve (1) 336 miles (541km), (-3) 385 miles (620km)

Background: Originally designated WG.13, the Lynx is the only helicopter to have been designed by Westland; it was also the first metric British design. Planned as a multirole military, naval and civil machine in the 4.5-ton class, it quickly proved outstanding in such matters as flight performance, agility (including aerobatics) and mission versatility, and in the Falklands its toughness was also apparent (in contrast to some other helicopters).

As part of the Anglo-French Helicopter Agreement of 1967 Aérospatiale were awarded 30 per cent of the manufacturing task, this being the intended French proportion of purchases. In fact France has so far bought 12 per cent, and competed with the Lynx wherever possible: nevertheless, the British machine has sold to 11 air forces and navies. First generation Lynx are all broadly similar, being divided into skid-equipped army versions and wheel-equipped naval models, each group having appropriate avionics and weapons.

In 1984 Westland flew the first second-generation Lynx-3 (not to be confused with the earlier Lynx HAS.3 of the Royal Navy). The Lynx-3 is a larger, heavier and more powerful machine being developed in army and navy versions.

Like all parts of the Lynx, the engines, gearboxes and rotors were designed to incorporate state-of-the-art late-1960s technology. The compact three-shaft engines have electrically de-iced inlets and are fed from bag tanks with a fuel capacity of 1,616lb (733kg) — 2,205lb (1,000kg) in the case of the Lynx-3 — with every conceivable arrangement for front-line fuelling/defuelling. The main gearbox has conformal gears and set new standards in compact design with few parts, while the main rotor hub is machined from a single titanium forging and its four extension arms are attached direct to tubular ties whose end-fittings are bolted to the blade root.

Each rotor blade has a stainless-steel two-spar box to which is bonded a Nomex-filled glassfibre rear section. The Lynx-3 blades are entirely of filament-wound composite construction with advanced BERP (British Experimental Rotor Programme) tips. The tail rotor has a light-alloy spar (all-composite in the Lynx AH.7 and Lynx-3, with rotation reversed to reduce noise). Current Lynx have a fixed half-tailplane at the top on the right side of the swept fin. the Lynx-3 has a large symmetric tailplane of inverted aerofoil profile at the bottom of the tailboom, the army variant also having end-plate fins; all these tail surfaces are fixed.

The fuselage is a streamlined pod-and-boom, mainly light alloy but with much glassfibre. The two hinged cockpit doors and large sliding cabin doors are all jettisonable. Behind the pilots' seats the minimum cabin length is 81in (2.06m), width 70in (1.78m) and height 56in (1.42m); the Lynx-3 cabin is 12in (0.3m) longer. Normal loads in the Lynx AH.1 include 10 armed troops, three stretchers and attendant or a cargo load of 2,000lb (907kg) internal of 3,000lb (1,361kg) external. Lynx-3 internal payload is 3,400lb (1,542kg).

Westland offer a tremendous variety of customer options, but standard kit includes a GEC Avionics autopilot-autostabilisation system. Missile-armed versions have various targeting system options, but the British Army AH.1 and 7 have the Hughes Tow sight (made by BAe) on the cockpit roof. In 1986 BAe received a £60m contract to add a full night-vision capability. Standard ECM dispenser is ALE-39. The Lynx-3 can have TADS/PNVS or other sensors in the nose, on the roof or in an MMS, and an IRCM jammer will be carried. All data will be digital, via 1553B bus.

The 60 anti-tank AH.1s of the British Army each carry eight Tow anti-tank missiles plus eight reloads in the cabin, or a team of three gunners with their own launcher and missiles; in addition, all the weapons depicted in the accompanying illustration have been cleared for use. The Lynx-3 is expected to carry eight or 16 Hellfire anti-tank missiles instead of Tow, plus Stinger air-to-air missiles.

Almost all future development is concentrated on the formidable Lynx-3, which though initially a dedicated anti-armour helicopter is also the obvious starting point for an important new generation of multirole tactical helicopters.

Above: An Army Lynx equipped for the anti-armour mission, with roof-mounted sight and quad Tow missile launchers. The cabin can accommodate eight reloads for the missile launchers or an anti-tank team of three gunners with their own missiles and launchers.

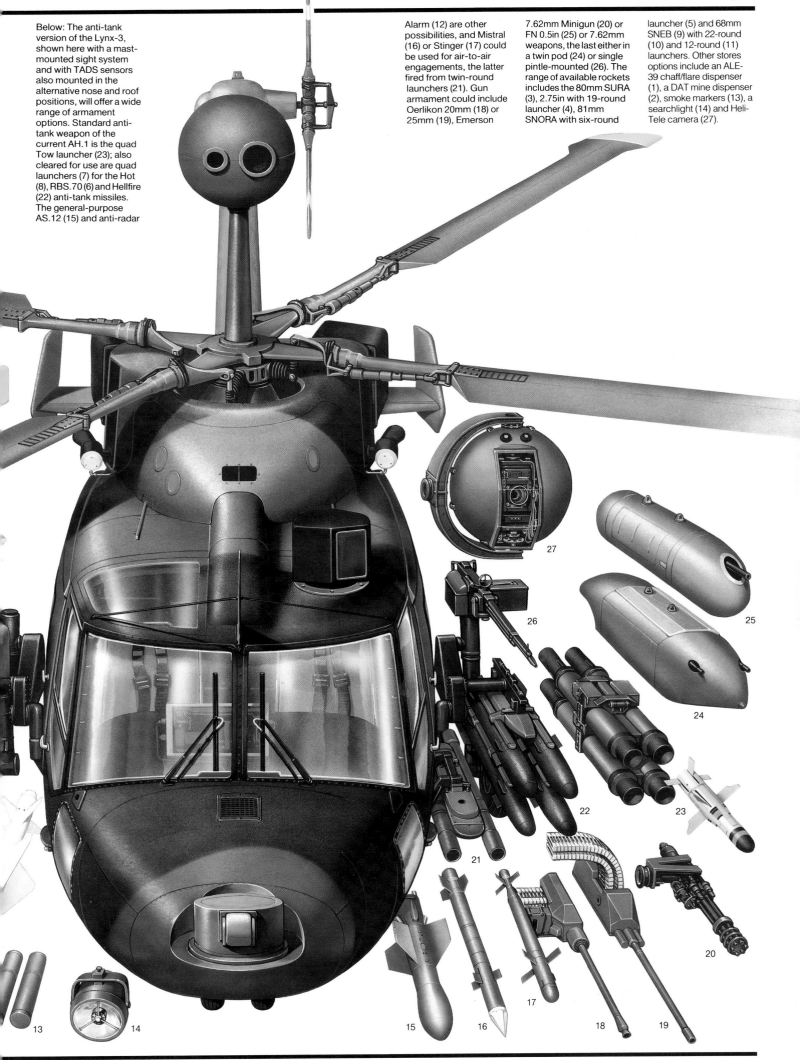

Below: The anti-tank version of the Lynx-3, shown here with a mast-mounted sight system and with TADS sensors also mounted in the alternative nose and roof positions, will offer a wide range of armament options. Standard anti-tank weapon of the current AH.1 is the quad Tow launcher (23); also cleared for use are quad launchers (7) for the Hot (8), RBS.70 (6) and Hellfire (22) anti-tank missiles. The general-purpose AS.12 (15) and anti-radar

Alarm (12) are other possibilities, and Mistral (16) or Stinger (17) could be used for air-to-air engagements, the latter fired from twin-round launchers (21). Gun armament could include Oerlikon 20mm (18) or 25mm (19), Emerson

7.62mm Minigun (20) or FN 0.5in (25) or 7.62mm weapons, the last either in a twin pod (24) or single pintle-mounted (26). The range of available rockets includes the 80mm SURA (3), 2.75in with 19-round launcher (4), 81mm SNORA with six-round

launcher (5) and 68mm SNEB (9) with 22-round (10) and 12-round (11) launchers. Other stores options include an ALE-39 chaff/flare dispenser (1), a DAT mine dispenser (2), smoke markers (13), a searchlight (14) and Heli-Tele camera (27).

2S5 and DANA

2S5

Origin: USSR
Armament: One 152mm gun
History: Developed to meet the requirements of the Soviet Army; entered service in late 1970s; not yet seen in public and not known to have been exported

Background: For many years after the end of World War II the Soviet Union relied almost exclusively on towed artillery weapons to provide fire support for its tank and motorised rifle divisions. Since the mid-1970s, however, a complete range of self-propelled guns and howitzers have been developed, although not all have entered service and only two, the 2S1 and 2S3, have made public appearances in Red Square.

Towed artillery is very cheap to build, operate and maintain but the crew and weapon are very vulnerable to small arms fire and shell splinters, the weapon usually takes several minutes to come into and be taken out of action, the vehicle is difficult to operate in an NBC environment and, above all, it lacks the cross-country mobility to keep up with mechanised units, which can easily leave their fire support

behind. According to US Intelligence sources the Soviet Union has been producing 1,000 self-propelled artillery weapons a year since 1984, with additional systems being produced in other Warsaw Pact countries, and it is estimated that by 1986 the Soviet Union had some 28,000 artillery weapons larger than 100mm, of which about 24,000 were towed and the remainder self-propelled.

The 122mm 2S1 and 152mm 2S3 are widely deployed but no information is available on the 2S2 or

2S6. The 155mm 2S5 self-propelled gun has never appeared in public, but is believed to be based on the chassis of the GMZ mine layer and has a long-barelled 152mm gun mounted in an open mount at the very rear of the chassis with the engine compartment at the front; before firing starts a large spade is lowered to the ground at the rear. It is believed that the 2S5 fires an HE or nuclear projectile to a maximum range of 29,527 yards (27,000m) or a rocket-assisted projectile to 40,463 yards (37,000m).

The 2S4 is a 240mm self-propelled mortar with the tube being carried in the horizontal position on the hull top and swung through about 120 39 so that it points to the rear. The mortar is breech-loaded and has a very low rate of fire of about one round per minute and a maximum range of 13,889 yards (12,700m). Types of mortar bomb fired include tactical nuclear, chemical, high explosive and concrete piercing.

The 203mm 2S7, which entered service in 1977, has a new chassis with the fully enclosed crew

Left: The Soviet 152mm 2S3 self-propelled gun-howitzer is the Soviet counterpart to the American 155mm M109 series. It has been exported to East Germany, Iraq and Libya and fires ammunition of the separate loading type, including nuclear rounds.

Right: The 2S5 is yet another of the more recent Soviet artillery systems that has yet to make its first public appearance, although photographs taken in East Germany have been released. In addition to firing conventional projectiles, including rocket assisted rounds, the 2S5 has a tactical nuclear capability.

compartment overhanging the front of the vehicle and the weapon being mounted on the hull at the rear. A large power-operated spade is lowered to the ground before firing commences and there is also a hydraulically operated loading device as the projectiles and charges are so heavy. No firm details of the types of ammunition fired by the 2S7 have been released but they would include chemical, high explosive and nuclear of which a maximum range of 32,808 yards (30,000m) has been quoted.

DANA

Origin: Czechoslovakia
Crew: 7 (estimate)
Armament: One 152mm howitzer; one 12.7mm anti-aircraft machine gun
Armour: Classified
Dimensions: Length including main armament 34ft 2in (10.4m); hull length 29ft 1in (8.87m); width 9ft 9in (2.97m); height 11ft 7in (3.52m)
Combat weight: 50,706lb (23,000kg)
Ground pressure: Not available
Engine: Tatra T-928 V-12 multi-fuel developing 345hp (257kW) at 2,200rpm
Performance: Road speed 50mph (80km/h); range 621 miles (1,000km); vertical obstacle 1ft 10in (0.6m); trench 6ft 7in (2m); gradient 60 per cent
History: Developed to meet requirements of Czechoslovakian Army with chassis being based on automotive components of the Tatra 815 (8 × 8) truck chassis. Entered service with Czechoslovakian Army in 1981 and also exported to Libya

Background: It is often believed in the West that members of the Warsaw Pact all use the same common equipment, but this is not always the case and there are many examples of countries like Czechoslovakia, Hungary and Poland developing their own equipment. For example, Czechoslovakia and Poland jointly developed the OT-64 (8 × 8) amphibious armoured personnel carrier which they use in place of the Soviet BTR-60PB; more recently Czechoslovakia has developed an 8 × 8 self-propelled howitzer called DANA which is the only wheeled self-propelled artillery weapon currently in service. (South Africa has developed the G6 (6 × 6) self-propelled artillery system, but this has yet to enter service, and a European company is developing a 6 × 6 155mm or 203mm self-propelled artillery system as a private venture.)

For many countries a wheeled self-propelled artillery weapon has great advantages over its tracked counterpart, being cheaper to design and build and easier to operate and maintain; the DANA also uses automotive components such as engine, transmission, suspension and wheels that are already in production for other applications. A wheeled weapon also has much greater strategic mobility, especially where there is a well established road network, and enables weapons to be quickly deployed from one part of the country to another.

Although the DANA uses automotive components of the famous Tatra 815 cross-country truck, it has a quite different layout with the fully armoured and enclosed cab at the front, the armoured turret in the centre and the engine and transmission at the very rear; all eight wheels are powered, with steering being power-assisted on the front four wheels. A central tyre pressure regulation system is standard and this allows the driver to adjust the tyre pressure to suit the type of ground being crossed.

Before firing commences three stabilisers are lowered hydraulically to the ground, one at the rear and one on each side between the second and third road wheels. The 152mm howitzer fires separate-loading ammunition to a maximum range of 18,700 yards (17,100m) or 26,246 yards (24,000m) with a rocket-assisted projectile. A 12.7mm machine gun is mounted on the turret roof for local and anti-aircraft defence.

Left: The 152mm DANA (8 × 8) self-propelled howitzer has been developed to meet the requirements of the Czechoslovakian Army and uses automotive components of the Tatra 815 cross-country truck. DANA entered service in 1981 and has been exported to Libya. It features a central tyre pressure regulation system operated by the driver.

SP-70 and GCT

SP-70

Origin: West Germany, Italy and the United Kingdom
Crew: 5
Armament: One 155mm howitzer; one 7.62mm anti-aircraft machine gun; four smoke dischargers each side of turret
Armour: Classified
Dimensions: Length including main armament 33ft 7in (10.235m); hull length 25ft 1in (7.637m); width not available; height not available
Combat weight: 95,953lb (43,524kg)
Ground pressure: Not available
Engine: MTU MB 871 turbo-charged 8-cylinder diesel developing 987hp (736kW)
Performance: No details released
History: Development started in 1973, but in late 1986 the whole SP-70 project was cancelled

Background: The United Kingdom was project leader for the towed 155mm FH-70 while West Germany was project leader for the self-propelled version called the SP-70. Full development began in 1973 and by that time the basic ordnance had already been well proved and it appeared to be a simple matter to design a new chassis and a new fully enclosed turret with an automatic loading system to enable a high rate of fire to be achieved. The West German Army had a requirement for 400 systems while Italy wanted 90

Right: The cancellation of the 155mm SP-70 project in late 1986 after the expenditure of almost £270m has left each of the three countries involved — West Germany, Italy and the UK — searching for new 155mm self-propelled artillery systems. The British Army was the first to issue a formal request to industry in December 1986; proposals were returned in mid-1987.

and the United Kingdom 221.

West Germany was responsible for the complete powerpack and chassis, ordnance with cradle extension, flick rammer and loading system, while the United Kingdom was responsible for the welded aluminium turret, the ammunition handling system (which held 32 projectiles), the sighting system and the traverse gearbox, and Italy was responsible for the auxiliary power unit, fuel system, combined balancing and elevating system and the elevation mass. By 1986 the SP-70 would still not work correctly all the time and from all accounts the required high rate of fire, essential on the battlefield today, could not be achieved consistently.

Accordingly, late in 1986 the three countries agreed to go their own way. The British Army is now studying four proposals to meet its future requirements, including the purchase of more M109A2s from the United States, the new private venture AS-90 from Vickers Shipbuilding and Engineering, the M109UK being promoted by Royal Ordnance and a version of the SP-70 offered by Vickers Defence Systems. West Germany is purchasing more M109A2s which will be fitted with the ordnance of the FH-70 and other modifications, and Italy is considering a number of options; OTO Melara is already upgrading a number of Italian Army M109s and has already produced a large number

of 155mm Palmaria self-propelled howitzers for the export market.

There are probably many lessons to be learned from the demise of SP-70, but the fact is that after 15 years of development and the expenditure of some £88 million by each of the three countries all that remained was 15 prototypes which did not always work.

GCT

Origin: France
Crew: 4
Armament: One 155mm gun; one 7.62mm or 12.7mm anti-aircraft machine gun; two smoke dischargers each side of turret
Armour: 3.14in (80mm) max
Dimensions: Length including main armament 33ft 8in (10.25m); hull length 22ft 0in (6.7m); width 10ft 4in (3.15m); height 10ft 8in (3.25m)
Combat weight: 92,593lb (42,000kg)
Ground pressure: Not available

Engine: Hispano-Suiza HS 110 12-cylinder water-cooled super-charged multi-fuel developing 720hp (537kW) at 2,000rpm
Performance: Road speed 37mph (60km/h); range 280 miles (450km); vertical obstacle 3ft 0in (0.93m); trench 6ft 3in (1.9m); gradient 60 per cent
History: Developed to meet the requirements of the French Army under the name GCT (Grande Cadence de Tir) with first prototype being completed in 1972 and first production vehicles in 1977. In service with France, Iraq and Saudi Arabia

Background: Whereas West Germany, Italy and the United Kingdom developed the 155mm FH-70 towed howitzer first and then the self-propelled SP-70, France developed the self-propelled gun first following up much later with the towed TR.

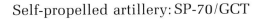

Above: By mid-1987 GIAT had built about 300 GCT self-propelled artillery systems for the French, Iraqi and Saudi Arabian armies. In the French Army each GCT regiment has four batteries of five GCT weapons with each battery tied into the ATILA artillery fire control system.

The GCT is essentially a slightly modified AMX-30 MBT chassis fitted with a new fully enclosed power-operated turret mounting a 155mm gun with a double baffle muzzle brake. Turret traverse is a full 360° and the ordnance can be elevated from —4° to +66°, and a very high rate of fire can be achieved with the help of the automatic loader in the turret rear which contains 42 projectiles and charges. A typical ammunition load would consist of 36 high explosive and six smoke or 30 high explosive, six illuminating and six smoke. The wide range of projectiles that can be fired by the weapon includes Type 56/59 HE, smoke phosphorus, training and illuminating shells, a projectile carrying six anti-tank mines (under development), and rocket-assisted and base bleed rounds for extended range performance, the last having a maximum range of 31,676 yards (28,500m).

Mounted on the turret roof is a 7.62mm machine gun, for which a total of 2,050 rounds are carried, or a 12.7mm M2 HB with 800 rounds. The GCT can be brought into action in under two minutes and takes one minute to come out of action. The maximum rate of fire with the automatic loader is 8 rds/min; in the event of failure the weapon can be loaded manually at two or three rounds a minute, and the turret can be reloaded in 15 minutes.

The ability to fire a large number of rounds is of crucial importance as modern target location systems can detect where the rounds are being fired from; this information can be passed to friendly artillery units and counter battery fire started within seconds. The actual gun is, however, only one part of an overall artillery system, which also includes target acquisition systems, artillery fire control and command and control systems and ammunition resupply.

Below: Propellant for GCT rounds is in combustible cartridge cases (1) and projectiles that can be fired include Copperhead (2), HE Type 56/59 (3), Smoke F1A (4), Training (5), HE Type F1 (6), Smoke (7), Training F1 (8), Illuminating F1 (9), mine dispensing (10), GIAT HE Base Bleed (11), HE Rocket Assist (12), Luchaire HE Base Bleed (13) and ERBER HE (14). In addition, the GCT carries percussion detonators (15). The SP-70 had 76mm smoke grenades (16) while GCT has 80mm smoke grenades (17); 12.7mm machine gun ammunition (18) is in belts.

M109

Origin: USA
Crew: 6 on weapon
Armament: One 155mm howitzer; one 12.7mm M2 HB anti-aircraft machine gun
Armour: Classified
Dimensions: Length including main armament 29ft 11in (9.12m); hull length 20ft 4in (6.19m); width 10ft 2in (3.1m); height 10ft 9in (3.28m)
Combat weight: 55,000lb (24,948kg)
Engine: General Motors Detroit Diesel Model 8V-71T turbo-charged diesel developing 405bhp (303kW) at 2,300rpm
Performance: Road speed 35mph (56.3km/h); range 217 miles (349km); vertical obstacle 1ft 9in (0.53m); trench 6ft 0in (1.83m); gradient 60 per cent
History: Developed to meet the requirements of the US Army in the mid-1950s with first production vehicles completed in 1963; current production model is M109A2. In service with Austria, Belgium, Canada, Denmark, Egypt, Ethiopia, West Germany, Greece, Iran, Iraq, Italy, Jordan, South Korea, Kuwait, Libya, Morocco, the Netherlands, Norway, Pakistan, Peru, Portugal, Saudi Arabia, Spain, Switzerland, Taiwan, Tunisia, the United Kingdom and the United States (Army and Marines)

Background: During the early 1950s the standard 155mm self-propelled howitzer of the US Army was the M44. This suffered from several major disadvantages, including a very short operational range, since it was powered by a petrol engine, and the fact that the 155mm weapon was installed in an open topped crew compartment at the rear with a traverse of 60° left and right. Originally it was intended to develop a new self-propelled howitzer with the ordnance mounted in a turret that could be traversed through a full 360°: the M44 was to be replaced by a version with a 156mm howitzer while the M52 105mm self-propelled howitzer was to be replaced by a version with 110mm ordnance. In the end it was decided to remain with the existing 155mm and 105mm calibres as the ammunition was in such widespread use.

Prototypes of the new 105mm howitzer were designated T195 while the 155mm version was the T196, both of which were powered by petrol engines, but further development resulted in the T195E1 and the T196E1 with more fuel-efficient diesel engines. In the end the T195E1 was type classified as the M108 and the T196E1 as the M109. The M108 only served with the US Army for a few years as it was decided to concentrate on the M109; most of the M108s were supplied to other countries and even in 1987 these remained in service with several armies.

Since production started in 1962 the M109 series of 155mm self-propelled howitzers has become the most widely used weapon of its type in the world and is being constantly modified to meet the changing operational requirements of the artillery.

The original M109 was manufactured at the Cleveland Army Tank Plant in Ohio, a facility owned by the Army but run by private contractors — originally the Cadillac Division of the General Motors Corporation, which was followed by the Chrysler Corporation and finally the Allison Division of General Motors Corporation; the last orders were placed in fiscal year 1969.

The M109 has a hull and turret of welded aluminium armour construction that provides the crew with protection from small arms fire and shell splinters; the driver is seated front left, with the engine compartment to his right and the turret at the rear. The 155mm howitzer has a very short barrel with a large fume extractor and muzzle brake and fires a wide range of separate-loading ammunition, including high explosive, smoke, tactical nuclear, chemical, rocket-assisted high explosive and illuminating. The standard HE M107

Above and right: The M109 is the most widely used 155mm self-propelled howitzer in the world, well over 3,000 having been built so far. Since it was first introduced into service in 1963 it has been constantly improved and the Howitzer Improvement Programme (HIP) is expected to become operational later this decade in both the United States and Israeli Armies. Recently the US Army has fielded the M992 Field Artillery Ammunition Support Vehicle (FAASV) which feeds fuzed projectiles and charges through its rear door and into the gun compartment of the M109 so enabling it to maintain a full supply of on-board ammunition. The ammunition used by the M109 is of the separate loading type consisting of charge (2) and projectiles, the charge being set off by an igniter (1). Rounds available include laser-guided Copperhead (3), M483A1 improved conventional munition, shown with fusible lifting lug (4), M109 HE (5), ADAM area denial artillery munition (6), RAAMS remote anti-armor minw system (7), NC (8), M485 illuminating (9), M825 smoke, white phosphorus, with fusible lifting lug (10), M110 Agent H/HD (11) and rocket-assisted HE (12). Ammunition for the 12.7mm M2 HB machine gun is in belts (13).

round has a maximum range of 15,966 yards (14,600m).

The M109A1 is basically an M109 with a new and longer ordnance (or barrel) and other modifications which allow the HE M107 projectile to be fired to a range of 19,794 yards (18,100m). All M109A1s were conversions of original M109s, while the M109A1B produced by BMY for the export market from the early 1970s was essentially an M109 incorporating all the modifications and improvements of the M109A1.

The M109A2 was placed in production by BMY in 1978 both for the US Army and for overseas sales and is essentially the M109A1 with additional improvements in reliability, availability, maintainability and durability plus some key safety improvements. The US Army's M109A3 is the M109A1 with the same improvements of the M109A2, these modifications being carried out by the Army itself at its own depots.

Using the chassis of the M109 BMY has designed and built the Field Artillery Ammunition Support Vehicle (FAASV), which is designed to carry nearly 100 155mm projectiles and charges and feed them to the M109 when the latter is in the firing position. The FAASV was developed as a private venture but was subsequently adopted by the US Army as the M992 and is also in service with several other countries,

including Egypt, which has a command post vehicle based on a similar chassis.

As the M109 series is to remain in service with the US Army well into the 1990s another improvement programme is now under way in which Israel, one of the largest users of the M109 series, is also involved. This Howitzer Improvement Programme includes not only major improvements in the automotive

and survivability areas but may also include a new 54-calibre ordnance as a replacement for the current 39-calibre weapon which would enable ranges of 49,212 yards (45,000 metres) to be achieved.

In recent years new types of 155mm ammunition have been developed to further improve the capabilities of the M109 series. These include a rocket-assisted projectile, the Copperhead cannon-

launched guided projectile, projectiles carrying bomblets or anti-tank mines and a new tactical nuclear projectile.

Many countries have modified the vehicle to meet their own unique requirements and South Korea, Italy and the Netherlands have all been involved in some degree of local production. The M109 has proved very reliable and will remain in service well into the next century.

Above: M109 155mm self-propelled howitzer on exercise at Fort Riley, Kansas. In the US Army the M109 is normally deployed in batteries of eight guns, with each regiment having three batteries.

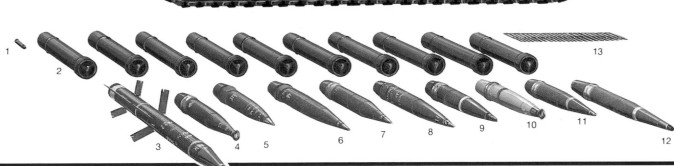

Pershing and Lance

PERSHING

Origin: USA

Pershing 1a
Dimensions: Length 34ft 6½in (10.4m); diameter 3ft 3⅓in (1.2m)
Launch weight: 10,295lb (4,670kg)
Performance: Range 112.5-460 miles (180-740km); CEP 492 yards (450m)
Warhead: Weight 650lb (295.5kg); types 60kT, 200kT and 400kT nuclear

Pershing II
Dimensions: Length 34ft 5½in (10.5m); diameter 3ft 3⅓in (1.02m)
Launch weight: 16,400lb (7,454.5kg)
Performance: Range 1,125 miles (1,800km); CEP 49 yd (45m)
Warhead: Weight 650lb (295.5kg); types 5-50kT selectable yield

Background: The two-stage solid-propellent inertially guided MGM-31 Pershing 1a missile is only used by the West German Air Force, which has a total of 72 firing platforms organised into two Flugkorpergeschwader, each of four staffeln, with nine Pershing 1a launchers apiece. There are a small number of reloads for some of these launchers as the total buy of missiles (including yearly operational testing rounds) was 137. Each firing battery consists of an articulated truck and trailer combination which serves as the TEL, a transporter for the programme tester and generator units, a firing battery control centre vehicle and a radio terminal set vehicle with an inflatable antenna. Usually the missiles are launched from pre-surveyed sites. The nuclear warheads are held under a dual-key arrangement.

In 1984 the US Army began replacing the Pershing 1a missiles with the Pershing II as an improvement to its intermediate

range theatre nuclear weapons capability. The new missile is considerably more accurate than its predecessors, using a nose cone-mounted all-weather radar correlation unit to compare radar returns from the ground with a pre-recorded on-board radar profile of the target area. Automatic comparisons of the live radar returns and the pre-recorded data provide control signals to actuate the control vanes which distinguish the Pershing II reentry vehicle from that of the older Pershing 1a. The improved accuracy allows the W50 high yield air burst warhead of the Pershing 1a to be replaced by a new variable lower yield air or ground-

Above: A Pershing II being launched from its semi-trailer during trials in the United States. Pershing II uses its on-board systems to hit targets up to 1,125 miles (1,800km) away with pin-point accuracy. The original M656 (8 × 8) trucks used to transport the Pershing 1A system are replaced by MAN trucks for Pershing II.

Above: The Pershing 1A is used only by the West German Air Force while the latest Pershing II is deployed by the US Army in West Germany as well as in the United States. Pershing II is much more accurate; fitted with an improved nuclear warhead, it is launched from a semi-trailer.

Above: A Lance surface-to-surface missile is launched from its M752 amphibious full tracked erector-launcher, a member of the M113 family. It can also be carried and

launched from a light trailer which can be slung under helicopters such as the CH-47 Chinook. A new enhanced radiation warhead is being developed.

burst W85 warhead. Prime contractor for both versions of Pershing is Martin Marietta of Florida.

By late 1985 all three Pershing battalions of the US Army in West Germany had re-equipped with the Pershing II. Each battalion has four firing batteries of three platoons, each of which has three erector/launchers towed by West German MAN (8 × 8) high-mobility cross-country trucks.

LANCE

Origin: USA
Dimensions: Length 20ft 3in (6.2m); diameter 1ft 10in (0.6m)
Launch weight: 3,920lb (1,778kg) with conventional warhead; 3,373lb (1,530kg) with nuclear warhead
Performance: Range 3-43 miles (4.8-70km) with conventional warhead, 3-75 miles (4.8-121km) with nuclear warhead; CEP 500 yd (455m)

Warhead: Weight 1,000lb (457kg) conventional, 467lb (212kg) nuclear; types M251 cluster bomblet, M234 10kT, 50kT or 100kT nuclear

Background: First thought of in 1962, the MGM-52 Lance was first test-fired in 1965 with production starting in 1971, and it entered

service with the US Army in 1971 as the replacement for the MGR-1 Honest John. Prime contractor was LTV Corporation, with FMC being responsible for the tracked launcher and Rocketdyne for the motor.

Lance is the standard NATO battlefield support missile system and is in service with the armies of the UK (one regiment of 12 launchers), West Germany (four battalions each of four launchers), Italy (one battalion of six launchers) and Belgium (one battalion of six launchers) using M84 nuclear warheads under dual-key arrangements and with the Netherlands Army (one battalion with six launchers) using the air-burst M251 cluster munition warhead filled with 836 0.95lb (0.43kg) BLU-63 anti-personnel/anti-material fragmentation bomblets. In the latter form it has also been exported to Israel for probable use in the air defence suppression role against Arab SAM sites.

The missile system is normally deployed on two tracked members of the M113 APC family, the M752 self-propelled erector-launcher vehicle with one ready-to-fire missile and the M688 loader transporter with two reloads and a loading hoist. Thi version is fully amphibious being

propelled in the water by its tracks. There is also a lightweight trailer launcher for Lance which can be towed by a light truck and is fully air transportable under a helicopter such as the Boeing Vertol CH-47 Chinook.

The inertially guided Lance has a two-part storable liquid propellent rocket motor and is spin-stabilised in flight by the expulsion of propellent gases through control vents in order to increase its accuracy. The normal nuclear weapons used in the warhead are the W70 Mod 1 and W70 Mod 2 systems with yields of 10kT, 50kT or 100kT. The Americans also have a stockpile in the United States of the W70 Mod 3 variant which has two yield option of about 0.8kT and 1.6kT. The major difference lies in the fact that the Mod 3 has an enhanced radiation feature which makes it into a neutron bomb for use against manned armour targets; it creates little blast or damage. During wartime the W70 Mod 3 payloads would be forward deployed as required for US Army.

Lance is used in battalions at Corps level by most of the NATO users, but the Israelis have organised a dedicated Lance brigade which has three launcher battalions and is used as an Army level unit.

Below: The Lance SSM was developed as the replacement for the Honest John unguided rocket and is more mobile, has a much greater range and is far more accurate. Lance is normally fitted with a tactical nuclear warhead, although Israel and the Netherlands use a conventional warhead. All the tactical nuclear warheads are under dual-key control and cannot be used by its European operators – the UK, West Germany, Italy and Belgium – without the consent of the US.

Pluton and Hades

Type: Battlefield support missile
Dimensions: Length 25ft 1in
(7.64m); diameter 25.6in (0.65m);
wing span 55.5in (1.41m)
Launch weight: 5,330.6lb (2,423kg)
Performance: Effective range 10.6-
75 miles (17-120km), CEP 164-341
yards (150-330m)
Warhead: Weight about 1,100lb
(500kg); types 15 or 25kT yield
AN51 nuclear

Background: Although fielded at
Corps level the Pluton *armement
pre-stratEgique* (pre-strategic
weapon) is actually under direct
Army command and requires the
authorisation of the French
President before it can be deployed
or fired, the idea being that its use
would show France's resolve to use
its full nuclear retaliatory capacity
if the course of action being pursued
by the enemy continued.

There are a total of five
operational Pluton Regiments 3, 4,
15, 32 and 74 RA each with an HQ
company, three launcher batteries,
a transport unit and a mechanised
infantry protection company with
ten AMX-10P ACPs. In peacetime
the guidance systems, warheads
and nuclear payloads are stored
separately from missiles. In
wartime the missile can be
assembled on the AMX-30 MBT-
derived tracked launcher either
prior to deployment or in the field,
with the components being

delivered by two heavy Berliet
trucks.

A modified Berliet GBC truck
which acts as the battery's
command, control,
communications and intelligence
(C31) centre is equipped with the
IRMC 2A data transmission system:
this uses the third-generation
digital Iris 35M general purpose
computer to process information
and program the missile guidance
systems once they are installed.
The IRMC 2A is also linked to the
Regimental command network as
well as to the Corps HQ.

These liasons are handled by two
Command teams which are
remotely located from the battery
command posts, one normally co-
located with the Regimental HQ
company receiving and
transmitting firing orders and
integrating the batteries into the
overall operational planning, while
the other is located elsewhere
maintaining absolute electronic
silence as a reserve ready to take
over if the Regimental Command
HQ and team were destroyed or
driven off the air by enemy action. If
necessary real-time target data can
be provided to the batteries by
Corps level remotely piloted
vehicles (RPVs) which can carry
out surveillance operations behind
enemy lines using data links, IR
line-scan sensors and optical
reconnaissance cameras.

For a rear area target the 25kT
yield warhead would be used in
either ground or air-burst
configuration, depending on how
well protected it was, while for area
targets near the forward line of
troops such as troop or vehicle
concentrations the 15kT warhead
in air-burst configuration would be
used. It is also possible that an
enhanced radiation ('neutron
bomb') warhead exists.

A total of 42 launcher vehicles
have been built to equip the five

regiments, provide a small attrition
reserve and allow for operational
training and development needs.
The missile itself is of the single-
stage inertially guided type with a
solid propellant dual-thrust rocket
propulsion motor.

A replacement system known as
Hades is already under
development for initial
deployment in 1992. Originally all
the Pluton Regiments were to be
replaced by only four Hades units,
with the latter being grouped

Left: The Pluton missile is
transported by and
launched from an
armoured tracked chassis
based on the AMX-30
MBT and is fitted with a
tactical nuclear warhead
which is under French
Government control. A
total of four Pluton
regiments are in service
and the missile can be
fitted with a 15kT or 25kT
tactical nuclear warhead.

together under the operational command of a single artillery Division with its own support and air defence regiments for self defence. Control of this Division would be undertaken by the French Armed Forces Chief-of-Staff in accordance with the French Nuclear doctrine.

However, as a result of budgetary considerations this programme may well have to be reduced to just three Regiments fielded at Corps level, the reduction in overall

numbers being compensated for by the use of a wheeled launcher vehicle with at least one reload round being carried; additional rounds would be available from the Regimental supply unit, and the missile would have a range of around 220 miles (352km) and be armed with a 60kT yield nuclear warhead. The first flight tests of the missile are due in 1987-88 with the weapon expected to show a significant increase in accuracy over the Pluton.

The Hades system will consist of a semi-trailer towed by a 4x4 tractor vehicle, the semi-trailer carrying a ready-to-launch missile and a reload round. For firing the missile has to be raised to the vertical position. The tractor/trailer combination will carry all of the necessary fire control equipment including a data transmission unit so that when a Hades launcher arrives at a preselected firing point the crew does not have to perform any manual operations outside the

launch cab, a necessary precaution in what may well be a possibly hostile radiation or chemically contaminated environment.

The prime contractor for Hades, as well as for the Pluton system, is Aérospatiale, under the guidance of the Direction des Engins. All the nuclear warheads for both systems are the responsibility of the Commissariat à l'Energie Atomique (Atomic Energy Commission) which designs, tests and builds the production model.

Right: Hades is currently under advanced development to replace the Pluton system and will be transported and launched from a semi-trailer towed by a 4×4 truck, each of which will carry two missiles. In addition to having a much longer range and being more accurate, Hades will also have a more powerful tactical nuclear warhead.

Above: Pluton entered service with the French Army in 1974. It has a dual-thrust solid propellant rocket motor which gives a range of up to 75 miles (120km).

MLRS

Origin: USA
Dimensions: Length of rocket 12ft 11in (3.94m); diameter 8.66in (227mm)
Weight: Phase I rocket 675.4lb (307kg) Phase II rocket 566.5lb (257.5kg) Phase III rocket about 550lb (250kg)
Range: Phase I rocket 20 miles (32km) Phase II rocket 25 miles (40km) Phase III rocket 28.125 miles (45km)
Warhead weight: Phase I (bomblet carrier) 333.8lb (154kg); Phase II (anti-tank mine carrier) 235.4lb (107kg); Phase III (terminally guided submunition) about 231lb (105kg)

Background: The concept phase for a new multiple rocket launcher system for the US Army began in 1976 and by 1980 Vought had a contract to develop its system. In production and in service with the USA and ordered by France, Italy, the Netherlands, West Germany and the United Kingdom.

The MLRS is based on the three-man M987 Fighting Vehicle System Carrier; weighing 55,420.2lb (25,191kg) fully loaded, it is fitted

with a lightly armoured cab with its own NBC defence system and the launcher fire control unit and computer. The vehicle is based on the M2 Bradley IFV chassis and carries a Launcher/Loader Module (LLM) which has a twin-boom crane unit for the self-loading and unloading of the two 4,994lb (2,770kg) fully loaded six-round Launch Pod Containers (LPCs). Ripples of up to twelve rockets can be fired at any one time, though re-aiming has to be automatically performed between each launch by the onboard fire control system as a result of the displacement of the vehicle by the launch forces released.

The launcher, or Self-Propelled Launcher Loader (SPLL) as it is formally known, is in service with the US Army in West Germany and South Korea as well as in the continental United States, and well over half the 300 plus SPLLs planned for the 41 batteries had been delivered by mid-1987. By 1980 the US Army had already made the MLRS programme a multinational one, and a second production line is

Above: Each Vought Multiple Launch Rocket System has 12 rockets in the ready to launch position; once expended these are replaced by fresh pods, each holding six rockets. The US Army has already fielded over half its intended 41 MLRS batteries and each US division — except airborne, light and air assault divisions — has one combined M110A2/MLRS battalion.

Above and right: The Vought Multiple Launch Rocket System (MLRS) is already operational with the US Army in the continental United States, Europe and South Korea. The Netherlands has ordered the system direct from the United States while France, West Germany, Italy and the United Kingdom have formed a consortium to make the complete

system and its rockets in Europe. The basic MLRS rocket (1) has a warhead (2) that carries 644 M42 (3) submunitions with HEAT warheads for top attack of armoured vehicles. For the longer term the US Army has started to develop the long-range TACMS (4), which is designed to have a conventional warhead. The West German Army will use MLRS to deliver

AT-2 anti-tank mines: each MLRS rocket would have 28 mines (5) in seven units of four (6); the warhead (7) is similar to that of the standard MLRS submunition. In the future a new warhead with terminally guided submunitions (8) is being developed by a consortium drawing on the expertise of both European and US companies.

to be set up in Europe. Apart from a few initial systems bought from Vought the European nations involved in the work will receive, from 1991 onward, the United Kingdom 67 (out of 71 total) SPLLs, West Germany 200 (202), France 55 (56) and Italy 20 (20). In addition, the Netherlands has ordered 30 SPLLs from the American production line.

In practically every case the army involved will use the MLRS to replace elderly tube artillery, a doctrine which is diametrically opposite to all that the Soviets have done since they introduced MRLs during World War II.

There are three types of warhead. The basic Phase I type, which is already in service and will be the standard type for all MLRS users, carries a total of 644 0.5lb (0.23kg) ribbon-stabilised M77 dual-purpose shaped-charge fragmentation bomblets, derived from the M42 type used in the conventional warhead variant of the Lance SSM and capable of penetrating light armour plate. The targets assigned to Phase I rockets are artillery and missile batteries, airfields, the assembly

areas of mechanised infantry units, radar sites and choke points such as road and rail junctions or river crossing points.

The Phase II warhead, which was developed by West Germany and has entered production for its army and, eventually, Italy, is designed specifically to engage armour concentrations. It consists of 28 Dynamit Nobel AT-2 anti-tank mines in seven submunition carriers that are ejected at a pre-determined height of around 3,940ft (1,200m) above the target area; individual mines are then released from the carriers some seven seconds later and are slowed down by parachutes so that they land with the correct orientation on the ground. On impact the parachute is released and the mine's trigger wires armed, and if not exploded by an armoured vehicle the mine will automatically detonate after one of six available pre-set intervals has elapsed. A single SPLL can lay 336 mines into an area 1,100 yd by 5,500 yd (1,000m by 5,000m) within a minute of the firing sequence starting at a range up to 25 miles (40km) from its launch

position. The AT-2 is designed to penetrate up to 5.5in (140mm) of armour plate.

The final warhead, the Phase III type, had only just entered its full-scale development stage by mid-1987 as a joint project between US, German, French and British companies, and initial deployment with MLRS users was not due until 1992. The payload will be six millimetre-wave active radar terminally guided submunitions. Over the general target area a time fuze will release the weapons, which then begin individual glide manoeuvres to allow their radars to acquire a target. Once a valid one is detected the submunition initiates a terminal top-attack dive onto the target, where its contact fuze detonates the shaped charge warhead.

Other warheads known to be under examination by the Americans include a binary chemical type which has a payload of 91.9lb (41.8kg) of chemicals which form a semi-persistent nerve gas agent when mixed, and the MLRS-SADARM, which has similar

characteristics to the Phase II head but carries six sense and destroy armour (SADARM) submunitions.

For the future, Vought has been selected to develop the new Army Tactical Missile System (TACMS) as the non-nuclear armed successor to the Lance tactical battlefield support missile. TACMS is designed to be carried and fired by the M987 MLRS SPLL with a single missile in its container-launcher replacing an LPC, and it is intended that the weapon will initially carry a payload of scatterable or terminally guided submunitions to attack enemy second-echelon forces. Provisional estimates for TACMS give a length of 13ft (3.96m) and a diameter of 2ft (0.61m), and an advanced single-stage solid propellant rocket motor should give a maximum range of 150 miles (240km). Further warheads will include types designed to attack hard targets, SAM sites and airfields. It is hoped that the first TACMS missile will be in service by 1991/92, and only software changes in the MLRS fire control computer should be required to integrate it into the overall system.

SS-1 Scud, SS-21 Spider and SS-23 Scarab

SS-1 SCUD

Origin: USSR
Dimensions: (Scud B) length 37ft 4¾in (11.4m); diameter 2ft 9in (0.84m)
Launch weight: 14,043lb (6,370kg)
Performance: Range 50-112 miles (80-180km) with nuclear warhead; 50-174 miles (80-280km) with conventional warhead; CEP 1,017-1,640 yd (930-1,500m) depending on range
Warhead: Weight 1,892lb (860kg); types HE, chemical, training, 40kT or 100kT tactical nuclear

Background: Classed as an operational tactical missile system by the Soviets, the NATO-designated SS-1 Scud B (Soviet designation R17E) entered service in the mid-1960s as a product-improved version of the earlier SS-1A Scud A (Soviet designation R-7) and SS-1B Scud B (Soviet designation R-17). Early Scuds were mounted on an obsolete tank chassis but current models are carried by and launched from an 8 × 8 chassis with good cross-country mobility.

Deployed by the Soviets at army and front levels in brigades of three TELs and three reload vehicles, Scud is being replaced by the SS-23 Spider. However, it is still in service with all the Warsaw Pact nations and has been exported to Egypt, Iraq, Iran, Libya, North Korea, South

Above: Soviet Scud-B missiles on their MAZ (8 x 8) transporter, erector, launchers (TEL) during a training exercise. In wartime they would be widely separated to avoid detection and destruction.

Below: The SS-23 Scarab has been developed as the replacement for the SCUD and started to replace the SS-1 system in 1985. It is transported and launched from an 8 x 8 cross-country chassis. When in travelling configuration the missile lies within the protection of the hull like the SS-21.

Left: The SS-21 Spider is now replacing the old FROG-7 missile and is more accurate and has a longer range. Each Soviet tank and motorised rifle division has two batteries of SS-21s and the system has already been exported to Czechoslovakia, East Germany, Iraq and Syria. It is transported and launched from a fully amphibious 6 x 6 chassis· which is also used as the basis for the SA-8 SAM system which is also now in service.

Yemen and Syria. The first combat use was by Egypt during the 1973 Arab-Israeli war, since when it has been used by both sides in the Gulf war as one of the main weapons in the 'Battle of the Cities' and by Libya, which fired two against an Italian island in the southern Mediterranean following the American raids on Libya in 1986.

In all cases the weapon has proved to be of more use against area targets such as cities than when aimed at specific targets such as command centres. As far as is known only HE warheads have been used to date.

SS-21 SPIDER

Origin: USSR
Dimensions: Length 19ft 8in (6.0m); diameter 2ft 10in (0.85m)
Launch weight: 3,000kg (6,614lb)
Performance: Range 8.7-74.6 miles (14-120km); CEP 50-110 yd (50-100m)
Warhead: Weight 450kg (992lb); types 10kT and 100kT nuclear, HE, anti-personnel bomblet and persistent chemical agent

Background: The NATO-designated SS-21 Spider — Soviet name Tockha (Point) — entered full service in 1978 and is a more accurate and longer-range replacement for the FROG-7 tactical missile. It is armed within a fully protected shelter located in the belly of a lightly armoured 6 × 6 derivative of the same Type 593

Below: Although the Scud B is now being replaced by the longer-range SS-23 system, it remains in service with many countries and has recently been used by both Iraq and Iran in the Middle East conflict. So far only high explosive warheads have been used in combat and delivery of these has proved to be inaccurate.

vehicle that is used as the basis for the SA-8 Gecko mobile SAM system.

The transporter-erector-launcher (TEL) is fully amphibious and requires four stabilising jacks to be lowered to the ground before a launch can occur; the double doors in the roof are opened before the missile is raised into the vertical position at the rear of the vehicle prior to missile launch. The missile is inertially guided and is of the single-stage solid-propellent type.

In the Soviet Army the SS-21 is deployed in the rocket battalions of the tank and motorised rifle divisions; each battalion has two firing batteries with two TELs apiece. The batteries also contain their own logistic support and command elements, including meteorological radars, and there is at least one reload per TEL.

The relatively new SS-21 has already been exported to the armies of Czechoslovakia, East Germany, Iraq and Syria, the last two countries having only conventionally armed warheads. By early 1987, according to the British Ministry of Defence, about 100 SS-21 missile launchers had been deployed in East Germany and Czechoslovakia.

SS-23

Origin: USSR
Dimensions: Not known
Launch weight: Not known
Performance: Range 50-311 miles

(80-500km); CEP 328 yd (300m)
Warhead: Weight 2,200lb (1,000kg); types HE, chemical, anti-material, cluster munition or 200kT tactical nuclear

Background: Development of the NATO-designated SS-23 began in 1975 as the replacement for the SS-1 Scud series; the first service trials were undertaken in 1980 with full service introduction occurring in 1985. The missile is carried in a fully protected shelter located within the belly of an eight-wheeled MAZ chassis, and the TEL (transporter-erector-launcher) probably requires stabilising jacks to be lowered before a missile can be launched. The missile has to be raised into the vertical position at the rear of the vehicle.

The missile is inertially guided and is of the solid-propellent type, which allows a much faster time into action and refire periods than liquid-fuelled models. Used solely by the Soviet Army, it is deployed in the rocket brigades of the Army and Front level as a one-to-one replacement for the Scud. By early 1987 significant numbers were in service but according to the British Ministry of Defence none had been deployed with Soviet formations stationed in East Germany or Czechoslovakia. By the middle of the year there had been substantial progress in talks aimed at eliminating such weapons.

BM-21 and RM-70

Origin: USSR

Dimensions: Length (standard rocket) 10ft 7in (3.23m); length (short rocket) 6ft 3in (1.9m); diameter 4.8in (122mm)

Weights: Standard rocket 169.8lb (77kg); short rocket 101lb (45.8kg)

Range: Standard rocket 12.7 miles (20.4km); short rocket 6.83 miles (11km)

Warhead: 42.8lb (19.4kg) types HE fragmentation, incendiary, smoke, chemical and submunition

History: The concept of the Multiple Rocket Launcher, or Katyusha, was first introduced by the Soviets during World War II. Today the 40 round 122mm (4.8in) and its derivatives are standard Warsaw Pact MRL systems. Known users of the BM-21 include Afghanistan, Algeria, Angola, Bulgaria, Chad, China, Cuba, Egypt, Ethiopia, East Germany, Hungary, India, Iran, Iraq, Israel, North Korea, Libya, Morocco, Mozambique, Nicaragua, Pakistan, Poland, Syria, Tanzania, USSR, Vietnam, North and South Yemen and Zambia

Background: The BM-21 system, which first entered service in the early 1960s, is mounted on a URAL 375 (6 × 6) cross-country truck chassis which is fitted with a central tyre pressure regulation system to allow the driver to adjust the tyre pressure to suit the type of ground being crossed. As such the 40-tube 4.8in (122mm) BM-21 is cheap and easy to produce and is deployed en masse either as an offensive salvo-fire weapon against area targets such as troop and/or vehicle concentrations or as a defence suppression weapon against artillery and mortar battery positions. The Soviets view their MRL as a supplement rather than a replacement for the tube artillery.

Versions of the BM-21 have been manufactured in China (40-round truck-mounted Type 81, 40-round tank chassis-mounted Type 81 and 24-round truck-mounted Type 83 systems); Egypt (40-round reverse-engineered copy, 21- and 30-round modifications and the locally produced Sakr-18 and Sakr-30 systems); India (40-round LRAR systems); North Korea (30-round local model designated BM-11); and Romania (21-round version on a Bucegi SR-114 truck chassis). There is also a 36-round Soviet variant mounted on a ZIL-131 truck chassis

known by the NATO designation M1976 and a special airborne 12-round launcher on a GAZ-66 (4 × 4) vehicle which is known as the M1975.

The BM-21 is normally found in the Soviet Army in single battalions of 18 launchers integrated into the divisional artillery regiments of both tank and motorised rifle divisions. Most models have seen combat action throughout the world in conflicts in Africa, the Middle East, the Far East and Central America, and Israel has captured a number of BM-21s and has used the system against its former Arab owners on a number of occasions.

Two types of rocket can be fired, the only difference between the long and short rounds being in the size of solid propellant rocket motor fitted. It is the sight and sound of the rockets exploding which causes the greatest shock, and when used against low-technology armies, especially in Africa, a salvo of BM-21 rockets has often caused considerable panic and confusion, allowing the attacking forces to win the battle easily. Against more sophisticated forces, however, a barrage will often bring retaliation in the form of an air strike

or counter-barrage by similar MRLs or tube artillery. In Western Europe the Soviets would use their MRL battalions as primary delivery platforms for chemical agents, especially substances like hydrogen cyanide gas, which cause degradation of NBC filters and enable follow-up attacks by other agents to penetrate defensive clothing and vehicle protection systems and kill the personnel. In order to reduce the 10 minute manual reloading time of the BM-21 the Czechoslovakians took the 40-round BM-21 launcher and mounted it on their cross-country capable 8 × 8 TATRA 813 truck chassis with a reload pack of 40 rockets between it and the vehicle's armoured cab to produce the RM-70. When the launcher is brought back to zero elevation after firing and aligned with the new rockets the latter are automatically loaded in just under two minutes. Subsequently the East Germans also adopted the RM-70 as their standard MRL with further units being exported to the Soviet Union and Libya. The RM-70's only known combat use is believed to have been by Libya during its ongoing border war with the French-

backed government of Chad. Some RM-70 systems have also been fitted with a front-mounted dozer blade to clear fire positions and battlefield obstacles.

The replacement for both the BM-21 and other obsolete calibre systems in the Soviet Army level artillery brigades is the 16-round 8.66in (220mm) BM-27 system on ZIL-135 8 × 8 cross-country truck chassis. The BM-27 has a 792lb (360kg) rocket with high explosive fragmentation, chemical or submunition warheads and is designed primarily to support Operational Manoeuvre Groups during breakthrough operations at ranges of up to 25 miles (40km). A rapid reload capability is provided by two further ZIL-135 vehicles, each with 16 reload rounds and a reloading arm on its rear platform, for each launcher vehicle. Reloading still takes between 15 and 20 minutes, but for such a large-calibre rocket is much faster than for any of the predecessor systems. The BM-27 has seen combat service in Afghanistan against the rebel forces and has been delivered in small numbers to Syria and Iraq. Warheads available include chemical, high explosive and submunition types.

Above: The Chinese have developed a number of variations of the 122mm BM-21 multiple rocket system, including this version based on the chassis of their new 152mm self-propelled gun. Mounted at the rear of the chassis is the 40-round launcher, while a pack of reload rockets is carried in front. The launcher has powered traverse and elevation and all 40 rockets can be fired in 20 seconds. Special single-round 122mm rocket launchers have been developed for guerilla units.

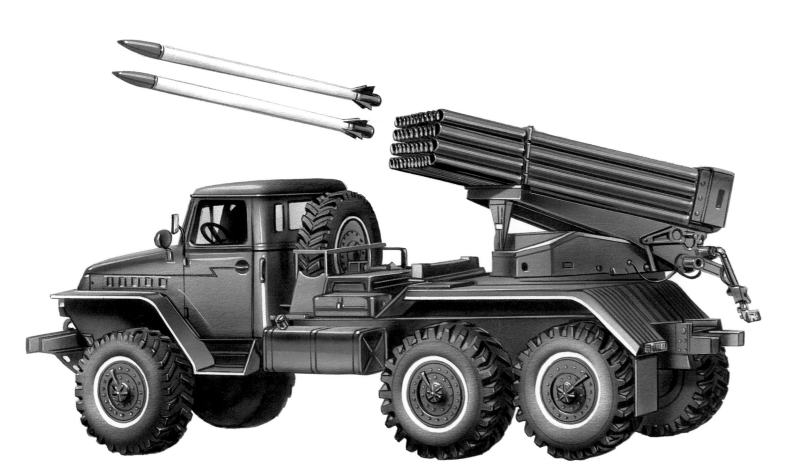

Left: The RM-70 fires the same rockets as the Soviet BM-21 but is mounted on a Tatra 8 x 8 chassis with an armoured cab and has greater cross-country mobility as well as a higher rate of fire. The 40-round launcher is mounted at the rear of the chassis with a reload pack of 40 rockets being carried to the immediate rear of the cab. Once the original 40 rockets have been fired another batch of 40 new rockets can be loaded automatically into the launch tubes and readied for firing in about two minutes.

Above: The BM-21 122mm (4.8in) has been the standard multiple rocket system of the Soviet Army for many years, but it is now being supplemented by more modern systems. It is mounted on a 6 x 6 cross-country chassis to allow for rapid deployment. Many other countries have built copies of the BM-21 on various other chassis, and the system is in widespread service. Although less accurate than artillery, the BM-21 can deliver a massive amount of firepower in a rapid salvo.

TR, FH-70 and Soltam

TR

Origin: France
Calibre: 155mm (6.1in)
Length of barrel: 244.1in (620cm)
Weight in action: 23,479lb
(10,650kg)
Muzzle velocity: 2,723 ft/sec (830m/
sec)
Rate of fire: 3 rounds in first 18 secs;
6rds/min for 2 mins; 120 rounds per
hour
Range: RAP 36,089 yd (33,000m)
Shell weight: 96.45lb (43.75kg)
History: Developed to replace
existing 155mm Model 50 howitzers
in French Army; first shown in 1979
and first production guns issued to
French motorised infantry divisions
in 1984. The French Army will
eventually have 79 TR guns

Background: The French TR towed
gun (le Canon de 155mm Tracté) was
developed after the 155mm GCT self-
propelled gun but it uses the same
family of ammunition and the barrel
and ballistics are very similar.

In many ways the TR is typical of
many 155mm gun-howitzers now in
service. It has a barrel 40 calibres
long and the carriage is equipped with an
auxiliary power unit that drives the
main wheels and powers some of the
carriage services such as opening
and closing the heavy trail legs.
Where the TR differs from other

Above: FH-70 of the British Royal
Artillery in firing position with a
truck unloading a unit load
container of ammunition. The
British Army has three regiments of
towed FH-70, based in the UK.

Below: Part of the
ammunition system of the
FH-70 consists of the
propelling charge (1) and
three projectiles, HE (2),
illuminating (3) and smoke
base ejection (4). The last
has smoke canisters that
fall to the ground giving a
dense smoke cloud in
less than one minute.

Below: GIAT 155mm TR
in firing position with three
of the many types of
projectile that it can fire.
The HE projectile (1) is
fitted with a nose plug
which is unscrewed and
replaced by a fuse before
loading. Both the base
bleed (2) and rocket-
assisted (3) rounds
provide extended range.

1   2   3

1

2   3   4

weapons is that it fires an entirely different range of ammunition from the NATO standard now in use elsewhere, and in order to provide the weapon with more appeal in the general export market the TR's manufacturers, GIAT, are now developing a version that can fire NATO ammunition. The current ammunition includes a standard round with a maximum range of 26,247 yd (24,000m) but base-bleed and rocket-assisted projectiles are also available and these provide considerably increased range.

The TR is a heavy weapon that requires a large 6 × 6 truck to tow it and a crew of at least eight men. Under its own on-board power it can travel at a speed of 5mph (8km/h).

FH-70

Origin: West Germany/Italy/United Kingdom
Calibre: 155mm (6.1in)
Length of barrel: 237in (602cm)
Weight in action: 20,503lb (9,300kg)
Muzzle velocity: 2,713ft/sec (827m/sec)
Rate of fire: Burst 3 rounds in 13 sec; normal 6rds/min; sustained 120 rounds per hour
Maximum range: 26,247 yd (24,000m)
Shell weight: 95.9lb (43.5kg)
History: Developed from 1968 onward as a joint project between three nations. Production was carried out by all three member nations with West Germany taking 216, Italy 164 and the United Kingdom 71. More have been sold to Saudi Arabia and Japan

Background: The FH-70 was developed to meet the requirements of three nations and each nation undertook a part of the overall development. The result is typical of many current towed 155mm gun-howitzers.

The FH-70 has heavy split trails and a barrel 39 calibres long. Many of the carriage services are carried out by hydraulics driven from an on-board auxiliary power unit which also drives the main wheels for short moves. For long moves the barrel is swung around to locate over the joined split trails which have wheels under them to assist movement and when opening and closing.

The FH-70 fires standard NATO ammunition of all kinds, from high explosive to cargo rounds, and ammunition development is still continuing. Other development in West Germany involves a new barrel 46 calibres long to increase range to 39,370 yd (36,000m), a flick rammer to increase the rate of fire and a new range of propellent charges.

FH-70 has proved to be reliable and robust in service, though it requires a powerful tractor to tow it.

It has also proved to be an export success as sales to Saudi Arabia and Japan have proved. However, its self-propelled version, SP-70, was cancelled at the end of 1986.

SOLTAM

Origin: Israel
Calibre: 155mm (6.1in)
Length of barrel: 839P 262.6in (667cm); 845P 303in (770cm)
Weight in action: 839P 23,920lb (10,850kg); 845P 25,794lb (11,700kg)
Muzzle velocity: 2,713ft/sec (827m/sec)
Rate of fire: Rapid 4rds/min; sustained 2rds/min
Shell weight: 95.9lb (43.5kg)
History: Developed from the Soltam M-71, from which it differs in having an on-board auxiliary power unit

Background: The M839P and M845P differ in barrel length, the barrel of the former being 39 calibres long and that of the M845P 45 calibres long. Both are based on the Soltam M-71, a 155mm towed howitzer which originally used the carriage of a Finnish Tampella 122mm (4.8in). The use of an auxiliary power unit mounted on the left-hand trail leg enables an ammunition handling crane and other items to be added to the carriage and also powers the main

carriage wheels; the maximum barrel elevation is also increased to 70°. If the main diesel power unit fails it can be driven by a back-up electrical motor using on-board batteries, or driven by a system of hand levers. The basic towed M-71 without the power unit is still produced both for the Israeli Army and for export and has an identical ballistic performance to the powered versions, though the 39-calibre barrel is more common.

The Soltam howitzers fire standard NATO ammunition. With base-bleed enhanced-range projectiles the M839P is stated to reach 33,900 yd (31,000m) and the M845P 42,651 yd (39,000m), though accuracy will be marginal at such extreme ranges.

The power unit provides the M839P and M845P with considerable mobility but the add-on units make the weapon a rather cumbersome load. This has not prevented the Soltam design from being used as the basis of a number of similar weapons such as the ODE 155 now under development in Singapore. It is also rumoured that the M845P has been used as a design study in China.

Left: For travelling the ordnance of the 155mm TR is traversed to the rear and clamped in position over the closed trails. It is towed by a Renault TR 10,000 (6 x 6) truck which also carries ammunition.

Left: The Soltam M-68 155mm gun/howitzer is known to be in service with the Thai Marines and fires standard NATO projectiles including illuminating (1), shown with fuse plug, and rocket-assisted (2), shown complete with fuse. A self-propelled model of the M-68 is in service with the Israeli Army on Sherman tank chassis under the designation L-33.

D-30 and S-23

D-30

Origin: USSR
Calibre: 121.92mm (4.8in)
Length of barrel: 191.9in (487.5cm)
Weight in action: 6,944lb (3,150kg)
Muzzle velocity: 2,428ft/sec (740m/sec)
Rate of fire: 7-8rds/min
Maximum range: HE 16,842 yd (15,400m); RAP 23,950 yd (21,900m)
Shell weight: FRAG-HE 47.97lb (21.76kg)
History: Designed as the replacement for the old M-30 howitzer, the D-30 has been exported widely and may be encountered in many parts of the world

Background: Although categorised as a howitzer the D-30 is really a gun-howitzer judged by its barrel length and the use of variable-charge ammunition, and is a simple weapon that is made to appear complicated by the employment of an unusual carriage system that has three trail legs. In action the three legs are separated and spread so that the entire weight of the weapon rests on them as the wheels are raised off the ground; there is also a centrally located firing jack that is lowered to the ground as the wheels are raised. To improve stability when firing the ends of the trail legs are secured by stakes that are hammered into the ground.

It does not take long to emplace the weapon as a trained crew can get the D-30 into action in about one and a half minutes; however, getting it out of action again takes longer as the stakes have to be removed first. The emplaced trail arrangement provides a full 360° top carriage traverse and makes the D-30 a useful anti-armour weapon; it is provided with special HEAT projectiles for this role, and a hit from one of these projectiles would disable most tanks.

A weight-saving feature of the D-30 is that it is towed by the muzzle, which has a folding towing eye under the multi-baffle muzzle brake for the purpose. This towing method lowers the centre of gravity of the towed load and also reduces the length of the tractor-weapon combination. The normal D-30 tractor is a light or medium 6 × 6 truck and the usual crew is seven.

In order to reduce ammunition logistic supply requirements the D-30 can fire many of the projectiles used by the old M-30 howitzer, which dates from 1938; these include high explosive shells and smoke and illuminating rounds. It can also fire a high-explosive rocket-assisted projectile to increase the maximum range. The weapon has few frills and the small shield is provided only to protect the gun mechanism, not the gun crew. The recoil mechanism is unusual among Soviet artillery weapons in being located over the barrel instead of underneath, the latter being the usual location.

The D-30 is a very simple weapon to operate and relatively cheap to produce so it is widely used as a training gun, and each Soviet Army tank division has two battalions of 18 guns; more are used by the motorised rifle divisions. The D-30 has been sold or donated to many countries, as well as some African and Far Eastern freedom fighter organisations, and is produced in China — and exported — by NORINCO as the Type D30. The Egyptian Army has so many D-30s that is has investigated the use of the weapon on a locally produced self-propelled platform, while Syria has mounted D-30s on obsolete T-34/85 tank chassis and at one time the Egyptians did the same. The Soviet 122mm 2S1 (M1974 or SO-122) self-propelled howitzer has a barrel very similar to that of the D-30, which it is replacing in Soviet service, and fires the same ammunition.

Above: China and Egypt both now produce copies of the Soviet D-30 howitzer—this is a Chinese example — and these are being offered for export. It was used in some numbers during the Vietnam conflict and proved to be accurate and hard hitting.

Left and below: For many years the 122mm D-30 field gun has been the backbone of Soviet artillery regiments, but it is now being replaced by the self-propelled 2S1 weapon. When deployed in the firing position the wheels are raised clear of the ground, enabling the weapon to be traversed rapidly through 360° for laying on a new target. The D-30 is normally towed by a 6 x 6 truck or MT-LB which also carries the crew and ammunition. The latter is of the separate loading type and consists of brass cartridge case (1) and propelling charges (8 and 9), plus projectiles. Shown here are HE fragmentation (2), HE full (3) HE reduced (4), HEAT (5), APFSDS (6) and Smoke (7) rounds for the D-30.

S-23

Origin: USSR
Calibre: 180mm (7.086in)
Length of barrel: 346.5in (880cm)
Weight in action: 47,288lb (21,450kg)
Muzzle velocity: 2,592ft/sec (790m/sec)
Rate of fire: 1rd/min max; 1 round every 2 minutes sustained
Maximum range: 33,246 yd (30,400m)
Shell weight: FRAG-HE 185.4lb (84.09kg)
History: Developed from a naval gun and first seen in public in 1955, so for many years known to Western Intelligence as the M1955

Background: The S-23 is a massive weapon, so massive that for many years it was thought to be a 203mm (8in) long-range gun, and it was only when some were captured from Syria by the Israelis that the true calibre was found to be 180mm. This is a standard Soviet naval calibre, indicating that the S-23 was developed from a naval gun.

The barrel of the S-23 has a length of about 49 calibres, which helps to impart a high muzzle velocity and a long range, and the range can be increased substantially by the use of rocket-assisted projectiles that confer a maximum possible range of 47,900 yd (43,800m), though at such ranges accuracy would be poor. The barrel is equipped with a pepperpot muzzle brake in an attempt to keep the recoil forces as low as possible, but the heavy split trail carriage still has to absorb most of them. The large

sliding breech block is also a very substantial component to withstand the high chamber pressures involved.

Getting the S-23 in and out of action must be a considerable task, requiring the use of a heavy tracked tractor — the AT-T or a similar vehicle — and each gun has a crew of 16 men; more tractors are needed to carry the ammunition. The main carriage wheels are dual and are filled with sponge rubber. The trail legs are carried on a small single-axle limber to offset some of the weight from the towing vehicle, and in action the S-23 is supported on a base plate that lifts the gun off its main wheels. When on tow the barrel is withdrawn to the rear over the trail

legs to make the load more manageable. The barrel has to be run out to its normal position when coming into action, which takes time. No shield is fitted as none would normally be required at the ranges at which the S-23 is normally deployed.

Once emplaced the S-23 has a low rate of fire, mainly because of difficulties in loading the heavy projectiles: the highest rate possible is only one round a minute, and one round every two minutes is more usual. The projectiles are fired using a variable bag charge system, the usual round being a fragmenting high explosive (FRAG-HE) shell, but also available are a concrete piercing shell and a nuclear shell with a yield

of 0.2kT. The nuclear shell is one of the main reasons for fielding the S-23, and every Soviet Army heavy artillery brigade in an artillery division has at least one battery holding 12 S-23s. The S-23s are also used in the coastal defence role, where their long range could be put to good use and where their bulk and weight would be less of a disadvantage.

The S-23 has been exported by the Soviet Union to nations such as Egypt, Syria and India. There are also reports of them being used by Iraq and no doubt the Israeli Army makes use of those it has captured. The replacement for the S-23 is probably a 152mm towed gun, the M1976, which became operational in 1981.

Above: Soviet D-30s in action. The introduction of various types of artillery locating devices has led to towed artillery losing its place on many battlefields since it is becoming too vulnerable.

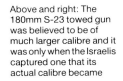

Above and right: The 180mm S-23 towed gun was believed to be of much larger calibre and it was only when the Israelis captured one that its actual calibre became known. The S-23 fires separate loading ammunition consisting of a projectile and charge (2 and 7). Types of projectile include HE (1), FRAG-HE (3), rocket-assisted (4), tactical nuclear (5) and concrete-piercing (6) rounds. It is normally crewed by a 16-man detachment and towed by a heavy tractor such as the AT-T.

M198 and Light Gun

M198

Origin: USA
Calibre: 155mm (6.1in)
Length of barrel: 240in (609.6cm)
Weight in action: 15,791lb (7,163kg)
Muzzle velocity: 1,850ft/sec (564m/sec)
Rate of fire: Maximum 4rds/min; sustained 2rds/min
Maximum range: HE 19,850 yd (18,150m); RAP 32,808 yd (30,000m)
Shell weight: HE 94.6lb (42.91kg)
History: Development started in 1968 and first prototypes were ready in 1972. Standardised as the M198 in mid-1978, first examples were issued later the same year. Now in service with the US Army and Marine Corps and with several other nations including Saudi Arabia, Pakistan, Tunisia, Australia and Thailand

Background: The M198 was developed by several government and civilian agencies and production has been carried out by Watervliet Arsenal, Rock Island Arsenal and ConDiesel Mobile Equipment, among others. Although categorised by the Americans as a lightweight weapon — it can be air-lifted under a CH-47D helicopter — it is really a hefty load and it lacks the auxiliary power unit and hydraulic actuating circuits featured on most comparable towed 155mm howitzers. The M198 requires at least a 6 × 6 truck to tow it over rough ground and manhandling the howitzer int a firing position is a considerable task requiring a gun crew of at least 11 men. However, it is a reliable and accurate weapon that has given good service so far and has been exported to several customers. It is still in production for overseas customers.

The design of the M198 is orthodox. For firing the split trail

Above: US Marine Corps M198 system in firing position. Unlike most other 155mm systems the M198 does not have an auxiliary power unit, which makes it difficult to move across beaches. The crew have to rely on their strength to bring it into action.

bottom carriage wheels are raised off the ground using a hand-operated hydraulic pump, and the howitzer then rests on a firing base under the front axle and on the trail axle spades. This improves firing stability at all elevation angles as the carriage wheels have a rather narrow track. For normal towing the barrel points forward but it can be reversed over the trails for storage purposes.

The barrel — the Cannon Assembly M199 — can be elevated by hand to an angle of 72° for firing to close ranges but on-carriage traverse is limited to a total of 45°. The fire control system has direct-fire sights to deal with targets such as armoured vehicles at short ranges.

One of the main strengths of the M198 is its ability to use virtually the entire range of American 155mm ammunition. This large family extends from the usual high explosive, smoke and similar orthodox projectiles to such things as tactical CS shells, cargo rounds

containing scatterable land mines or radio communication jammers, binary chemical agent shells and the laser-guided Copperhead anti-armour munition, and includes tactical nuclear projectiles. All are fired using a variable charge system and to achieve the maximum range of 32,808 yd (30,000m) a rocket-assisted projectile is used, a rocket motor in the shell base firing just as the projectile reaches the limit of its initial firing velocity. However, accuracy is poor at extreme ranges.

The US Army has now called for a new version of the M198 light enough to be lifted under a Black Hawk helicopter but still using the basic ordnance of the M198 and having a similar overall ballistic performance. BMY is currently designing a suitable light carriage using various advanced techniques and modern light materials but no hardware had appeared by mid-1987.

LIGHT GUN

Origin: United Kingdom
Calibre: 105mm (4.14in)
Length of barrel: 124.8in (317cm)
Weight in action: 4,100lb (1,860kg)
Muzzle velocity: 2,323ft/sec (708m/sec) max
Rate of fire: 8rds/min for 1 min; 6rds/min for 3 min; 3rds/min sustained
Maximum range: 18,810 yd (17,200m)
Shell weight: HE 35.49lb (16.1kg)
History: Developed to replace the 105mm Pack Howitzer used by the Royal Artillery. First production examples issued late 1974. Now in widespread use following active service in the 1982 Falklands campaign, and ordered by the US Army with a new barrel under the designation M119.

Background: The Light Gun was designed at the Royal Armament and Research Establishment at Fort

Below: The M198 fires a wide range of separate loading ammunition including chemical (1), smoke (2), anti-personnel (3) and practice (6) rounds with their associated propelling charges (4 and 5). To engage targets at longer range rocket assisted projectiles or the more accurate base bleed rounds can be fired. The M198 can also fire the Cannon Launched Guided Projectile to engage enemy tanks with the actual target being illuminated by a forward observer with a laser designator for terminal guidance.

Right: Royal Ordnance 105mm Light Gun of the British Army during exercises in Norway. The Light Gun can be carried slung under a Puma helicopter or towed behind a Land Rover; when being towed across snow it is often fitted with skis. The US Army has adopted the 105mm Light Gun with the shorter barrel, which uses US ammunition with a shorter range.

be rapidly traversed through 360° to engage any target that may appear from any direction, a useful facility in mobile warfare.

For towing, the weapon's barrel is traversed to the rear over the trails, which allows the centre of gravity to be kept low for towing but means that the barrel has to be swung forward again when coming into action. This entails removing and replacing one of the carriage wheels, but the procedure takes only a few seconds using a racing hub on the wheel concerned.

On several occasions during the Falklands campaign the Light Gun proved itself capable of firing for long periods without problems. The L118 version has a maximum range well in excess of any comparable gun but the ordnance can be changed in order to fire the American M1 family of 105mm ammunition. This conversion, the L119, is the one selected by the US Army.

The ammunition fired by the L118 Light Gun is special to it, though it is also fired by the Abbot self-propelled gun. Rounds include high explosive, smoke, marker smoke of various colours, several types of practice shell, illuminating and anti-armour HESH. The Americans are developing a rocket-assisted shell for their guns to improve the maximum range of their shorter-ranged M1 ammunition. The British Light Guns use a five-charge propellent system with an extra super charge to achieve maximum range. Minimum range is 2,734 yd (2,500m) and is achieved by using high angles of barrel elevation and fitting spoiler vanes on the shell nose to degrade its ballistic performance.

The Light Gun requires only a light truck for towing, and British Army units use over-snow vehicles and mount the gun on skis in Arctic regions. The US Army will use a version of its Hummer as the tractor for its M119 Light Guns.

Halstead in Kent. After a period of development the first production examples were ready in 1974 and since then the Light Gun has been used by the British Army and adopted by many others. It has been ordered by the US Army for their new light divisions as the M119.

The Light Gun makes extensive use of light alloys to keep down overall weight, the carriage uses a bowed tubular steel trail, and it is possible to carry a Light Gun slung under a Puma helicopter. In action the carriage wheels rest on a circular firing platform that allows the gun to

Left: The Royal Ordnance 105mm Light Gun fires the same wide range of ammunition used by the Abbot self-propelled gun including HE (1), smoke (2), marker (3) and illumination (4), as well as US HESH (5) and HE (6) rounds, all of which are of the separate loading type using brass normal (7) or extended-range super (8) cartridge cases.

1   2   3   4   5   6   7   8

Crotale, Shahine and AMX-13 DCA

CROTALE

Origin: France
Dimensions: Length 9ft 6in (2.89m); diameter 5.9in (15cm); wingspan 1ft 9in (0.54m)
Launch weight: 187lb (85kg)
Performance: Effective range 0.31-6.21 miles (0.5-10km); effective altitude 46-13,123ft (15-4,000m)
Speed: Mach 2.3
Warhead: 30.86lb (14kg) proximity- and IR contact-fuzed HE fragmentation

Background: Developed originally for South Africa as the Cactus all-weather low-altitude mobile SAM system, the missile was ordered by the French Air Force under the name Crotale, and by late 1985 11 countries had brought the system in five versions. The original version, produced in 1969, was called the 1000 series, with the 2000 series arriving in 1973, the 3000 series in 1975, the 4000 series in 1983 and the 5000 series in 1985. The main difference is that the vehicles of the first three series are not ready for action as soon as they come to a halt, but have to be connected together by data transmission cables allowing a maximum separation of 2,624ft (800m). In contrast the 4000 series

Above: The Shahine SAM system consists of two key components, the firing unit with six missiles in the ready to launch position (left) and the acquisition unit (right). A typical Shahine section would have two acquisition and four firing units and these would normally be tied into an overall air defence command and control system which could include the Royal Saudi Air Force's AWACS airborne warning aircraft and fighters. Replacement missiles are loaded from a 6 × 6 truck with the aid of a crane.

Above: The Crotale SAM system was originally developed by Thomson-CSF to meet the requirements of South Africa but has now been adopted by the French Air Force for air base defence as well as being exported in substantial numbers. It consists of two key vehicles, the firing unit shown here with four missiles in the ready to launch position and the acquisition vehicle, each based on a similar 4 × 4 chassis which has limited cross-country mobility and three hydraulic jacks for stabilisation.

are fitted with radio data links, which allows them to go straight into action, and to be up to 1.86 miles (3km) apart so as to defend more airspace. The 5000 series has further improvements, including the ability to mount up to four short-range point defence SAMs on the side of two of the R440 missile containers to meet saturation attacks.

A typical Crotale battery has one P4R 4 × 4 wheeled acquisition vehicle with an 11.1 mile (18km) range E-band radar and two P4R firing vehicles, each with a 10.6 mile (17km) J-band tracking radar and four command-to-line-of-sight missiles in container-launcher tubes. The radar can track one target and guide up to two missiles simultaneously, and a back-up fire control system is fitted. No reloads are carried and fresh containers have to be brought up by truck and loaded with a light crane.

SHAHINE

Origin: France
Dimensions: Length 12ft 0in (3.15m); diameter 1ft 11in (0.59m); wingspan 6in 15.6cm)
Launch weight: 232lb (105kg)
Performance: Effective range 0.31-7.145 miles (0.5-11.5km); altitude limits 45-22,000ft (15-6,800m)

Speed: Mach 2.5
Warhead: Weight 30.86lb (14kg) contact- and proximity-fuzed HE-fragmentation

Background: The Shahine low-altitude SAM system was developed in the late 1970s to meet a Saudi Arabian requirement for an all-weather air defence system. At present the system has two components, a mobile version which is based on a modified AMX-30 MBT chassis, and a static shelter version based on a three-axle trailer. Both use interchangeable launcher and radar acquisition units as the installation rings are common to both. The acquisition unit has an 11.495 mile (18.5km) range E-band surveillance radar with moving target indicator capability; up to 40 targets can be registered in the computer control system, with the 18 highest threat evaluations being handled simultaneously. A TV system provides monitoring of the accompanyinng launcher systems and a secondary optical target acquisition facility.

The launcher itself has a 10.56 mile (17km) range J-band fire control radar which can simultaneously track a target and command-guide one or two missiles to it. In heavy ECM environments a back-up TV

system is used instead. Six containers with ready-to-fire R460 missiles are carried; once fired they have to be replaced from a resupply vehicle which is fitted with a hydraulic crane. First AMX-30 production systems to the original Saudi order were delivered in 1980 with a second order for an improved version being delivered in both trailer and AMX-30 versions.

AMX-13 DCA

Origin: France
Dimensions: Length 17ft 9in (5.4m); width 8ft 2in (2.5m); height 12ft 6in (3.8m) with radar operating, 9ft 10in (3m) with radar retracted
Combat weight: 37,919lb (17,200kg)
Crew: 3
Engine: 8-cyliner SOFAM Model 8Gxb water-cooled petrol developing 250hp (184kW)
Performance: Max road speed 37.2mph (60km/h); max road range 186 miles (300km); fording 2ft 0in (0.6m); vertical obstacle 2ft 2in (0.65m); trench 5ft 7in (1.7m)
Armament: 2 × 30mm HS831A cannon, 600 rounds carried; elevation/depression —5°/+85°, traverse 360°

Background: Developed in the mid-1960s for the French Army on an

AMX-13 light tank chassis, a total of 60 production vehicles were delivered between 1968 and 1969 for use by corps-level air defence regiments to protect high-value point targets and vehicle transit routes. The SAM S 401A turret carries two 30mm cannon, all the optical, electrical and hydraulic systems required to lay them, and a D-band Oeil Noir 1 search and range-finding radar. The data obtained by this is then fed into a corrector system which computes the offset required between the line of fire and the line of sight to ensure that the guns are aimed correctly at the target. A maximum effective engagement range of 2.17 miles (3.5km) is possible.

In 1975 Saudi Arabia placed an order for 53 examples of an improved version mounted on the AMX-30 MBT chassis. This uses a TG230A turret fitted with a D-band Oeil Noir 1 radar and carries a total of 1,500 rounds of ammunition. These vehicles are used in conjunction with the Shahine low-level SAM system to provide a mobile integrated battlefield air defence network for the Saudi Army. Further development of this turret has resulted in the SABRE system which can be mounted on a variety of tracked and wheeled chassis.

Left: The Shahine surface-to-air missile system was developed by Thomson-CSF to meet the requirements of Saudi Arabia and is mounted on an AMX-30 MBT chassis for improved cross-country mobility and armour protection. Saudi Arabia also has a trailer-mounted version of Shahine that can rapidlly be moved around the country by C-130 Hercules transport aircraft.

Above: The AMX-13 DCA twin 30mm self-propelled anti-aircraft gun system is only in service with the French Army although a later model, based on the larger AMX-30 chassis, is used by Saudi Arabia.

Both systems fire belted 30mm ammunition (1) of various types (2 to 6) depending on the type of mission to be undertaken. Further development has resulted in the SABRE turret which has been

tested on a wide range of chassis such as AMX-10RC, AMX-30 and Chieftain, SABRE has yet to enter production, but it can mount twin 30mm Hispano-Suiza or Oerlikon cannon.

Wildcat, Roland and Gepard

WILDCAT

Origin: West Germany
Crew: 3
Armament: 2 × 30mm cannon in power-operated turret with traverse of 360° and elevation from —5° to +85°
Armour: Classified
Dimensions: Length 22ft 7in (6.88); width 9ft 9in (2.98m); height (radar down) 9ft 0in (2.74m)
Combat weight: 40,785lb (18,500kg)
Engine: Mercedes-Benz 8-cylinder turbo-charged diesel developing 320hp (238kW)
Performance: Road speed 49.7 mph (80km/h); range 373 miles (600km); vertical obstacle and trench not available; gradient 60 per cent
History: The Wildcat was developed as a private venture by an international consortium headed by Krauss-Maffei. Two prototypes have been built and tested but the system was not in production or service by mid-1987.

Background: Krauss-Maffei built all the Gepard twin 35mm air defence

systems for the Belgian, West German and Netherlands armed forces. A highly effective all weather system, Gepard is too heavy and sophisticated for many countries and Krauss-Maffei as project leader has designed and built the Wildcat mobile air defence system.

Wildcat consists of a 6 × 6 chassis using automotive components of the West German Army's Transportpanzer 1 vehicle fitted with a one-man power-operated turret armed with two Mauser 30mm MK 30-F cannon, each having 380 rounds of ready-use ammunition (340 for air targets and 40 APDS-T for ground targets) with additional ammunition being stowed in the hull. The 30mm cannon can engage aircraft and helicopters out to a range of about 3,280 yd (3,000m).

The second prototype Wildcat turret has been installed on a Swiss MOWAG Shark (8 × 8) chassis. The Wildcat is being offered with a number of fire control systems to meet different operational requirements ranging from clear weather to all weather.

Above: Roland being launched from an XM985 tracked chassis based on the M109 self-propelled gun during trials in the USA. At present the US Army has one battalion equipped with the Roland 2 system; this is manned by the New Mexico National Guard and assigned to Central Command. Production US Rolands are pod-mounted on the rear of a 6 x 6 cross-country truck chassis.

Below: French Army Roland 2 SAM system launching a missile. In addition to the two missiles in the ready to launch position a further eight missiles are carried in the hull in two four-round drum type magazines, one on each side. The West German Army uses the Marder chassis for its Roland 2 SAMs.

Above: The Wildcat twin 30mm system has been developed as a private venture by a consortium headed by Krauss-Maffei of Munich, but as of mid-1987 no firm production orders had been placed. The twin 30mm Mauser cannon, also used in the Greek Artemis system, use the belted ammunition (4), including practice (1), APDS-T (2) and HEI-SD-T (3) rounds, also used by the A-10 attack aircraft's GAU-8 gun.

ROLAND

Origin: France/West Germany (specifications for West German Roland 2 on Marder chassis)
Crew: 3
Armament: Twin launcher with two Roland in ready to launch position and eight missiles in reserve
Armour: Classified
Dimensions: Length 22ft 8in (6.91m); width 10ft 6in (3.2m); height (radar down) 9ft 7in (2.92m
Combat weight: 71,650lb (32,500kg)
Ground pressure: 13.22lb/sq in (0.93kg/cm2)
Engine: MTU MB 833 Ea-500 6-cylinder liquid-cooled diesel developing 600hp (447kW) at 2,000 rpm
Performance: Maximum road speed 43.5 mph (70km/h); range 323 miles (520km); vertical obstacle 3ft 9in (1.15m); trench 8ft 2in (2.5m); gradient 60 per cent
History: Roland was developed to meet the requirements of the French and West German armies from 1964 by Aérospatiale of France and MBB

of West Germany. Originally two versions were developed, the clear-weather Roland 1 and all-weather Roland 2 but the latter is the only version now produced. The West German Army use Roland on a Marder chassis while France uses a modified AMX-30 MBT chassis. Other users include Argentina, Brazil, Iraq, Nigeria, Spain, Venezuela, and the United States, with more than 600 systems ordered or delivered

Background: Roland 2 is a highly mobile surface-to-air missile system which can operate on its own or as part of an overall air defence system. It has both tracking and surveillance radars and carries a total of 10 missiles; the maximum range of the missiles is 6,890 yd (6,300m), but latest missiles have a range of 9,296 yd (8,500m). In addition to the systems on Marder and Roland chassis, a shelter version on a MAN (8 × 8) cross-country truck has been developed, and this has been selected to defend key air bases in West Germany. The shelter version

can also be used in the static role, and this version was used by Argentina in the Falklands to defend Port Stanley.

GEPARD

Origin: Switzerland/West Germany
Crew: 3
Armament: 2 × 35mm cannon in power-operated turret with traverse of 360° and elevation from -10° to + 85°
Dimensions: Length including main armament 25ft 4in (7.73m); hull length 22ft 6in (6.85m); width 11ft 0in (3.37m); height excluding radar 9ft 10in (3.0m); height with radar 13ft 3in (4.03m)
Combat weight: 104,277lb (47,300kg)
Ground pressure: 13.51lb/sq in (0.95kg/cm2)
Engine: MTU MB 838 Ca M500 10-cylinder multi-fuel developing 830hp (618kW) at 2,200 rpm
Performance: Road speed 40.3mph (65km/h); road range 342 miles (550km); vertical obstacle 3ft 9in (1.15m); trench 9ft 10in (3m); gradient 60 per cent

History: Following trials with prototype systems armed with twin 30mm and twin 35mm cannon the latter was selected by the West German Army, for which 420 vehicles were built by Krauss-Maffei. Belgium ordered 55 vehicles and the Netherlands ordered 95, the latter having Hollandse Signaalapparaten instead of Siemens tracking and surveillance radars

Background: The Gepard all-weather self-propelled air defence system was designed and built to replace the US-supplied M42 twin 40mm self-propelled anti-aircraft gun system and is provided with a computerised fire control system, tracking and surveillance radars and a land navigation system. The twin 35mm Oerlikon-Bührle cannon have a cyclic rate of fire of 550rds/min each, and each cannon is provided with 310 rounds of anti-aircraft and 20 rounds of armour-piercing ammunition. The guns have an effective range of 3,827-4,374 yd (3,500-4,000m).

Below: West German and Belgian Gepards have different radars to the Dutch Gepard although both use the same twin 35mm Oerlikon Buhrle cannon. A total of 620 rounds of anti-aircraft and 40 anti-armour rounds are carried in belts (1). Types of ammunition fired include target practice (2), APDS-T (3), SAPHEI-T (4), HEI-T and HEI (5 and 6). A special break-up training round is also available.

Bofors 40mm L/70 and ZSU-23-4 Shilka

BOFORS 40mm L/70

Origin: Sweden
Crew: 4-6
Armament: One 40mm cannon with traverse of 360° and elevation from −4° to +90°
Dimensions: Length travelling 23ft 11in (7.29m); width travelling 7ft 4in (2.22m); height travelling 7ft 9in (2.34m)
Combat weight: 12,566lb (5,700kg)
History: Entered production in 1950/51 and still in service with Argentina, Belgium, Brazil, Chile, Denmark, Djibouti, Ecuador, Finland, France, West Germany, India, Indonesia, Iran, Ireland, Israel, Italy, Ivory Coast, Libya, Malaysia, Netherlands, Nigeria, Norway, Peru, Portugal, Singapore, Somalia, South Korea, Spain, Taiwan, Thailand, Turkey, Uganda, Venezuela and Yugoslavia

Background: The Bofors 40mm L/60 — the latter figure indicates the length of the barrel in calibres — was developed in the 1930s and proved one of the most effective towed anti-aircraft guns of World War II, with production being undertaken in many countries and self-propelled and naval versions also being developed.

The Bofors 40mm L/70 was developed shortly after the end of the war and was subsequently adopted by many countries, some of which, including India, Italy, the Netherlands, Spain and the United Kingdom, produced the gun under licence. In some countries, for example the United Kingdom, the weapon has been replaced by surface-to-air missile systems, but many others have upgraded the gun by the introduction of new ammunition, such as the High Capacity High Explosive (HCHE) or Pre-Formed High Explosive (PFHE) rounds, or more advanced fire control systems such as those used by the Contraves Skyguard replacement for the older Super Fledermaus or the Dutch Signaal Flycatcher.

The basic 40mm L/70 has manual elevation and traverse with 24 rounds of ready-use ammunition in clips of four rounds and a further 96 rounds in reserve in the ammunition racks at the rear of the mount. Other models have full powered control with an on- or off-carriage generator. In the most advanced system the mount is unmanned, with an off-carriage fire control system providing target information. Effective anti-aircraft range of the gun is about 2,734 yd (2,500m). The carriage has four road wheels and when in the firing position is stabilised by four jacks, one at each end of the carriage and one either side on outriggers. The US Army's abandoned Sgt York DIVAD system used two 40mm Bofors guns and there are numerous naval versions.

More recently, as a private venture, Bofors has developed the Trinity air defence system for both naval and self-propelled applications; this fires even more advanced ammunition and has a sophisticated fire control system than enables it to down missiles. The ordnance of the 40mm L/70, inverted and with some modifications, is being used to arm one of the Swedish Army's new family of Combat Vehicle 90 armoured vehicles.

ZSU-23-4 SHILKA

Origin: USSR
Crew: 4
Armament: 4 × 23mm cannon in power operated turret with traverse of 360° and elevation from −4° to +85°
Armour: 0.35-0.59in (9.2-15mm)
Dimensions: Length 21ft 6in (6.54m); width 9ft 8in (2.95m); height without radar 7ft 5in (2.25m); height with radar up to 12ft 6in (3.8m)
Combat weight: 45,194lb (20,500kg)
Ground pressure: 9.81lb/sq in (0.69kg/cm2)
Engine: Model V-6R 6-cylinder in-line diesel developing 280hp (208kW)
Performance: Road speed 27.3mph (44km/h); range 280 miles (450km); vertical obstacle 3ft 7in (1.1m); trench 9ft 2in (2.8m); gradient 60 per cent
History: Developed in the early 1960s and entered service in 1966. In service with Afghanistan, Algeria, Angola, Bulgaria, Cuba, Czechoslovakia, Egypt, Ethiopia, East Germany, Hungary, India, Iran, Iraq, Jordan, Kampuchea, North Korea, Libya, Mozambique, Nigeria, Peru, Poland, Somalia, Syria, USSR, Vietnam, North and South Yemen and Yugoslavia

Background: Until the introduction of the ZSU-23-4 the standard self-propelled anti-aircraft gun system of the Soviet Army, apart from the twin 14.5mm KPV machine guns installed on modified BTR-152 (6 × 6) and BTR-40 (4 × 4) chassis, was the ZSU-57-2 twin 57mm gun developed from the towed 57mm S-60. The main disadvantages of the ZSU-57-2 were its low rate of fire and lack of an on-board fire control system.

The ZSU-23-4 has a chassis similar to that of the SA-6 Gainful surface-to-air missile system and is armed with four 23mm AZP-23 cannon whcih are almost identical to those used on the ZU-23 twin 23mm towed system. In the ZSU-23-4 application the barrels are water-cooled and have a cyclic rate of fire of 800-1,000rds/min, but in practice bursts of a maximum of 30 rounds are fired; a total of 2,000 rounds are carried. The

Below: The Bofors 40mmL/70 light anti-aircraft gun entered service from the late 1940s and since then both the gun and its associated ammunition and fire control systems have been constantly upgraded to take into account the changing threat. The 40mm L/70 gun fires various types of fixed ammunition, including AP-T (1), PF-HE-T (2), PF-TP-T (3), and MPT (4).

23mm cannon can be used in both anti-aircraft and ground roles and have a maximum effective range of about 1,750 yd (2,500 m). Mounted on the turret roof at the rear is a Gun Dish radar which carries out search, detection, automatic tracking and other fire control functions; targets can be acquired on the move but the vehicle normally comes to a halt before opening fire.

The ZSU-23-4 has seen extensive combat service in the Middle East and was one of the most effective systems of the 1973 Middle East war when used in combination with other air defence weapons including SAMs. The latter would force Israeli aircraft to fly very low, whereupon they would encounter the ZSU-23-4s and man-portable SA-7 SAMs. The ZSU-23-4 is being replaced by a new self-propelled air defence system based on a T-72 MBT chassis called the ZSU-X by NATO. This is very similar in appearance to the West German Gepard used by the Belgian, West German and Netherlands armies and is armed with twin 30mm cannon and fitted with both tracking and surveillance radars.

Left: Crew of an East German ZSU-23-4 carrying out routine maintenance work in the field. The weapon was used successfully in the 1973 Middle East conflict to engage Israeli aircraft forced low by Egyptian SAMs.

Left: The ZSU-23-4, developed as the replacement for the clear weather ZSU-57-2 system, is used in large numbers by the Warsaw Pact and many other countries that have received Soviet aid. It has an all-weather fire control system and is armed with four 23mm water-cooled cannon in a power operated turret. It is now being supplemented by the ZSU-30-2 system armed with twin 30mm cannon.

SA-4, SA-6, SA-8, SA-9 and SA-13

SA-4 GANEF

Dimensions: Length (SA-4a) 28ft 11in (8.8m), (SA-4b) 27ft 2½in (8.3m); diameter 35.4in (0.9m), max span 102in (2.6m)
Launch weight: 5,500lb (2,500kg) approx
Performance: Effective range (SA-4a) 5.8-45 miles (9.3-72km), (SA-4b) 0.7-31.25 miles (1.1-50km); max altitude limit (SA-4a) 88,583ft (27,000m), (SA-4b) 78,740ft (24,000m); speed Mach 4.0
Warhead: 297lb (135kg) proximity-fuzed HE fragmentation

Background: First displayed in the Red Square Parade on May Day, 1964, the ZRK-SO Krug (NATO code name SA-4 Ganef) medium- to high-altitude SAM system was not fully deployed until 1969 in brigades as the air defence element for Front (two brigades), Tank and Combined Arms Armies (one brigade each).

The missile has four solid-fuel booster motors which fall away when the kerosene-fuelled ramjet sustainer motor's ignition speed is reached. Initial target detection is achieved by the Long Track radar, which passes the hostile track to the continuous-wave fire control and command guidance Pat Hand radar of a battery for engagement. A single missile is launched and guided to the target by the radar guidance beam with the terminal phase being handled by the round's own semi-active seeker head.

Right: The SA-6 Gainful SAM system (second right) proved to be highly effective in the 1973 Middle East conflict as it forced Israeli aircraft to fly low within the range of the ZSU-23-4 self-propelled anti-aircraft guns system and SA-7 Grail SAMs.

Below: The SA-13 Gopher SAM system, replacement for the SA-9 Gaskin. The latter was based on the BRDM-2 (4 x 4) chassis, but the SA-13 is based on the MT-LB multi-purpose armoured vehicle and has four missiles in the ready to launch position, though only one can be fired at a time.

SA-6 GAINFUL

Dimensions: SA-6a length 19ft (5.8m); diameter 13.2in (0.335m); wingspan 49in (1.245m); tailspan 60in (1.524m)
Launch weight: 1,276lb (580kg)
Performance: Effective range 2.3-15 miles (3.7-24km); effective altitude limits 262.5-47,244ft (80-12,000m); speed Mach 2.5
Warhead: 176lb (80kg) contact- and radar proximity-fuzed HE fragmentation

Background: First seen in the November 7, 1967, Red Square Parade, RK-SD Kub (NATO designation SA-6 Gainful) is a mobile, air-portable and amphibious low- to- medium-altitude SAM system mounted on a modified ZSU-23-4 self-propelled anti-aircraft gun chassis. In Soviet service the SA-6 is now found at divisional level in the anti-aircraft regiment. The latter has a Regimental HQ with one Thin Skin-B and two Long Track radars and five SA-6 batteries, each with an SSNR Straight Flush G/H/I-band fire-control radar vehicle and four SPU launcher vehicles with three ready-to-fire missiles apiece; in wartime two additional SPUs would be added.

In 1979 the SA-6b variant entered service on a new SPU which carries its own guidance radar. Initially deployed on the basis of one SPU per SA-6a battery, the system effectively doubled the number of targets the battery could engage at one time. Both systems are being complemented in Soviet service by the new SA-11 Gadfly, which is based on the American Standard missile family.

SA-8 GECKO

Dimensions: Length 10ft 2½in (3.1m); diameter 8¼in (0.21m); wingspan 23.6in (0.6m)
Launch weight: 374lb (170kg)
Performance: Effective range (SA-8a) 1-7.5 miles (1.6-12km), (SA-8b) 1-9.4 miles (1.6-15km); effective altitude limits 32.8-42,651ft (10-13,000m); speed Mach 2.0
Warhead: 88lb (40kg) proximity- and contact-fuzed fragmentation

Background: The ZRK-SD Romb (NATO designation SA-8 Gecko) low-altitude SAM system entered Soviet service in 1974 and was first seen in public during the November 1975 Red Square Parade. The SA-8 has replaced towed AA guns in a number of divisonal anti-aircraft regiments because of its greater mobility, each regiment having 20 fire units.

Known by the NATO code name Land Roll, the radar complex has a rotating H-band early warning and search radar, a pulsed J-band target tracking radar below that and two small I-band dish antennas to transmit guidance command signals to the missiles. Each SPU can engage a single target with a two missile salvo operating on different frequencies to overcome ECM and avoid guidance problems.

SA-9 GASKIN

Dimensions: Length 5ft 11in (1.8m); diameter 4.72in (0.12m); wingspan 15in (0.38m)
Launch weight: 66lb (30kg)
Performance: Effective range 0.5-4.1 miles (0.8-6.5km); effective altitude limits 44.9-5,906ft (13.7-1,800m); speed Mach 1.5
Warhead: 5.7lb (2.6kg) proximity- and contact-fuzed HE fragmentation

Background: The ZRK-BD Strela 1 (NATO designation SA-9 Gaskin)

Below: The SA-4 Ganef is a medium- to high-level SAM system which is deployed by Bulgaria, Czechoslovakia, East Germany, Hungary, Libya, Poland and the USSR. Each battery has one Pat Hand radar system and three launchers, each with two Ganef missiles. If the Pat Hand H-band continuous wave fire control and command guidance radar system is knocked out missiles cannot be launched.

low-altitude SAM system was developed in parallel with the ZSU-23-4 self-propelled anti-aircraft gun and entered service in 1968. It is issued to the anti-aircraft batteries of Warsaw Pact motorised rifle and tank regiments on the basis of four SPUs and four ZSUs to give a total of 16 SPUs and 16 ZSUs per division. The SPU is based on the BRDM-2 scout car chassis with the chain-driven belly wheels removed and the turret replaced by one with four ready-to-launch infra-red guided SA-9s in container-launcher boxes; four reloads are carried. The original SA-9a used an uncooled seeker but the latest SA-9b has a cryogenically cooled seeker to provide greater lock-on capability.

SA-13 GOPHER

Dimensions: Length 7ft 2in (2.2m); diameter 5in (0.127m); wingspan 15.75in (0.4m)
Launch weight: 121lb (55kg)
Performance: Effective range 0.3-6.1 miles (0.5-9.7km); effective altitude limits 32.8-10,499ft (10-3,200m); speed Mach 1.5
Warhead: 8.8lb (4kg) contact- and proximity-fuzed HE fragmentation

Background: First deployed in the mid-1970s, the ZRK-BD Strela 10 (NATO code name SA-13 Gopher) low-altitude SAM system is replacing the less capable SA-9 Gaskin on a one-for-one basis in motorised rifle and tank regiment anti-aircraft batteries. The amphibious tracked SPU is based on the MT-LB chassis and can also use either the SA-9 or a mixture of SA-9 and SA-13 container-launcher boxes on the four launcher rails. A simple range-only radar is fitted to prevent missile wastage on targets outside engagement range. The SA-13 uses a cryogenically cooled all-aspect IR-seeker which operates in two frequency bands to give high discrimination against defensive flares and decoy pods.

Below: The SA-8 Gecko replaced the 57mm towed anti-aircraft gun and is in service in two versions, the SA-8a shown here, with missiles on open launchers, and the SA-8b, which has the missiles in long boxes for both transport and launch. SA-8 Gecko is a stand-alone system.

Rapier

Origin: United Kingdom
Dimensions: Length 7ft 4in (2.23m); diameter 5.2in (133mm); wingspan 1ft 3in (0.38m)
Launch weight: 93.7lb (42.6kg)
Performance: Effective range Towed Rapier 875-7,500 yd (800-6,858m); Tracked Rapier 432.5-7,500 yd (400-6,858m); altitude limits 150-10,974ft (15-3,658m); speed Mach 2.0
Warhead: 3.1lb (1.4kg) HE semi-armour piercing with contact fuze
History: Development of Rapier began in the early 1960s with the first production rounds being issued to RAF Regiment and British Army in 1971. Since then it has been sold to Australia, Brunei, Indonesia, Iran (Army and Air Force), Oman, Qatar, Singapore, Switzerland, Turkey, the United Arab Emirates, the United States Air Force and Zambia. Well over 23,000 rounds have been produced and more than 10,000 have been launched during trials, training and in combat by the British and Iranian armed forces during the Falklands and Gulf wars respectively

Background: In its basic form the Towed Rapier system consists of the fire unit with an on-board surveillance radar, an optical

tracker, a secondary sight, a generator and a tactical control unit, all of which are connected by cable and towed by two lightweight ¾- or 1-ton vehicles which carry a total of 13 rounds in sealed containers. The system can only engage targets in daylight conditions, and to meet the threat of day/night and all-weather attack a third vehicle is added which tows a DN181 Blindfire radar tracker unit with its own generator. This frequency-agile monopulse radar produces a very narrow beam which is used to track both target and missile in order to achieve a very high single-shot kill probability. The number of rounds carried by the unit is also increased to 17, and the Blindfire radar can be added to an optical Towed Rapier system as required, so that the British Army has only a 33 per cent Blindfire capability for its Towed Rapiers whereas the RAF Regiment, protecting valuable airfield targets, has a 100 per cent capability.

In 1974 a tracked version of Rapier began development to meet the requirements of the Shah of Iran's armed forces. This was subsequently cancelled in 1979 by the new Iranian government after the Shah was deposed but the system was

subsequently adopted by the British Army, the first order being placed in 1981 for for 50 units. In 1983 a further 20 were ordered so as to equip three Light Air Defence Regiments with four batteries each, two with 12 Towed systems apiece and two with 12 Tracked systems each. The tracked system, based on an M548 chassis designated RCM748, has a crew of three and is fitted with a Darkfire thermal imaging system for day/night capability; an all-weather Blindfire radar can be added as needed. The Tracked Rapier vehicle carries eight rounds in the ready-to-fire position compared with the Towed Rapier's four, and each launcher also has a resupply M548 which carries a further 20 rounds in their sealed containers. To maintain and support the vehicle in the field a two-man Forward Area Support Team (FAST) M548 variant is deployed with each battery.

For the mid-1990s and beyond Rapier manufacturer British Aerospace is developing the Rapier 2000 system, which will equip two Army Air Defence regiments and three RAF Regiment squadrons; this introduces an eight-round towed launcher, a steerable infrared optronic tracker in place of the

current on-launcher surveillance radar, a new trailer-mounted 3D surveillance radar with built-in IFF and an updated Blindfire tracking radar. The system will also fire the new Mk 2A Rapier missile with a smart proximity-fuzed fragmentation warhead for use against RPVs, ARMs and cruise missiles and the Mk 2B with contact-fuzed hollow-charge warhead for use against aircraft and helicopters. The range is increased to 8,750 yd (8,000m) and each system is able to fire and guide two-round salvoes whereas the current system is able to guide only one. The Mk 2 round is also compatible with existing launchers.

It is also hoped to upgrade the current Towed Rapier launcher during the late 1980s with the Darkfire tracker system, a new surveillance radar with a 50 per cent increase in range, a console tactical control unit and a six-round launcher. BAe has also developed privately the Laserfire system, which offers 85 per cent of the performance of the towed system at a much lower cost using a millimetre-wave surveillance radar, an automatic laser tracker and four ready-to-fire Rapier Mk 1 missiles on a two-man

The British Aerospace Rapier is produced in two basic versions, towed (below) and tracked (right). The latter is only in service with the British Army. The basic Rapier is a clear weather system, but with the addition of a Marconi Blindfire radar it has an all-weather capability. So far more than 600 towed Rapiers have been built and the weapon is in service with more than a dozen countries as well as the British Army and Royal Air Force. Towed Rapier has seen combat in the Middle East and with the British Army in the course of the 1982 Falklands campaign.

self-contained fire unit which can be mounted either on a vehicle such as a medium sized Bedford truck or on the ground. By April 1987 no firm orders for Laserfire had been received.

In the spring of 1987 it was announnced that British Aerospace had teamed with two US companies, FMC Corporation and United Technologies, to bid for the US Army's LOS-Forward-Heavy air defence system requirement following the cancellation of DIVAD. This team is proposing a modified version of Tracked Rapier for the short term and a more advanced system based on the Bradley chassis for the longer term.

Right: A well camouflaged Tracked Rapier in British Army service, with launcher traversed right and operator using sight in cab roof. This version of Rapier, with eight missiles ready to launch, is unique to the British Army, though a US Army variant has been proposed.

M163 Vulcan and Patriot

M163 VULCAN

Origin: USA
Crew: 4
Armament: One six-barrel 20mm cannon inn power-operated turret with traverse of 360° and elevation from −5° to +80°
Armour: 0.47-1.49in (12-38mm)
Dimensions: Length 15ft 11in (4.86m); width 9ft 4in (2.85m); height including turret 9ft 0in (2.74m)
Combat weight: 27,082lb (13,310kg)
Ground Pressure: 9.52lb/sq in (0.61kg/cm2)
Engine: Detroit Diesel Model 6V-53 6-cylinder water cooled diesel developing 215hp (160kW)
Performance: Road speed 42.25mph (67.6km/h); range 302 miles (483km); vertical obstacle 2ft 0in (0.61m); trench 5ft 6in (1.68m);

gradient 60 per cent
History: Developed in the mid-1960s, the M163 Vulcan entered US Army service in 1968 and was subsequently exported to Ecuador, Israel, South Korea, Morocco, the Philippines, Sudan, Thailand, Tunisia and North Yemen. A similar system mounted on the Commando 4 × 4 APC chassis is in service with Saudi Arabian National Guard

Background: The M163 basically consists of an M113 APC fitted with a one-man power-operated turret which has an M61A1 Vulcan six-barrel cannon, gyro lead computing sight and a range-only VPS-2 radar mounted on the right-hand side. The chassis is designated M741 and differs only in minor details from the M113A1, while the cannon, a development of the standard USAF Vulcan aircraft gun, has two rates of

fire, 1,000 and 3,000 rounds per minute; the former is used in the direct-fire ground role while the latter is used for air defence. The gunner can select bursts of 10, 30, 60 or 100 rounds and the maximum effective anti-aircraft range is 1,750 yd (1,600m) and maximum ground range 3,280 yd (3,000m) using M53 AP-T, M54 HPT, M56A3 HEI or HEIT combat rounds.

From June 1984 the US Army fielded the Product Improved Vulcan Air Defence System (PIVADS), which has an improved fire-control system and the ability to fire the new Mk 149 APDS round, which increases the effective engagement range to 2,843 yd (2,600m) against aircraft.

The M163 saw combat use in the ground role in Vietnam as a convoy escort vehicle, proving particularly useful in breaking up ambushes

because of its very high rate of fire with the 1,100 ready-to-fire rounds available and the 1,000 reserve rounds inside the hull. The Israelis also used it during their 1982 Peace for Galilee invasion of South Lebanon, when several Syrian aircraft were engaged and destroyed during air attacks on Israeli armoured columns.

The 20mm Vulcan's main drawback is its lack of all-weather capability. It was to have been replaced by the Sgt York DIVAD system, but that has now been cancelled, so the Vulcan will soldier on for some years yet.

PATRIOT

Origin: USA
Dimensions: Length 17ft 5in (5.31m); diameter 16in (406mm); wingspan 3ft (0.92m)

Left: A US Army gunner mans his 20mm M163 Vulcan self-propelled anti-aircraft gun system with range only radar to the right of the mount. When engaging aircraft targets cyclic rate of fire is 3,000 rds/min, while 1,000 rds/min are fired against ground targets.

Left: The US Army uses two versions of the Vulcan 20mm anti-aircraft gun system, the M163 self-propelled on an M113 chassis and the M167 towed system. The major drawbacks of the Vulcan system are its very short range and lack of all weather capability. It was to have been replaced by the cancelled Sgt York DIVAD twin 40mm gun system.

Launch weight: 2,195lb (998kg)
Performance: Effective range 3.125-4.28 miles (65-68.5km); altitude limits 328-78,740ft (100-24,000m); speed Mach 3.0
Warhead: 221lb (100kg) HE-fragmentation with proximity fuze
History: Originally known as SAM-D. The development period extended from 1965, when the requirement was first specified, to 1980 due to the complexity of the system. Since then the weapon has entered service with the US Army (four battalions activated by late 1986) and has been ordered by the Netherlands, West Germany and Japan as their replacement for the MIM-14 Nike Hercules. Total procurement for the US Army will be 103 fire units and 6,200 missiles, of which 14 fire units and 840 missiles will be loaned to the West Germans in addition to their own

14 fire units and 779 missiles purchased under a NATO air base defence agreement.

Background: The Patriot fire unit contains all the elements necessary to engage a target: the MPQ-53 phased-array radar set performs all the surveillance, IFF interrogation, acquisition, target tracking and guidance functions which in

previous systems, such as Nike Hercules and Hawk, required up to nine separate radars; the manned MSQ-104 enagement control station houses the weapon system's fire and operational status control computer; the MJQ-24 electric power plant; and eight four-tube launchers with Patriot rounds in their ready-to-fire canisters. A Patriot battalion consists of six of these firing units.

The single-stage phased array command guided and semi-active homing solid-propellent missile carries an HE-fragmentation warhead and is capable of TVM (track via missile) radar guidance. In the summer of 1986 a Patriot fire unit equipped with modified software for the anti-tactical missile role successfully intercepted a Lance surface-to-surface missile in flight. A development programme to provide for modifications to existing US Army and NATO SAM systems was initiated as part of the US Army's Tactical Missile Defence (TMD) plan, the need being for the SAMs to be able to intercept the increasingly accurate Soviet tactical missiles before they could inflict an incapacitating first strike on NATO's rear area logistics and airfield infrastructures, prime targets on the Central Front.

Left: The Patriot SAM system has been developed to replace the Nike Hercules and supplement the Hawk SAMs. Patriot is now operational in West Germany and the United States and has also been selected by West Germany, Japan and the Netherlands. Compared with Nike Hercules it is much more mobile and can engage more targets. With additional development it will be able to engage tactical battlefied missiles such as the Soviet SS-21 and SS-23.

Artemis and Breda Twin 40L70

ARTEMIS

Origin: Greece
Crew: 2-3
Armament: Two 30mm cannon with powered traverse of 360° and powered elevation from —5° to +85°
Dimensions: Length travelling 25ft 9in (7.85m); width travelling 7ft 9in (2.38m); height travelling 7ft 10in (2.39m)
Combat weight: 12,320lb (5,600kg)
History: Development of the Artemis began in the late 1970s with production beginning inn 1985 for the Greek Army, Navy and Air Force. Although the prime contractor is the Hellenic Arms Industry, much assistance has been provided by KUKA of West Germany (carriage), Mauser of West Germany (cannon) and Philips of Sweden (fire control system); first deliveries were made in 1986. The first version to enter service is a towed model but a self-propelled version may be developed in the future

Background: The Artemis 30 is a twin 30mm cannon mounted on a twin-axle split type carriage; for travelling purposes the generator which powers the system is fixed to the axle nearest the towing arm, but when deployed the combined assembly is removed and located some distance away from the mount. The rear axle is power-retracted upward and the whole system is then lowered and levelled by means of three hydraulically operated pads, of which two are on outrigger arms. The system has three modes of operation: remote via external fire control system; local via a gunner seated behind the central mount support and using a periscope for ground targets and a gyroscopic angle predicting sight for air target engagements; and emergency local when no power is available via the gunner, with weapon aiming by hand wheels and firing by a foot trigger.

The Mauser 30mm Model F cannon can fire the 30mm × 173 GAU/8A family of ammunition, inncluding HEI-SD, HEI-SD-T and break-up rounds, as used by the A-10 ground attack aircraft. Typical engagement range of the gun in a battery is 2,187-3,828 yd (2,000-3,500m) with maximum range being 5,468 yd (5,000 m). The fire control system uses a laser/optronic director head mounted on a small trailer; this feeds information into a truck-mounted fire control centre which relays gun-laying data and firing commands to three or four guns via a land line. At night an infra-red sensor can be fitted, while for all-weather use a monopulse tracking radar can be installed on the director, and further development work will add a guided weapon capability to the network in the long term. Actual detection of targets is handled by a Battle Coordination Post which uses long-range search radars to obtain the target track and designation data needed by the fire-control centre before an engagement can commence. A total of 500 rounds (250 for each cannon) are carried in the on-mount ammunition hoppers.

BREDA TWIN 40L70

Origin: Italy
Crew: 2-4
Armament: Two 40mm Bofors L/70 cannon with powered traverse through 360° and elevation from —13° to +85°
Dimensions: Length travelling 26ft 5in (8.05m); width travelling 10ft 6in (3.2m); height travelling 9ft 1in (3.7m)
Combat weight: 24,222lb (11,010kg) approx
History: The Breda Twin 40L70 field mounting is a land version of the company's well established twin 40mm naval anti-aircraft gun system, which is used by more than

Right: The Artemis twin 30mm anti-aircraft gun system is normally unmanned during firing operations with aiming and firing being accomplished by remote control. Mounted on the carriage is an integral generator.

Left: The 30mm Mauser Model F cannon fire standard ammunition including HEI-SD (High Explosive Incendiary - Self Destruct) (1), TP (Target Practice) (2), HEI-SD-T (tracer) (3), TP-T (target practice tracer) (4) and break up (5) rounds, all of which are linked in belts.

1   2   3   4   5

Above: Two Breda 40mm Twin 40L70 anti-aircraft guns on the firing range with the Flycatcher radar fire control system in the right background. So far the twin 40L70 air defence system has only been purchased by Venezuela. The guns are the same as those installed on Venezuelan Navy frigates as a close-in weapon system.

20 navies. Only Venezuela has bought the land system to date, with 36 systems delivered.

Background: The field mounting consists of a 360° training platform supported by six outrigger jacks when the carriage is emplaced for firing; the upper section of the mount is completely enclosed in a watertight reinforced glass fibre cupola and under the platform is a magazine with four horizontal layers housing 444 rounds in clips of four. These are fed by two independent hoisting systems which feed the clips into the guns above and the magazine trains with the guns, so the system is fully automatic: no-one needs to be on the mount when the gun is in action, and even if one gun is out of action the other can continue to fire. Gun training is by on-board electrical motors driving epicyclic gearboxes, the power for which is provided by an external 440V AC generator. External connections also have to be made to the fire control system which controls the engagement.

The most common fire control system is the Dutch Flycatcher, which is used to detect, identify and automatically track targets flying at low or medium altitudes using I-band and K-band radars with a complementary TV tracking system. A general-purpose on-board computer handles targets up to Mach 2.0 then performs the necessary calculations to lay the guns, and a Flycatcher can control up to three twin 40mm Breda mounts. Other fire control systems that can be used include the Contraves Skyguard and Super Fledermaus.

All the standard Bofors 40mm anti-aircraft ammunition types can be used, including the latest proximity-fuzed designs, and typical engagement ranges for effective anti-aircraft fire are around 3,828-4,375 yd (3,500-4,000m). As well as being highly effective against aircraft and helicopters the system could well be used to down cruise missiles, as one of the key roles of the original naval version is the destruction of anti-ship missiles. The 40mm Breda system is well suited to the defence of key areas such as airfields and oil depots, but is perhaps too heavy for extensive field deployment, where transport by aircraft or helicopter is a key requirement. With this in mind Breda have more recently developed the twin 30mm air defence system, which can be used with a variety of fire control systems.

1 2 3 4

Above: Camouflaged Twin 40L70 land version of Breda's widely used anti-aircraft gun system. The field mounting has its own power supply and 444 rounds of ammunition which is fed to the guns automatically at a rate of 330 rounds per barrel per minute. Pre-fragmented proximity fuzed shells (1) are the most effective against aircraft targets, but armour piercing tracer (2) and HET (3) rounds are also available for other targets, as well as practice rounds (4).

Right: Artemis twin 30mm anti-aircraft gun being towed by a truck carrying the battery command centre. The Artemis system has been developed to meet the requirements of the Greek Army, Navy and Air Force and uses both West German (30mm cannon and mount) and Swedish (fire control system) technology.

Stinger, Blowpipe, Javelin and SA-7

STINGER

Origin: USA
Dimensions: Length 5ft 0in (1.52m); diameter 2.76in (70mm); wingspan 5.5in (140mm)
Launch weight: 34.76lb (15.8kg)
Performance: Effective range 220-5,500 yd (200-5,000m); altitude limits 11-5,250 yd (10-4,800m)
Warhead: 6.6lb (3kg) HE-fragmentation with proximity fuze
History: Stinger, a man-portable infra-red guided shoulder-launched SAM which is designed to engage low-altitude high-speed jet, propeller-driven or helicopter targets, is in service with Chad, Denmark, West Germany, Italy, Japan, South Korea, Netherlands, Saudi Arabia, Turkey and United Kingdom

Background: Developed in the 1970s, the FIM-92a Stinger has replaced the earlier tail-chase IR-guided FIM-43A Redeye in the US Army, US Marine Corps, US Navy and US Air Force light air defence and special forces units. Stinger is

Above: The Shorts Javelin, now replacing the earlier Blowpipe SAM, has a number of advantages including more powerful warhead and extended range.

proving to be highly effective in the hands of Afghan guerilla forces, who have downed some 100 Soviet aircraft and helicopters.

Further development of the FIM-92A's all-aspect IR seeker resulted in the Fiscal Year 1983 FIM-92B production variant which is also known as Stinger Post (Passive Optical Scanning Technique) with enhanced capabilities.

BLOWPIPE

Origin: United Kingdom
Dimensions: Length 4fft 7in (1.39m); diameter 3in (76mm), span (wings) 10.6in (270mm)
Launch weight: 24.2lb (11kg)
Performance: Effective range 765.5-3,937 yd (700-3,600 m); altitude limits 32.8-2,190 yd (30-2,000 m); speed Mach 1.6
Warhead: 4.84lb (2.2kg) HE-fragmentationn with contact fuze

Right: The Shorts Blowpipe was the first man-portable SAM to enter service with the British Army and has been exported to a number of countries. Some have
also found their way to Afghanistan, where local guerillas found them difficult to operate without prior training in the system's launch procedure.

Right: The Stinger was developed as the replacement for the older Redeye SAM and large numbers of Stingers have recently been supplied to Afghan guerilla units, where they have forced
Soviet aircraft and helicopters to fly much higher. The Stinger is a man-portable system but it does need comprehensive training to ensure the selected target is shot down.

Above: The SA-7 (Grail) is probably the most widely used shoulder-launched SAM in the world, although in the Soviet Army it is now being replaced by the SA-14
Gremlin. The SA-7 has been supplied to many guerilla units which have used it to shoot down numerous aircraft, the targets often being civilian-operated.

History: Blowpipe was developed in the 1960s by Short Brothers Missile Systems Division to meet the requirements of British Army. In service with 10 other countries including Argentina, Canada, Chile, Ecuador, Malawi, Nigeria, Oman, Portugal and Thailand. Some have also found their way to Afghanistan

Background: The Blowpipe system is entirely self-contained, with no external power requirements, and consists of two main components, the aiming unit and the missile within its launcher container. Reloading, which takes only seconds, involves clipping the arming unit onto a new missile/canister combination; the aimer then lifts the complete system to his shoulder and acquires the target in his monocular sight, fires the missile and flies it into the target using his thumb controller. The missile is fitted with flares which in the early stages of flight are automatically detected by a sensor in the arming unit in order to gather the missile to the centre of the aimer's field of view. A contact fuze explodes the missile within the target.

JAVELIN

Origin: United Kingdom
Dimensions: Similar to Blowpipe
Launch weight: 26.4lb (12kg) approx
Performance: Effective range 328-4,920 yd (300-4,500m); altitude limits 11-3,280 yd (10-3,000m); speed Mach 1.8
Warhead: 6.05lb (2.75kg) HE-fragmentation with proximity fuze
History: Javelin has started to replace Blowpipe in the British Army and Royal Marines and has been exported to at least one country

Background: Javelin evolved from the earlier Blowpipe SAM but has a semi-automatic line-of-sight command (SACLOS) guidance system coupled with a new higher-impulse two-stage solid-propellent rocket motor to increase the engagement envelope, a larger warhead and a new fuzing system that can be deactivated by the operator to enable him to steer the missile away from friendly aircraft or an incorrectly engaged target without the warhead detonating.

During an engagement all the operator has to do is keep the target centred in his sight and the command guidance signals are automatically generated and sent to the missile's control surfaces via a radio link. To engage future low-level aircraft and attack helicopter threats the British Army is taking delivery in the early 1990s of Shorts' Starstreak high-velocity SAM systems on Stormer APCs. Each Starstreak missile contains three highly accurate manoevrable darts with explosive warheads.

SA-7 GRAIL

Origin: USSR
Dimensions: Length 4ft 3in (1.29m); diameter 3.94in (100mm)
Launch weight: 20.24lb (9.2kg)
Performance: Effective range (SA-7a) 49.2-3,830 yd (45-3,500m); (SA-7b) 49.2-6,125 yd (45-5,600m); altitude limits (SA-7a) 164-1,640 yd (150-1,500m); (SA-7b) 27.3-4,700 yd (25-4,300m); speed (SA-7a) Mach 1.5; (SA-7b) Mach 1.95
Warhead: (SA-7a) 3.96lb (1.8kg); (SA-7b) 5.5lb (2.5kg) HE-fragmentation with contact fuze

History: Designed as a platoon self-defence weapon, the two-stage solid propellent NATO-designated SA-7a Grail (Soviet name Strela-2; designation 9M32) entered service in 1966 with the enhanced capability SA-7b version (Soviet designation 9M32M) following in 1972. Since its introduction it has been supplied to practically all the Soviet-supplied client states and every Warsaw Pact army and has found its way to a number of terrorist and guerilla groups

Background: The SA-7 uses a simple optical sighting and tracking device with the operator activating the IR seeker when he has acquired a target; an indicator light denotes seeker lock-on and he then fires the missile, which adopts a tail-chase flight profile.

Improved versions of the SA-7 are being manufactured by Egypt as the Sakr Eye and by China as the HN-5 series. Since the early 1980s the SA-7 has undergone replacement by the SA-14 Gremlin system, and in 1987 a further portable SAM, the SA-16, was revealed to be in service with Soviet Army; the last is believed to be laser-guided.

Above: The Shorts Javelin man-portable SAM has now started to replace the older Blowpipe in the British Army and later this decade a version with four missiles in the ready to launch position on a Spartan tracked APC will enter service, giving the system greater mobility. Javelin is also carried on Royal Navy ships.

Armbrust, RPG-7 and Dragon

ARMBRUST

Origin: West Germany
Dimensions: Length 2ft 9in (0.85m); calibre 3.1in (78mm)
Weight: Launcher plus round 13.86lb (6.3kg)
Range: 330 yd (300m) anti-armou; 1,640 yd (1,500m) max
Projectile: Warhead weight 2.178lb (0.99kg); types HEAT, HE-fragmentation anti-personnel; armour penetration 11.8in (300mm) plus; muzzle velocity 722ft/sec (220m/sec)
History: Developed as a private venture by MBB and in limited use with a few countries including West Germany and United States (Delta Force)

Background: The Armbrust (crossbow) is a lightweight disposable man-portable shoulder-launched recoilles weapon which can safely be fired in confined spaces with obstructions as close as 2ft 7in (0.8m) behind the operator. The noise created is similar in type and intensity to a pistol shot and there is none of the flash, smoke or blast which normally characterise the operation of such a weapon. The reason is the use of around 5,000 small plastic flakes as a rearward-ejected counter-mass to balance the forward momentum of the projectile, and the fitting of pistons which are driven by the propellent gases released on firing to seal the launcher's ends so that the flash, smoke and blast are eliminated and the noise is substantially reduced.

Up to four rounds can be carried comfortably by a single man with a launch tube being discarded after each engagement. A simple reflex sight is fitted, though for special operations it is possible to fit a computerised sight to ensure a very high hit probability at a considerable range. The non-disposable sights are carried in addition to the round.

RPG-7

Origin: USSR
Dimensions: Length 3ft 3in (1.0m); calibre 1.57in (40mm)
Launcher weight: 15.43lb (7kg)
Performance: Range 330 yd (300m) against moving target, 545 yd (500m) against stationary target; muzzle velocity 393.7ft/sec (120m/sec)
Projectile: Weight 4.96lb (2.25kg); types PG-7 HEAT, PG-7M HEAT, OG-7 HE anti-persnnel; armour penetration (PG-7) 12.6in (320mm), (PG-7M) 15.75in (400mm)
History: Similar to the earlier RPG-2 in having a calibre of 1.57in (40mm), the RPG-7V was introduced into service as an anti-tank rocket with a diameter of 3.35in (85mm). The system is widely deployed all over the world especially by guerilla forces and terrorist groups

Background: The RPG-7 operator screws the cylinder containing rocket propellant into the warhead section, loads the complete round into the muzzle of the launcher unit, then uncovers the nosecap of the warhead and extracts the safety pin. A pull on the trigger fires the round, which is fairly accurate when no crosswinds are present. In 1968 a folding version, the RPG-7D, was introduced into service for use by the Soviet Airborne troops.

By the late 1970s the RPG-7 was being replaced in Soviet and Warsaw Pact service by the RPG-16, which is 3ft 7in (1.1m) long, of 2.3in (0.58mm) calibre and fires a 6.6lb (3kg) one-piece 3.15in (80mm) diameter rocket capable of piercing over 14.8in (375mm) of armour plate at ranges up to 875 yd (800m). This weapon was supplemented in service by the single-shot throwaway RPG-18 and RPG-22 light anti-armour weapons, which are telescoped open and used to engage targets out to a range of approximately 275 yd (250m). A number of countries have built their own versions and others have begun manufacture of ammunition for it.

DRAGON

Origin: USA
Dimensions: Length 2ft 3in (0.744 metres); diameter 5in (127mm); wingspan 12.9in (330mm)
Weight: System 30.4lb (13.8kg); missile 13.7lb (6.2kg)
Performance: Range 66-1,200 yd (60-1,100m)
Warhead: 5.4lb (2.45kg) HE-shaped charge capable of penetrating 23.6in (600mm) of armour plate
History: The McDonnell Douglas M47 Dragon anti-tank guided weapon concept started life in 1964 and inn 1970 the McDonnell Douglas Corporation (MDC) was given approval to start a multi-year procurement programme for the system. By Fiscal Year 1975 a two-source basis was established with Raytheon as the second partner, the latter finally becoming the sole source with MDC as the prime contractor. Production of this first-generation Dragon by MDC ended in 1977 and by Raytheon in 1980. It is in service with the US Army and Marine Corps, Iran, Israel, Jordan, Morocco, the Netherlands, North Yemen, Saudi Arabia, Spain, Switzerland, Thailand and Yugoslavia. It has seen combat use with Iran, Israel and Morocco, primarily against Soviet-supplied armoured vehicles

Background: The Dragon ATGW can be fired at stationary or moving targets within its operational range with the gunner being required to do no more than keep his sight cross-hairs on the tank or other target until the missile hits. Typical targets that can be engaged include armoured vehicles, fortified bunkers, concrete gun emplacements and similar hardened targets. The complete launcher consists of a bipod to rest

Above: The Armbrust man-portable anti-tank system was developed as a private venture by MBB but has not been built in large numbers. One of its most useful features is that it can be fired from within a building as it has no backblast, an attribute that makes it suitable for ambush situations.

the front missile container-launcher on, a tracker unit and the missile container-launcher itself. On completion of an engagement the container-launcher and bipod assembly are discarded and the tracker is placed on another assembly ready for the next target. Both day and night vision sight trackers are available.

For the future the US Marine Corps has initiated a Product Improvement Program for its Dragon launchers; initially this involves the retrofitting of all its first-generation Dragon missiles with an improved shaped-charge warhead to produce what is known as second-generation Dragon. For the US Army a new replacement system under development, the Advanced Anti-Tank Weapon System-Medium (AAWS-M), will be usable on battlefields covered by obscurant chemicals and electro-optical decoy systems.

Left: The Soviet RPG-7 anti-tank rocket system is the most widely used weapon of its type in the world and is used by numerous guerilla forces. Its main drawback is its backblast, which means that it cannot be fired in a confined space. Its HEAT warhead will not penetrate new Western armour.

Above: The Dragon is the standard medium-range ATGW of the US Army and Marine Corps but has many drawbacks when compared with other systems such as Milan, including short range, lack of armour penetration and the fact that it is difficult to control. A major weapon enhancement programme is now under way.

Carl Gustaf, AT-4, Tow and Milan

CARL GUSTAF

Origin: Sweden
Dimensions: Length 3ft 8in (1.13m); calibre (84mm)
Weight: M2 31.3lb (14.2kg); M2-550 33.1lb (15kg); M3 17.6lb (8kg)
Performance: Range 545 yd (500m) against stationary target, 435 yd (400m) against moving target, 1,095 yd (1,000m) against personnel; muzzle velocity 790-1,230ft/sec (240-375m/sec) depending on ammunition type
Projectiles: 6.8lb (3.1kg) FFV545 illuminating; 6.8lb (3.1kg) FFV469 smoke; 5.72lb (2.6kg) FFV65 HEAT; 6.8lb (3.1kg) FFV441 HE-shrapnel; 6.6lb (3kg) FFV551 rocket-assisted HEAT; 15.4lb (7kg) FFV597 over-calibre rocket-assisted and the 7.04lb (3.2kg) FFV502 HE-dual-purpose combined hollow-charge and fragmentation round
History: Manufactured by FFV of Sweden, the M2 has been adopted by some 22 countries as an anti-tank and infantry support crew-served weapon and has been continuously developed to meet changing operational requirements

Background: Normal crew is two men, one of whom carries the launcher and the other eight rounds of ammunition. The breech-loaded weapon has a basic optical sight on the left side.

To improve the system the M2-550 was developed: this uses a new telescopic sight and the rocket-assisted FFV551 HEAT round which increases the range to about 765 yd (700m) against armoured targets by flattening the trajectory and increasing the maximum round velocity. A new lightweight version is known as the M3 Carl Gustaf.

AT-4

Origin: Sweden
Dimensions: Length 3ft 3in (1m); calibre 3.31in (84mm)
Weight: Total 13.2lb (6kg)
Performance: Range 330 yd (300m); muzzle velocity 985ft/sec (300m/sec)
Projectile: Weight 6.6lb (3kg); type HEAT; armour penetration 11.81in (300mm) plus
History: The AT-4 has been developed as a disposable light anti-tank weapon and entered

production for Sweden and the USA in 1986.

Background: The FFV AT-4 is a lightweight glass-reinforced plastic launch tube fitted with a firing mechanism and sight and containing a new form of HEAT round which has behind-armour secondary effects. The AT-4 has been adopted by the US armed forces as the replacement for the old M72 Light Anti-tank Weapon (LAW) and will also be made in the USA by Honeywell.

TOW

Origin: USA
Dimensions: Length (BGM-71A/B) 3ft 10in (1.174m); BGM-71C 5ft 1in (1.55m); BGM-71D 5ft 8in (1.714m); diameter 6in (152mm); wingspan 13.5in (343mm)
Weight: Basic launcher 172.7lb (78.5kg); BGM-71D launcher 204.6lb (93kg); BGM-71A/B missiles 49.6lb (22.5kg); BGM-71C missile 56.65lb (25.7kg); BGM-71D missile 61.95lb (28.1kg)
Range: BGM-71A 70-3,280 yd (65-3,000m); BGM-71B/C/D 70-4,100 yd (65-3,750m)
Warhead: BGM-71A/B/C 7.7lb (3.5kg) HEAT; BGM-71D 13lb (5.9kg) HEAT
Armour penetration: BGM-71A/B 23.6in (600mm); BGM-71C 27.6in (700mm); BGM-71D 31.5in (800mm) plus
History: The Hughes BGM-71A Tube-launched, optically-tracked wire command-link guided (Tow) heavy anti-tank weapon system entered the design stage in 1962 and reached operational service in 1970. Since then it has been adopted by more than 36 countries and seen combat service in the Middle East and Far East in both air - and ground-launched modes

Background: Tow is a semi-automatic command-to-line-of-sight system, which means that all the operator has to do is keep the cross-hairs of his sight on the target and flight control commands are automatically transmitted via the wire-guidance link. The basic BGM-71A, the first model produced, was superseded in 1976 by the extended-range BGM-71B. In order to meet the threat of new Soviet armour the

Below: The FFV AT-4 is a man-portable anti-tank weapon that fires a HEAT (high explosive anti-tank) warhead with behind-armour secondary effects shown here in flight (1) and loaded (2) configurations. It is currently being produced for both the United States and Swedish Armies in large numbers, but it will not defeat active armour.

Below: The Swedish FFV Carl Gustaf weapon can fire a HEAT round, shown here in flight configuration with its fins opened out (1), a new over-calibre

HEAT round which has a larger warhead with nose probe (2), or a wide range of other ammunition types including HEAT FFV 551 (3), illuminating (4),

smoke (5), HE (6), and HE dual purpose (7), enabling a range of targets to be engaged.

Left: Euromissile Milan deployed in typical firing position, with loader on the left ready with a new missile, gunner firing and observer on the right.

weapon had to undergo a two-stage upgrade programme. The first part resulted in the new BGM-71C Improved Tow with a new 5in (127mm) diameter warhead fitted with a telescopic nose fuze that pops out after launch to give an optimum stand-off armour penetration capability. I-Tow was followed by the BGM-71D Tow-2 missile which has a 6in (152mm) diameter warhead with a large telescopic nose fuze probe, improved guidance features and an updated propulsion system.

MILAN

Origin: France/West Germany
Dimensions: Length 2ft 6in (0.769m); diameter 3.54in (90mm); wingspan 10.4in (265mm)
Weight: Complete system 60.9lb (27.7kg); missile 14.7lb (6.65kg)
Performance: Range 27-2,190 yd (25-2,000m)
Warhead: Milan 1 2.64lb (1.2kg)

HEAT; Milan 2 3.96lb (1.8kg) HEAT
Armour penetration: Milan 1 25.6in (650mm); Milan 2 41.7in (1,060mm)
History: Entered production in mid-1970s and now in service with 36 countries. Produced under licence in India, Italy and UK

Background: The Euromissile Milan is an advanced second-generation man-portable spin-stabilised anti-tank guided weapon designed for use mainly from defensive positions. It is a SACLOS wire-controlled missile using infra-red tracking to allow a computer to generate the control signals. The weapon has seen combat service in Chad, the Falklands, Iran and Iraq, and the MIRA thermal imaging sight has been developed for use by the French, West German and British armies. The missile is self-contained in its own tube which is automatically discarded following a launch; once the engagement is over a new tube is fitted to the launcher/guidance unit. To meet new Soviet armour developments Euromissile started production in 1984 of the Milan 2 with a warhead of greater diameter.

Left: The Hughes Tow heavy anti-tank missile has been built in larger numbers than any other missile in the West. It is also launched from armoured vehicles and helicopters. Three types

of Tow missile have been produced: Tow-2 (1), Improved Tow (2) and the original Tow (3). A new warhead is under development to counter new Soviet reactive armour developments.

Below: Milan firing post fitted with the MIRA night sight to enable targets to be engaged under all conditions. The current production version of the Milan missile has a larger diameter warhead with a probe for increased armour penetration. Milan is built in France, . West Germany, India, Italy and the UK.

SA-80, M16 and AK-74

SA-80

Origin: United Kingdom
Calibre: 5.56mm (0.223in)
Length: IW overall 30.9in (70.5cm); IW barrel 20.4in (51.8cm); LSW overall 35.43in (90cm); LSW barrel 25.43in (64.6cm)
Weight loaded: IW 10.98lb (4.98kg); LSW 14.5lb (6.5kg)
Type of feed: 30-round box magazine
Muzzle velocity: IW 3,084ft/sec (940m/sec)
Rate of fire: IW 650-800rds/min; LSW 700-850rds/min
Effective range: IW up to 437 yd (400m); LSW up to 1,094 yd (1,000m)
History: Originally developed from a family of 4.85mm (0.191in) weapons and intended to replace existing rifles and sub-machine guns in the British armed forces. The first 5.56mm full production examples were issued during 1987

Background: The SA 80 is also known as the Enfield Weapon System and comprises two main weapons, the L85A1 Individual Weapon (IW), or Endeavour, and the larger L86A1 Light Support Weapon (LSW), or Engager. The IW is a combat rifle of the bullpup type with the magazine located behind the trigger group to make it short, compact and handy. The LSW may be termed a light machine gun but can be regarded as a machine rifle; it is intended to provide longer range support fire for infantry sections and can fire from an open or closed bolt

whereas the IW fires from a closed bolt only.

Both weapons share many common components and the same general bullpup layout but the LSW has a longer barrel and a light folding bipod. Both use an optical sight but some non-infantry versions of the IW will have orthodox metal sights with the rearsight incorporated into a carrying handle over the receiver. The IW and LSW both use an all-in-

line layout and have very similar gas-operated mechanisms. They are produced by Royal Ordnance Small Arms Division at Enfield Lock.

M16

Origin: USA
Calibre: 5.56mm (0.223in)
Length: Overall 38.97in (99cm); barrel 20in (50.8cm)
Weight: 7lb (3.18kg)

Above: British infantry advance with Royal Ordnance Individual Weapons; the man standing is also carrying a Royal Ordnance 51mm mortar which is already in service with the British Army. The Individual Weapon, which has a day optical sight fitted as standard, can also be fitted with a night sight and has a 30-round magazine which is also used by the Light Support Weapon.

Below: When fitted with the M203 grenade launcher attachment (3) under the barrel, the M16 can fire a wide range of 40mm grenades (1 and 2), such as smoke, high explosive and even armour piercing. The latest version is the M16A2 which has a number of improvements

and can fire the new SS109 round. It was first issued to the US Marine Corps, with the Army receiving its first weapons early in 1987.

Type of feed: 20- or 30-round box magazine
Muzzle velocity: 3,280ft/sec (1,000m/sec)
Rate of fire: 700-950rds/min cyclic
Effective range: 437 yd (400m)
History: The original Armalite AR-15 was designed by Eugene Stoner in the early 1960s; adopted by the US Army in 1967 as the M16, later to become the M16A1. The latest model is the M16A2, and the main producer has been Colt Industries

Background: The Armalite AR-15 was designed to make use of the new 5.56mm (0.223in) cartridge that became the M193. This enabled the weapon to fire on full automatic without the recoil forces making the fire inaccurate. The US Army and Air Force adopted the AR-15 as the M16 but combat experience in Vietnam showed the need for a bolt return plunger to ensure the bolt was closed if the rifle jammed after fouling produced by prolonged firing. The M16A1, the main production model to date, uses a 20- or 30-round box

magazine with the 30-round version being the most favoured. The M16A2 fires the new NATO standard 5.56mm (0.223in) SS109 round and has a heavier barrel. It also has a revised flash hider at the muzzle. The ammunition fired by the M16A1 was designed to have an effective combat range of some 437 yards (400m), the maximum expected to be effective in combat.

Several attempts have been made to produce a light machine gun version but none has been adopted in any numbers, though carbine and sub-machine gun versions have been produced for use by Special Forces. There is also a special version intended to be fired from the firing ports of the M2 Bradley IFV; this has a telescopic wire butt and is known as the M231.

AK-74

Origin: USSR
Calibre: 5.45mm (0.2145in)
Length: AK-74 overall 36.6in (93cm); AKS-74 butt folded 27.16in (69cm);

barrel 15.75in (40cm)
Weight: 7.93lb (3.6kg) unloaded
Type of feed: 30-round box magazine
Muzzle velocity: 2,953ft/sec (900m/sec)
Rate of fire: 650rds/min cyclic
Effective range: 328-437 yd (300-400m)
History: Small-calibre development of the 7.62mm (0.3in) AK-47 and AKM series that first appeared in 1959; now widely used by the Soviet armed forces and some other Warsaw Pact nations

Background: Taking the basic form of the classic 7.62mm AK-47 and AKM rifles as a starting point, the decision was taken to adopt a new Soviet 5.45mm cartridge and the AK-47 design was scaled down to fire it. Consequently the AK-74 closely resembles the AK-47 and AKM rifles but is slightly smaller and lighter overall.

The AK-74 differs in detail from the earlier weapons but uses the same basic gas-operated mechanism. It has a revised and very

efficient muzzle brake to reduce recoil forces and the magazine is manufactured from a distinctive light tan-coloured plastic. It also has a solid wooden butt but a variant known as the AKS-74 intended for use by airborne and other special forces has a tubular skeleton butt that folds along the left-hand side of the weapon. There is also a light machine gun version known as the RPK-74 which has a longer barrel, a 40-round magazine and a light bipod. A much shortened sub-machine gun version known as the AKR has been encountered in Afghanistan.

The bullet fired by the AK-74 is unusual in having a steel core that is so arranged that the bullet nose will bend even if it strikes a soft target. This will enable the bullet to tumble and so inflict wounds much larger than the small calibre could otherwise inflict.

The AK-74 and AKS-74 are now the standard assault rifles for the Soviet armed forces and some other Warsaw Pact armies.

Below: The EWS (Enfield Weapon System), or SA-80, comprises two weapons, the Individual Weapon (IW) shown here and the Light Support Weapon (LSW). The former is now replacing the 7.62mm rifle in the British Army and fires standard 5.56mm ammunition (1) and can be fitted with a bayonet (2), the scabbard of which (3) can be used as a wire cutter.

Left: The AKS-74 is the latest in the long line of famous AK-47 rifles which have been produced in larger numbers than any other rifle since World War II. It fires a new 5.45mm cartridge that has a steel core. The LMG version is called the RPK-74 and has a bipod and 40-round magazine.

Valmet M76, FA MAS and Galil

VALMET M76

Origin: Finland
Calibre: 5.56mm (0.223in) or 7.62mm (0.3in)
Length: Overall 36in (91.4cm); barrel 16.53in (42cm)
Weight loaded: 9.94lb (4.51kg)
Type of feed: 15-, 20- or 30-round box magazines
Muzzle velocity: 5.56mm 2,953ft/sec (900m/sec); 7.62mm 2,359ft/sec (719m/sec)
Rate of fire: 650rds/min cyclic
Effective range: 383-437 yd (350-400m)
History: Originally manufactured in the late 1950s as a Finnish-produced version of the Soviet AK-47. Adopted by the Finnish armed forces and produced for export in various forms and calibres from 1976 onwards

Background: The Valmet Corporation decided to produce a local version of the Soviet 7.62mm (0.3in) AK-47 in the late 1950s. The first example, the M60, differed from the Soviet original in several respects, the main one being that it had no wooden parts as plastic was used instead. The receiver was machined from solid steel and the muzzle brake differed considerably from that of the Soviet design. The M60 rifle was adopted by the Finnish armed forces and became the M62, which differed from the M60 in few details but had a trigger guard.

Commercial sporting and hunting versions of the M60 and M62 were produced but in 1976 the M76 appeared as a deliberate marketing ploy to attract exports. The M76 can be produced in several versions to suit customer requirements, and the two basic models are calibred either for NATO or American 5.56mm cartridges or the Soviet 7.62mm round. To add to these variations the M76 can be fitted with a variety of butt stocks: the M76T has a tubular butt stock, the M76F has a folding stock, and while the M76P has a plastic stock the M76W uses wood. Three sizes of box magazine are available. A design variant of the M76 is the M78, which uses a longer and heavier barrel fitted with a light bipod for sustained fire.

FA MAS

Origin: France
Calibre: 5.56mm (0.223in)
Length: overall 29.8in (757mm); barrel 19.21in (488mm)
Weight: 7.96lb (3.61kg)
Type of feed: 25-round box magazine
Muzzle velocity: 3,150 ft/sec (960m/sec)
Rate of fire: 900-1,000 rds/min cyclic
Effective range: 328 yd (300m)
History: Produced by GIAT at the St Etienne Arsenal and first issued to the French armed forces in 1979, it is intended to be the standard French service rifle. More than 250,000 produced by mid-1987.

Background: The French FA MAS rifle has several claims to fame, and is almost certainly the shortest and most compact of any service rifle in current use. It also uses an unusual dellayed blowback locking mechanism that is not used inn any other weapon of its type. The reduced legth is made possible by the use of the bullpup layout with the 25-round box magazine situated behind the trigger group, but even so the weapon is equipped with a small folding bipod to enable aim to be steadied when firing or when launching grenades.

The FA MAS has a very distinctive appearance due to the long handle over the receiver. This houses the fore nd rear sights and also protects the cocking lever, which travels centrally along the top of the weapon. The length of barrel that

Below: The M76 is the latest version of the Valmet assault rifle and is offered in both 5.56mm (0.223in) and 7.62mm (0.30in) calibres with a variety of butt stocks, including the tubular one shown here and plastic, wood or folding models.

The M78 has a longer and heavier barrel and is fitted with a bipod for use in the LMG role. All accept magazines holding 15, 20 or 30 rounds.

Above: The FA MAS rifle is available in a range of variants. As well as the regular weapon using NATO standard 5.56mm ammunition (1) there is a training version firing 4.5mm lead pellets, plus short-barrel and 2.23mm versions. It can also be used without preparation to launch a range of grenades (2,3,4 and 5) using ordinary ball ammunition.

Above: French infantry dismount from their AMX-10P infantry fighting vehicle using their FA MAS 5.56mm assault rifles. Since 1979 more than 250,000 weapons have been delivered to the French armed forces and some foreign nations. The FA MAS can also fire a variety of bullet trap rifle grenades including smoke, high explosive and training models. The rifle has a 25-round box magazine.

protrudes from the main body can be used to launch rifle grenades of several types, including an anti-armour grenade with a range of 87 yd (80m); special sights are used when grenades are launched. The muzzle is also used to mount a very knife bayonet. The fire control mechanism has a three-round burst fire capability in addition to the usual semi-automatic (single shot) and full automatic; the cartridge used is the M193.

Short as the FA MAS is there is a carbine version known as the Commando intended for use by special forces. This has an attenuated barrel only 15.95in (405mm) long and there is no provision for launching grenades. There is also a low-cost training version which uses compressed air to fire target pellets on single shot only, and a 2.23mm model.

GALIL

Origin: Israel
Calibre: 5.56mm (0.223in) or 7.62mm (0.3in)
Length: 5.56mm overall 38.54in (979mm); stock folded 29.21in (742mm); barrel 18.1in (460mm) 7.62mm overall 41.34in (1,050mm); stock folded 31.89in (810mm); barrel 20.98in (533mm)
Weight: 5.56mm 8.6lb (3.9kg); 7.62mm 8.7lb (3.95kg)
Type of feed: 5.56mm 12-, 35- or 50-round box magazines; 7.62mm 12- or 25-round box magazines
Muzzle velocity: 5.56mm 3,215ft/sec

(980m/sec); 7.62mm 2,789ft/sec (850m/sec)
Rate of fire: 650rds/min cyclic
Effective range: 5.56mm 547 yd (500m); 7.62mm 656 yd (600m)
History: Designed by Israel Galil and first issued in 1973, the Galil rifle was intended to replace a wide range of existing weapons and is produced in several forms and two main calibres by Israel Military Industries

Background: The three main models of the Galil are the AR assault rifle (data above), the ARM which has a bipod and is used as a light machine gun — the bipod also doubles as a handy wire cutter — and the SAR, which is a shortened assault rifle. All models are based on the Soviet AK-47 but closely resemble the Finnish M60 series.

The Galil has many detail design differences from other AK-47 variants. All versions have a folding tubular skeleton stock and all can be used to fire rifle grenades from a specially designed muzzle attachment, a 12-round magazine holding ballistite cartridges being provided for the purpose. The usual magazine holds 25 or 35 rounds, the 50-round magazine being used mainly with the ARM model.

A special 7.62mm sniper version of the Galil has been developed; this is a hand-built model with a heavy barrel, a bipod, a revised muzzle brake and a telescopic sight mounted on a side bracket. The South African 5.56mm (0.223in) R4 rifle is based on the Galil.

Above: The Galil assualt rifle is produced in both 7.62mm (0.30in) and 5.56mm (0.223in) calibres, the latter being standard issue in the Israeli armed forces. It is very similar to the Soviet AK-47 rifle and can have a variety of banana-type magazines including one holding 50 rounds (1) or a 12-round (2) type holding ballistite cartridges which are used to fire various rifle grenades (3, 4 and 5).

M249, RPK, MG3 and M60

M249

Origin: Belgium
Calibre: 5.56mm (0.233in)
Length: Overall 40.94in (1,040mm);
barrel 18.35in (466mm)
Weight loaded: 22lb (10kg)
Type of feed: 200-round belt or 30-round M16A1 box magazine
Muzzle velocity: 3,000ft/sec (915m/sec)
Rate of fire: 750-1,000 rds/min cyclic
Effective range: 875 yd (800m)
History: Originally the FN Minimi and adopted by the US armed forces as their M249 Squad Automatic Weapon (SAW)

Background: The M249, which only entered service with the US Army and Marine Corps in 1987, is based on the FN Minimi, which uses the basic gas-operated mechanism of the Belgian FNC assault rifle allied to a new light machine gun form. The M249 differs only in detail from the original and uses the optional feed system that accepts either 200-round belts or a 30-round M16A1 box magazine, the belts being carried in plastic boxes clipped under the weapon. It fires the new NATO SS109 ammunition, but earlier versions fire the M193 round. Although the M249 is fitted with a bipod it can be fired from a tripod. If the barrel becomes hot from firing it can be rapidly changed; a handle is provided for barrel changing and carrying, and the butt stock may be fixed or sliding.

A short version of the original FN Minimi known as the Para has a shortened barrel and a sliding butt stock. There is also a version intended for use on armoured vehicles. The Minimi is also used by Canada, Australia and Indonesia.

RPK

Origin: USSR
Calibre: 7.62mm (0.3in)
Length: Overall 40.75in (1,035mm);
barrel 23.27in (591mm)
Weight loaded: 15.65lb (7.1kg)
Type of feed: 30- or 40-round box magazine or 75-round drum
Muzzle velocity: 2,402ft/sec (732m/sec)
Rate of fire: 660rds/min cyclic
Effective range: 875 yd (800m)
History: Based on the AKM assault rifle. Entered service during the early 1960s and now in widespread use by various Warsaw Pact nations

Background: The Soviet RPK light machine gun may be regarded as an enlarged AKM assault rifle, using the gas-operated mechanism from the AK-47 allied to an AKM receiver with a longer and heavier barrel plus a bipod. The trigger mechanism has been revised and a large wooden butt shaped for a comfortable left-hand grip when firing bursts is provided, and although the barrel is fixed, so that automatic firing has to be carried out in short bursts to prevent overheating of the barrel, this hardly restricts the use of the weapon as it is normally employed as a light section fire support weapon. Although the RPK is sighted up to 1,094 yd (1,000m) it is normally used at much shorter combat ranges and some examples have been seen equipped with infra-red night sights.

The RPK can use the normal 30-round box magazine of the AK-47 and AKM or a larger 40-round box. It can also be used with a special 75-round drum magazine that fits into the usual magazine slot. A version with a folding butt stock, known as the RPKS, is used by airborne troops and other special forces requiring such compactness.

MG3

Origin: West Germany
Calibre: 7.62mm (0.3in)
Length: Overall 48.23in (1,225mm);
barrel 20.9in (531mm)
Weight: As LMG 24.36lb (11.05kg)
Type of feed: Variable-length belts
Muzzle velocity: 2,690ft/sec (820m/sec)
Rate of fire: 700-1,300rds/min cyclic
Effective range: As LMG 875 yd (800m); as HMG 2,406 yd (2,200m)
History: Originally the World War II MG42, put back into production postwar. Still in production

Background: When the Federal German armed forces became part of NATO they began to rearm and adopted the wartime MG42 as their standard machine gun; eventually it became the current widely-used MG3, the only change from the MG42 being the adoption of the new NATO 7.62mm (0.3in) cartridge and small manufacturing alterations.

The MG3 is a general purpose machine gun that can be mounted on a bipod or a tripod, and for sustained fire the air-cooled barrel has a rapid-change system. The mechanism, of the locking roller type, is both efficient and reliable and is capable of delivering high rates of fire.

Numerous types of vehicle mountings have been produced and pairs of MG3s can be coupled for air defence mountings. Ammunition is fed into the weapon in factory-filled belts of various types with varying lengths to suit the required role. The gun is manufactured under licence in Greece, Pakistan, Spain and Turkey. Attempts have been made to produce a light version using alumunium alloys but so far none has entered large scale production.

M60

Origin: USA
Calibre: 7.62mm (0.3in)
Length: Overall 43.5in (1,105mm);
barrel 22in (560mm)
Weight: 23.17lb (10.51kg)

Above: The RPK is the standard LMG of the Soviet armed forces and has been exported in large numbers. It can use the standard 30-round magazine of the AK-47 assault rifle, a 40-round box or even a 75-round drum magazine. A folding bipod is fitted as standard.

Above: The 7.62mm MG3 is the standard machine gun of the West German and many other armies and is a further development of the famous MG42 weapon of the Second World War. In addition to the standard infantry version shown here fitted with a bipod, there are also vehicle-mounted versions and single and twin anti-aircraft mounts.

Above: A US soldier using his 7.62mm M60 machine gun with empty cartridge cases being ejected to the right of the weapon. When not required the bipod folds up under the barrel to save space. A carrying handle is provided on top of the weapon.

Type of feed: Variable-length belts
Muzzle velocity: 2,805ft/sec (855m/sec)
Rate of fire: 550rds/min cyclic
Effective range: As LMG 1094 yd (1,000m); as HMG 1,969 yd (1,800m)
History: The M60 is a composite design that entered service with the US armed forces during the late 1950s and is still in production

Background: The M60 was a design amalgamation of several types of machine gun into a new weapon. It uses an all-in-line layout and on the early production versions the barrel and bipod were connected and had to be changed together when the barrel got hot, a drawback which was later removed. Other drawbacks were a poor sighting system and long ammunition feed belts which were a disadvantage in the light machine gun role; the carrying handle also proved to be too flimsy for hard use. Overall, the M60 has proved to be too heavy as a light machine gun while the barrel is too light to deliver sustained fire for long periods when used as a heavy tripod-mounted weapon.

Gradual design changes have removed most of the worst features of the M60 and it is still widely used in several forms, including a tank coaxial weapon and as a helicopter weapon on pintles or in pods. The M60 was widely employed during the Vietnam conflict and has been adopted by Australia, Taiwan, South Korea and several other nations. Saco Defense Industries have produced a lightened model known as the M60E3 for use as a light machine gun, but this has not been adopted.

Right: The M249 Squad Automatic Weapon (SAW) is the US version of the Belgian FN Minimi and is currently being produced in the United States. In addition to using the standard 30-round M16 magazine it can also accept a 200-round box as shown here. A bipod is also provided.

Above: The 7.62mm M60 is the standard machine gun of the United States armed forces although when first introduced it did have a number of shortcomings. The weapon is air-cooled, belt-fed and fitted with a bipod. There are also versions for mounting on armoured fighting vehicles and in helicopters doors.

MO-120-RT-61, L16A2 and M-240

MO-120-RT-61

Origin: France
Calibre: 120mm (4.72in)
Length of barrel: 81.89in (2,080mm)
Weight in action: 1,283lb (582kg)
Rate of fire: 10-12rds/min
Maximum range: 8,897 yd (8,135m)
Bomb weight: HE 41.23lb (18.7kg)
History: Introduced in 1961.
Produced by Thomson-Brandt and
now widely used by many nations

Background: The Thomson-Brandt
rifled 120mm mortar may be
regarded as an exercise in how to
produce a light artillery piece at a low
cost, being complex but relatively
light compared to artillery weapons
and able to deliver very accurate fire.
It has to be towed by its tractor
vehicle to its firing site as it is too
heavy for man handling, which can
restrict the choice of firing position,
and when emplaced on its large and
heavy base plate the carriage retains
its wheels. Hand-loading the rifled
bombs is not easy because of the
height of the barrel muzzle and
sometimes a short ladder has to be
employed, but all the disadvantages
are overcome by the fact that the
rifled mortar is a very accurate
weapon in action. It is often used by
light forces who could not otherwise

take any form of artillery with them
into action.

The rifled barrel is a massive single
forging that is finned along its entire
length to dissipate the heat produced
when firing and is strong enough to
be used as a lever to get the base plate
out of the ground after prolonged
firing. A lunette is inserted into the
muzzle for towing, usually by a light
wheeled vehicle.

The bombs fired have a pre-
engraved driving band that has to be
engaged in the barrel rifling as they
are loaded. Apart from the usual high
explosive, smoke and illuminating
bombs the ammunition family
includes a rocket-assisted bomb with
a maximum range of 14,217 yd
(13,000m); an anti-armour bomb is
also available, and smooth-bore
120mm bombs can be fired.

L16

Origin: United Kingdom
Calibre: 81mm (3.19in)
Length of barrel: 50.4in (1,280mm)
Weight in action: 83.6lb (37.94kg)
Muzzle velocity: 974ft/sec (297m/
sec) max
Rate of fire: 15rds/min max
Maximum range: 6,179 yd (5,650m)
Bomb weight: HE 9.26lb (4.2kg)
History: Entered service in 1961; in
service with more than 15 countries

by 1987. Saw extensive use in the
1982 Falklands campaign

Background: The L16A2 has proved
one of the best mortars in service
anywhere and has been approved by
the US Army as the M252 for use by
its new light divisions. It uses a
mount known as a 'k' mount and has

Above: Royal Ordnance 81mm
mortar in action. To enable it to be
transported over rough terrain it
can be quickly disassembled into
three main components, baseplate,
barrel and bipod. British
Aerospace is developing the Merlin
terminally guided mortar bomb
intended to attack the tops of tanks.

Right: The Thomson-
Brandt 120mm rifled
mortar is widely used by
many countries in place of
105mm towed artillery and
is currently being
evaluated by the US Army
as a replacement for its
very old 4.2in mortars. In
addition to HE bombs (2)
other types can be fired
including smoke (1) and
illuminating.

Below: The Royal
Ordnance 81mm L16 has
been the standard mortar
of the British Army for
many years and has been
adopted by many other
armies, more recently the
US Army. The mortar fires
HE (1) and Smoke White

Phosphorus (2) bombs to
a maximum range of
6,179 yards (5,650m).
The standard version is
used in the ground role
but it can also be installed
in armoured fighting
vehicles such as the
FV432 and M113.

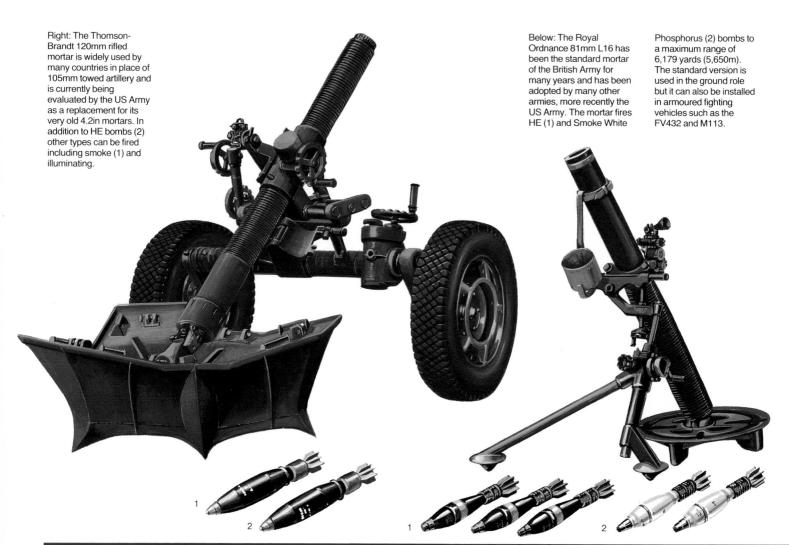

a circular base plate. The barrel is made of a special nickel steel alloy that enables sustained firing of up to 15 bombs a minute without dangerous overheating; the barrel is finned at the base to dissipate heat. The high-explosive bombs fired produce extensive fragmentation effects on target.

The L16A2 can be broken down into three main loads for man-packing — this method was used in the Falklands — or carried in light vehicles. The British Army deploys it in specially equipped FV432 tracked carriers in its mechanised battalions. British L16A2 teams now use hand-held fire control computers that provide speed of response and greater accuracy, and a trained mortar team can take the weapon into and out of action within a few minutes.

Bombs fired from the L16A2 include high explosive, smoke, illuminating and practice, and by varying the propellent charge system and the barrel elevation ranges as short as 181 yd (166m) can be reached. Under development is an anti-armour bomb known as Merlin which uses a radar seeker head to guide itself onto tank targets. Bombs able to reach ranges of over 6,000 metres (6562 yd) are also being developed, as is a new type of mount.

M-240

Origin: USSR
Calibre: 240mm (9.45in)
Length of barrel: 210.2in (5,340mm)
Weight in action: 9.149lb (4,150kg) approx
Rate of fire: 1rd/min
Maximum range: 10,600 yd (9,700m)
Bomb weight: 286.6lb (130kg)
History: In service since the early 1950s and developed using World War II tactical experience as a guide. Retained in service for use against strong points and built-up area targets

Background: The M-240 heavy mortar may be regarded as a form of artillery weapon as it is meant to be used only at heavy artillery brigade

level. It is a large and cumbersome weapon that requires an area of flat and level ground from which to fire and at least 25 minutes are required to bring it into action, even when use is made of the winches on the carriage. The time is taken mainly by the need to pack the base plate into firm earth, and slightly less time is needed to get the weapon out of action. The normal towing vehicle is a tracked tractor and the usual mortar crew is at least 11 men.

The big, heavy bombs are breech-loaded after the long smooth-bored barrel is split and hinged forward horizontally to receive them. Each bomb is carried to the breech by four men using a carrying yoke and inserted along a guide; the barrel is raised, the sights are checked, and only then is the M-240 ready to fire. This loading procedure reduces the rate of fire to only one bomb a minute at best. Recoil forces are absorbed by shock absorbers on the carriage and the massive base plate.

The high-explosive bombs used are almost 59in (1.5m) long, and weigh 286.6lb (130kg), of which 75lb (34kg) is explosive payload. These powerful bombs are used to demolish strong points or targets in built-up areas that other types of artillery could tackle only with difficulty.

Left: The M-240 240mm is the largest towed mortar in service with the Soviet Army and has also been exported to several other countries. It suffers from a number of drawbacks such as slow rate of fire and short range and is therefore more likely to be used in urban fighting. A self-propelled 240mm mortar is now in service.

Tactics

Below: A Tow team and M61 tanks participating in exercise Border Star 85 are menaced by an A-10. The modern battlefield embraces three dimensions.

Introduction

All armies study operational methodology, and whether they refer to land warfare as a science or as an art most of them find the study of military history a rewarding undertaking, believing that they can derive from the past valuable lessons and principles for the future and usually managing to deduce from their studies precepts which form the fundamental principles for their own current and future operational and tactical doctrine. Not surprisingly, these principles differ from army to army, being dependent on factors such as national history, geography, international obligations and so on.

The **Soviet** Army probably studies war, in both general and specific terms, more than any other, and its detailed study of military history focusses especially on its campaigns during World War II. Its principles of war consequently include elements derived directly from the Soviet experience:

Mobility and high tempo of operations: this principle always features first and requires the Soviet forces to achieve and sustain rapid movement; it encompasses manoeuvre forces, fire support and logistic elements.

Combat activeness: this is the doctrine of the offensive — the constant attempt to seize and retain the initiative.

Concentration of effort: this can be achieved in space — for example, by massing troops to assault over a narrow front — or in time, such as by the use of geographically dispersed artillery units to produce heavy concentrations of fire.

Surprise and security: the Soviet Army sets great store by achieving both strategic and tactical surprise, and views security as an integral part of surprise, going to extreme lengths to ensure the security of plans and operations.

Conformity of the goal: the main thrust of this principle is that the goal of an operation must be compatible with the combat situation; that is, it must be achievable with available forces and means and must take cognisance of space and time.

Coordination: this principle seeks to ensure that all elements of the force work together in combat.

Preservation of the combat effectiveness of friendly forces: this principle considers the conservation of the fighting strength of own troops — by protecting them, by returning wounded men and damaged vehicles to combat and by utilising captured equipment as it becomes available — though it does not prevent Soviet generals being more profligate with manpower than their counterparts in other armies.

US Army doctrine stipulates that the primary purpose of an offensive operation is to destroy the enemy's defensive system by breaking through and driving rapidly into the rear areas: once that has been achieved artillery, air defence weapons, command posts and other elements of command and control systems, as well as logistical support, can be destroyed. To this end the US Army lays down six fundamental principles:

See the battlefield: this involves the entire spectrum of intelligence from knowledge of the enemy's organisation, capabilities and current deployment, to information on terrain and climate.

Concentrate overwhelming combat power: this entails identifying the enemy's weak points; massing armoured mechanised and artillery assets to overwhelm them at the chosen spot; and using terrain, camouflage, smoke, ECCM and movement by night to achieve such concentrations.

Suppress enemy defensive fire: concentration of force renders own troops vulnerable to direct, indirect and air defence fire, and action must be taken to suppress this before it starts.

Shock, overwhelm and destroy the enemy: attacks must be prosecuted with all speed, bypassing defensive positions when possible, leapfrogging stalled attacking elements and exploiting an enemy's weaknesses until he is utterly defeated.

Attack the enemy rear: once through the enemy's forward positions, armoured forces must press on into his rear areas to destroy field artillery, air defences, C^2 locations, logistic locations and reserves.

Provide continuous mobile support: accompanying artillery, air defence weapons, engineers, signals and logistic units must be able to keep pace with the forward manoeuvre elements to maintain the momentum of the advance.

British Army tactical doctrine has long been based on ten principles of war; the first is paramount, but the remainder occur in no particular order of priority:

Below: The widespread provision of wheeled and subsequently tracked vehicles for infantry formations was one step toward the mobility that is fundamental to all modern army doctrine, but the helicopter introduced a new level of speed to troop deployment. Here US Army Blackhawks carry light vehicles in an air-mobile assault.

Above: Knowing where you are is at least as important as being able to get there. A US Army tank commander studies a map in the turret of an M60.

Right: A tank formation on the move in poor weather. Being able to carry on the assault whatever the conditions is a fundamental tactical consideration.

Selection and maintenance of the aim: this pre-eminent principle reflects the absolute importance of clarity of purpose at strategic, operational and tactical levels.

Maintenance of morale: the morale of one's own forces is of vital importance to the continuation of a campaign.

Offensive action: offensive action is the only way in which a commander can obtain ultimate success — defensive action can only be a stepping-stone to victory, it cannot achieve victory on its own.

Surprise: this factor is necessary to cause confusion and upset·the enemy's equilibrium, thus enabling a commander to seize and retain the initiative.

Concentration of force: success will normally result from the concentration of superior force at the decisive time and place.

Economy of effort: in many ways the corollary of concentration of force, this warns against the unnecessary dissipation of resources; it may involve taking calculated risks in less critical areas and adopting the defensive or conducting delaying actions in some areas in order to attack in others.

Security: this entails far more than denial of information to the enemy, encompassing the defence of bases, the protection of flanks, the maintenance of a favourable air situation and the provision of reserves.

Flexibility: this requires commanders and units to respond effectively to changes in the situation as operations develop.

Cooperation: all military operations require close cooperation between different elements of the ground forces and many also need cooperation between land and air or sea forces also.

Administration: all operational and tactical plans depend on sound and reliable logistic support.

It is clear from the above that three important and very experienced armies agree on, for example, the need for concentration of force, offensive action and surprise. The Soviet Army is the only one to emphasise high tempo, while the British formally recognise the importance of morale as a principle, though it would be wrong to deduce from this that the others neglect such a critical factor. The British Army is also the only one of the three to include flexibility as a principle. Of course there are further factors which could be included as principles: other armies stipulate boldness and some would go so far as to encourage the taking of risks.

The principles serve as the basis for operational and tactical doctrine. For example, the Soviet Army has applied the principles of mobility and high tempo of operations and combat activeness to a doctrine which calls for an average rate of advance of 18 miles (30km) per day in conventional warfare and of 30 miles (50km) per day in nuclear conditions.

Unit designation symbols

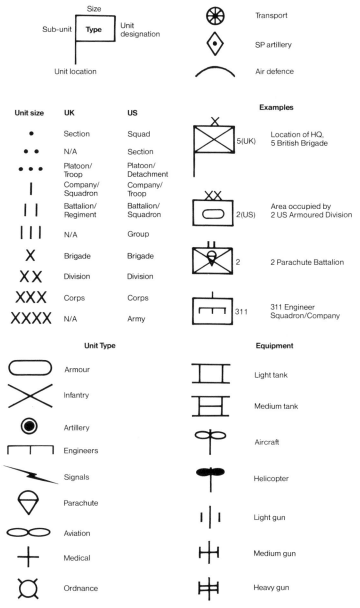

Unit size	UK	US
•	Section	Squad
• •	N/A	Section
• • •	Platoon/Troop	Platoon/Detachment
I	Company/Squadron	Company/Troop
I I	Battalion/Regiment	Battalion/Squadron
I I I	N/A	Group
X	Brigade	Brigade
XX	Division	Division
XXX	Corps	Corps
XXXX	N/A	Army

Transport
SP artillery
Air defence

Examples

5(UK) — Location of HQ, 5 British Brigade

2(US) — Area occupied by 2 US Armoured Division

2 — 2 Parachute Battalion

311 — 311 Engineer Squadron/Company

Unit Type

Armour
Infantry
Artillery
Engineers
Signals
Parachute
Aviation
Medical
Ordnance

Equipment

Light tank
Medium tank
Aircraft
Helicopter
Light gun
Medium gun
Heavy gun

The Suez Canal, 1973

After its successes in the 1967 Middle East war Israel was faced with a classic contradiction. The country was determined to retain the territorial gains in the Sinai, the Gaza Strip, the West Bank, Jerusalem and the Golan as buffers against possible future Arab aggression, but this ensured that the Arabs would never rest until they were recovered, so that the apparent means of security were actually the seeds of inevitable insecurity.

Following their 1967 defeat the Arab leaders and their military forces had no option but to adopt a long-term policy of rebuilding and re-equipping. The new leader of Egypt, Anwar Sadat, who succeeded Nasser on his death in November 1970, agreed with President Assad of Syria to pursue a strategy with limited but realistic aims: to compel Israel to withdraw from territory occupied in 1967, recognise Palestinian rights and agree to the resolution of the refugee problem. From this stemmed a military strategy designed to demonstrate Arab military determination both to themselves and the world at large and involving the seizure of the Golan Heights and the East Bank of the Suez Canal, but without advancing far enough to threaten Israel's national existence; a concurrent oil embargo would impose economic pressure on the West. It was a sound, well thought-out strategic concept, and it very nearly succeeded.

THE MILITARY SITUATION

The military solution to Israel's need to defend the line of the Suez Canal would have been to use a mobile surveillance screen near the canal itself, with armoured formations held well back in the Sinai ready to counter-attack Egyptian penetrations, but political pressures forced the Israelis to adopt a forward defensive position known as the Bar-Lev Line.

There was a series of fortified posts along the east bank of the canal, each garrisoned by a half-platoon and reinforced by the remainder of the platoon in an emergency, and Israeli engineers had constructed a large sand ramp, very close to the edge of the eastern bank, which constituted a major obstacle to any vehicle landing. A natural sand ridge a few miles to the east was the setting for a series of larger strong points, each to be garrisoned by an infantry company on mobilisation. Immediately available mobile reserves were provided by tanks, with fire positions prepared for troops of three tanks each at the forward platoon posts and a further series of positions 500-1,000m behind the bank posts, giving them support and covering the gaps. Further back still were positions to give depth and to defend the important passes through the Western Hills — the Sudr, Mitla, Giddi and the Khatmia. These were to be occupied by reserve brigades on mobilisation.

Two north-south roads had been constructed to enable reinforcements and reserves to be deployed quickly. The Artillery Road ran immediately behind the line of company posts, some 6 miles (10km) from the canal, while the Lateral Road was even further back, about 18 miles (30km) from the canal.

The force defending the canal was the Sinai Division whose HQ was at Bir Gifgafa, but other command posts had been built ready for occupation on mobilisation. In late 1973 this division comprised an under-

strength infantry brigade in the forward positions, backed by one armoured brigade giving immediate support to the infantry brigade, with the remaining two armoured brigades well to the east, many hours from the canal area.

The important commanders were all Armoured Corps officers, who found themselves faced with a dilemma in that their training and natural instincts urged them to rely on mobile warfare, but the political constraints forced them into a semi-static strategy, even though much depended upon mobile, aggressive tank forces. However the static environment, reinforced by the inevitable inertia which overtakes troops who try to maintain a high degree of readiness over a protracted period, led to a gradual increase in rigidity of thought and outlook: coupled with the disdain in which the Israeli Army held the Egyptians after the previous wars, this in turn led to a dangerous degree of complacency which almost resulted in defeat.

An Egyptian analysis of the situation in early 1973 credited the Israelis with air superiority, high standards of training and motivation, technical ability and the assured support of the United States. Against these were a reluctance to fight a long war or to incur heavy casualties coupled with long lines of communication, partiuclarly to the Suez front, and over-confidence. These factors, together with large-scale Soviet arms supplies, particularly of surface-to-air missiles, led the Egyptians and

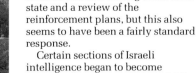

Left: The crucial factor in the Egyptian success – the breaching of the sand walls on the eastern bank of the Canal – was the idea of a junior engineer officer.

Syrians to conclude tnat a well-planned and carefully coordinated attack could succeed.

On the Suez front the Egyptians knew a great deal about the Israeli positions: their problem was how to concentrate sufficient force to be able to carry out a surprise attack across the canal, seize bridgeheads, break out from the bridgeheads and seize and hold the Western Hills, before the Israeli reinforcements could arrive following mobilisation.

Since the 1967 war the Egyptian armed forces had undergone a major re-equipment programme, all its new material coming from the Eastern bloc. The Army received Scud-B and Frog missiles, together with AT-3 Sagger and AT-2 Swatter anti-tank missiles, RPG-7 shoulder-launched rockets and large numbers

Above: Another factor in the Egyptian plan was the build-up of vast concentrations of military equipment without alarming the Israelis until the very last moment.

of SA-2 Guideline, SA-3 Goa, and SA-6 Gainful anti-aircraft missiles; the SAMs were used to set up one of the strongest air defence systems ever known, covering Cairo, several other major cities and the Suez Canal, and field units were supplied with SA-7 Grail missiles and ZSU-23-4 tracked guns for use in the forward areas. Training, particularly of junior officers, was given a high priority, and great care was exercised in the selection of senior commanders and staff officers.

EGYPTIAN PREPARATIONS

The Egyptians concentrated their assault force under the guise of their annual mobilisation exercise, which was publicly scheduled to end on

All aspects of the plan were carefully coordinated and when the Egyptians struck they inflicted the worst military reverse the Israelis have suffered.

October 8, 1973, and a disinformation campaign was mounted to allay US and Israeli suspicions. Apparently random activity such as troop movements and lifting minefields was all, in fact, part of the detailed plan, which was extremely successful, and by October 5 all was ready.

On the other side the Israelis had had one or two suspicions, but were generally reasonably complacent. A major Arab attack during the fasting period of Ramadhan seemed unlikely, although the Sinai Divison did go on to a low-level alert on October 1 as a result of the exercise — a standard and not especially demanding military precaution. The general commanding the Israeli Southern Command toured the forward positons on October 2 and

ordered a further raising of the alert state and a review of the reinforcement plans, but this also seems to have been a fairly standard response.

Certain sections of Israeli intelligence began to become concerned as the attack neared. The sudden departure of Soviet civilians and families from Egypt and Syria and the sailing of Soviet ships from Egyptian and Syrian ports was noted by Israeli Naval Intelligence, and some junior intelligence officers were predicting war by October 3 or 4, but their reports were rejected as alarmist. On October 5 the Israeli Southern Command began to realise that the build-up opposite them was becoming distinctly threatening, but a request to implement the reinforcement plan was rejected as provocative.

On the night of October 5/6 the Egyptians and Syrians made their final dispositions and the Israelis put their active army on the highest state of alert, though there was still no mobilisation order. In the early hours of October 6 Israeli military intelligence obtained a copy of the Egyptian operation order, but this was a somewhat outdated copy; the attack time it gave as 1800 hours had been changed to 1400 hours some weeks previously, and led the Israelis to think they had more time than was actually the case. A series of meetings took place, and partial mobilisation was ordered at 1000 hours, but proposed pre-emptive strikes were cancelled as the Prime Minister, Golda Meir, needed to ensure that Israel was demonstrably the victim of aggression.

THE CROSSING

At 1330 hours (H−30 minutes) Cairo Radio broadcast a news flash about an Israeli raid on Zafaıani on the Red Sea coast, and this was followed by a formal complaint to the United Nations Security Council at 1400 hours. The news was, of course, a complete fabrication, but it gave the excuse for the crossing of the canal as a reprisal.

The assault started at 1405 hours with a massive air strike against Israeli artillery and command positions, combined with an artillery bombardment of the Bar-Lev Line. At 1435 hours commandos crossed the canal, followed by infantry, engineers and a few amphibious and ferried tanks, while heliborne raiding parties headed for the Khatmia, Giddi and Mitla passes.

The main problem at this stage was to deal with the massive sand embankment erected by the Israelis, and the answer was provided by a junior officer of the Egyptian engineer corps — powerful water monitors, which simply washed the barrier away. Soviet-supplied pontoon bridging was quickly in position and the first bridges were in use in the Second Army area before midnight. By the end of this phase the Egyptians were firmly on the far bank of the canal and all the bridgeheads were linking up with each other, but only in certain places, mainly in Second Army in the North,

Left: After their success in the first few days, the tide turned against Egypt and they suffered heavy losses, symbolised by these knocked-out Soviet-built tanks.

Above: In 1973 the Israeli Armoured Corps was one of the most dynamic elements in the army. Every tank they could lay their hands on was put to good use,

whether it was modern British Centurions, captured Soviet T-54s or these old World War II Shermans, updated with new guns and engines.

had they reached and taken the ridge overlooking the Artillery Road. The helicopters carrying commandos to set up blocking positions in the passes through the Western Hills had suffered badly — they were operating outside the SAM umbrella — and a courageous attempt by 130 Marine Amphibious Brigade to relieve the Giddi Pass raiders had been repulsed when it accidentally ran into an Israeli armoured brigade on its way south.

Some 80,000 men were across the canal by last light (1930 hours) for a loss of 208 killed, and by dawn many more troops plus some 500 tanks were also across. During October 7 more tanks crossed the canal despite heavy Israeli air attacks.

On October 7 Israeli reinforcements began to arrive, demonstrating the efficiency of their mobilisation drills. Israeli battle plans laid down that a counter-attack was to be launched 48 hours after any Arab attack, a requirement based on the assumption that there would be 72 hours notice in which to mobilise and deploy, and despite the fact that

its basic assumption was invalid in this case the Israeli commanders proceeded to implement the doctrine. The price of this example of military blindness was failure.

The Israeli operation on October 8 was not helped by a muddled plan and confusing orders. Two Israeli armoured divisions drove south in echelon and passed across the front of the Egyptian positions, exposing their right flanks as they did so; the Egyptians seized the opportunity and destroyed many tanks — 70 out of 170 in the northern Israeli division alone. The Egyptians also dealt very conclusively with two further Israeli attacks on October 9.

So far the Egyptians had been outstandingly successful. They had achieved surprise, crossed the canal, linked up their bridgeheads and kept resolutely within their SAM umbrella. Moreover, they had made a large dent in the Israeli reputation of invincibility, and while they had failed to take the passes and had not advanced as far as planned they were relatively secure. However, they had failed in one respect that was to be

almost fatal in the following days: there was a gap at the junction of Second and Third Armies, one which the Israelis were to detect and to exploit.

Unfortunately, their very success involved strong pressure to exploit it. Junior officers wanted to sweep forward to the Western Hills, while President Assad appealed to President Sadat on October 11 to attack and draw Israeli forces, particularly air power, to the South, thus relieving pressure on his forces in the Golan. As a result the Egyptian commander was pressured into sending Egypt's two armoured divisions across the canal on October 12/13. The attack was put in on October 14, but instead of a concentrated effort for a decisive blow they attacked all along the line and nowhere in overwhelming strength. The Egyptian forces achieved some local successes early on, but they had soon lost over 200 tanks to Israeli tanks and a further 60 to air strikes, and in the evening orders were issued for a return to the bridgeheads.

THE ISRAELI COUNTERSTROKE

With Egyptian confidence shaken and their own somewhat restored, the Israelis counter-attacked on October 15. Major-General Sharon hit the junction between Second and Third Armies and was able, in classic Israeli armoured style, to penetrate to the canal, while a parachute brigade landed on the far side near Deversoir. The Egyptian Second Army closed the corridor behind Sharon, isolating his division temporarily in two bridgeheads either side of the canal, but Major-General Adan's division broke through, bringing supplies and, more importantly, a bridge to Sharon, and by October 19 both divisions were on the Egyptian side of the canal. Israeli attempts to take Ismailia to the northwest were repulsed by Egyptian paratroops and armoured forces, but Adan made slightly better progress southward towards Cairo.

A ceasefire applied from 1852 hours on October 22 was disregarded

The Egyptian attack: 1700, October 6

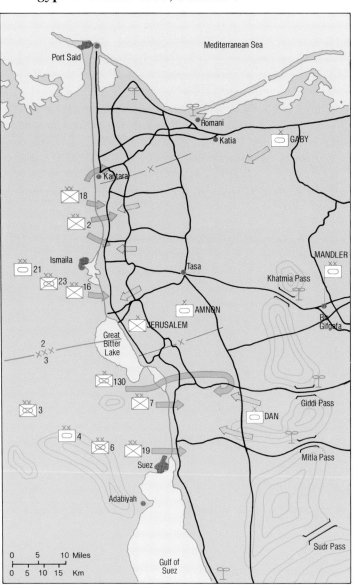

Late afternoon, October 7

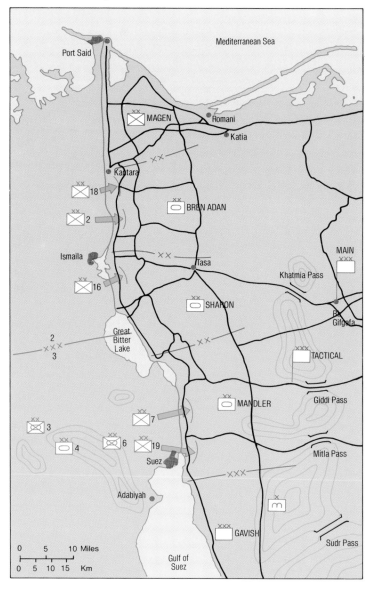

Above: The situation three hours after the Egyptians crossed the canal on a five-division front. Israeli defensive plans were based on strongpoints on the banks and on the assumption that reserves would be able to use the north-south roads.

Above: The situation on the day following the Egyptian assault as the Israelis regrouped and tried to contain the situation, while the mobilisation and deployment of their reserves proceeded apace at home. Meanwhile, Egyptian morale remained high.

by both sides, and the Israelis sent strong reinforcements across the canal and Adan continued to drive south and succeeded in isolating the Third Army. An attempt to take the city of Suez was repelled by the Egyptians just before a second, effective ceasefire came into effect at 0700 hours on October 24.

CONCLUSIONS

The Egyptian plan and its early implementation were superb. Despite the best that Israeli and US intelligence could do strategic and tactical surprise was achieved, and considering how many people in the Egyptian and Syrian high commands must have been involved this was a remarkable achievement. Moreover, even when Sadat took the calculated risk of telling the Soviet ambassador 48 hours before H-hour and the Soviets insisted on evacuating their nationals, the secret still held. In fact, it is extraordinary that the Soviets apparently did not know what was going on at this late stage. The lesson is clear: even in this day of ultra-sophisticated surveillance, it is still possible for a combination of good planning, a sound deception plan and well-trained troops to achieve both strategic and tactical surprise.

Nor should the scale of the Egyptian control and logistic achievement on the canal be underestimated. To concentrate so many troops and equipment prior to H-hour, to carry out the crossing and install so many bridges, and then to pass troops and equipment over them and on into the Sinai was masterly.

General Ismail has been criticised in some quarters for failing to exploit his success, especiallly after the victory on October 8. However, he seems to have realised clearly the limitations of his own troops and to have understood the Israeli mastery of mobile warfare and air superiority, and it was only when he was forced into the attack on October 14 that matters began to go wrong for the Egyptians. His ground troops found themselves beyond the SAM umbrella, on ground which the Israelis knew well, and were defeated. Then, as has happened so often in war, came the fatal error of a failure at a junction between two major formations.

The Israelis learnt some bitter lessons from the war in the south. They showed that even such an imaginative, experienced, highly motivated and well trained army can suffer from over-confidence and from the stultifying effects of protracted garrison duty in fixed positions. They also demonstrated that even the best intelligence staffs can ignore or misinterpret crushingly obvious intelligence pointers, especially when they fail to fit in with preconceived ideas. This problem, known as cognitive dissonance, occurred in the USA in the lead-up to Pearl Harbor and, more recently, in Britain in the weeks preceding the Argentinian invasion of South Georgia and the Falkland Islands.

At the end of it all, however, these battles on the Suez Canal in 1973 restored the Egyptian Army's pride in itself. It had carried out some very successful operations and its infantry had stood firm against Israeli armour attacks, although not always successfully. It was this restoral of confidence that led first to the disengagement agreement of 1974, in which the Israelis withdrew to a line a few miles east of the canal and then to the Camp David agreement in which the Egyptians recovered virtually all of the Sinai.

The 1973 war also showed how modern equipment and logistics enable the balance of advantage on the battlefield to swing back and forth with dramatic frequency. Apparent Israeli impregnability up to October 6 was followed by a period of sudden Egyptian dominance up to October 14, when the Israeli position looked distinctly shaky. Then the pendulum swung back, and by October 16 the Israelis were over the canal in places. Such rapid advances and sudden reverses underline the need for resilient command and control systems and for the mental agility to allow commanders and units to change direction suddenly, to regroup and to change plans instantly.

October 8: Planned Israeli counterattack

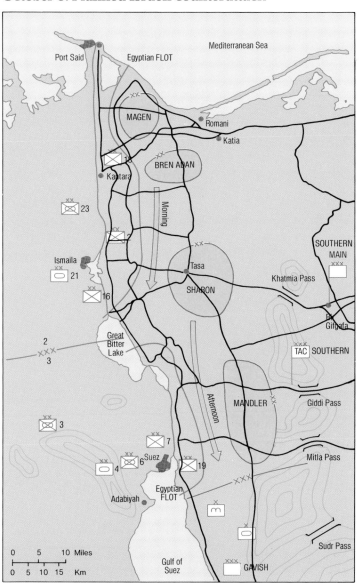

Above: On October 8 the Israeli commanders acted in a manner that was not only uncoordinated but – surprisingly, in an army with such traditions – dogmatic and doctrinaire. As a result many tanks were lost while the Egyptians remained unruffled.

October 14: Final Egyptian exploitation

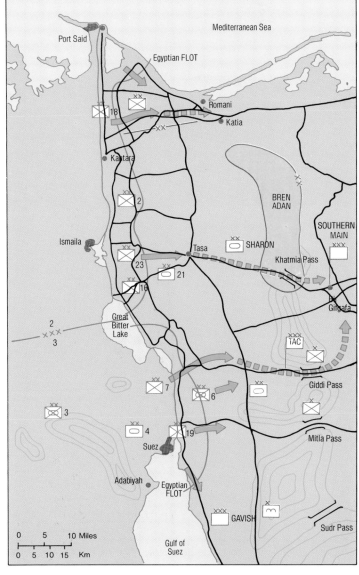

Above: The high point of the Egyptians' operation came on October 14 as they pushed forward into the Sinai, leaving the SAM umbrella which had served them so well up to this point. Had matters rested here, the campaign would have been a triumph.

Combined Arms Operations

All the more sophisticated armies, particularly those likely to fight in Central Europe, organise themselves in such a way that they can deploy combined arms formations made up of tank and mechanised infantry units. The British Army in West Germany, for example, has brigades consisting of armoured regiments and infantry battalions, each of which is a coherent fighting unit in its own right, but rapid regrouping can mix these units to suit the tactical situation, so that a tank-heavy battle group could be formed using the armoured regiment headquarters and two tank squadrons, with an infantry-heavy battle group elsewhere within the brigade.

Since the mechanisation of the infantry for the majority of roles became an accomplished fact in the 1960s, the distinction between tank and infantry has blurred, and permanent combined arms units may soon be established, though such a step would be resisted desperately by the traditionalists in many armies. In the meantime, artillery, engineer and aviation arms must also be integrated in any tactical grouping.

The designations of military formations and units frequently cause confusion, since some nations have retained traditional designations. For example, most armies designate the basic unit a battalion; this is normally commanded by a lieutenant-colonel or a major and is some 400 to 600 men strong. However, while the US and most other armies have infantry, tank, artillery and other battalions, the British Army, while using the designation battalion for the infantry, terms armoured, artillery and engineer units regiments.

The grouping of several battalions is designated a brigade in some armies and a regiment in others; confusion arises from the fact that in some armies, such as the British, brigades are commanded by brigadier-generals while in others, for example the US Army, the commander is a colonel. In armies such as those of France and the Soviet Union, which use the regiment as a tactical formation, it is commanded by a colonel and the battalion commanders are majors. The next level, the division, is almost invariably commanded by a major-general and is normally the largest formation to be trained and fought as a combined arms team.

It is important to note that even where titles and organisations in different armies may appear to be superficially similar there can be considerable differences in strengths of manpower and equipment, and thus in fighting potential — a Soviet Army division, for example, is somewhat smaller than a US Army heavy division.

ARTILLERY

Artillery units have become tactically more responsive since the 1960s, as self-propelled weapons have facilitated more rapid reactions and greater ranges, and terminal

Above: The combination of tank and infantry units is absolutely essential on today's battlefield and these two combat arms are now so interdependent as to be virtually inseparable, although no army has yet taken the plunge and organised permanent mixed formations. Here Swedish S-tanks and Pbv-302 APCs operate together.

Above: An absolutely indispensable element of any combined arms grouping is artillery, whose flexible, accurate and effective fire support remains essential to offence and defence alike. Their elaborate command and control systems are designed to ensure rapid and overwhelming response.

Below: Infantry/armour cooperation has its limits and tanks and jeep-borne infantry would be unlikely to operate like this on a battlefield.

effects have increased as larger calibres have come into use. One of the particular advantages of artillery is its tactical flexibility, allowing fire to be moved or concentrated to the full extent permitted by the command and control system, and all armies include artillery units in their brigade or equivalent organisations, usually in the form of self-propelled 155mm regiments or battalions. Further artillery resources — heavy guns and howitzers, rocket launchers and tactical missiles — are held at division, corps and army or front level, where they can be used under the control of the HQ to which they belong or allocated to subordinate formations for specific operations or tasks. The artillery arm also provides air defences.

ENGINEERS

It is a truism demonstrated afresh in every war that there are never enough engineers. The mobility resulting from mechanisation depends on engineer preparation and repair of routes, particularly the building of bridges and the clearance of obstacles, and the renewed popularity of mine warfare has placed further demands on engineers. All armies include engineer units in their forward brigades or regiments.

AVIATION

There has been phenomenal growth in the deployment of helicopters by armies, some of which also have small fixed-wing aircraft elements. The helicopter is providing a new dimension to land warfare, adding to its traditional roles of liaison, reconnaissance and troop transport an important new capability to deal with armour. The result is that substantial resources have to be devoted to countering anti-tank helicopters, and since the best weapon for finding, attacking and destroying a helicopter is generally held to be another helicopter, the day of the helicopter fighter has already arrived.

Right: Also essential to combined arms operations are support troops such as the engineers who made this bridge and the logistics troops in the trucks crossing it.

Above: Newest members of the combined arms teams are aviation units, whose helicopters add a new dimension to battlefield operations. Carrying out liaison, reconnaissance, transportation and anti-tank missions, they are of increasing importance. Anti-helicopter tactics are being added to their repertoire.

Most armies have aviation units in their forward brigades, either as integral components or placed in direct support for specific operations.

US ARMY DOCTRINE

The US Army has long been concerned that battle plans to counter Warsaw Pact forces failed to take sufficient account of Soviet capabilities, particularly the fact that as aggressors the Soviets would start off with the initiative and use their speed of advance and multi-echelon tactics to maintain the momentum of their attack. Current US Army operational doctrine, approved in 1982 and based on the Air Land Battle 2000 concept, is much more aggressive than earlier doctrines, seeking to secure the intiative from the aggressor as early as possible and then use it dynamically to defeat him. The doctrine depends upon four tenets:
Initiative to make the enemy react to US forces and not vice versa.
Depth, a three-dimensional concept whose essential elements are time, distance and resources.
Agility, or the ability to act and react faster than the enemy.
Synchronisation, involving coordination with higher and lower echelons, other services and allies.
At the operational level the doctrine calls for a three-level view of the battlefield, with three concurrent, inextricably related and equally important battlefields labelled deep, close-in and rear. Deep battle involves delaying, disrupting or, preferably, destroying second, third and subsequent enemy echelons. Because it is a focal point in the C³I systems, especially in relation to joint-service and allied HQs, the key level in the deep battle is corps, although division and

brigade may also fight a less ambitious deep battle.
Fundamental to the US Army's offensive operations are five characteristics, namely concentration, surprise, speed, flexibility and audacity. The first four are self-explanatory, while the fifth is seen as entailing a balance between a justifiable tactical risk and a gamble.
The new doctrine also calls for a change in style of defence and seems to emphasise an aggressive defence without actually specifying how this differs from earlier approaches. The aim is to halt the enemy's advance and force him to deploy, whereupon he will be counter-attacked, probably by the designated reserves, which may constitute up to one third of the force.

US TACTICAL UNITS

The US Army's basic combat units are the tank battalion and the mechanised infantry battalion. The tank battalion deploys 58 M1 Abrams tanks, with 48 allocated to the four tank companies, each of which has three four-tank platoons. There is also an HQ which includes an Armoured Cavalry Platoon with seven M3 Bradleys and six 81mm mortars.
The mechanised infantry battalion consists of 844 men organised into four rifle companies, an anti-armour company and an HQ company. Each rifle company has three platoons, whose three nine-man squads are mounted in M2 Bradley IFVs. The anti-armour company has three platoons of three sections each, each with an Improved Tow vehicle, and the HQ company includes a scout platoon and a mortar platoon with six 81mm mortars.

Tanks and anti-tank weapons are used to destroy enemy tanks and other fighting vehicles, while the infantry's task is to destroy enemy infantry and to provide security for tanks in close country and at night. The two elements are usually grouped together according to the tactical situation under tank or infantry battalion HQs into combined arms battalion task forces, which can either be tank heavy — where the basic unit is the tank battalion with proportionately smaller infantry sub-units added — or infantry heavy.

A relatively new element is the Combat Aviation Brigade, which consists of two attack helicopter battalions, a general support aviation company, a combat aviation company and a reconnaissance squadron. The attack helicopter units are air manoeuvre units which use highly mobile, responsive air combat vehicles as part of the combined arms team, and are tasked with destroying armoured vehicles and dismounted infantry. They manoeuvre and practise fire and movement exactly like ground-borne units to engage the enemy from the front, sides and rear.

The other main combat element is the artillery, which is responsible for providing fire support for the manoeuvre elements. In a division the divisional artillery has one 155mm SP howitzer battalion for each manoeuvre brigade, plus an MLRS battery and an air defence artillery battalion. Divisions will be allocated support by heavier weapons under corps and army group control according to the tactical situation.

SOVIET ORGANISATION

The Soviet tactical doctrine of a high tempo of operations, which basically means the rapid achievement of combat objectives, involves an unremitting emphasis on a rate of advance of around 25 to 30 miles (40 to 50km) per day in conventional operations. It also entails continuity of attack, the principle means of achieving which is the concept of echelons, for which there is no direct Western equivalent. The defence is given scant consideration in Soviet military thinking; it is never practised at levels above the divisional, and even at lower levels it is seen as a very temporary expedient, to be adopted by units making brief pauses in their advance or who are temporarily held up by the enemy.

Soviet attack formations are normally organised into three groupings designated first echelon, second echelon and reserve. The first echelon includes the main elements of the force, probably between half and two thirds of its strength, and most of the tanks and artillery. The second echelon has as its primary task the maintenance of momentum, especially on the main axis, and can be tasked to reach the same objective as the first echelon if that becomes necessary; alternatively, if the first echelon attack is successful the second echelon can be used for

immediate exploitation either on the main axis or in a new direction.

The second echelon follows some distance behind the first, remaining in tactical march column until it is committed. Typical distances between first and second echelons are: battalions 0.6-1.9 miles (1-3km); regiments 3.1-9.3 miles (5-15km); and divisions 9.3-18.6 miles (15-30km). The reserve, usually very small by Western standards — a

Above: An AH-1S Cobra attack helicopter flies top cover for a column of M113 APCs. Helicopters are also able to reconnoitre ahead of such formations.

Right: A class carries out an indoor tactical exercise at one of the many officer schools in the USSR, where strict training ensures uniformity of doctrine. The tank models characteristically depict an attacking formation.

Below: A Soviet Army infantry squad in a BTR-60 wheeled APC. Some Western commentators suggest that Soviet troops may prove unreliable in a future conflict, but their evidence for this claim is flimsy.

reinforced battalion for a division, for example — is held ready for unanticipated tasks. Other specialised reserves, such as an anti-tank reserve, may be created to deal with an unexpected armoured resistance.

A distinctive Soviet operational and tactical characteristic is that of only reinforcing success. Thus, in a regimental attack where two battalions were fighting hard but

Below: A joint armour/infantry attack during an exercise in the Red Banner Siberian Military District. Such combined attacks are routine for the Soviet Army.

failing to make any progress while the third was making slow progress, it is the third that would be supported, first by the regimental second echelon and then, in all probability, by the division's second echelon.

The basic permanent tactical element of the Soviet Army is the regiment, which is commanded by a colonel and equates to brigades in Western armies. The three main types of combat regiment, tank, motor rifle and airborne, each have a headquarters and three battalions of the basic arm, together with combat support — air defence, reconnaissance, engineer and signal — companies and combat service support (logistics) units. In addition, the tank regiment includes a motorised rifle company, the motor rifle regiment has a tank battalion and each airborne regiment includes a company of BMD assault combat vehicles.

There are two types of tank battalion. The tank battalion of a tank regiment has 31 MBTs in three companies of ten, while independent tank battalions and the tank battalions of motor rifle regiments have 40 MBTs each (13 per company); each tank platoon has three tanks. The tank battalions also have an HQ, a logistics platoon and a medical section, but no integral fire support. Motor rifle battalions consist of three motor rifle companies, each with 10 APC/IFVs, a mortar company of six 120mm mortars and logistic sub-units.

To achieve the tempo of activity and the rate of advance required, Soviet tactical units emphasise quick attacks, especially from the line of march, rapid crossing of obstacles, the use of heliborne or parachute troops ahead of the forward units, and movement by night as well as by day. These require tight and comprehensive control, and movement discipline is very strict, being closely supervised by the Commandant's Service, who are roughly equivalent to Western military police.

The Soviet Army practicses the detachment of complete units from one formation to another to suit the tactical situation. However, these do not appear to regroup into battalion-level task forces, as is the practice in many Western armies.

A significant development at the operational level in Soviet thinking in recent years is a return to the concept of the Operational Manoeuvre Group (OMG). Originally developed during World War I, the OMG, which might be based on a formation such as a tank division but supplemented with other units according to the operational situation, is intended to achieve a major penetration and then operate deep inside enemy — that is, NATO — territory. The OMG differs conceptually from the second echelon described above in that it is not simply an instrument of punching through to an objective or of limited exploitation, but is intended to operate on its own. This means that a NATO formation looking for the second echelon in the rear of the Soviet FLOT would not be able to find it.

It is unlikely that an OMG would be committed immediately on the outbreak of hostilities, but it would be launched as soon as it was possible to gauge where it could best be deployed, the apparent intention being to blast a corridor for it through the enemy tactical zone, using massive artillery and air strikes.

An OMG operating inside NATO territory on the Western side of the FLOT would be detected and counter-attacked, but a sufficiently powerful OMG would require such large forces to pin it down and then destroy it that it would cause a critical redeployment of forces that would otherwise have been meeting the main Warsaw Pact attacks. The significant difference between the OMG and other forces intended to fight in an enemy's rear area, such as Spetznaz, Special Forces, guerrillas, and so on, is that the OMG is intended to fight as a coherent fighting formation and not in a series of small bodies.

The logistic support of such a large body would become a major problem after a few days, especially if it was moving long distances and using substantial quantities of ammunition, and the commander would have to either divert considerable numbers of troops to keep a resupply corridor back to the Warsaw Pact lines open or live off captured supplies. The latter is certainly a possibility, especially as he would probably be operating in an area where there would be a number of NATO resupply depots, but there would be a large element of risk involved.

Soviet dismounted infantry section formation

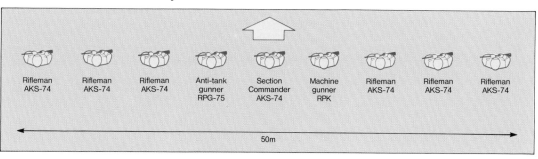

Above: A Soviet infantry section advancing, typically, in line. The section leader is in the centre, where he can best exercise command and control, with the machine gun group on his right

and the anti-tank group on his left. The section covers some 50m and would be an easy target for artillery or machine gun fire, but the formation is suited to Soviet tactical doctrine.

Below: A platoon advances in line in open country about 100m behind the tank, the platoon HQ following behind the centre section and the empty APCs bringing up the rear 200-400m further back.

Platoon advance in line

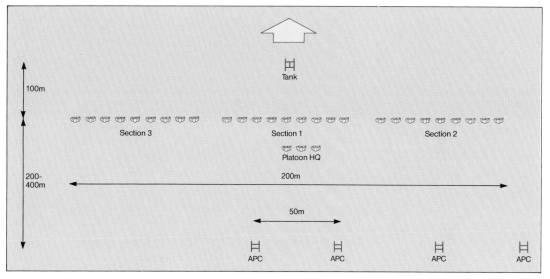

Platoon advance in open country – echelon to right

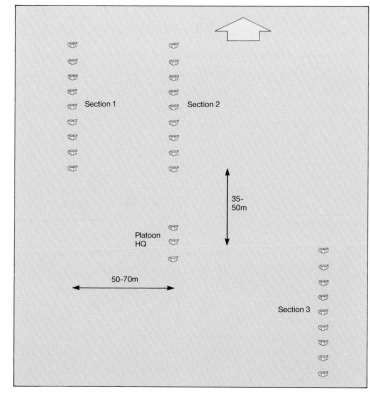

Above: An alternative formation used in open country is for the three sections to advance in echelon to the right, with the

platoon HQ again positioned in the centre of the formation. In line or abreast are the standard patterns: fire and movement is rarely used.

Platoon advance in close country – two-up

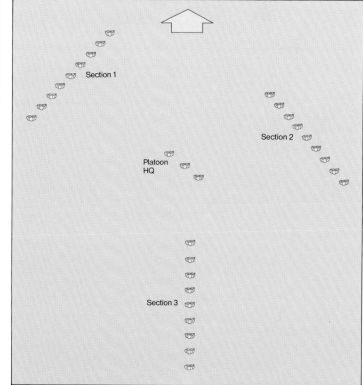

Above: In close country a typical disposition of the platoon is for the two forward sections to be echeloned to left and right as

shown, while the third section follows in line behind the platoon HQ, located as usual in the centre of the formation.

Soviet Tactics

The Soviet Army is a staunch believer in the use of surprise to mislead the enemy and to catch him off balance. Combat reports from Afghanistan have not been published in the West, and this example taken from the Soviet Army journal *Soviet Military Review* depicts an exercise scenario, but it can be taken to exemplify what a Soviet battalion commander would seek to achieve in combat.

THE SITUATION

Soviet units (Red) are advancing in a northerly direction, but the withdrawing enemy (Blue) has managed to set up a defensive position on Hills 116 and 110. These positions are occupied by a company each, supported by ATGW.

The 1st Tank Battalion, with 1st Artillery Battalion under its command, had been advancing north along the axis of the road from Savelnevo to Nyrkovo. On coming under fire 1st Tank Company has carried out a quick attack from the line of march in the direction Snopovo-Nyrkovo, but this failed and the company is pinned down at Position A. The remainder of the battalion halted behind Hill 110 awaiting the outcome of 1st Tank Company's engagement, and on its failure the battalion commander moves forward to Hill 115.

THE PLAN

The battalion commander's plan is to blank off the position on Hill 110 by fire and then to attack Hill 116 with two companies, but he needs to disguise his intentions and surprise the enemy. His plan is, therefore, to move 1st Tank Company from its exposed position at A to the forward edge of the Bolshaya Wood (B) where it will appear to be preparing to attack Hill 110.

At the same time 2nd Tank Company, halted behind Savelyevo at C, will move across the open ground between Ovalnaya Wood and Bolshaya Wood, entering the latter as if going to join up with 1st Tank Company for a battalion attack, but will then swing around through Bolshaya Wood, exiting behind Hill 99 to return unseen to Ovalnaya Wood to Position D.

Meanwhile, 3rd Tank Company will advance under cover from

Below: Soviet infantrymen advance in line supported by BMP-1 IFVs. There has been intense, open and honest discussion in Soviet military journals about the best tactics for the use of IFVs; the result is that the idea of the vehicles charging the objective, guns blazing, before the infantry has debussed has been discarded.

River-crossing Operations

Soviet Army tactical doctrine is based on extremely rapid advances intended to keep the enemy off balance, so it is very important that they maintain the momentum of such an advance and that obstacles, particularly water obstacles such as rivers, streams and canals, are crossed as quickly as possible. The Soviets estimate, for example, that in north west Europe any advancing force would encounter numerous water obstacles, on average one over 20ft (6m) wide every 12 miles (20km), one up to 328ft (100m) wide every 22-37 miles (35-60km), one 328-984ft (100-300m) wide every 62-93 miles (100-150km) and one over 984ft (300m) every 155-186 miles (250-300km).

The Soviet Army possesses a vast range of engineer equipment to ensure that such obstacles are crossed with the minimum of fuss and delay, including tank-launched bridges such as the MTU-20, a Class 50 scissor-bridge, mounted on a T-55 chassis and capable of spanning a 59ft (18m) gap. The TMM Class 60 truck-launched tactical bridge consists of four sections which

together are capable of spanning a 130ft (40m) gap, with a water depth not exceeding 10ft (3m).

The PMP pontoon bridge set has a maximum length of 36 links, but each division holds 16 river and two shore links, and six boats, giving it the capability of constructing a 387ft (118m) Class 60 bridge, a 740ft (225m) Class 20 bridge or various other combinations of length and weight classification. Other equipment includes the PTS tracked amphibious transporter, which can carry a payload of 9.84 tons (10,000kg), and the GSP tracked amphibious ferry, consisting of two non-interchangeable left- and right-hand units which, when joined together, can carry a tank, which is capable of firing while afloat.

Most of these mechanical equipments have parallels in most Western armies, but while the great majority of Soviet reconnaissance vehicles, self-propelled guns and armoured personnel carriers are amphibious, the most important fighting vehicle of all the — MBT — is not.

Soviet tanks, like most Western tanks, are capable of wading to a

Soviet surprise action

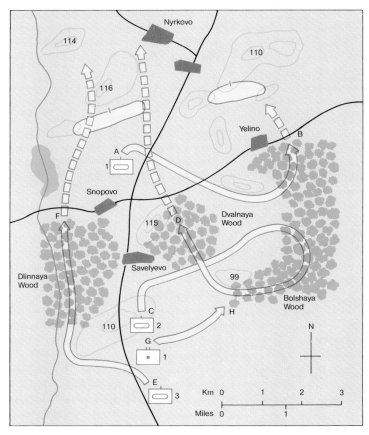

Above: A Soviet officer's concept of a battalion attack from the line of march (fully described in the text). The constant pressure on the enemy, the unceasing search for weak points and the close cooperation between tanks, infantry and artillery all have but one aim – to enable the advance to continue.

Right: Closed-down BMPs move forward to deliver their infantry squads to their final assault positions in an attack on an 'enemy' strong point. The advent of APCs/IFVs has revolutionised infantry tactics and forced reconsideration of some deeply inbred and passionately held attitudes in all armies.

Position E through Dilnaya Wood to Position F. Finally, the direct support artillery battalion, having halted on the line of march at G will deploy to a fire position at H from where it can support the attacks. Observing these moves, the enemy assumes that the attack will be from Yelino towards Hill 110. Consequently, he reinforces that position with the ATGWs from Hill 116.

THE ATTACK

The attack opens with 1st Artillery Battalion bringing down covering fire on the enemy position at Hill 116, while 1st Tank Company fires on the other enemy position on Hill 110 from B, with the particular task of preventing the enemy from redeploying his ATGWs once he has detected the main thrust line. As the attack starts 1st Tank Company loses one of its Tank Platoons, withdrawn by the Battalion Commander into battalion reserve.

The main attack then takes place, with two companies up. 2nd Tank Company assaults on the line Ovalnaya Wood (D)-Nyrkovo, while 3rd Tank Company is on the line Snopovo-Hill 114. As 2nd and 3rd Tank Companies pass over Hill 116, 1st Tank Company attacks on the line Yelino-Nyrkovo, taking out the enemy on Hill 110 en route.

Left: Even narrow rivers and canals constitute obstacles to an advancing army and crossing operations need preparation and engineer support. Here a US Army MBT is crossing an engineer-installed bridge; most armies possess such equipment.

Above: Tracked bridgelayers (AVLBs) can lay bridges rapidly and recover them afterwards, though rather less quickly. However, their span is limited to about 60ft (18.3m). The scissors type shown here makes a prominent target as it is laid.

maximum depth of 5ft (1.4m), and they are also capable of crossing rivers with the aid of a snorkel tube. This method is virtually never regarded as a tactical operation in Western armies, all Western tanks that have a deep-wading capability use wide snorkel tubes, and the capability is seldom practised in peace. There have been several unconfirmed reports that Soviet tank units have mutinied rather than carry out this apparently hazardous operation, and while Soviet films and videos show tanks approaching rivers in neat columns, driving into the water, disappearing from sight briefly and emerging on the far side of the river ready to drive off, firing as they go, the operation is nothing like as simple as it appears.

THE CROSSING

Careful reconnaissance of a proposed crossing site is essential. Snorkelling tanks are vulnerable to underwater obstacles, soft river beds and swift currents, any of which can cause the tracks to slip or the driver to lose control, especially by stalling the engine. In addition, the snorkel tube can be damaged, with potentially disastrous results, by floating debris, broken ice and, of course by artillery or mortar fire.

For planning purposes the maximum permissible current is 7mph (11km/h) and the maximum depth envisaged is 18ft (5.5m). The entrances and exits to the crossing must also be carefully selected and, where necessary improved by engineers; maximum slope on the entry side is 25° and on the exit 15°.

For operational underwater crossings the small diameter OPVT combat snorkel is fitted over the loader's periscope. A special wide snorkel tube, for use in training only, is wide enough for a man to escape through.

The tanks incorporate fixed equipment for such crossings, including watertight seals for the engine compartment covers, air cleaner shutters, gun ports and sighthead. Additional equipment is carried dismounted on the tank. Such removable items of underwater driving equipment include the snorkel tube (normally carried in one or two sections behind the turret), exhaust valves, seals for any apertures such as the radiator top antenna mounting, coaxial machine gun slit and gun sights, muzzle seals for the main gun and machine guns, and rubber sealing cords for the commander's hatch. There are also oxygen masks and lifebelts for each crew member.

Left: PT-76 reconnaissance tanks swimming a river on an exercise. The Soviet Army has vast numbers of vehicles capable of swimming with little or no preparation.

PREPARATION

Preparation time of an MBT unit for crossing a water obstacle varies according to the type of tank involved but normally is about 90 minutes and takes place some 4 miles (6km) back from the river. The first requirement, at least in peacetime, is that a tank must have a minimum of 620 miles (1,000km) to go before its next scheduled overhaul.

The tank crew begins its preparation for underwater fording by carrying out a full technical maintenance, checking the communications equipment rubberised sealing, ensuring that all washers and plugs are watertight and that the turret and driver's hatches do not jam. They also check that the pressure in the compressed air cylinders is not less than 120kg/cm². Because they are going to be driving blind on the river-bed, they then carry out a check for lateral deviation, ensuring that the tank does not veer more than 16ft (5m) off course while being held straight by

the driver moving in first gear over a 110yd (100m) level course.

The crew then install the removable equipment and ensure that all slits are watertight using a special sealing compound. The turret is locked in position and the ring is sealed with an inflatable rubber device, and special valves are attached to the exhaust system to allow the exhaust gases to escape but prevent water from entering; the remaining exposed working parts are smeared with resin. The bottom section of the snorkel is then attached, a piezometer is mounted in a special opening in the turret roof and the watertight integrity of the tank is tested. With the rest of the crew outside the tank the driver starts the engine, adjusts it to run at precisely 650rpm and leaves via the loader's hatch, sealing it after him. The commander then closes the end of the snorkel and the crew carries out a visual inspection of the seals and after 3 minutes the commander checks the piezometer to ensure that it registers within 300mm Hg.

When all is ready the snorkels are dismounted and tanks move in company to a forward site about a mile from the crossing site, where it takes about two minutes to remount

Soviet submerged river-crossing procedure

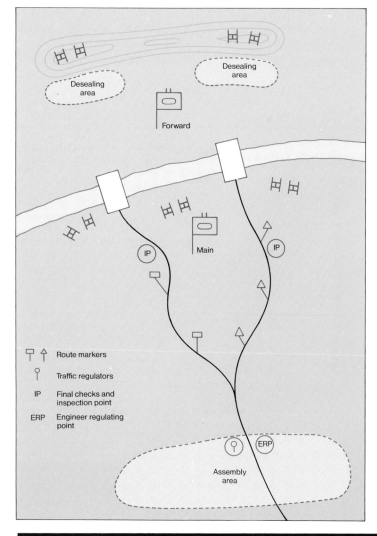

Route markers

Traffic regulators

IP   Final checks and inspection point

ERP   Engineer regulating point

Left: Soviet Army underwater river-crossing operations using snorkels. Two crossing sites are prepared, the primary and the reserve, and all movements from the assembly area, through the river and on to the desealing area are closely controlled.

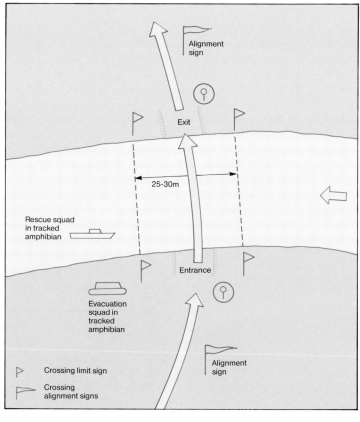

Crossing limit sign

Crossing alignment signs

Above: Crossings are marked with flags, and recovery tanks and boats are positioned ready to spring into action should a tank have serious difficulties. As the crews are blind, a tank stopping in mid-stream will cause a snarl-up with tactical consequences.

Right: A Soviet GSP heavy amphibious ferry carrying a T-54 MBT. The ferry is formed from two vehicles, and those for each side are not interchangeable.

the snorkel tube, carry out final integrity checks and adjustments, and establish radio contact with the crossing site commander.

All Soviet training literature stresses that the tank must be driven smoothly and at a constant speed — normally 100m per minute — entering the water without jerks and moving strictly in the direction of the leading marks. The tanks travel in first gear with their engines at 1,500-1,600rpm, and in no circumstances must engine speed be allowed to fall below 1,100rpm, otherwise it will stall, block the crossing for following tanks and have to be pulled out of the water by recovery teams, all of which makes the operation even more vulnerable to hostile action.

The tank is driven in a straight line on a preassigned magnetic bearing; the crew use the gyrocompass inside the vehicle, and course corrections can be radioed to the tank by the crossing commander from his position on the bank. Such careful driving is necessary because the tracks tend to slip on the slippery river bottom and to ensure that the tank emerges at the correct exit site. The interval between tanks is about 33 yards (30m).

In combat, after leaving the water the snorkel is jettisoned by means of explosive charges and the tank can then, if operationally necessary, go straight into action without the crew leaving the tank. However, the engine compartment hatches must be opened at the first opportunity to prevent overheating and at the earliest opportunity the crew needs to spend about 20 minutes restoring the tank to its normal state.

RESCUE AND RECOVERY

Rescue and recovery parties are certainly deployed on peacetime exercise, and their presence is equally essential in war, though in the latter case the reason would be as much to keep the stream of tanks moving as to save life. The parties consist of divers, boatmen and tractor operators, and a special multipurpose engineer rescue set is used to ensure the rescue of the crew from a submerged but not flooded tank. The primary requirement is to identify as early as possible a tank with problems and then to get frogmen down to fix ropes and pulleys so that recovery can start at once.

TACTICS

It is highly unlikely that an underwater crossing by tanks would be attempted without a bridgehead on the far bank, since the tanks are so vulnerable while entering and leaving the water and only if no other form of crossing were possible and time was of the essence would an underwater attempt be made.

The battalion commander normally receives his orders by

Above: Artillery units cross a Soviet floating bridge during an exercise in Poland. Such bridges are very vulnerable to artillery fire and air attack. Each pontoon is carried by a 2.5-ton truck, which also launches it.

Below: Soviet engineers construct a TMM Class 60 bridge. A bridge set comprises four 33.5ft (10.2m) sections with 9.8ft (3m) trestles; a 130ft (40m) bridge takes 12 men 40-60 minutes to lay by day, or 60-80 minutes by night.

radio, which designate the crossing area. The fording sites are each controlled by a crossing commander, normally from the attached engineer unit, and a command post is set up on each side of the obstacle, usually with the commander in the forward CP and the deputy commander on the near bank. As is usual Soviet practice, all routes are heavily and clearly marked by the Commandant's Service, and there are elaborate markings at the fording sites themselves, flags by day and green lamps at night.

The fording sites must be dominated by fire and amphibious tanks are sent to take up fire positions on the far bank. MBTs also take up fire positions on the near bank. Artillery and mortar fire are used to support the crossing, along with ground-attack aircraft and helicopter gunships.

Infantry Battalion Attack: Wireless Ridge

East Falklands

The Wireless Ridge attack by 2nd Battalion, The British Parachute Regiment (2 Para) on June 13-14 during the 1982 Falklands War is an excellent example of an action by a highly trained, fit and experienced unit. This action is of particular interest because 2 Para was the only unit to carry out two full-scale battalion attacks during the war and thus the only one to be able to put into practice the lessons learned at Goose Green on May 28. It is also of interest because it was a pure infantry affair, with no armoured personnel carriers and only a very few light tanks engaged.

The Falklands War had started with the Argentinian invasion of the islands on April 2, 1982, and the British Task Force sailed for the South Atlantic only three days later. The island of South Georgia was repossessed on April 25 and the landing at San Carlos on East Falkland took place on May 21. Back in the United Kingdom 2 Para and 3 Para had been part of 5 Infantry Brigade, but both had been hastily transferred to 3 Commando Brigade on the formation of the Task Force. Following the landing at San Carlos 2 Para became the first unit of the force to be involved in a major land battle, at Goose Green on May 28. The battle lasted just under two days and ended in the total defeat of the Argentine garrison, but at the cost of numerouus casualties in 2 Para, including the Commanding Officer, who died at the head of his battalion.

On the arrival of 5 Infantry Brigade in the Falklands 2 Para was transferred back and led the drive towards Port Stanley on the southern axis. The men were flown forward, a company at a time, to Fitzroy Settlement on June 1 in the sole surviving Chinook helicopter and were still in the area on June 8 when the landing ship *Sir Galahad,* carrying 1st Battalion, Welsh Guards, was attacked by Argentian Skyhawks; the ship was lost with 97 men. Throughout this time all forward British units were patrolling actively to identify Argentinian positions and minefields in anticipation of the final drive on Port Stanley.

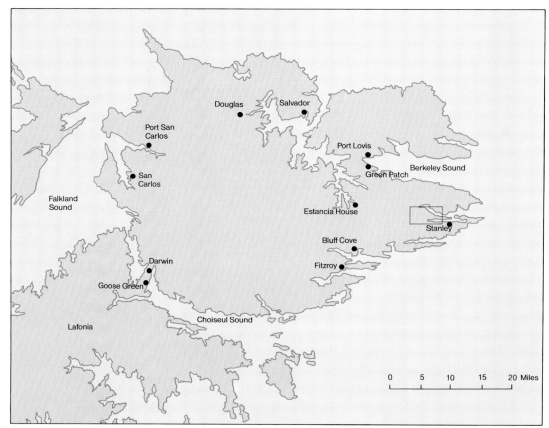

THE MILITARY SITUATION

The Argentinians appeared to be in a strong position. They occupied the hill features to the east of Stanley, dominating all the open, coverless approaches to the capital. They had had plenty of time to dig in, lay mines, construct wire barriers, plan defensive fire missions and prepare themselves for the battles which had become inevitable once the British had landed at San Carlos. They had had time to build up a major supply base at Port Stanley and had plenty of ammunition and supplies, with much shorter delivery distances than the British, who were ever further from their logistic base at San Carlos. On the other hand, communications to Argentina were becoming ever more tenuous, although C-130 Hercules transport aircraft were able to get into and out of Stanley airfield right up to the night before the surrender.

An Argentinian infantry regiment occupied the features to be attacked by 2 Para. The headquarters and one company were on Ring Contour 250, with two companies on Wireless Ridge itself and further positions on Ring Contour 100 and a small feature

Above: Virtually all land operations in the South Atlantic War took place in the northern half of the East Falklands, and were conducted with but one aim — the capture of Port Stanley.

Below left: A British 105mm Light Gun, which was the only land artillery weapon used. Fire support also came from RN and RAF aircraft and from warships, the latter proving very effective.

Below: British troops advance near Port Stanley over typical Falklands terrain. The going is far more difficult than it may appear from this photograph.

to the north east of Mount Longdon. They were mostly well dug in and had fire support from the 155mm guns located among the civilian houses on the hill above Port Stanley; these guns were always rapid and accurate in their response to calls for fire support.

The terrain on East Falkland is bleak. The peaty ground is covered in low scrub, except for the occasional rock outcrops, particularly on the ridge lines, and the unique rock runs; there are no trees, bushes or natural cover for infantry. The vicinity of Port Stanley is dominated by a series of hills; most are smooth-sided, but with rough rocks and water pools at their summit. Sapper Hill lies to the south west, and from it a ridge extends eastward through Mount William and Two Sisters to the dominating feature, Mount Kent. At the head of Stanley Harbour lies the mount of Moody Brook and the ruined Moody Barracks, which had been the home of the Royal Marines detachment until the Argentinian invasion. From Moody Brook there ran, at the time of the war, one of the very few rough tracks, to Estancia House. To the north of Moody Brook was Wireless Ridge, a long, relatively low feature, once the site of the high-frequency radio antennas of the Falklands radio staion from which it took its name.

On June 11 2 Para, now returned to 3 Commando Brigade, moved by helicopter from Fitzroy Settlement on the south coast of East Falkland to a lying-up position west of Mount Kent, which by that time had been occupied by part of 42 Commando, Royal Marines. At 2300 hours 2 Para set off on foot to an assembly area to the north of Mount Kent, ready to support either 3 Para in their attack on Mount Longdon or 45 Commando, Royal Marines, whose mission was to take the position known as Two Sisters; however, both attacks were successful and 2 Para were not called on. Consequently, the morning of June 12 found 3 Para, 45 Commando and 42 Commando firmly established on Mount Longdon, Two Sisters and Mount Harriet respectively, with the units of 5 Infantry Brigade ready to pass through to attack Tumbledown, Mount William and Sapper Hill. The ultimate objective was the island's capital, Port Stanley, now only a few miles away.

In 3 Commando Brigade 2 Para moved forward about nine miles (15km), skirting Mount Longdon on its north west side but keeping to the south of the Murrell River. They reached an assembly area in the lee of a steep escarpment which offered some cover from the sporadic shelling by the effective Argentinian

Above: A British paratrooper with his 80lb (36kg) load. A French general once observed that "the British infantry is the finest in the world; fortunately there are not many of them."

Below: A 105mm Light Gun battery during the final battles for Port Stanley. Ammunition expenditure was very heavy; by the final day stocks were at critical levels but proved just sufficient.

artillery, where the battalion, as always, dug in. In mid-afternoon orders were received for an attack on Wireless Ridge that night, but they were quickly followed by others postponing the attack to the following night.

At Goose Green 2 Para had been very short of supporting fire, having had only three 105mm guns, one Royal Navy frigate and the battalion's mortars, and the latter had run out of ammunition in the middle of the morning. In this battle they were to have considerably more, including two batteries of 105mm Light Guns in direct support, the mortar platoons of both 2 and 3 Para, each with six 81mm mortars, naval gunfire support from HMS *Ambuscade*, a Type 21 frigate armed with a 4.5in gun, a troop of two Scimitar and two Scorpion AFVs, and the battalion's own machine-gun platoon and Milan anti-tank missile platoon.

As a diversion the Special Air Service (SAS) carried out an attack on Navy Point, the old naval stores and fuel depot at the very eastern end of the Wireless Ridge position. Transported by boats of the Royal Marine's Rigid Raider Squadron, they were illuminated by a searchlight from an Argentinian hospital ship and came under heavy fire from anti-aircraft guns defending the airport. Most of the boats were lost in the process, but, nevertheless, this had the desired effect of confusing the Argentinians.

As always in this short campaign ammunition resupply was a severe problem for the British, but 2 Para improvised a porterage unit, formed from 35 men on less essential tasks, which delivered ammunition to the weapons positions and carried back the wounded on the return journey.

THE ATTACK

In the early afternoon of June 13 four Argentinian Skyhawk aircraft flew in low from the west to attack the headquarters of 3 Commando

Wireless Ridge, 13/14 June 1982

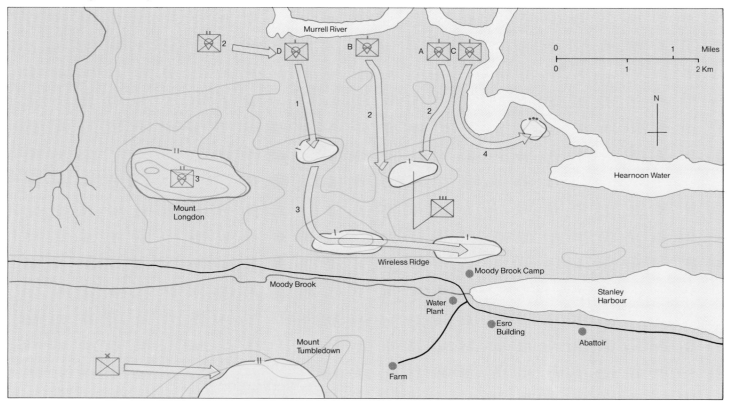

Above: The battle for Wireless Ridge was a classic action carried out by the only British infantry unit to conduct two full battalion attacks. The commanding officer utilised all the resources at his disposal and his sound original plan, amended as circumstances changed during the attack, led to total success.

Brigade. Intense fire from the ground prevented their attack from being pressed home too closely, but they did delay a number of moves in preparation for the coming attack, especially the registration of targets by artillery and mortars.

The commanding officer's plan was for a four-phase 'noisy' attack: Phase 1 was to be the capture by D Company of a small feature north east of 3 Para on Mount Longdon; Phase 2 was a two-company attack by A and B Companies on the Argentinian regimental headquarters on Ring Contour 250; D Company would then advance due south to its Phase 3 objective, Wireless Ridge itself, and then swing east, clearing the ridge line as far as the knoll above the Moody Brook barracks building. Finally, C Company would sweep along the low ground to the Ring Contour 100, a small feature commanding the Murrell River and Hearndon Water.

As 2 Para moved out at last light — 2030 hours local — to the forming-up points the commanding officer received a report that intelligence staffs had just discovered the existence of a minefield in front of A and B Companies' objective. At this late stage, however, there was no alternative but to go ahead and hope for the best.

The artillery fire plan started at 2115 hours local time on June 14 and

Right: An Argentinian 155mm towed howitzer, the heaviest land weapon used during the campaign. It remains in Port Stanley, a reminder of a war of long ago.

D Company crossed its start line at 2145 hours for its Phase 1 attack. The company reached its first objective with little trouble, finding that the enemy had withdrawn, leaving a few dead in their slit trenches. While they reorganised on the objective, enemy 155mm airburst fire began to fall on D Company's new position, a reminder of the efficiency and quick reactions of the Argentinian artillery. With D Company secure, A and B Companies began their advance, the latter passing through what transpired to be the minefield discovered by Intelligence. Some sporadic fire came from a few Argentinian trenches, but was quickly silenced; 17 prisoners were taken and several men killed in this phase of the battle, while the remainder fled. A and B Companies immediately started to dig in, and as usual an accurate and fairly intense enemy artilllery bombardment began; it was to continue for some nine hours. At this point the commanding officer amended his plan slightly, bringing forward C Company's Phase 4 move to take Ring Contour 100; this was achieved with no casualties, the Argentinians having abandoned the position.

It was now time for D Company to carry out its second Phase 3 attack and just as this was about to start the commanding officer received a new piece of information: rather than one enemy company at the other end of the ridge there were two. This was hardly likely to impress the Paras, who by this stage of the campaign had established a considerable moral ascendancy over the Argentinians,

but in the early minutes of this final phase of the battle D Company did receive some casualties as the enemy fought back with unexpected vigour, withdrawing from one bunker at a time. A few casualties also resulted from a supporting fire mission landing direct on D Company. As the Paras poured onto the position, however, the enemy suddenly broke and ran, being continuously harassed off the position by the British Scorpions and Scimitars, and chased by the exhilarated Paras.

As D Company began to reorganise it too came under artillery as well as remarkably effective small-arms fire from Tumbledown Mountain and Mount William to the south, which had not yet been captured by 5 Infantry Brigade. The enemy could be heard trying to regroup in the darkness below the ridge and to the south in the area of Moody Brook. At daybreak a counter-attack was

undertaken by some 40 men up the hill from the area of Moody Brook, but this final gesture petered out after a few minutes under a hail of small-arms and machine gun fire, which was just as well: 2 Para had very little ammunition left and were preparing to resist the attack with grenades and bayonets.

This seems to have been the signal to many Argentinians that the war was over, and shortly afterwards increasing numbers of disheartened and disillusioned Argentinian soldiers were observed streaming off Mount William, Tumbledown and Sapper Hill to seek refuge in Port Stanley. A and B Companies of 2 Para were now brought forward onto Wireless Ridge and the battalion's attack was successfully concluded. The Paras had lost three dead and 11 wounded. Lack of time and opportunity precluded counting the Argentinian casualties, but it has been estimated that, of an original strength of some 500, up to 100 may have been killed; of the balance, 17 were captured and the remainder fled.

ANALYSIS

It is unfortunate that the earlier battle of Goose Green, and the fall of Port Stanley that immediately followed the Wireless Ridge action, have overshadowed this classic battalion attack. However, the taking of Wireless Ridge illustrates the standards which can be achieved by a well led and well trained unit: 2 Para totally defeated a force of at least equal strength, who were well-prepared and dug in and who were occupying a series of dominating features. The commanding officer's plan was well conceived and executed, and was sufficiently flexible to absorb the changes necessary to cope with the additional enemy company on the Wireless Ridge feature as well as bringing forward Phase 4.

The battalion involved, 2 Para, had been on the go ever since its traumatic experience at Goose Green at the start of the land campaign, but had learned its lessons well. It also gave the lie to the frequent and ill-informed allegation that parachute units do not have staying power: it is significant that at every stage they paid assiduous attention to battle procedures, carrying out aggressive patrols when temporarily in a static position, advancing with enthusiasm to every attack, and reorganising and digging in immediately on arrival at an objective.

It may be argued that the days of such classic infantry battalion attacks are over, and that the infantry should be concentrating on combined-arms operations, mounted in APCs and moving rapidly across country in support of tanks. However, as well as the British in the Falklands the Americans in Vietnam and Grenada, the Soviets in Afghanistan, the Israelis in the Middle East and the Iranians and Iraqis in the long-running war have all found themselves mounting such operations.

Above: British infantry advance across the Falklands. Many lessons were learned from this campaign, particularly concerning personal equipment such as boots, puttees — worn by these men — socks and rucsacks.

Left: An abandoned Argentinian infantry position on Mount Longdon is examined cautiously by a British soldier. The Argentinian troops had plenty of time in which to set up their defences around Port Stanley, and many of them were well sited and soundly prepared.

Below: The terrible debris of defeat — abandoned Argentinian rifles, automatic weapons and ammunition in the Falklands in August 1982. The Argentinian Army was sadly ill-prepared for the task set it by the military junta safely back in Buenos Aires.

Air Mobility

The helicopter is having an increasing effect on the tactics of the modern battlefield, particularly for the rapid deployment and redeployment of tactical reserves, and in anti-tank warfare. A significant development over the past decade has been the gradual move away from the idea that any infantry unit can be made air mobile simply by providing it with helicopters: an increasing number of armies are appreciating that the role requires an integrated force of dedicated helicopters and specialised air assault troops.

The US Army is forming three types of Combat Aviation Brigade (CAB) to fight the Air Land Battle. The first is integral with the heavy divisions — primarily those in Europe — and has 137 helicopters, including 50 attack, 54 reconnaissance and 33 assault/transport. The second is part of the light divisions of the Rapid Deployment Force, and has only 97 aircraft, but with a higher proportion

Above: Italian troops rush to board an AB 412. Helicopters give an exceptional degree of tactical flexibility, being capable of redeploying men or equipment over long distances very rapidly.

Below: An exercise at Fort Hood, Texas, with US Army AH-1G attack helicopters escorting tanks in a Central Front tactical setting. Gunships are now essential for the anti-tank mission.

Above: US Army UH-60 Blackhawks ferrying vehicles and equpment in a rapid redeployment exercise. In 1987 the US Army possessed some 8,970 helicopters, about 1,000 of them Blackhawks.

Right: US Army troops emplaning in UH-60 Blackhawks. Large-scale use of helicopters in tactical operations was pioneered in Vietnam and the lessons learned have been applied since.

of assault/transport UH-60s. The third is at Corps level, with around 270 aircraft, 126 attack, 96 assault/transport and 64 cargo/transport. A US corps in Germany with three divisons will thus have about 680 dedicated aircraft.

The CAB with a heavy division, with approximately 1,200 officers and soldiers, is designed to consolidate the aviation assets of the division as well as to provide an additional control headquarters. The principal units in the CAB are its two attack helicopter battalions, each equipped with 21 AH-64 Apache attack helicopters and 13 OH-58 Kiowa reconnaissance helicopters. There is also a general support aviation company, which has 16 OH-58 Kiowas, 8 UH-60 Blackhawk transports and six EH-60A electronic warfare machines. There is also a reconnaissance squadron.

The French Army has grouped its helicopters into brigades within the Rapid Deployment Force (FAR), and with the recent introduction of the MBB PAH1 helicopter armed with six HOT ATGW, anti-tank defence is now the primary role of the West German Army's *Heeresfliegertruppe*. Each corps in the *Bundesheer* has a regiment of 176 helicopters, each comprising 56 PAH1, 40 assault/transport UH-1D and 42 medium transport, and 30 reconnaissance MBB-105. Although not integral with the aviation regiment, there is an airborne brigade in each corps, one of whose primary tasks is to fight a series of delaying actions against hostile armour thrusts to give the main force time to deploy. The British Army has long experience in the combat use of helicopters and has a strong Army Air Corps (AAC), whose primary task is currently seen as anti-tank defence.

The Soviet Army has also formed specialised air assault brigades in which its air assets have been concentrated. These brigades comprise four infantry battalions — two equipped with BMD — together with artillery, SAM, anti-tank and

Above: French paratroops deploying from a Puma helicopter. The French Army developed the tactical use of helicopters during the counter-revolutionary war in

Algeria and currently incorporates a large helicopter arm, the ALAT, with some 660 aircraft, including one air-mobile division with a total of 240 aircraft.

support units. The helicopter assets of the Tactical Air Armies have been transferred from air force to army command. These air assault brigades would be an essential element in the deployment of Operational Manoeuvre Groups (OMG) and would operate in an aggressive manner in support of a Soviet advance. A particular capability is the introduction of the Hokum helicopter fighter which will be tasked to destroy opposing helicopters, especially those operating in the airborne anti-tank role, or deploying ground-based anti-tank teams.

Below: A UH-60 Blackhawk landing during an exercise to pick up and redeploy a patrol. The current generation of helicopters are extremely capable in comparison with those of past decades, though speeds have not increased markedly, but future aircraft promise to be much faster, greatly increasing productivity.

Below: The Soviets have long had a fascination with sheer size and, as in other fields, their helicopter fleets include the largest in the

world. These Mil Mi-6s, in service since the early 1960s, have a maximum payload of 26,455lb (12,000kg) carried internally or

19,841lb (9,000kg) externally, far beyond the capability of any existing or projected Western helicopter.

Airborne Forces

There is no doubt that World War II was the heyday of the parachute forces, and there has been a gradual rundown in parachute capability since then. However, many armies retain parachute forces, by far the largest being the Soviet Army's seven airborne divisions, followed by the USA, Poland, France and West Germany with one parachute division each. Other armies retain smaller capabilities: for example, the UK and Belgium each have three parachute battalions, though only two of the British battalions are in the parachute role at any one time.

Parachute troops have proved their value time and again in operations outside Europe, and while the merits of using parachute forces in a general war setting, particularly on the Central Front, are questionable, parachuting remains a valuable capability in operations outside Europe.

Over the past 40 years parachute insertion has been used in the Suez operation, in the Indo-Pakistan war in 1971 and in CRW operations in Indochina, Algeria and Malaya, as well as in counter-hostage operations in places such as the Congo. Because of their high standard of training and aggressive tactics, parachute troops are frequently used in special operations, even if they are not parachuted in. For example, the Soviets used 103rd Guards Airborne Division to capture Prague Airport in 1968, while 105th Guards Airborne Divsion was the principle force in the seizure of Kabul in 1979.

In all armies the parachute troops form an élite force. They invariably have special selection procedures and maintain a markedly higher standard of physical fitness than standard 'line' infantry battalions. Paratroop units tend to have high esprit de corps, which is sustained and supported by the 'parachute mystique' and distinctive items of dress such as winged badges and the red (or, in the case of Soviet Army, blue) beret.

SOVIET PARACHUTE TACTICS

According to the Soviet *Dictionary of Basic Military Terms*, airborne assault is defined as: "Troops airlifted to the enemy rear to conduct combat activities there. According to its scale an airborne assault can be either tactical, operational or strategic. The assault can be effected either by parachute or from landed aircraft (fixed-wing or helicopters), or by a combination of both.' In the Soviet system the Airborne Forces are an independent arm of service, subordinated in peace to the Ministry of Defence and in war to the Supreme Command.

Strategic airborne assaults could involve two or more airborne divisions attacking objectives deep in the enemy rear, such as ports or airfields, under the direction of the Ministry of Defence. At the operational level an Airborne Assault force could be up to divisional size operating at distances up to 60 miles (100km) beyond the

Above: Soviet paratroops are among the Army's elite units and are grouped into no less than seven airborne divisions, composed of 21 parachute battalions.

Below: ASU-85 self-propelled guns are among the wide range of special-to-role equipment developed specifically for the Soviet parachute forces.

Above: US paratroops wait to board an aircraft at night during a Team Spirit exercise. The US Army currently has one airborne division, the 82nd, with nine

battalions in the parachute role. The division is based at Fort Bragg in North Carolina, but can be deployed anywhere in the world at very short notice.

Right: South Korean paratroops landing after being dropped by USAF C-130s. South Korean paratroops are concentrated in seven special forces brigades.

FLOT, in support of Frontal operations, undertaking missions such as the seizure of bridgeheads, the destruction of enemy nuclear delivery means or cooperation with Operational Manoeuvre Groups. Tactical airborne assaults could be undertaken by heliborne forces up to battalion size, operating against enemy targets within some 20 miles (32km) of the FLOT.

According to Soviet doctrine a parachute operation requires extensive preparation and coordination, together with aerial and, wherever possible, covert ground reconnaissance. Aircraft routes are selected with great care to avoid ground-based air defences and air interception, and considerable air assets would be designated to support the fly-in to ensure the suppression of air defences as well as to keep enemy interceptors away from the lumbering transports.

Air drops are normally made at night, with the dropping zones (DZ) being marked by specially trained pathfinder groups, who use electronic and visual markers to guide the transport aircraft. A typical DZ is about 2.5 miles (4km) long and 2 miles (3.2km) wide: a battalion would need one such DZ, a regiment two and a division up to six. DZs are normally as close as possible to the objective and may sometimes actually be on the objective itself. Unlike other parachute forces, Soviet airborne troops often drop their heavy equipment either first, or concurrently with the first wave, which normally also includes command posts and air defence, engineer and anti-tank units, and is responsible for eliminating enemy resistance and for protecting follow-up drops.

US PARACHUTE TACTICS

The US Army's airborne forces are concentrated in XVIII Airborne Corps, comprising 82nd Airborne Division, the parachute force, and 101st Airborne Division (Air Assault), an air-mobile force. The 82nd Airborne Division consists of three brigades, each of three parachute battalions, together with the field artillery battalions and a tank battalion and an integral Divisional Support Command. Divisional air support includes 48 AH-1S Cobras armed with Tow missiles, 90 UH-60 Blackhawk transport helicopters and 59 OH-58 Kiowa reconnaissance helicopters.

The 82nd Airborne Division can be delivered anywhere in the world by air insertion using either C-141 Starlifters or C-130 Hercules aircraft. The division has repeatedly demonstrated its ability to operate from C-141s flown direct from the Continental USA to the Central Front, jumping into a tactical location in West Germany after a non-stop flight.

Having seized an objective the division would be subjected to heavy counter-attacks and a divisional tactical response termed the Airborne Anti-Armor Defence (AAAD) has been developed. Terrain coupled with natural and man-made obstacles is used to create islands of mutually supporting anti-armour weapons teams, backed up by artillery and close air support, and it is intended that enemy armour would be channelled into killing zones where they could be destroyed piecemeal from the flanks and rear. This concept requires an anti-tank system capable of air delivery and with effective ranges out to 3,280 yd (3,000m), as well as integral air support and an armoured counter-attack force. In addition, any sophisticated enemy can also be expected to throw considerable air assets at a major airborne landing, making air defence a major requirement for the 82nd.

Left: US and Bolivian paratroops carry out pre-flight checks prior to taking part in a joint exercise. Many small armies maintain one or two parachute battalions for special roles.

Above: Paratroops streaming from a C-130 Hercules, the West's most widely used aircraft for airborne operations. It can deliver men or heavy equipment loads from high or low levels.

Parachute Operations: Rescue at Kolwezi

Zaïre, the former Belgian Congo, was a major international problem through most of the 1960s and 1970s after being granted independence with undue haste by the Belgians in 1960. The ensuing disorders led to United Nations intervention and widespread military action: finally the army chief of staff, General Mobutu, became President in 1965, and although he had considerable success in bringing order to his country he still had to deal with sporadic outbreaks of trouble, particularly in Shaba Province, formerly Katanga, the breakaway province once under the control of Moise Tshombe.

THE MILITARY SITUATION, 1978

On May 13, 1978, a force of some 4,000 'Tigers' of the Front National de Liberation du Congo (FNLC) swept into Kolwezi, the provincial capital of Shaba, inflicting heavy casualties on the Army garrison and cutting all communications to the capital, Kinshasa. An orgy of bloodshed and rape then followed, and hundreds of European men, women and children were murdered or kidnapped, leading to a major international outcry. Consequently, on May 14 President Mobutu formally requested help from France, to which they responded both rapidly and effectively.

THE RESCUE OPERATION

On May 17, 1978, at about 1000 hours, the French quick-reaction force, 2nd Foreign Parachute Legion Regiment (2ᵉREP), based at Calvi on the island of Corsica, was placed on six hours, notice to move. The executive order to move did not arrive until 0130 hours the following morning, and by 0830 hours the regiment had moved to the Solenzara air base and was ready to go. The first echelon left that afternoon on five DC-8 airliners chartered from

Above: French paratroops wait to board a Zaïrean C-130 transport aircraft at Kinshasa Airport. A complication was that they had never jumped from C-130s nor had they used the US-pattern T-10 parachute, but they jumped successfully into the operational area within 24 hours of leaving their base in far-off Corsica.

Below: En route to Kolwezi the French paratroops look studiously nonchalant, even though they had little idea of the conditions they would find on the ground.

Left: Men of 2e REP collect their weapons after landing near Kolwezi. Without their rapid arrival many more people, both European and Zaïrean, would have been killed by the insurgents.

Below: Legionnaires of 2e REP move through the scrub near Kolwezi looking for the 'Tigers' or their unfortunate victims, most of whom died in the most dreadful manner.

various French civil airlines. The balance of the unit, together with the heavy weapons and vehicles, followed later in USAF C-141 Starlifters and C-5 Galaxies.

The DC-8s arrived at Kinshasa airfield that evening. The legionnaires were greeted with the news that the situation in Shaba Province was so serious that they must emplane almost immediately in four Hercules and two C.160s of the Zaïrean Air Force for the 1,240-mile (2,000km) flight to Kolwezi: their task would be to carry out a 'humanitarian combat mission' to rescue all civilians trapped in and around Kolwezi. Little firm information could be given about the situation on the ground, apart from the fact that the 'Tigers' were on the rampage. Few of the men of 2ᵉREP had ever jumped from C-130s (they were, of course, familiar with the C.160) and an additional complication was that they would all have to use the unfamiliar American T-10 parachute.

The men of 22ᵉREP worked through the night to get things organised and were then piled somewhat haphazardly into the aircraft, and a bad situation was made worse when one of the C.160s blew a tyre during the take-off run and aborted. All the aircraft then returned to the pan, where the legionnaires were taken out of the disabled aircraft and told to push their way into the remaining five machines. So, with 80 paratroops stuffed into aircraft designed to take 66, carrying strange parachutes, after a long journey from Corsica and having had little or no sleep for 48

Right: Parachute forces have an inherent and unparalleled flexibility during rapid deployment missions such as this. Indeed, their future roles may well lie in such non-European deployments, rather than on the Central Front, where the aircraft used to deliver them are very vulnerable.

Right: A 2e REP command post in the bush. This was the regiment's first operational jump since Dien Bien Phu in 1954, but they showed that they had lost none of their elan or professionalism.

hours, the small rescue force set off on a bumpy four-hour flight to Kolwezi.

The drop, 2ᵉREP's first operational jump since Dien Bien Phu, took place at a height of 650ft (200mm). The selected DZ was some 1,100 yd (1,000m) from the objective, but for unexplained reasons the Zaïrean pilots dropped the French paratroops directly onto the objective. Fortunately all went well: and there was no immediate response to their arrival, and 1ᵉCie occupied the Lycee John Paul XXIII, 2ᵉ the hospital and a workshop, and 3ᵉCie the Hotel Impala and an overpass. The paras dug in rapidly, conscious that their heavy weapons were on a later flight.

During the night there was sporadic action and when, in the early hours of the following morning,

the four C-130s and a lone C.160 arrived overhead with further men from the regiment, the commanding officer decided that the situation did not warrant the risk of a night jump. He therefore sent the aircraft off to nearby Lubumbashi, whence they returned at dawn to drop the men and equipment in a successful second jump. During all of this the legionnaires had been getting on with the job of bringing order back to the city, rescuing prisoners and dealing with the 'Tigers' of the FNLC.

By midday on May 20, just two days after taking-off from Corsica, the situation in Kinshasha was sufficiently under control for 4ᵉCie to move out to Metal Shaba, a township some distance to the north. There they bumped a major hostile force, which put in a counter-attack against them, using lorryborne infantry

supported by two Soviet-built light tanks. They were given short shrift by the Legion, but the encounter was indicative of the possible threat to the small French force.

At first light on May 21 the majority of the 2ᵉREP's transport arrived from Lubumbashi, with the remainder following during the course of the day. Mobile at last, the companies spent the next few days scouring the countryside, searching for rebels and their prisoners. Groups of Europeans were found, many half-crazed with fear as a result of their harrowing experiences with the 'Tigers', and a large group of rebels was totally eliminated on May 25. On May 28 2ᵉREP was ordered to hand over to incoming Belgian, Moroccan and Zaïrean troops and move to Lubumbashi in preparation for a return to Corsica in USAF C-141s.

Artillery

Artillery has been the single greatest cause of battle casualties in every major twentieth-century war and it remains a crucial component of modern tactical forces. Modern artillery weapons are more effective, more mobile and more adaptable than ever before, though they demand complex command and control systems and means of long-range target acquisition and place serious demands on the resupply system.

Tactical artillery—that is, artillery deployed at corps level and below—is normally integral to the formations it serves and includes tube-artillery (guns and howitzers), rocket launchers, mortars and missiles. In addition, all armies have heavier artillery units, commanded at higher levels, which can be used either under higher control or allocated to corps or divsions for use in specific operations.

The first task of artillery is fire assault, in which fire is used to annihilate or neutralise enemy personnel, weapons or combat material representing either area or point targets. Harassing fire involves firing at pre-selected targets in a random fashion in order to make movement difficult for the enemy and to promote a feeling of uncertainty. Tactical artillery doctrine in most armies sees two major fire missions: interdiction, which covers action against the enemy's rear areas and secondary echelons, and the direct support of manoeuvre units. An approximate demarcation line between these two tasks would be about 20 miles (30km) beyond the FLOT, with missiles and rockets predominating beyond that distance and guns inside.

ARTILLERY DEPLOYMENT

All armies deploy their artillery in regiments or battalions subdivided into companies or batteries, the latter formation usually including six guns. The artillery commander is normally located alongside the commander of the formation he is

Above: Towed artillery still has major applications in less demanding environments, a fact demonstrated here during the US invasion of Grenada in 1983.

Below: Field deployment of a Soviet artillery unit in support of a motor-rifle battalion. Soviet artillery units are among the most effective in the world.

Soviet towed artillery battalion deployment

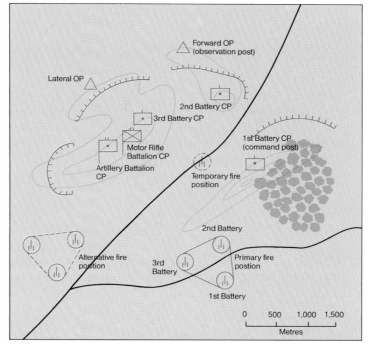

Each battery consists of six guns or howitzers, and fire missions are carried out in accordance with strict norms governing sector coverage per gun and per battery, separation distance of guns and batteries, ammunition expenditure, speed of travel and the length of time allowed to crews of each type of ordnance for setting up and vacating fire positions.

supporting — for example, an artillery battalion commander would travel with the brigade commander, while the battery commanders would be with the infantry battalion commanding officers — and the batteries are deployed and moved separately. Field artillery batteries also deploy forward observation parties to observe and correct the fall of shot, and these move well up with the forward troops.

All artillery arms operate on the principle of moving one battery at a time with the others firm on the ground and able to fire in support of the unit whose battery is moving. Frequent moves are necessary not only to position the guns where they can provide the best support, but also because a major task for all artillery is counter-battery fire, and staying too long in one place invites retaliation from the opposing artillery. To concentrate the fire of all available guns when and where required, artillery arms require comprehensive communications systems, and the need for rapid response necessitates the increasing use of computers.

Divisional artillery in the US Army is some 2,300 men strong and follows the traditional concept of direct support for the manoeuvre elements. Each 155mm battalion routinely supports one of the division's brigades, and can split any battery into two elements, each capable of independent operation, while the MLRS battery provides the division with an organic rocket capability as well as a longer-range capability to fight the Deep Battle concept. A recent change has removed the 203mm howitzer battery from divisional to corps control, thus easing the division's logistic problems.

The division's air defence artillery battalion concentrates on the defence of the brigade areas, leaving corps ADA assets to defend the division rear area. However, ADA organisation and tasks are being redefined following the cancellation of the Sgt York divisional air defence weapon system.

SOVIET ARTILLERY

The artillery arm of the Soviet Army is one of the most skilful and best organised in any army, with a host of different types of unit at every tactical and operational level of command. Artillery also gives the Soviets free rein to practise their concept of war as a science rather than an art and it is subject to the most detailed study and the allocation of a comprehensive set of norms for the calculation of every detail of artillery fire planning.

First echelon divisions will normally be allocated, in addition to their own organic artillery, army-controlled artillery assets together with the fire of artillery units from

Left: The traditional image of Soviet artillery seen here, with towed guns deployed in straight lines in the open, is now completely out of date.

second echelon divisions. Within the division organic and attached artillery will normally be allocated to forward regiments, especially those on the main axis, and these regiments, in their turn, may place some or all of these assets in support of leading battalions. Second echelon divisions, regiments and battalions are not normally reinforced with additional artillery until they are committed; indeed, their organic artillery will normally be used to augment the fire of first echelon artillery, especially in the area of main effort.

The command and organisational structure which ensures flexibility in the concentration of artillery fire is established by temporary, mission-oriented artillery groupings such as divisional or regimental artillery groups. These usually consist of at least two artillery battalions, which may or may not deploy the same type of weapon. At each command level there is a Commander of Rocket Troops and Artillery (CRTA) who exercises control over all organic and allocated artillery within the formation and who moves always with the manoeuvre force commander.

Soviet gunners conduct several well-defined fire missions:

Fire assault, used mainly during the preparation phase of an attack with the aim of annihilating or neutralising enemy personnel, weapons and combat material.

Fire concentration, used against a single target or against several targets in a single area.

Successive fire concentration, used in support of advancing troops to neutralise known targets on the flanks of or ahead of the line of advance.

Controlling fire, used during the intervals between fire assaults, with random single rounds or bursts to prevent the target from returning to action or escaping.

Barrage fire, used against preselected linear targets to prevent movement by enemy infantry or tanks. **Defensive rolling barrage,** using successive shifts of a heavy curtain of fire from one preselected, observed line to another, during an enemy tank or combined arms attack.

Offensive rolling barrage, involving successive shifts of high-density fire from one line to another ahead of advancing units during an attack.

Overlapping fire, which involves high density fire directed at artillery and mortar positions between the end of the preparatory fire and fire

Above: Soviet artillery commanders plan according to a well defined set of tactical norms, which define types of weapon to be used, type of fire, firing rates and numbers of shells for a given area or target. Such procedures enable them to respond quickly.

support periods, to enable own troops to seize forward positions.

Fire concentration is calculated in terms of hectares (one hectare is an area of 10,000m², equivalent to 2.47 acres), and each artillery weapon is calculated to be able to neutralise a specific area determined by the time allowed and the type of target. For example, a 122mm howitzer battalion shelling exposed personnel can cover an area of 18 hectares (44.5 aces) in three or four minutes, but only three or four hectares (7.4-9.88 acres) in five minutes if they are under cover.

In a successive fire concentration coverage would be:

Weapon	hectares/acres
100mm gun	3/7.4
130mm gun	3/7.4
152mm gun	3-6/7.4-14.8
122mm howitzer	4/9.9
152mm howitzer	6/14.8

Right: One possible field deployment for a Soviet SP artillery unit. The use of self-propelled guns and howitzers enables battery positions to be taken up rapidly; once they are in place fire missions can be executed and the position vacated before hostile fire can be brought to bear.

Below: The 122mm 2S1, the first of the new generation of Soviet SPs to reach operational status, has proved a great success. It is unlikely that many towed artillery pieces would be used in major theatres in any future conflicts.

In an offensive rolling barrage fire is delivered on successive linear targets for five minutes on each main line and for one or two minutes on intermediate lines. Sectors on the line are assigned on the following basis:

100/130mm guns	m/yards
Per weapon	20-25 /22-27
Per battery	150/164
Per battalion	450/492

Howitzers	
Per weapon	35/38
Per battery	200/219
Per battalion	600-650/656-710

There are further norms for deployment governing the distance by which units and individual weapons are separated:

Mortars	Separation (m/yd)
Weapons	15-60/16-66

Soviet SP artillery deployment

Batteries	N/A
From FLOT	500-1,500/547-1,640

Guns/howitzers

Weapons	20-40/22-44
Batteries	400-2,000/437-2,187
From FLOT	
Regimental	1-4,000/1,094-4,374
Divisional	3-6,000/3,280-6,562

MRLs

Weapons	15-50/16-55
Batteries	1-2,000/1,094-2,187
From FLOT	3-6,000/3,280-6,562

Ammunition expenditure is also carefully calculated. For example, during a successive fire concentration 100mm and 130mm guns and 122mm howitzers would be expected to fire three rounds per hectare per minute, while for 152mm howitzers and 160mm mortars the equivalent figure is two rounds.

Using such norms a fire plan can be prepared giving very precise details on the targets, the types of fire, the length of each fire mission and the numbers of rounds to be fired by each weapon.

Artillery units are calculated to travel at a speed of about 12.4mph (20km/hr) in daylight and 9.3mph (15km/hr) in darkness, and the time taken by a towed battery to set up is about 20-25 minutes by day and 30 minutes by night; a self-propelled battery obviously takes less time. Time to vacate a position is about 12 minutes, and again this will be less for an SP unit. The time spent in any one location depends upon the tactical situation, especially on the enemy's counter-battery capability, and could be as short as 20 minutes in some circumstances.

For many years Soviet artillery took up linear positions in the open. This is still done to a certain extent, but the introduction of self-propelled guns and howitzers has led to more flexible arrangements.

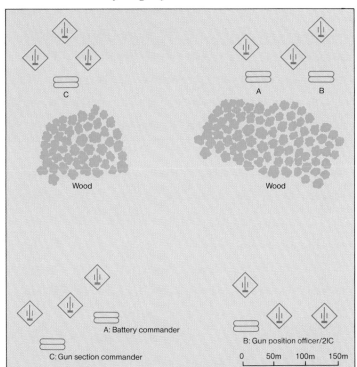

A: Battery commander
B: Gun position officer/2IC
C: Gun section commander

0   50m   100m   150m

Low-intensity Warfare

Any examination of the use of ground forces since the end of World War II shows that while there have been many conventional international conflicts the major form of military ativity has been combatting attempts by an internal group to take over or change the form of government of a country by force. Many of these campaigns have been combatted by the security forces of the government of the country alone, but in other cases outside military assistance has been called in, occasionally resulting in the supporting power virtually taking over, as in South Vietnam and Afghanistan.

Frequently armed forces fighting in a counter-insurgency (COIN) or counter-revolutionary warfare (CRW) campaign have used wrong or inappropriate tactics, or have attempted to use technology to make up for tactical deficiencies. All such cases have led to disaster, and it is interesting that the Vietnamese have proved no more successful in putting down the Cambodian insurgency and the Soviets no more successful in Afghanistan than were the Americans in South Vietnam, even though the lessons of Vietnam seemed so clear.

The insurgent sees time as a weapon that he can use against the government: the longer a campaign goes on, he reasons, the more the masses will tend to criticise the government for failing to find a solution. On the other hand, there is no time pressure on insurgents, who can keep on for extraordinarily protracted periods. Indeed, the sheer persistence of some insurgents is astonishing: the Malayan Communists have been in the jungles of Malaysia since 1948, while across the South China Sea the Philippine Communists have been fighting for only a few years less. Several times these Communist movements seem to have been totally defeated, but on each occasion they have lain dormant for a few years, recruited and retrained, and started again.

A noteworthy feature of this type of campaign is that in many cases the insurgents have not had to inflict military defeat on the security forces in order to achieve their aim; indeed, in some campaigns the insurgents have been virtuallly defeated in a military sense, but through political determination and willpower they have succeeded. Thus, the Algerian FLN was defeated in the field by the French Army, but the will of the French people to carry on had been so sapped by the campaign that it could no longer be sustained.

INSURGENT TACTICS

Insurgents normally start their campaigns with some form of political party and no form of military organisation at all. Nevertheless, given the will and a reasonable degree of support they can build up a large and effective military force. The Vietnamese Peoples' Liberation Army, for example, was founded on December 22, 1944, by a history professor

Above: A Mujahideen recoilless rifle crew fire on an Afghan Army position at Nahrin, eastern Afghanistan, during the continuing counter-insurgency conflict.

Below: Members of the Shan State Army in the southern Shan state of Burma display a motley collection of weaponry during a pause in their guerilla campaign.

Right: Minimal personal equipment is a characteristic of guerillas such as these Karen National Liberation Army men on the march in eastern Burma.

whose first unit consisted of 34 men armed with a hotchpotch of rifles and pistols. Just ten years later the VPLA was a sophisticated, well trained and well armed force comprising six infantry divisions of some 10,000 men each, some 20 independent infantry regiments and a similar number of independent battalions; there was also a heavy division equipped with field guns and howitzers, heavy mortars and anti-aircraft guns. The erstwhile professor, now General Vo Nguyen Giap, was able to deploy elements of this force first to isolate and then to defeat the French in a set-piece battle at Dien Bien Phu and thus break their will to go on.

Most insurgent movements organise themselves on similar lines to the VPLA, which followed the precepts of Mao Tse-tung. In this organisational system there are three levels:

Popular troops (or people's militia), raised in villages under insurgent control and often those under nominal government control as well. Members pursue their normal civil occupations until called out, when they undertake local offensive or defensive operations, frequently in support of the regional troops or the main force. One of their main tasks is acting as porters for the main force.

Regional troops are full-time troops with the task of protecting bases and villages and supporting the main force when it is operating in their area.

The main force, which is composed of professional soldiers formed into battalions and regiments.

Insurgents' strategy generally follows four stages, again based upon Mao's teachings but modified to suit local conditions. The first is the organisational stage in which the insurgents establish their political and military infrastructure and carry out minor military actions. In the second stage, the strategic defensive, the insurgents increase the pace of military action over as wide an area as possible, thus compelling the security forces to dissipate their effort, becoming strong nowhere and weak everywhere. In the third phase, the strategic stalemate, the insurgents keep up the pressure on the security forces, but meanwhile reorganise and retrain to produce a main force which can then undertake the fourth stage, the strategic offensive, in which the insurgent army drives the incumbent government and its military forces to defeat.

In an insurgent campaign there are no front lines and rear areas as there are in more conventional wars, except, perhaps, in the final days of stage four: until then the government and insurgent forces move around the country carrying out relatively isolated operations. The tactics of the insurgent force combine normal low-level infantry operations, such as attacks on towns and police stations, with what the government desribes as terror attacks on the civil population. The main tactic of the insurgent is to attack where least expected and to disengage as soon as the object of the operation has been achieved. There is no merit, only considerable danger, to the insurgents in standing and fighting; far better for them to fade into the countryside and live to fight another day.

It should not be thought, however, that insurgents are always successful. Even a finally successful movement such as that in Indochina made miscalculations and suffered on the road to victory. A particular example was the Tet Offensive of 1968. Following a row in the Central Committee in Hanoi in 1967 the North Vietnamese leadership decided to try to short-circuit the normally slow and sure process of

revolutionary war and stake everything on a major offensive in Tet 1968. The Chinese and General Giap argued against such a plan, but the Russians — who have never understood revolutionary warfare — were for it. The aims were to promote a popular uprising, to cause the collapse of the South Vietnamese armed forces and to destroy the USA's military and political position. The offensive was a major disaster for the NVA and the Viet Cong, who failed to achieve military success anywhere and suffered great losses in manpower and equipment, although the hysterical reactions of the Western press did serve to undermine the USA's resolve in the long run.

COUNTER-INSURGENCY TACTICS

The forces of government have found revolutionary warfare difficult to counter, but they have been by no means always the losers. The British in Malaya (1947-60) the Greeks (1944-49), the Philippines (1946-54) and the Colombians (1945-65) demonstrated that victory is possible, but there is no universal panacea, no tactical secret which once understood and applied will guarantee success.

One major lesson from the successful campaigns, however, is that there is no purely military solution. Thus, the CRW campaign must be a combined politico-military undertaking, in which political measures to deal with complaints or injustices are just as important to eventual success as military victories.

On the military side, however, it is necessary for those involved to understand that the techniques being used by the insurgents require special reactions. The heavy-handed use of conventional military force will very rarely succeed — indeed, it is almost invariably counter-productive - and a more subtle and sophisticated approach is necessary. In particular, it is a proven error to believe that modern technology can be used to make up for deficiencies in tactics. However, when outright military action is taken it must be rapid, efficient and effective, and modern technology may provide assistance.

Above: The other side of the coin. March 1985 found troops of the US Army's 101st Airborne Division carrying out small unit training in the La Ceiba area on the north coast of Honduras. The series of Universal Trek exercises also involved beach landings. **Below: Another aspect of Universal Trek was resupply by USAF C-130s such as this example seen coming in low.**

Special Forces Operations

At the lowest level of modern land warfare comes a variety of military operations conducted not against a formal enemy in a war setting, but against terrorists, kidnappers or small groups of dissidents. Such operations can take place under a variety of conditions. For example, the retaking of hostages being held by armed kidnappers can in some circumstances be a purely police operation; in others, where the number or quality of armaments is too great for the police to handle or where distance is involved, it is quite clear that only the military have the capability to undertake the mission. Thus, the Israeli hostages being held in Entebbe (July 1976) were so far from their homeland that only a fully military operation could cope with any hope of success, while the British retaking of the Iranian Embassy in 1981 was at the interface of police/military jurisdiction.

According to Risk International Inc, *(The New York Times,* April 24, 1984) during the calendar year 1983 authenticated terrorist global activities included 119 kidnappings (7 killed), 1,120 bombing incidents (813 killed), 1,231 other attacks on installations, 362 assassination incidents (725 killed) and 5 hijackings (4 killed). The pace has slackened slightly since that year, and although firm statistics are not yet available it would seem that since the 1986 US attack on Libya there has been a marked reduction.

Increasingly, military forces have been dragged into this arena and not only have tactics had to be developed to cope, but in many cases it has been found that special units have had to be formed to undertake such missions. Thus, among the leading tasks of units such as the British SAS, the US Delta forces and their numerous counterparts elsewhere is the anti-terrorist mission.

ANTI-HOSTAGE OPERATIONS

Clearly, in the majority of hostage-taking operations the primary arm of the State, certainly in democratic countries, must be the police. Thus, operations such as the British Balcombe Street siege, and the Libyan Embassy operation which followed the shooting of a Metropolitan Policewoman are quite properly dealt with by the police so long as they have the capability to do so. Once a significant number of the opponents are armed, however, the military inevitably become involved.

A factor which exacerbates the difficulties is that contemporary terrorists are able to conduct their activities on a global scale and frequently strike at targets on the territory of a third party who has no involvement in the basic problem at all. Thus, for example in April-May 1980 a group of anti-Khomeni terrorists from Arabistan in southern Iran attacked and occupied the Iranian Embassy in London, England, forcing the British — who had absolutely no connection with the dispute—to try to bring it to some sort of a conclusion.

A major difficulty for the security forces is that the terrorists generally have the tactical intitiative in the sense that they choose when and where to strike, frequently lying dormant for months or even years then striking suddenly at a totally unexpected target. Indeed, the places chosen by terrorists to carry out their operation and to hold their hostages range from aircraft, which have long been popular targets, to ships such as the *Achille Lauro,* trains in the case of the Molluccan terrorists in the Netherlands, buses — a target of Arab terrorists in Israel —and buildings, exemplified by the Iranian Embassy siege.

Most nations now have at least one special unit to deal with such situations, either an adaptation of an existing unit, such as the British SAS, or a new unit, and such units have been found to need not only specially trained squads of troops within their own organisations but also specially trained support and logistics units, trained to their own high standards for the same type of operations. The USA, for example has designated 23rd Air Force a Special Operation Force (SOF) unit to support forces such as Delta.

The detailed tactics of the military units involved in counter-terrorist operations are naturally highly classified, but observation of past undertakings suggests some of the tactical principles that are used. The first is that there must be total understanding, cooperation and determination to succeed between the politicians, the police and the military forces involved in the operation. Second, there must be detailed and painstaking reconnaissance to establish just where the opponents and their hostages are located, and in what condition they are. The third is that any assault must be very carefully

timed and should take place when other less violent channels have been exhausted and there is no further alternative, for example when the terrorists have started killing hostages. Fourth, when it does take place the assault must be carried out with maximum violence and surprise. The fifth is that a psychological operation must be mounted against the terrorists to wear them down and soften them up, preferably to hand over their hostages without further violence, but, in the last resort, in anticipation of military action. Finally, all units involved in this area make maximum use of technology to help them in their task.

Dealing with these situations is no simple matter and there have been spectacular failures. For example, the West German attempt to resolve

the Black September attack on the Israeli boxing team at the 1972 Olympic Games in Munich ended in tragedy at a spectacular shoot-out at the Furstenfeldbruck military airfield. Similarly, an Egyptian commando attack on a hijacked airliner in Malta resulted in a large number of deaths. It is, however, arguable that where authorities have been less than firm with terrorists the result has been a spate of further attacks, whereas firm action which results in the capture or death of the terrorists, even if it involves the death of a number of the hostages, is actually the best kind of action to take. Certainly the civil and military authorities involved in such decisions are placed in some very difficult practical and moral situations where any course of action must involve risk.

Above: A special forces soldier descends the outer wall of a building. One of the crucial tasks in counter-terrorist operations is gaining rapid and effective access to the building, aircraft or train where the terrorists have established themselves. Many specialised techniques and items of equipment have had to be developed to enable this task to be accomplished.

THE IRANIAN EMBASSY SIEGE

The Iranian Embassy at 16 Princes Gate, London, opposite Hyde Park, was taken over at 1130 hours on Wednesday April 30, 1980, by six terrorists. At the time of the takeover there were 29 people in the Embassy: four British men and 22 Iranian men and women. Three of the Iranians escaped in the first few minutes.

The men were all from Arabistan, an area of Iran some 400 miles (643km) from Teheran, which had long resisted the rule of the Aryan northerners. Most had supported Ayatollah Khomeini's takeover from the Shah, only to find the newcomer as ruthless a suppressor of minorities as his predecessor. The terrorists represented a group entitled the Democratic Revolutionary Movement for the Liberation of Arabistan (DRMLA), a Marxist-Leninist group based in Libya, whose cause was regional autonomy (not independence) for Arabistan. The UK was in no way involved in this dispute.

The six men involved included the leader, Oan, aged 27, and five others all in their early twenties. Three were armed with 9mm automatic pistols, one had a 0.38in revolver and the remaining two had 9mm sub-machine-guns; the group also had a number of Chinese-made hand-grenades. The terrorists' demand was for the release of 91 prisoners being held by the Iranian authorities in Arabistan, something over which the British authorities had absolutely no jurisdiction. The time limit was 1200 hours Thursday May 1: midday the following day.

Following the violent takeover of the Embassy a sick Iranian woman was released late on the Wednesday night and a sick Englishman the following morning; the first deadline (1200 hours) was postponed when the police transmitted a message from the terrorists to the Press and a second deadline (1400 hours) passed without a move from either side. By the Friday morning there had been numerous contacts between the terrorists and the police, some direct and some through intermediaries, but by now specific threats were being made against the lives of some of the hostages. Negotiations continued throughout the Saturday and a major advance was made when the terrorists agreed to release two hostages in return for a broadcast on the radio of a statement of their aims. One hostage was released in the early

Left: Men of the West German Border Police special counter-terrorist unit GSG-9 practice scaling and entering a typical modern building.

Below: Smoke billows from the Iranian Embassy building during the very brief and totally effective entry operation by the British SAS working in four-man teams.

Above: A picture that electrified the world as black-clad SAS troopers were seen briefly on the balconies of the buildings adjacent to the Iranian Embassy.

evening and another after the statement had been broadcast on the BBC Nine O'Clock News, word for word as given by the terrorist leader to the police. The atmosphere inside the Embassy became almost euphoric, helped by a good meal sent in by the police.

Through the Sunday the British Government discussed the situation with various Arab ambassadors, but no agreement could be reached on a possible role for them in finding a solution to the crisis. Inside the Embassy the major event of the day was the release of an Iranian hostage who had become very ill. On Monday the terrorists were noticeably more nervous and a shouted discussion between two British hostages and the police at noon did little to ease the tension. At about 1330 hours Oan's patience apparently snapped and he shot Abbas Levasani, one of the Embassy staff, in the course of a telephone conversation with the police.

Any doubts about whether anyone had actually been killed were resolved just after 1900 hours when the dead body was pushed through the front door of the Embassy and a pair of policemen rushed forward and carried it away on a stretcher.

MILITARY INTERVENTION

The police had obviously tried their best to identify just where the hostages and their captors were, and what they were all doing; doubtless classified surveillance devices were used. The SAS were therefore as ready as it was possible to be in the circumstances when, in accordance with normal British legal practice, the police formally requested the military to deal with the situation.

The plan was to use three of the customary four-man SAS teams; two teams were to take the rear, descending by rope from the roof, one team to reach the ground and the second the first-floor balcony. Both would then break in using either frame charges or brute force. The third team was to be at the front, crossing from a balcony at 15 Princes Gate to No 16. Once inside, all three teams were to rush to reach the hostages before they could be harmed. Other teams were to be outside the building in support of the twelve men inside.

Everything possible was done to heighten the impact of the attack. The 12 SAS men were dressed from head to foot in black, including their rubber anti-gas respirators, and looked extremely menacing. The combination of explosions, noise, smoke, speed of action and the appearance of the men was all intended to strike confusion and dread into the minds of the terrorists and succeeded brilliantly.

The SAS men had pored over plans of the buildings in minute detail and had also spent many hours studying photographs of the hostages. But in the end — as every soldier knows — all the training and planning have to be translated into action.

At 1926 hours precisely the men of the rear attack force stepped over the edge of the roof and abseiled down. The first two went down each rope successfully, but one of the third pair became stuck, a hazard known to abseilers everywhere. In the front the SAS men appeared on the balcony of No 15 and climbed over to the Embassy, giving the world's press and the British public an image of the SAS which will endure for years.

Suddenly, grenades exploded, lights went out and all was noise and confusion. Some parts of the embassy caught fire and the SAS man caught on the rope was cut free and dropped onto a balcony — a risk preferable to that of being roasted alive.

The SAS men swept through the building. Two terrorists were quickly shot and killed. One started shooting the hostages in an upstairs room but stopped after causing a few wounds. Within minutes five of the six gunmen were dead, with the sixth sheltering among the newly freed hostages. All survivors were rushed downstairs into the garden, where the remaining terrorist was identified and arrested. Not one hostage was killed in the attack which was a major success in the West's fight against the evils of terrorism.

Index

Page numbers in bold type refer to subjects of illustrations or captions.

2S1 152mm, **40,124-5**, 142
2S3, 43-4, **124-5**
2S5, **40**, 44, 124-5
2S7 203mm, **40**, 44, **124-5**

A

A-10, **48**
A 129 Mangusta, **120-1**
AB412, **194**
AFVs, see Light AFVs; Tanks
AGT-1500, **22**, 82
AH-64 Apache, **49**, 63, **116-7**, 195
AIFS, 42
AIFV, 58, 105
AK-74, AKS-74, **167**
AMX-10 PAC, 31
AMX-10RC, **31**, 33, **100-1**
AMX-13 DCA, 30, **147**
AMX-30, **88**, 147
AMX-32, 89
AMX-40, **16**, **88-9**
AN/USD-501 drone, 47
APDS rounds, 19, **20**, 34
  see also illustrations and captions relating to specific weapons
APFSDS rounds, **16**, **19**
  see also illustrations and captions relating to specific weapons
AS-90, 126
ASU-57, **195**
AT-2 anti-tank mines, **39**, **134**, 135
AT-3 Sagger, 14, 58, **108**, 113
AT-4 Spigot, 109, 113
AT-4 (FFV), **164**
AT-5 Spandrel, 58, 103, **109**
AT-8 Cobra, 21, 55
AT-8 Songster, **84-5**
ATGWs, see Missiles
Abbot (FV433), 110, **145**
Abrams (M1) **18**, **82-3**
ADAM, 42, **128**
Advanced Indirect Fire System (AIFS), 42
Aérospatiale
  Hades, **132-3**
  Lynx, 122
  Puma, **62**
  Roland, **52**, **148-9**
  Super Puma, **195**
Afghanistan, **202**
Agusta Mangusta (A 129), **120-1**
Agusta Bell AB412, **194**
Air defence, 48-55
  anti-helicopter defence, 55
  detection, 50
  identificiation, 51-2
  infantry, 61
Air Land Battle 2000 concept, 183, 184
Air mobility, 194-5
Airborne forces, **196-9**
  see also Parachute Regiment; REP; SAS; Special forces
Aircraft
  aviation units, 183
  surveillance, 47
  see also Helicopters; specific designations
Algeria, FLN, 202
Altair RPV, **47**
Alvis Scorpion, **30**, **74**, **98-9**, 191, 192
HMS Ambuscade, 191
Ammunition, 19-21
  artillery, 40-3
  Soviet, **19**
  stowage, **21-2**
  see also designations of specific types, eg APFSDS; also illustrations and captions relating to specific weapons
Amphibious operations,

24, 186-7, **188**
  river crossings, Soviet Army **186-9**
Anti-hostage operations, 75, 77, **198-9**, **204-5**
Anti-tank guided weapons (ATGW), see Missiles
Anti-tank warfare and weapons, 34-9
  infantry anti-tank weapons, 60-1
Anti-terrorist operations, **74-7**, **204-5**
Apache (AH-64), **49**, 63, **116-7**, 195
Argentina, see Falklands campaign
Armalite rifle, 167
Armament, see Guns; for armament of specific vehicles, see vehicle designation
Armament firing simulator, **18**, **83**
Armbrust, 36, **162**
Armour, see vehicle designations
Armour-Piercing Fin Stabilised Discarding Sabot (APFSDS) rounds, **16**, **19**
  see also illustrations and captions relating to specific weapons
Armoured fighting vehicles, see Light AFVs; Tanks
Armoured Infantry Fighting Vehicle (AIFV), 58, 105
Armoured personnel carriers (APCs), 56-9
Army Air Corps, 195
Artemis, **158-9**
Artillery, 40-5
  anti-tank, **34**, 37
  for low intensity warfare, 75
  organisation of units, 182, 184, 200-1
  tactics, **200-1**
Atelier de Construction d'Issy-les-Moulineaux, 100
ATILA artillery fire control system, 127
Austria
  Kurassier SPAT, 36
  SK 105, **18**, 30, **96-7**
Autoloaders, 21
Aviation units, 183
  US combat aviation brigades, 184
  see also Aircraft; Helicopters
Avco Lycoming AGT-1500, **22**, 82

B

BGM-71 TOW, **2-3**, **34**, **80**, **164-5**
  M901 ITV, **104**
BM-21, **138-9**
BM-24, 45
BM-27, 45, 139
BMD, **75**, **113**
BMP-1, BMP-2, 14, **56-8**, **108-9**, 186, 187
BO-105, **49**, 63, **183**, 195
BRDM, 14, **102-3**
BTR-60, BTR-70, **112**, 184
Barrel-length, 17
  Battlefield helicopters, 34, 63-4, **116-23**
  anti-helicopter defence, 55
  see also specific designations
Battlefield nuclear weapons, 70-1
  ER weapons, 34, 35, 70
Belgium
  M249 LMG, 60, **170-1**
  SS 109 rifle rounds, 59
BILL, **8-9**, **37**, 60
Black Hawk (UH-60), **176**, **194-5**
Blazer, **38-9**, 83

Blindfire (DN181) radar, **154**
Blowpipe, **160-1**
Bofors
  90mm, 97
  BILL, **8-9**, **37**, 60
  HEAT rounds, **36**
  L/70 40mm, **150**, 158, **159**
  RBS70, **53**
  Trinity air defence system, 150
Border Star 85 exercise, 78-9
Bradley (M2/M3), **80**, **105-7**, 111
Breda Twin 40L70, **158-9**
Bren 7.62 LMG, 110
Bridges, bridgelayers, Soviet army, 186, **187**, **189**
Britain, see United Kingdom
British Aerospace
  Laserfire, 154
  Rapier, **53**, **154-5**
British Light Gun, 75, **144-5**, **190**, 191
Browning M2HB 12.7mm, **21**, 140
Burmese insurgents, **202-3**

C

C1 MBT, **92**
C-5 Galaxy, 199
C-130 Hercules, **197**
C-141 Starlifter, 199
CH-47 Chinook, **45**, 62
CL-289 RPV, **13**, 47
CN/CS gas, 77
Cadillac-Gage
  power control system, **28**
  Stingray, 18, **99**
    engine, **22**
  V-150 armoured car, **32**
Calibres, **16-17**
Canadair
  AN/USD-501, 47
  CL-289 RPV, **13**, 47
Camp David agreement, 181
Canada
  LAV-25, **59**, 75, **106**
Cannon Launched Guided Projectile, 144
Carl Gustaf 84mm, 36, **164**
Centurion, 94
Challenger, **86-7**
Chemical warfare, **72-3**
Chieftain, **86**
China
  Types 63, 77, **96**
  Type 81 rocket launcher **23**, 45
Chinook (CH-47), **45**, 62
Chobham armour, 38
Chrysler M1 Abrams, **18**, **82-3**
Cleveland Army Tank Plant, M109, 40, **41**, **43-4**, 126, **128-9**
Cobra (AT-8), 21, 55
Cockerill 90mm turret, **30**, 32
Cognitive dissonance, 181
Colombian insurgency, 203
Combat aviation brigades, 184, **194-5**
Combat Engineer Vehicle (M728) **38**, 39, 83
Command, control and communications, 64-5, 181
  air defence, 55
  see also Organisation of military formations and units
Commando, see Cadillac Gage
Condor CV-12, 86
Copperhead (M712), **34**, 37, **128**, 129
COTAC fire control system, 89
Counter-insurgency (COIN) warfare, **202-3**
Counter-terrorist operations, **74-7**, **204-5**
Crews, MBTs, 26-7
Crotale, **146-7**

Cummins VTS-903T engine, 106
Czechoslovakia, DANA, **41**, 44, **125**

D

D-20 152mm, 43
D-23, **40**
D-30 122mm, **142-3**
Daimler Ferret, 101
Daimler-Benz OM403A engine, 102
DANA, **41**, 44, **125**
Defoliants, 73
Depleted uranium, 19
Design
  MBTs, 16-29
Designations of formations and units, 182
Destruction of tanks, 34-9
Detroit Arsenal Tank Plant, M60, **16**, 22, **82-3**, **177**, **183**, 186
Detroit Diesel
  Model 6V-53, 104, 106, 156
  Model 8V-71T, 128
  Model 8V-92TA, 99
Diesel engines, **22-3**
  see also vehicle designations
Dimensions, tank design, 25-6
  for dimensions of specific weapons, see relevant designations
Ditches, anti-tank, 39
Doctrine, tactical
  Soviet Army, 184-5
  US Army, 183
Dornier/Canadair CL-289 RPV, 13, 47
Dragon (M-47), 90, **162-3**
Dress, paramilitary units and anti-riot police, 77
Drives, AFVs, 31, 32-3
Drones, 47
Dyamit Nobel AT-2 anti-tank mine, **39**

E

EBG combat engineer vehicle, 88
EBR75, **101**
ECM/ECCM, 50, 66, 68-9
EH-60 Quick Fix, 68
EH-60A EW, **195**
EMP, 70
ER weapons, 34, 35, 70
ERC90 F4 Sagaie, 100
ERFB rounds, 44
ESM, 68-9
EW, 66-9
  EH-60A EW aircraft, 195 equipment, 69
Egyptian Suez campaign, 1973, **178-81**
Electromagnetic pulse, 70
Electromagnetic spectrum, **66-8**
Electronic warfare, 66-9
  EH-60A aircraft, 195 equipment, 69
ELOP Matador tank fire control system, 29
Enfield Weapon System (SA-80), **164**
Engesa
  EE-3 Jararaca, 31
  EE-9, 32, 33
  EE-11, 32
Engines, **22-3**
  see also Diesel engines; Gas turbines; also specific makers or designations of engines or vehicles
Engineers, organisation of units, 182-3
Ericsson Giraffe radar, **50**
Euromissile
  Hot, **35**, **183**, 195
  Milan, **36**, **114**, **165**, 191

F

FA MAS, **168-9**

FAASV (M992), **41**, 44, **128**, 129
FBW, 120
FFV 028 anti-tank mine, **39**
  AT-4, **164**
  Carl Gustaf 84mm 36 **164**
FH-70, 44, 126, **140-1**
FIM-92 Stinger, **10-11**, **160**
FLIR, 116, 118, 120
FV432, 433, **110**
Falklands campaign, 145, **190-3**
  abandoned Argentinian equipment, **192**, **193**
  Argentinian foxhole, **193**
Federal Republic of Germany
  air mobility, 195
  Armbrust, 36, **162**
  BO-105, **49**, 63, **183**
  Fuchs, **58**, 115
  Gepard, **14-15**, **55**, 149
  Jagdpanzer 4-5 SPAT, 36
  Leopard I, **9**, 21, 22, 24, **90**
    derivative AFVs, **30**
  Leopard 2, **16**, 24, **90-1**
  Luchs, 58, **102-3**
  Marder, 31, 57, 93, **114-5**
  Rheinmetall 120mm smoothbore, **16**, **82-3**, **90-1**
    105mm, 93
    20mm, **114**
  Skorpion mine-laying system, **39**
  TH-301, 93
  Wildcat, **148**
Ferret, 101
FIAT
  C1 MBT, **92**
  OF-40, **17**, **92-3**
Fighting Vehicles Research & Development Establishment
  105mm Light Gun, 75, **144-5**, **190**, 191
  FV432, 110
Fighting Vehicle Systems Carrier, 45, 107, **134-5**
Finland, M76 7.62mm, **168**
Fire control systems, **27-9**, **40**, 54
  see also specific fcs designations; for installations in specific weapons, see weapon designations
Firepower, tank design, 16-22
Flares, 43
Flycatcher fire control system, 159
Folgore, 60, 61
Ford Motor Company (FMC)
  AIFV, 58, 105
  M2/M3, **80**, **105-7**, 111
  M113, 31, **56-7**, **104-5**
Formations, see Units and formations
Fox, **101**
France
  air mobility, **195**
  AMX-10 PAC, 31
  AMX-10RC, **31**, 33, **100-1**
  AMX-13 DCA, 30, **147**
  AMX-30, **88**, 147
  AMX-32, 89
  AMX-40, **16**, **88-9**
  Crotale, **146-7**
  FA MAS, **168-9**
  FH-70, 44, 126, **140-1**
  GCT 155mm, 43, 88, **126-7**
  GIAT, see under GIAT
  Hades, **132-3**
  Leclerc, **88**
  Mistrale, **53**
  MO-120-RT-61, **172**
  Pluton, **71**, **132-3**
  REP, **198-9**
  Shahine, 81, 88, **146-7**
  TR 155mm, **44**, 140
Frequency, **66-8**
FROG-7, **136**
Fuchs, **58**, 115

G

G-6 155mm, 44
GC45 155mm, 44
GCT 155mm, 43, 88, **126-7**
GKN
  FV432, **110**
  Warrior, **110-1**
Gainful (SA-6), 53, **152**
Galaxy (C-5), 199
Galil 5.56mm, **169**
Ganef (SA-4), **152-3**
Gaskin (SA-9), 103, **152-3**
Gas turbines, **22**, 23, 82, **85**
  for engines in specific vehicles, see vehicle designations
GAZ-41 engine, 102
GAZ-69 field car, 14
Gecko (SA-8), 136, 137, **152-3**
General Dynamics Stinger (FIM-92), **10-11**, 160
General Electric T700-701 engine, 116
General Motors Detroit, see Detroit
General Motors of Canada LAV-25, **59**, 75, **106**
Gepard, **14-15**, **55**, 149
Germany, see Federal Republic of Germany
GIAT
  AMX-10 PAC, 31
  AMX-10RC, **31**, 33, **100-1**
  AMX-13 DCA, 30, **147**
  AMX-30, **88**, 147
  AMX-32, 89
  AMX-40, **16**, **88-9**
  CS90, 31
  25 M 811 AA cannon, **55**
  120mm smoothbore, 16, 17
  155mm base bleed shell, **42**
  GCT 155mm, 43, 88, **126-7**
  TR 155mm, **44**, 140
GIAT/Lacroix projectors, 89
Glacis plate mounting, 17, **19**
Goose Green, 190, 193
Gopher (SA-13), **152-3**
Grail (SA-7), 14, 53, **160-1**
Grand Cadence de Tir (GCT), **43**, 88, **126-7**
Greece, Artemis, **158-9**
Gremlin (SA-14), **160**
Grenades, 60
  stun grenades, 77
Guerilla warfare, 203-3
  see also Low intensity warfare; Terrorist warfare
Guided weapons, see Missiles; Rocket artillery
Guns
  AFVs, 33
  anti-tank, 34, 35-7
  the tank gun, 16-18
  MBT secondary armament (Machine guns), 21
  see also Artillery; Firepower; also type, maker, or specific designation; for armament of specific vehicles, see vehicle designation
Gun/launchers, 19, 20, **84-5**
Gunships, 62-3, **116-23**

H

Hades, **132-3**
Havoc (Mi-28), **63**
HEAT rounds, **19-20**, 34, **36**, 38
  see also illustrations and captions relating to specific weapons
HEP rounds, see HESH rounds
HESH rounds, 19, **20**, 34
  see also illustrations and captions relation to specific weapons
HIMAG, **26**

Hagglund and Soner Ikv-91 SPAT, 36, **97**
Heckler and Koch
  G11 rifle, 59
  MP-5 SMG, 75, **77**
Helicopters, 34, 62-3, **116-23**
  and air mobility, 194-5
  anti-helicopter defence, 55
  see also Aviation units; specific designations
Hellenic Arms Industry, Artemis, 158-9
Hercules (C-130), **197**
High-explosive anti-tank, see HEAT
High-explosive plastic/ High-explosive squash-head, see HESH
High Mobility Agility Test Rig (HIMAG), **26**
Hind (Mi-24), 63, **118-9**
Hiroshima, **70**
Hispano-Suiza
  HS110, 88, 126
  HS115, 100
Hokum, **63**, 195
Hollow charge, see HEAT rounds
Honduras insurgency, **203**
Hook (Mi-6), 195
Howitzer Improvement Program (HIP), **128**, 129
Huey (UH-1), 63, 195
Hughes
  TOW (BGM-71), **2-3, 34, 80, 164-5**
  M901 ITV, **104**

I
IFF, 51-2
IFVs 56-9
IHADSS, 116, 120
Ikv-91 SPAT, 36, **97**
IMS computer, 120
IRA (Provisionals), 75
IRMC 2A data transmission system, 132
Image intensification, **46**
Immobilisation of tanks, 34-9
Incapacitating agents, 73
Infantry warfare, 56-61
  IFVs 56-9
  mechanised infantry battalions, US Army, 183-4
  personal equipment, **61**
  see also Wireless Ridge attack by 2 Para, 1982
IR detection, 50-1, 66
Insurgency, **202-3**
  see also Terrorist warfare
Iranian Embassy siege, 75, 77, **205**
Irish Republican Army, Provisional Wing, 75
Isotov TV3-117 engines, 118
Israel
  Galil 5.56mm, **169**
  Merkava, 82-3
  Sherman (M50), **179**
  Soltam 155mm, **141**
  Suez campaign, 1973, **178-81**
Italy
  AB412, **194**
  Breda Twin 40L70, **158-9**
  C1 MBT, **92**
  Folgore, **60**, 61
  Mangusta, **120-1**
  OF-40, **17, 92-3**
  Palmaria 155mm, 126

J
Jagdpanzer
  4-5, 36
  SK-105, **18, 30, 96-7**
Jaguar
  J60 engine, 98
  XK engine, 101
Jammers, 43, **67**
Japan, Type 74, 18
Javelin, **161**

K
KPVT 14.5mm, **102**
KT1, 23
Kanone, 114
Karen guerillas, **202**
Kinshasa rescue, 1978, **198-9**
Kiowa (OH-58), 195
Kolwezi, 1978, 198-9
Krauss-Maffei
  Gepard, **14-15, 55, 149**
  Leopard 1, **9, 21, 22, 24, 90**
    derivative AFVs, **30**
  Leopard 2, **16, 24, 90-1**
  Wildcat, **148**
Krupp MaK
  Leopard 1, **9, 21, 22, 24, 90**
    derivative AFVs, **30**
  Leopard 2, **16, 24, 90-1**
  Marder, 31, 57, 93, **114-5**
Kurassier SPAT, 36

L
L7 105mm, **16, 18, 21,** 31, **82-3, 90, 99**
L11 120mm, 16
L16 81mm, **61, 172-3**
L70 40mm, **150, 158, 159**
L118 Light Gun, 75, **144-5, 190, 191**
LARS-2, 45
LAV-25, **59,** 75, **106**
LAW (M72), 164
LAW 80, **37**
LLTV, 118
Lance (MGM-52), 70, **131**
Land Roll radar, 152
Laserfire, 154
Lebanese terrorist attack, 1983, 76
Leclerc, 88
Leopard 1, **9, 21, 22, 24,** 90
  derivative AFVs, **30**
Leopard 2, **16, 24, 90-1**
Levels of conflict, 12-13
Leyland L60, 86
Light AFVs, 30-3
  see also denominations of specific vehicles
Light Gun, Royal Ordnance 105mm (L118), 75, **144-5, 190, 191**
Light machine guns (LMGs), **60, 168-71**
Limited warfare, 74-5
Lockheed Altair RPV, **47**
Long Track radar, 152
Low-intensity warfare, 74-5, **202-3**
Luchs, **58, 102-3**
Lynx, **122-3**

M
M1 Abrams, **6-7, 18,** 23, **82-3**
  controls, **13**
  fire control system, 28
  interior, **29**
M2/M3 Bradley, **80, 105-7,** 111
M2 HB 12.7mm, **21, 56, 104, 106-7**
M16, 59, **166-7**
M24, 30
M41, 30
M42, **134,** 135, 149
M44, 128
M47, 90, **162-3**
M48, **82-3,** 90
M50, **179**
M52, 128
M60, **16, 22, 82-3, 177, 183, 186**
M60 MG, **170-1**
M68 105mm, **16, 18,** 21, 31, **82-3**
M71, **141**
M73, 21
M76, **168**
M77, 135
M85, **21**
M106, 104
M108, 128
M109, 40, **41, 43-4,** 126, 128-9
M110, 41, **81, 134**
M113, 31, **56-7,** 104-5
M125, 104
M163, 104, **156**
M193, 59
M198 155mm, **45, 144**
M231, 167
M-240 heavy mortar, **173**
M240 7.62mm, **21**
M249 LMG, 60, 170-1
M548, 105, 154
M551 Sheridan, 16, 30, **74**
M577, 104
M601A, 21
M650 203mm RAP, 41
M712 Copperhead, **34,** 37, **128,** 129
M718 RAAMS, 37
M728 Combat Engineer Vehicle, **38,** 39, 83
M830P, M845P, **141**
M901 ITV, **104**
M981, 104
M987, 45, 107, **134-5**
M992 FAASV, **41, 44, 128,** 129
MAN cross-country truck, 149
MB833 Ea-500, **114,** 149
MB838 Ca-500, **22,** 90, 149
MB871, 126
MB873 Ka-501, 90
MB883 Ka-500, 93
MBB
  BO-105, **49,** 63, **183,** 195
  PAH-1, 195
  Armbrust, 36, **162**
  PARM, **38**
  Roland, **52, 148-9**
MBT-70, 82
MCLOS, 38
MG3, LMG, **115, 170-1**
MGM-31 Pershing, **70-1, 130**
MGM-52 Lance, 70, **131**
Mi-6 Hook, **195**
Mi-8, 62
Mi-24 Hind, 63, **118-9**
Mi-28 Havoc, **63**
MICVS, 56-9
MLRS SPLL (M987), 45, 107, **134-5**
MP-5 SMG, 75, **77**
MSE communications system, 64-5
MT-LB, **57, 112-3**
MTU engines
  MB833 Ea-500, **114,** 149
  MB838 Ca-500, **22,** 90, 149
  MB871, 126
  MB873 Ka-501, 90
  MB883 Ka-500, 93
McDonnell Douglas, AH-64 Apache, **49,** 63, **116-7,** 195
  M47 Dragon, 90, **162-3**
Malayan Emergency, 202, 203
Mangusta (A 129), **120-1**
Manual Command to Line-of-Sight (MCLOS), 38
Marconi Blindfire radar, 154
Digital fire control system, 99
Marder, 31, 93, **114-5**
Matra Mistrale, **53**
Mauser MK 30F cannon, 148, **158**
MAZ, 136, 137
Mechanised infantry combat vehicles (MICVs), 56-9
Machine guns, 59-60
Merkava, 84, **94-5**
MICAH, 39
Milan, **36, 114, 165,** 191
Mines, **38,** 39
MIRA night sight, **165**
Missiles
  anti-tank, **34-38**
  SAMs, 52-4
    see also Rocket artillery; specific names
  Mistrale, **53**
Mobility, tank design, 16, 22-5
Mohawk (OV-1D), **47**
Monroe effect, 20
Mortars, 61, **172-3**
Motor rifle battalion,

Soviet, composition, 14
Mountings, 17
MOWAG
  Piranha, **33**
    see also LAV-25
  Shark, **33**
Mujahideen, **12, 202**
Multiple Launch Rocket System (MLRS), 45, 107, **134-5**
Muzzle brakes, **18**

N
NP 105A2, **19**
Nerve agents, 73
Neutralisation of tanks, 34-9
Non-lethal weaponry, 77
Noricum NP 105A2 APFSDS rounds, **19**
Norinco 40mm anti-tank launcher, **37**
Nuclear warfare, tactical, 70-1
  ER weapons, 34, 35, 70
Nuclear warheads, 70, 71, 130-3

O
OBUS-A 105mm, 20
OF-40, **17, 92-3**
OH-58 Kiowa, 195
OV-1D Mohawk, **47**
Obstacles, anti-tank, 34, 38-9
Oerlikon-Bührle 35mm, **149**
Olympic Games tragedy, 1972, 204
Operational manoeuvre groups, Soviet Army, 184-5
Organisation of military formations and units, 182-5
  artillery, 182
  aviation, 183
  engineers, 182-3
  Soviet organisation, 184-5
  US Army tactical doctrine, 183
  US Army tactical units, 183-4
  see also Command, control and communications
OTO Melara OF-40, **17, 92-3**

P
PAH-1, 195
Pbv 302, **4-5, 182**
PIVADS, 156
PKT 7.62mm, 102
PNVS, 116, 120
PT-76, 30, 96, **188**
Pack Howitzer, 144
Palmaria 155mm, 126
Panavia Tornado, **48**
Pandur, **33**
Panga, 101
Panhard
  EBR 75, **101**
  ERC 90 F4 Sagaie, 100
Panzerfaust, **38**
Parachute Regiment (2 Para) at Wireless Ridge, 1982, **190-3**
Paratroops, see Airborne forces; REP; SAS
PARM, 38
Pat Hand radar, 152, **153**
Patriot, **50, 156-7**
Payloads, artillery, 42-3
Performance, see vehicle denominations
Periscopes, 29
Pershing (MGM-31), **70-1, 130**
Philippines, insurgency, 202, 203
Piranha, **33**
  see also LAV-25
Plastic anti-riot rounds, 77
Pluton, **71**
Police, unconventional warfare, 76-7
Port Stanley, 190, 191, 193

Power output, MBTs, **22-3**
Poyaud V12X, 89
Propellant technology, 17
Provisional Irish Republican Army, 75
Protection
  tank design, 16, 25
  T-80, **85**
  chemical warfare, 73
  anti-terrorist, 75
Psychological agents, 73
Ptarmigan, **65**
Puma, **62**

Q
Quick Fix (EH-60), **68**
  EH-60A EW aircraft, 195

R
RAAMS, 37, 42, **128**
RADAG, 71
RAPs, 41
RARDEN 30mm, **100-1, 110-1**
RBS-70, **53**
RCM 748, 154
RDF/LT, 75
REC, 69
REP, **198-9**
RM-70, 75
ROBAT, 83
RPG-7, **162-3**
RPK LMG, 14, **170**
RPU-14 140mm, 45
RPVs, **13, 47, 48-9**
Radar, **46, 50-1**
Radiation, nuclear, 34, 35, 70
Radio-Electronic Combat (REC), 69
Rakete, 114
Ranger, **75**
Rangefinders, 27-8
Rapid Deployment Force Light Tank (RDF/LT), 75
Rapier, **53, 154-5**
Reactive armour, **85**
  Blazer, 38-9, 83
Recoil forces, 17-18
Recoilless weapons, 36-7
Renault TR 10,000 truck, 141
Rescue and recovery, amphibious operations, 189
Rheinmetall
  20mm, **144**
  105mm, 93
  120mm, **16, 82-3, 90-1**
Rifles, 59
RITA communications systems, 64, 65
River-crossing operations, Soviet Army, 186-9
Robots
  explosives disposal, **76**
  tanks, 27
Robotic Obstacle Breaching Assault Tank (ROBAT), 83
Rocket artillery, 44-5
Roland, **52, 148-9**
Rolls-Royce
  Condor CV-12, 86
  Gem, 120, 122
  K60 No.4 Mk.4F, 110
Royal Ordnance 105mm Light Gun, **144-5**
Royal Ordnance Leeds, see Vickers

S
S-23 180mm, **143**
S401A turret, 147
S-tank, **4-5, 17,** 23, 27, 36, **182**
SA-2 52-3
SA-4 Ganef, **152-3**
SA-6 Gainful, 53, **152**
SA-7 Grail, 14, 53, **160-1**
SA-8 Cecko, 136, 137, **152-3**
SA-9 Gaskin, 103, **152-3**
SA-13 Gopher, **152-3**
SA-14 Gremlin, **160**
SA-80, **164**
SACLOS, 38, 54, 161, 165
SAS, 75, 77, 191, **204-5**

SAW LMG, 60
SEAL, **74**
SINCGARS-V, 65
SK 105, **18, 30, 96-7**
SP-70 155mm, 43, 44, **126**
SPAT, 36
  see also vehicle denominations
SRC International, GC45 155mm, 44
SS-1 Scud, **136-7**
SS-21 Spider, **136-7**
SS-23, **136-7**
SU-100 SPAT, 36
SABRE turret, **147**
SADARM, 135
Sagaie (ERC 90F4), 100
Sagger (AT-3), 58, **108, 113**
Saladin, 99
Samaritan, 99
Samson, 99
San Carlos, 190
Scimitar, 30, 99, 131, 192
Scorpion, **30, 74, 98-9,** 191, 192
Scud (SS-1), **136-7**
Self-propelled artillery, 43-4
Self-propelled anti-tank guns (SPATs), 36
Self-propelled launcher loader (SPLL), see MLRS
Self-propelled recoilless guns, 37
Semi-Automatic Command to Line-of-Sight (SACLOS), 38, 54, 161, 165
Sensors
  remote, 46-7
  tanks, 27-9
Shahine, **81,** 88, **146-7**
Shan State Army, **203**
Shark, **33**
Shells, 40-3
  binary chemical, **72**
  for specific payloads, see weapon name
Sheridan (M551), 16, 30, **74**
Sherman (M50), **179**
Shilka (ZSU-23-4), 53, **54,** 55, **150-1**
Shorts
  Blowpipe, **160-1**
  Javelin, **161**
  Starstreak HVM, 99, 161
SIBMAS APC, **32**
Siemens MPDR radar, **50**
Sights, 28-9
Sikorsky UH-60 Black Hawk, **176, 194,** 195
Sir Galahad, Falklands campaign, 190
Size, tank design, 25-6
  for dimensions of specific weapons, see weapon denomination
Skorpion mine-laying system, **39**
Smoke screens, 42-3
Snipers' rifles, 59
Snorkels, 24, 187-9
Soft recoil system, 18
Soltam 155mm, **141**
Songster (AT-8), 84-5
Sopelem TN2-1 night vision goggles, **46**
South Africa, G-6 155mm SP, 44
Soviets, see USSR
Spandrel (AT-5), 103, **109**
Spartan, 99
Special forces, 74-5, **204-5**
  see also Airborne forces
Special Air Service (SAS), 75, 77, 191, **204-5**
Spider (SS-21), **136-7**
Spigot (AT-4), 109, 113, **164**
Starlifter (C-141), 199
Starstreak HVM, 99, 161
Steering, AFVs, **33**
Steyr
  7FA engine, 97
  Pandur, **33**
  SK 105, **18, 30, 96-7**
Stinger (FIM-92), **10-11,** 160
Stingray, **18, 99**
  engine, **22**
Stormer, 99

Stowage of ammunition, **21-2**
Straight Flush, 152
Streaker, 99
Striker, 99
Stun grenades, 77
Sub-machine guns (SMGs), 59-60
Suez campaign, 1973, **178-81**
  military situataion, 178-9
  Egyptian preparations, 179
  crossing, 179-80
  Israeli counterstroke, 180-1
  conclusions, 181
Sultan, 99
Super Puma, **195**
Surface-to-air missiles (SAMs), 52-4
  see also specific denominations
Surprise factor, 181, 186
Surveillance and target acquisition, 46-7
  counter-terrorist, 75
  see also specific aspects, eg Radar; Thermal imaging
Suspensions
  MBTs, **23-4**
  AFVs, 32
Sweden
  AT-4 (FFV), **164**
  Carl Gustaf 84mm, 36, **164**
  FFV 028, **39**
  Ikv-91 SPAT, 36, **97**
  L/70 40mm, **150**, 158, **159**
  Pbv 302, **4-5**, 182
  S-tank, **4-5**, **17**, **23**, 27, 36, **182**
  Trinity air defence system, 150
Swingfire, 99
Switzerland
  Piranha, **33**
    see also LAV-25
  Shark, **33**

T

T-54, **189**
T-64, 27, **84**
T-72, **19**, 20, **24**, 27
T-80, 20, 23, **26**, 27
TACMS, **134**, 135
TADS, 116, **122-3**
TAM, 31, **93**
TG230A turret, 147

TH-301, 93
TR 155mm, **44**, **140**
Tactical nuclear warfare, 70-1
  ER weapons, 34, 35, 70
Tactical units, see Units and formations
Tank battalions, US Army, 183-4
Tanks
  design, 16-29
    for low-intensity warfare, **75**
    the tank gun, 16-18
    see also Anti-tank warfare; Light AFVs; also specific designations
Target acquisition, 46-7
Tatra
  813, 138, **139**
  815, 125
T-928 engine, 125
Technology and land warfare , 13-15, 56
Teledyne
  Armoured Gun System, 18
  Continental AVDS-1790, 82, 94
Terrorist warfare, 74-7
  see also Insurgency
Thermal imaging, 46
Thermal Observation and Gunnery System (TOGS), 86, 87
Thin Skin radar, 152
Thomson-Brandt MO-120-RT-61, **172**
Thomson-CSF
  Air Defence System, 55
  Crotale, **146-7**
  Mygale search radar, 51
  Shahine, **81**, 88, **146-7**
Thyssen-Henschel
  Fuchs, **58**, 115
  Luchs, **58**, **102-3**
  Marder, 31, 93, **114-5**
  TAM, 31, **93**
  TH-301, 93
TOGA armour, **56**
Tornado, **48**
TOW, **2-3**, **34**, **80**, **164-5**
  M901 ITV, **104**
Towed artillery, 44
  see also specific designations
Tracks, 23, 24, 26
Tractors, armoured, **38-9**
Transportation of MBTs, **26**
  see also Amphibious operations
Transporter/erector/

launcher (TEL), **136-7**
Transportpanzer 1 (Fuchs), **58**, **115**
Trinity air defence system, 150
Trunnion pull, **18**
Tungsten, 19
Turrets, 17, **18**, 25-6
  advantages, 17
  Soviet tanks, 18-19
  see also specific vehicles
Type 5D20 diesel engine, 108, 113
Types 63 & 77, **96**
Type 74, 18
Type 81 rocket launcher, **23**, **45**

U

UH-1 Huey, 63, 195
UH-60 Black Hawk, **176**, **194-5**
Unconventional warfare, 74-7
  see also Insurgency
Units and formations organisation, 182-5; US, 183-4; Soviet, 184-5; symbols, 177
USSR
  2S1 152mm, **40**, **124-5**, 142
  2S3, 43-4 **124-5**
  2S5, **40**, 44, 124-5
  2S7 203mm, **40**, 44, **124-5**
  AK-74, AKS-74, **167**
  BM-21, 138-9
  BM-24, 45
  BM-27, 45, 139
  BMD, **75**, **113**
  BMP, **14**, **56-8**, **108-9**, **186**, **187**
  BRDM, 14, **102-3**
  BTR-60, BTR-70, **112**, 184
  D-20 152mm, 43
  D-23, 40
  D-30 122mm, **142-3**
  Hokum, **63**
  M-240 heavy mortar, **173**
  Mi-8, **62**
  Mi-24 Hind, 63, **118-9**
  Mi-28 Havoc, **63**
  MT-LB, **57**, **112-3**
  PT-76, 30, 96, **188**
  RM-70, 75
  RPG-7, 162-3
  RPK, 14, **170**
  RPU-14 140mm, 45
  S-23 180mm, **143**
  SA-4, **152-3**

SA-6, 53, **156**
SA-7, 14, 53, **160-1**
SA-8, 136, 137, **152-3**
SA-9, 103, **152-3**
SA-13, **152-3**
SA-14, **160**
SS-1 Scud, **136-7**
SS-21 Spider, **136-7**
SS-23, **136-7**
SU-100 SPAT, 36
T-64, T-72, T-80, **84-5**
ZSU-23-4, 53, **54**, 55, **150-1**
ZSU-X, 151
  air mobility, **195**
  tactical organisation, 184-5
  tactics, **186-7**
    parachute tactics, **196-7**
    river crossing operations, **186-9**
United Kingdom
  air mobility, 195
  Army Air Corps, 195
  AS-90, 126
  Blowpipe, **160-1**
  British Light Gun, 105mm, 75, **144-5**, 190, 191
  Challenger, **86-7**
  Chieftain, **86**
  FV432, 433, **110**
  Ferret, 101
  Fox, **101**
  Javelin, **161**
  LT 105mm, **16**, **18**, 21, 31, **82-3**, 90, **99**
  L16 81mm, **61**, **172-3**
  LAW 80, **37**
  Lynx, **122-3**
  Pack Howitzer, 144
  Parachute Regiment (2 Para) at Wireless Ridge, 1982, **190-3**
  Rapier, **53**, **154-5**
  SA-80, 164
  SAS, 75, 77, 191, **204-5**
  Scimitar, 30, 99, 131, 192
  Scorpion, 30, **74**, **98-9**, 191, **192**
  Starstreak HVM, 99, 161
  Vickers
    Mk.5, 18
    Mk.5 Weapon Control System, 28-9
  Warrior, **110-1**
USA
  A-10, 48
  AH-64 Apache, 49, 63, **116-7**, 195
  AIFV, 105
  C-130 Hercules, **197**

CH-47 Chinook, **45**, **62**
EH-60 Quick Fix, **68**
EH-60A EW, 195
M1 Abrams, **6-7**, **18**, 23, **82-3**
  controls, **13**
  fire control system, 28
  interior, **29**
M2/M3 Bradley, **80**, **105-7**, 111
M16, 59, **166-7**
M24, 30
M41, 30
M47, 90, **162-3**
M48, **82-3**, 90
M60 MBT, **16**, **22**, **82-3**, **177**, **183**, **186**
M60 MG, **170-1**
M68 105mm, **16**, 18, 21, 31, **82-3**
M109, 40, **41**, 43-4, 126, 128-9
M110, 41, **81**, **134**
M113, 31, **56-7**, 104-5
M163, 104, **156**
M198 155mm, **45**, **144**
M551 Sheridan, 16, 30, **74**
M601A, **21**
M901 ITV, **104**
M987 FVSC, 45, 107, **134-5**
MGM-31 Pershing, **70-1**, **130**
MGM-52 Lance, 70, **131**
MLRS, 45, 107, **134-5**
OH-58 Kiowa, 195
Patriot, **50**, **156-7**
Stinger (FIM-92), **10-11**, **160**
Stingray, 18, **99**
  engine, **22**
Teledyne Armored Gun System, 18
TOW, **2-3**, **34**, **80**, **164-5**
M901 ITV, **104**
UH-1 Huey, 63, 195
UH-60 Black Hawk, **176**, **194-5**
US Army
  air mobility, **194-5**
  CABs, 184, **194-5**
  doctrine, 183
  parachute tactics, **196-7** tactical units, 183-4
Ural truck, 138

V

V-6 R engine, 150
VCI, 93
Valmet M76, 168

Vickers
  AS-90, 126
  Challenger, **86-7**
  Chieftain, **86**
  Fox, **101**
  Mk.5, 18
  Mk.7 Weapon Control System, 28-9
Vietnam, 202, 203
  aircraft losses, 53
Volvo-Penta TD120 engine, 97
Vought
  M987 MLRS SPLL, 45, 107, **134-5**
Vulcan (M163), 104, **156**

W

W-46 engine, 84
Warheads, nuclear, 70, 71, 130-3
Warrior, **110-1**
Weapon control systems, **27-9**, **40**, **54**
  see also specific fire control system designations; for installations in specific weapons, see weapon designations
West Germany, see Federal Republic of Germany
Westland Lynx, **122-3**
Wheeled
  AFVs, 31-2
  APCs, 58-9
  SP guns, 44
Wildcat, 148
Wireless Ridge attack by 2 Para, 1982, **190-3**
  abandoned Argentinian equipment, **192**, **193**

X

XM803, 82
XM985, **148**

Y

YaMZ238V engine, 112
Yom Kippur War, 37, 38-9
  Israeli aircraft losses, 53

Z

ZIL, 14, 139
ZMZ-4905 engine, 112
ZSU-23-4 Shilka, 53, **54**, 55, **150-1**
ZSU-X, 151
Zaïre rescue, 1978, **198-9**

Picture Credits

Above: Martin Marietta ADATS (Air defence/anti-tank system).